Building the Web of Things

Building the Web of Things

WITH EXAMPLES IN NODE.JS AND RASPBERRY PI

DOMINIQUE D. GUINARD
VLAD M. TRIFA

MANNING

SHELTER ISLAND

Manning Publications Co.
20 Baldwin Road
PO Box 761
Shelter Island, NY 11964

Development editor:	Lesley Trites
Technical development editor:	Scott Chaussée
Copyeditor:	Linda Recktenwald
Proofreader:	Melody Dolab
Technical proofreader:	Valentin Crettaz
Typesetter:	Marija Tudor
Cover designer:	Leslie Haimes

ISBN: 9781617292682
Printed in the United States of America
1 2 3 4 5 6 7 8 9 10 – EBM – 21 20 19 18 17 16

brief contents

PART 1 BASICS OF THE IOT AND THE WOT 1

    1 ▪ From the Internet of Things to the Web of Things 3

    2 ▪ Hello, World Wide Web of Things 29

    3 ▪ Node.js for the Web of Things 59

    4 ▪ Getting started with embedded systems 83

    5 ▪ Building networks of Things 109

PART 2 BUILDING THE WOT 141

    6 ▪ Access: Web APIs for Things 143

    7 ▪ Implementing web Things 175

    8 ▪ Find: Describe and discover web Things 214

    9 ▪ Share: Securing and sharing web Things 248

   10 ▪ Compose: Physical mashups 279

contents

preface   xiii
acknowledgments   xv
about this book   xviii

PART 1 BASICS OF THE IOT AND THE WOT 1

1 *From the Internet of Things to the Web of Things   3*

1.1 Defining the Internet of Things   4

1.2 Enter the Web of Things   6

*Web of Things scenario: connected hotel   6
Comparing IoT and WoT   8 ▪ The Internet of Things—
a brief history   12*

1.3 Use cases—why connected objects?   14

*Wireless sensor networks and distributed
sensing   14 ▪ Wearables and quantified self   16 ▪ Smart
homes and buildings   17 ▪ Smart cities and energy grids   18
Smart manufacturing and Industry 4.0   19 ▪ Smart logistics
and supply chains   19 ▪ Marketing 2.0   21*

1.4 The Web of Things—a supercharged Internet of
Things 22

*Easier to program 23 ▪ Open and extensible standards 24
Fast and easy to deploy, maintain, and integrate 24
Loose coupling between elements 25 ▪ Widely used security and
privacy mechanisms 25 ▪ WoT—the shortcomings 26*

1.5 Summary 27

2 Hello, World Wide Web of Things 29

2.1 Meet a Web of Things device 30

The suspect: Raspberry Pi 31

2.2 Exercise 1—Browse a device on the Web of Things 32

*Part 1—The web as user interface 32 ▪ Part 2—The web as an
API 36 ▪ So what? 41*

2.3 Exercise 2—Polling data from a WoT sensor 42

*Part 1—Polling the current sensor value 42 ▪ Part 2—Polling
and graphing sensor values 43 ▪ Part 3—Real-time data
updates 44 ▪ So what? 45*

2.4 Exercise 3—Act on the real world 46

*Part 1—Use a form to update text to display 46 ▪ Part 2—
Create your own form to control devices 48 ▪ So what? 50*

2.5 Exercise 4—Tell the world about your device 50

So what? 54

2.6 Exercise 5—Create your first physical mashup 54

So what? 57

2.7 Summary 57

3 Node.js for the Web of Things 59

3.1 The rise of JavaScript: from clients to servers to things! 60

Pushing JavaScript to things 61

3.2 Introduction to Node.js 62

*Installing Node.js on your machine 63 ▪ Your first web server
in Node.js 63 ▪ Returning sensor data as JSON 65*

3.3 Modularity in Node.js 66

*npm—the Node package manager 67 ▪ Clean dependencies
with package.json and npm 68 ▪ Your first Node module 69*

3.4   Understanding the Node.js event loop   71

Multithreaded web servers   71 ▪ *Single-threaded, non-blocking*
web servers   71

3.5   Getting started with asynchronous programming   73

Anonymous callbacks   74 ▪ *Named callbacks   77* ▪ *Control*
flow libraries   78

3.6   Summary and beyond the book   81

4   *Getting started with embedded systems   83*

4.1   The world of embedded devices   84

Devices for hobbyists vs. industrial devices   84 ▪ *Real-time*
operating systems vs. Linux   85 ▪ *Summary and beyond the*
Pi   87

4.2   Set up your first WoT device—Raspberry Pi   88

Meet the Raspberry Pi   88 ▪ *Choosing your Pi   89*
Shopping list   90 ▪ *Setting up your Raspberry Pi   91*
Connecting to your device   96

4.3   Installing Node.js on the Raspberry Pi   97

Using Git and GitHub on the Pi   99 ▪ *So what?   99*

4.4   Connecting sensors and actuators to your Pi   99

Understanding GPIO ports   100 ▪ *Working with breadboards*
and electronic components   100 ▪ *Accessing GPIOs from*
Node.js   102 ▪ *Beyond the book   107*

4.5   Summary   108

5   *Building networks of Things   109*

5.1   Connecting Things   111

Network topologies   111 ▪ *Network classification models   113*

5.2   Networking protocols for Things   115

Spatial considerations   115 ▪ *Internet protocols and the*
IoT   116 ▪ *IoT personal area networks   120* ▪ *IoT wide area*
networks   124 ▪ *So, which one should I choose?   127*

5.3   Application protocols for Things   130

ZigBee and Bluetooth application stacks   130 ▪ *Apple HomeKit*
and Google Weave   132 ▪ *Message Queuing Telemetry*
Transport   132 ▪ *Constrained Application Protocol   135*
So, which one should I use?   135

5.4   The Web of Things architecture   136

*Layer 1: Access   136 ▪ Layer 2: Find   137 ▪ Layer 3:
Share   138 ▪ Layer 4: Compose   138 ▪ Why does the WoT
matter?   138 ▪ Beyond the book   139*

5.5   Summary   140

PART 2   BUILDING THE WOT 141

6   *Access: Web APIs for Things   143*

6.1   Devices, resources, and web Things   144

*Representational State Transfer   144 ▪ Why do we need a
uniform interface?   146 ▪ Principle 1: addressable
resources   147 ▪ Principle 2: manipulation of resources through
representations   151 ▪ Principle 3: self-descriptive
messages   154 ▪ Principle 4: Hypermedia as the Engine of
Application State   160 ▪ Summary—web Things design
process   163*

6.2   Beyond REST: the real-time Web of Things   163

*The WoT needs events!   164 ▪ Publish/subscribe   165
Webhooks—HTTP callbacks   166 ▪ Comet—hacking HTTP
for a real-time web   167 ▪ WebSockets   168 ▪ The future: from
HTTP/1.1 to HTTP/2   172*

6.3   Summary   173

7   *Implementing web Things   175*

7.1   Connecting devices to the web   176

7.2   Direct integration pattern—REST on devices   177

*Creating a WoT server   178 ▪ Resource design   180
Representation design   186 ▪ Interface design   189
Pub/sub interface via WebSockets   191 ▪ Summary—direct
integration pattern   194*

7.3   Gateway integration pattern—CoAP example   194

*Running a CoAP server   195 ▪ Proxying CoAP via a
gateway   196 ▪ Summary—gateway integration pattern   198*

7.4   Cloud integration pattern—MQTT over
EVRYTHNG   199

*Set up your EVRYTHNG account   201 ▪ Create your MQTT
client application   204 ▪ Use actions to control the power*

plug   206 ▪ *Create a simple web control application   208*
Summary—cloud integration pattern   212

7.5   Summary   212

8 Find: Describe and discover web Things   214

8.1   The findability problem   215

8.2   Discovering Things   217
Network discovery   217 ▪ *Resource discovery on the web   220*

8.3   Describing web Things   223
Introducing the Web Thing Model   225 ▪ *Metadata   227*
Properties   227 ▪ *Actions   229* ▪ *Things   231*
Implementing the Web Thing Model on the Pi   232
Summary—the Web Thing Model   238

8.4   The Semantic Web of Things   239
Linked data and RDFa   239 ▪ *Agreed-upon semantics:*
Schema.org   243 ▪ *JSON-LD   244* ▪ *Beyond the book   246*

8.5   Summary   247

9 Share: Securing and sharing web Things   248

9.1   Securing Things   250
Encryption 101   252 ▪ *Web security with TLS: the S of*
HTTPS!   253 ▪ *Enabling HTTPS and WSS with TLS on your*
Pi   255

9.2   Authentication and access control   260
Access control with REST and API tokens   260 ▪ *OAuth: a web*
authorization framework   263

9.3   The Social Web of Things   265
A Social Web of Things authentication proxy   266
Implementing a Social WoT authentication proxy   269

9.4   Beyond the book   276

9.5   Summary   278

10 Compose: Physical mashups   279

10.1   Building a simple app—automated UI generation   280
A universal user interface for web Things   281

10.2   Physical mashups   288
Boxes and wires mashups for the Physical Web: Node-RED   289

10.3   Using wizards for physical mashups: IFTTT   295

     Pushing intruder alert tweets to a Google spreadsheet   296
     Sending requests to a Thing with the Maker Channel   298
     Pushing intruder alert tweets to a Google spreadsheet   299

10.4   Beyond the book   300

     From simple mashups to big data mashups   300 ▪ *A better user
experience   301*

10.5   Summary   302

appendix   Arduino, BeagleBone, Intel Edison, and the WoT   303

     index   309

preface

Our biggest hope with this book is that we've done a good job of providing you with a deep overview of what the future of the Internet of Things (IoT) might look like. Despite the oceans of e-ink used every day to talk about the IoT, we know that practical and authoritative content about this topic is still hard to come by. We hope that this book will bring some order to the chaos by proposing a pragmatic and structured methodology to building IoT devices and services, one inherited from our own experience building large-scale commercial systems for connected devices.

Because every actor wants to get a slice of the future pie, there are literally hundreds of competing standards for connected devices. The "my protocol is better than yours" attitude has been the major cause of the fragmentation of the IoT world and the reason why it's plagued by constant wheel reinventions and a severe lack of proper innovation. All existing applications, tools, and mechanisms need to include support for every new protocol that appears. And with the hundreds of protocols already out there that need to be integrated and maintained—well, you get the idea!

When we started working on the Web of Things about a decade ago, our objective was to pause a bit and reflect on what could be done to realize the full potential of the IoT. At that time, it was clear that most projects tackled only smaller issues of the IoT. Few projects tried to look at the bigger picture of the IoT and ask, "What problems are we really trying to solve and how can we make it easier to innovate?"

Almost everyone was trying to build a global network optimized for devices and data-driven applications—from scratch! Web of Things people like us, on the other hand, decided to look into and learn from the most successful application layer of them all: the web. The web scales, it's open and easy to take part in, and best of all, it's versatile! If it's good enough for banking services, games, chat rooms, and changing the media industry, why wouldn't it be good enough for the Internet of Things?

Turns out, it is! We wrote this book to show you not only the *why* but also the *how*. We hope it will equip you with the understanding and tools necessary to thrive in a world where most physical objects have a digital life of their own thanks to web protocols. This book is about not reinventing the wheel where it isn't needed. And, as you'll see, it can be a lot of fun to reuse solid web protocols to build ever bigger, smarter, and simpler Things—to build the Web of Things!

DOM & VLAD

acknowledgments

We learned the hard way that writing a book is not as trivial as it seems. "Oh, we'll just refresh our PhD theses and we're done in a few weeks" has gradually turned into "OK, well, I guess we'll have to write these chapters from scratch over the next few months. What about the source code? Which source code? Let's just rewrite this whole thing in Node.js!" Nevertheless, the many weekends and late nights we spent putting together this book have been a lot of fun and a unique challenge. Distilling all the knowledge we acquired over a decade of R&D into a single book *and* making sure that book is easy to use has been a tough and very motivating aspiration.

Obviously, many people helped us in this adventure, and this book wouldn't have existed without their support and contributions, so it's time to give credit where it's due!

First and foremost, we'd like to thank the entire team at Manning. They've been both very demanding and incredibly encouraging, and their feedback on the content and form of this book throughout its evolution from some ideas to what you're holding in your hands has been extremely valuable. Thanks to Michael Stephens for believing in the book and encouraging us to make it great. Thanks to Lesley Trites for her continuous support and constructive feedback and suggestions all along: by the last chapter, it was clear that she'd become an expert in this field! Thanks to Candace Gillhoolley for her energy in finding new ways of marketing the book. Finally, thanks to Melody Dolab, Kevin Sullivan, and everyone else at Manning involved in the production of the book.

We'd also like to thank all the reviewers of the book for their constructive and encouraging remarks, in particular Scott Chaussée, who offered suggestions on the overall technical content, and Valentin Crettaz, who gave all chapters a full technical proofread. Many others provided invaluable feedback throughout the process: Alain Couniot, Alvin Scudder, Brent Stains, Gonzalo Huerta-Canepa, Harald Kuhn, Joel Kotarski, Lance May, Kenneth Fricklas, Mayur S. Patil, Philip Arny, Rocio Chongtay, Roy Legaard, Jr., Sander Rossel, Sebastian Haehnel, Steve Grey-Wilson, Troi Eisler, and William Wade.

Next we'd like to thank all the people who supported our research and work on the Web of Things. We've had the chance to work with those who pioneered the IoT, such as Professor Sanjay Sarma at MIT and Professors Friedemann Mattern and Elgar Fleisch at ETH Zurich. A special thanks goes to Friedemann, who was also our PhD advisor. He has been an incredibly inspiring mentor, giving us the freedom to explore the Web of Things.

Thanks to all our colleagues at EVRYTHNG: to our cofounders Andy Hobsbawm and Niall Murphy, to our first readers Albert Zaragoza and Joel Vogt, to Laura Lilienthal for boosting the marketing of our book, but also to the rest of the dream team. They all contributed to this book in one way or another, and we're very grateful for that! Building the Web of Things (WoT) with them for the last few years has been a blast, and we've barely scratched the surface of what it can do.

Thanks also to the entire WoT community and its pioneers. To the dozens of researchers we worked with over the years who graciously provided us their time, ideas, feedback, and pull requests—you are the Web of Things! We're unable to thank you individually here, but you should know that we're proud that you trusted and supported this vision from the beginning. Oh—and a big thanks to our detractors as well! The criticism we faced in the early days of our work was an essential ingredient and inspiration to making the WoT a reality. See, the web *did* make it to embedded devices after all!

Similarly, a big thank-you goes to many other communities who've helped us during the creation of this book, especially the Raspberry Pi and Node.js communities. In particular, thanks to Brian Cooke, Nick O'Leary, Matteo Collina, and Douglas Wilson.

For the logistics, we'd like to thank The Best Kebab at 233 Old Street in London, which provided us excellent halloumi and falafel wraps to fuel us through many long coding and writing sessions. It's fair to say this temple of kebabs has become our little tradition every Sunday. Also, a big thank-you to the British Library at Kings Cross in London for providing the most inspiring place to study—this is where the majority of the book was written.

FROM DOMINIQUE

I would also like to send a big thank-you to my family for their limitless love. Thanks to Mireille, Véronique, and Léonie, who never quite understood what I was writing this book about and yet found it pretty awesome from the word *go*! Thank you to Jean-Pierre, my dad, whose out-of-this-world skills in electronics were really central to making sure Vlad and I did not blow up the entire building! Thanks also for his great reviews of the entire book and code. Finally, a huge thank-you to Rachel, who accepted sacrificing so many weekends and pushed me with incredible love and patience to tick one more box on my bucket list: writing a book.

FROM VLAD

I would like to send a huge thank-you to Mariana (my mom) and Aurel (my pops) for being pretty much the best parents anyone could ask for and allowing me to spend countless nights in front of computers as a teenager. Also, thanks to my sweet *bunica* for being the most caring grandma and doing the opposite when asking me all the time to stop "destroying my eyes" by staring at computers all day long. Thanks to all my friends for, well, being awesome and understanding why I'm spending my weekends at the British Library or at the office instead of hanging out with them. Finally, a warm thank-you to Flavia for being my best friend and partner in life. Her support, encouragement, and general awesomeness have been the vital ingredients that helped this book become a reality.

about this book

Over the last few years, the Internet of Things (IoT) has become one of the most popular topics in the technology and business worlds. From blogs to executive reports to conferences, everyone seems to be asking the same question: "What is this IoT thing and how can I use it for my business and my life?"

Because the potential of the IoT is so massive, everyone is rushing to build a strategy or solution, which usually sounds like this: "Hey, let's connect everything in our building, supply chain, factory, office, and so on, so we can track and analyze this huge amount of data!"

Sounds great, but the question everyone should be asking first is, "*What* exactly do we want to connect and, more importantly, *why*?" The real challenge with the IoT has much less to do with the technology (the *how*) than the actual use case (the *what*). True, the IoT is so young that the landscape is highly fragmented. There are hundreds of tools, standards, devices, protocols, and IoT cloud platforms to choose from, and more are appearing every day. And with all the self-proclaimed IoT experts and bloggers who've appeared overnight, it's certainly not easy to separate the wheat from the chaff. Sure, you can easily find great tutorials online that will teach you how to connect your cat or car to the internet using an Arduino and some sensors, but when it comes to building an end-to-end, scalable, secure system and putting together the hardware, data collection, storage, processing, visualization, and interaction, it's a different story!

There are some great books about the IoT available. Some are very specific and technical; for example, they talk in great detail about hardware or data processing, but they don't address the bigger picture and how to build the IoT. Other books are written at a high level; they talk about most elements of the IoT but only superficially, so you won't learn how to use any of them.

This is exactly the void we wanted to fill. We wanted to write a book that was easy enough for an IoT novice to read, that covered all the tools needed in a complete end-to-end IoT toolbox, and that was technical enough so you would actually learn how to create each element yourself.

With this objective in mind, we decided to distill everything we've learned from working for over a decade in the Internet of Things as engineers, researchers, and entrepreneurs, so that you can become a proficient IoT developer with a minimum of effort. Our goal was to teach the skills required to build IoT prototypes, products, and applications by using the web ecosystem and infrastructure. And we're glad to say that *Building the Web of Things* is therefore the first and most comprehensive hands-on guide to learning about the intersection of the IoT and web technologies. After a broad introduction to the nuts and bolts of the IoT, such as devices, sensors, standards, and tools, we quickly move up the protocol stack and focus on the Web of Things—the Application layer of the IoT.

Roadmap

This book will provide you with the skills needed to architect and implement IoT products, applications, and services by using the scalability and flexibility of the web. With the right balance between theory and practice, you'll be able to rapidly navigate the complexity of the Web of Things and learn about a wide range of tools and techniques for connecting IoT devices to the web and building interactive applications on top. The book is divided into two parts for a total of 10 chapters.

Part 1 introduces the basics of the Web of Things. You'll learn about the underlying technologies, protocols, tools, and issues related to connecting all sorts of devices to the web. After reading part 1, you'll have a solid understanding of the many issues in today's IoT, the various techniques available, and when to use each one:

- Chapter 1 introduces the general idea of the Web of Things—what it is, why it's different from the Internet of Things, and when using a WoT approach is ideal.
- Chapter 2 offers a hands-on walkthrough of the WoT. You'll interact with a remote, web-connected device across the world and build simple web applications with a few lines of code.
- Chapter 3 is a succinct overview of why Node.js is a great framework for implementing web-connected devices. This chapter also offers an introduction to the key concepts of Node.js and how to run it on embedded systems.
- Chapter 4 is a quick overview of the hardware side of the IoT. You'll learn how to configure a Raspberry Pi (or other Linux device) and connect it to the web,

as well as how to wire various sensors and actuators to a Pi and how to write
Node.js code to access them.

- Chapter 5 is a broad and condensed overview of today's IoT landscape, focusing
  on the networking aspects. You'll learn about the various networking and communication protocols used today, how they relate to each other, and when to
  use each one. This sets the stage for the WoT architecture stack, its layers, and
  the role of each layer.

Part 2 builds on everything you learned in part 1 and teaches you how to implement
the various layers of the WoT stack. You'll already have a real device that's connected
to the internet after part 1. Now you'll learn how to design a clean web API for that
device and how to use a variety of tools to build interactive, scalable, and extensible
WoT products and applications:

- Chapter 6 introduces layer 1 (Access) of the WoT architecture and offers a solid
  introduction to the HTTP and REST APIs. You'll learn various features of HTTP
  such as content negotiation, error codes, and verbs, and how to use them to
  implement great APIs for web-connected products. You'll also learn how to use
  WebSockets to cover the real-time aspects of sensors and actuators.
- Chapter 7 shows how to implement the Access layer in different situations and
  how to put into practice the concepts introduced in chapter 6. You'll learn
  about integration patterns and look into the integration of other protocols,
  such as MQTT and CoAP to the WoT.
- Chapter 8 focuses on layer 2 (Find) of the WoT and describes how to employ
  the features of web-connected products so they can be automatically discovered
  and used by web clients. It also offers a brief overview of the Semantic Web and
  how it relates to the IoT.
- Chapter 9 describes layer 3 (Share) of the WoT and discusses the various considerations and issues involved in connecting the real world to the web. You'll learn
  about best practices of web security and how to safely share data and services of
  a product with trusted applications and users. You'll also learn about the Social
  Web of Things, or how to use social networks to build networks of Things.
- Chapter 10 focuses on layer 4 (Compose) of the WoT and shows how to rapidly
  build complex applications that merge data from various sources. You'll learn
  about physical mashups and how to build and scale them.

We use the Raspberry Pi as a reference device in examples throughout the book. However, we've also included an appendix with the basics for integrating three other popular embedded systems—the BeagleBone, the Intel Edison, and the Arduino—into
the Web of Things.

Who should read this book?

This book has been designed to provide a rich yet accessible introduction to the Internet of Things. We wrote it assuming that our readers have no prior experience with

building embedded devices and application development. We expect you to have only a basic understanding of how the web works and some skills in programming. Our primary objective is to rapidly equip you with a broad and sufficiently deep understanding of a number of technologies, techniques, and challenges you'll encounter when building complex web-based applications that interact with the physical world. You won't become an expert in embedded sensing or web application design, but you'll certainly gain a well-stocked toolbox of frameworks, tools, standards, and application design patterns, along with the know-how required to combine those building blocks to build production-ready web-based IoT applications and systems.

How to use this book

You should first read chapter 1 to get a broad overview of the Web of Things, how it's different from the Internet of Things, and why this difference matters. If you're not familiar with web APIs and JavaScript, we encourage you to follow the various exercises in chapter 2. If you're not familiar with Node.js, you should definitely read chapter 3. If you have no experience with embedded devices such as sensors or processors, be sure to read chapter 4. If you're new to networking protocols and standards and can't tell your Bluetooth from your TCP/IP, definitely read sections 5.1 and 5.2 in chapter 5; otherwise, you could jump directly to section 5.3. Even if you have some experience with REST APIs, you should read chapter 6 to understand how to create REST APIs for devices, followed by chapter 7 to learn how to implement those APIs. Afterward, you can read chapter 8 or 9 and then chapter 10 at the end.

Code conventions and downloads

This book contains many examples of source code both in numbered listings and inline with normal text. In both cases, source code is formatted in a `fixed-width font like this` to separate it from ordinary text.

You can find all the code samples used throughout the book on GitHub at github.com/webofthings/wot-book. The code is also available from this book's website, located at manning.com/books/building-the-web-of-things.

All the links listed in the book as well as news and more information are available at http://book.webofthings.io.

Other online resources

There are many outlets where you can find new inspiration:
- The Web of Things community is where all this started back in 2007. You'll find lots of articles, news, and other technical whitepapers about the WoT here: http://webofthings.org.
- The W3C is actively looking at standardizing the Web of Things. You'll find the latest developments in this field at http://www.w3.org/WoT/. With EVRYTHNG, Dom and Vlad are also part of this W3C standardization effort.

- Postscapes is a great site for news on the IoT. It's not limited to the WoT, but you'll find lots of inspiration and interesting projects there: http://postscapes.com/.
- The community site of Element14 is a great place to discover projects and tutorials for building all sorts of web-connected devices: http://www.element14.com/community/. For more hardware and electronics projects, make sure you follow *Make* magazine (http://makezine.com/) and Instructables (http://www.instructables.com/).

Author Online

Purchase of *Building the Web of Things* includes free access to a private web forum run by Manning Publications; you can make comments about the book, ask technical questions, and receive help from the lead author and from other users. To access the forum and subscribe to it, point your web browser to manning.com/books/building-the-web-of-things. This page provides information on how to get on the forum after you're registered, what kind of help is available, and the rules of conduct on the forum.

Manning's commitment to our readers is to provide a venue where a meaningful dialogue between individual readers and between readers and the author can take place. It's not a commitment to any specific amount of participation on the part of the author, whose contribution to the AO remains voluntary (and unpaid). We suggest you try asking the author some challenging questions lest his interest stray!

The Author Online forum and the archives of previous discussions will be accessible from the publisher's website as long as the book is in print.

About the authors

Dominique Guinard and Vlad Trifa are the cofounders of EVRYTHNG, a large-scale Web of Things cloud powering millions of web Things. They also cofounded http://webofthings.org, the earliest community and conference series for practitioners and researchers in web-connected devices. Both are veterans of WoT and IoT technologies and have pioneered this field at SAP, ETH, and MIT. In 2011, they were listed fifth among the world's top 100 IoT thinkers by Postscapes.

 **Dominique "Dom" Guinard** is the CTO and cofounder of EVRYTHNG, a large-scale Web of Things cloud platform that makes products smart by connecting them to the web. Dom holds a PhD from ETH Zurich, where he worked on the early concepts of the WoT architecture: an open Application layer for the Internet of Things. Early in 2012, his PhD thesis was granted the ETH Medal. Before this, Dom spent a decade working on a number of IoT projects: exploring large-scale RFID networks, in partnership with Sun Microsystems;

researching the role of mobile phones as IoT gateways, at the Auto-ID Lab of ETH Zurich with Nokia Research; bringing the EPCglobal RFID network to the Web of Things at the Auto-ID lab of MIT; and four years integrating tagged objects and wireless sensor networks with enterprise software at SAP.

 **Vlad Trifa** is the cofounder and EVP of Research and Development of EVRYTHNG. Widely published, he is a recognized expert in distributed embedded sensing and the integration of interactive devices with enterprise applications using web technologies. Previously, he worked as a researcher in urban and mobile computing at the MIT Senseable City Lab in the United States and in Singapore; in bioacoustics and distributed signal processing at UCLA; and in human-robot interaction and neuroscience at ATR in Kyoto, Japan. He also gained industrial experience in factory automation and enterprise computing while working as a research associate at SAP. Vlad graduated with a PhD in computer science from ETH Zurich and with an MSc in computer science from EPFL with a concentration in robotics, artificial intelligence, and machine learning.

Part 1

Basics of the IoT and the WoT

In part 1 we lay the basis of the Web of Things, what it is, and how it compares and relates to the Internet of Things. At the end of the first part you'll have a broad understanding of the problems and challenges of building Internet of Things systems.

Chapter 1 introduces the Web of Things approach and discusses the various advantages it offers in numerous use cases and contexts.

Chapter 2 offers a high-level yet hands-on first encounter with the Web of Things. You'll learn how to send requests to a real device in London and quickly write simple applications that interact with the device.

Chapter 3 describes why JavaScript is an excellent fit for embedded devices and the Web of Things and also provides a crash course on the Node.js framework and ecosystem.

Chapter 4 provides an introduction to the world of embedded systems, their various types, and their differences. Next, you'll become familiar with the Raspberry Pi platform, learn how to connect sensors and actuators to your device, and then control it from Node.js applications.

Chapter 5 is a broad introduction to the various approaches and methods for interconnecting physical objects. In particular, you'll learn about the benefits of and differences between the various networking protocols commonly used in the Internet of Things. At the end of the chapter, we propose a layered architecture for the Web of Things.

From the Internet of Things to the Web of Things

> **This chapter covers**
> - An introduction to the concept and history of the Internet of Things (IoT)
> - When and why we should digitally connect physical objects
> - The limitations of traditional approaches to the Internet of Things
> - How and why the Web of Things (WoT) is different and why it's promising

If you're holding this book in your hands, it's very likely that you've already heard the terms *Internet of Things (IoT)* and *Web of Things (WoT)*. Maybe you want to understand what this trend is all about. Or maybe you already understand why this topic has become so popular and you'd like to be part of it, but you're not sure where to start. Or—even further than that—you realize what the IoT could mean for your industry and you'd like to gain the hard technical skills needed to build web-connected products and services. If any of those ring true, you're in for a treat!

What is the IoT, anyway? When and where was it invented? What new types of applications and scenarios does the IoT enable? How will this change the technology and business landscape for the coming years? The next chapters will answer all these questions and many more. But don't throw away this book yet, because it won't just discuss theory. It will also cover in detail all the web technologies and tools that will help you make the Internet of Things a reality. On the other hand, we believe that starting with some background will help you better understand what the IoT really is and how you can use it in your own projects, not just stick to the superficial and stereotypical descriptions of it. Diving into the history of the IoT will help you understand the subtle difference between the Internet of Things and the Web of Things and especially why this distinction matters.

In the last few years, the Internet of Things has become one of the most promising and exciting developments in technology and business. The vision of a world where tiny computers with sensors and communication interfaces that are embedded in the infrastructure of our cities or in cars, offices, or clothes is likely to revolutionize every area of our lives—how we play, how we work and do business, and how we live. Until recently, IoT projects mostly focused on building small-scale, closed, and isolated deployments where devices were not designed to be easily accessible or reprogrammable. The bespoke coupling between devices and applications in a given use case means that any change to an existing deployment is complex and expensive. This limits both the maintenance and evolution of the Internet of Things because considerable resources (time, money, and technical skills) are required each time a new function is added.

In contrast, the web has become widely successful in the last two decades because it's simple to learn and use and it also emphasizes loose coupling between servers, browsers, and applications. The simple and clearly defined programming model of HTTP makes it possible for anyone to change pieces of the system without breaking the whole system. Therefore, building new web applications has been relatively inexpensive and accessible to a much larger group of technology enthusiasts.

The Web of Things is a specialization of the Internet of Things that uses what made the web so successful and applies it to embedded devices in order to make the latest developments in the Internet of Things accessible to as many developers as possible. On the Web of Things—just like on the web—anyone with a text editor and the basic understanding of web standards (HTML and HTTP) can quickly start connecting devices and objects to the web. But it also enables going to the next level and helps you to effectively build interactive and innovative real-world applications that blend the physical and digital worlds.

1.1   *Defining the Internet of Things*

Capturing the essence of the Internet of Things in one sentence is nearly impossible. The concepts have been around for decades and there are no clear boundaries to what the IoT is or isn't. Nevertheless, the broad definition of the Internet of Things vision is a world where the internet is much more than the collection of multimedia content it is today: it extends into the physical, real-time world using a myriad of small or even tiny computers. In short, the simplest definition we can offer for the Internet of Things is the following.

> **DEFINITION** The Internet of Things is a system of physical objects that can be discovered, monitored, controlled, or interacted with by electronic devices that communicate over various networking interfaces and eventually can be connected to the wider internet.

Two decades ago, a world where everyday objects could feel the world through sensors and then analyze, store, or exchange information existed only in science-fiction novels or in the Jetsons. Today, such scenarios are increasingly becoming reality, thanks to the colossal progress in embedded devices that brought into the world a new class of objects: smart things. A *smart thing* (which we'll refer to as a *Thing*—with a capital *T*—in the rest of this book) is a physical object that's digitally augmented with one or more of the following:

- Sensors (temperature, light, motion, and so on)
- Actuators (displays, sound, motors, and so on)
- Computation (can run programs and logic)
- Communication interfaces (wired or wireless)

Things extend the world we live in by enabling a whole new range of applications; see figure 1.1. By deploying a bunch of tiny and cheap—yet increasingly powerful—computers everywhere around us, it becomes possible to monitor and interact with the physical world with a much finer spatial and temporal resolution than ever before.

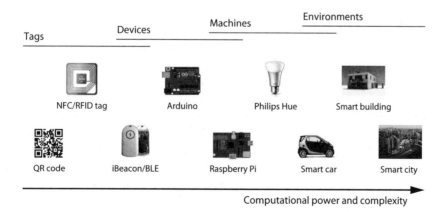

Figure 1.1 The Internet of Things landscape. The IoT is a network of Things, which are anything that can be connected in some form to the internet. From a box of oranges with an RFID tag, to a smart city, to every Thing in between, all digitally augmented objects make up the Internet of Things.

Concretely, the Things in the Internet of Things can range from simple tagged products such as your FedEx package with an Auto-ID tag (Automatic Identification methods such as bar codes, QR codes, and NFC and RFID tags) attached to it so it can be tracked from the shipping center to your door; to more elaborate, complex, and wirelessly connected products, devices, or machines such as security systems, your car, or a factory assembly line; and all the way up to a building or even a city. The *internet* part of the term means that the Thing (or at least its services or data about/from it) can be accessed and processed by other applications through the existing internet infrastructure. Note that this does not imply that the Thing itself must be directly connected to the internet. The communication network used can be an Auto-ID method, short-range radio (Bluetooth, ZigBee, and the like), or the Wi-Fi network in a building.

Unfortunately, building a single and global ecosystem of Things that communicate with each other seamlessly is virtually impossible today. There's no unique and universal application protocol for the Internet of Things that can work across the many networking interfaces available today. To put it bluntly, the Internet of Things of today is essentially a growing collection of isolated Intranets of Things that can't be connected to each other.

For the Internet of Things to become real, we need a single universal application layer protocol (think *language*) for devices and applications to talk to each other, regardless of how they're physically connected. Rather than inventing yet another protocol from scratch (as many IoT projects have been—and keep—doing), why not reuse something that's already widely used to build scalable and interactive applications, such as the web itself? This is what the Web of Things (and this book) is all about: using and reusing readily available and widely popular web protocols, standards, and blueprints to make data and services offered by Things more accessible to a larger pool of (web) developers.

1.2   *Enter the Web of Things*

As we'll describe in detail in section 1.4, the limitations of the Internet of Things become visible as soon as one wants to integrate devices from various manufacturers into a single application or system. To illustrate how the Web of Things can deal with these limitations, let's consider the life of Johnny B., the owner of a famous hotel chain in several cities around the world. Johnny would like to digitally connect all the appliances in all the rooms of all his hotels, so that he can monitor, control, and improve the management of his hotels from the deck of his yacht in the Bahamas via a single control center application. Meanwhile, this system could also offer a more pleasant and personalized experience to each guest in his hotels, as shown in figure 1.2.

1.2.1   *Web of Things scenario: connected hotel*

Building this smart hotel system will likely require electronic door locks made by company *Alpha*, security cameras from company *Beta*, and a control application to manage all of this made by company *Gamma*. Making these devices and systems talk and work

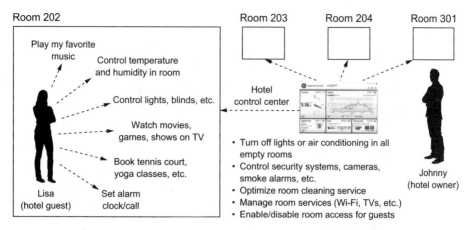

Figure 1.2 Johnny would like to digitally connect the appliances in all rooms of his hotel. First, guests could have access to a variety of services from controlling their room (lights, air-conditioning, entertainment, and so on), to booking hotel facilities, to ordering food and drinks—all of this on their mobile phones. Second, this system would allow Johnny to coordinate and optimize all aspects of his hotel in a centralized and efficient manner, without having to use a variety of siloed applications and tools.

with each other will require lots of custom system integration. Johnny could contract with a specialized company and spend his well-earned resources on a substantial project that will take months to complete. Such a complex and bespoke project will have the robustness of a Jenga tower (touch the wrong piece and all hell breaks loose): it will be swamped with bugs and hacks and therefore will be a nightmare to maintain and to extend. In this scenario, there's little doubt that Johnny will run out of money before he gets the system he wants.

If Johnny is into DIY (do it yourself), he can certainly decide to build the whole system himself. He'll need to buy all the equipment from the same company so he won't run into any incompatibilities. Unfortunately, it's unlikely that he'll find a single manufacturer that has all the sensors and equipment he needs. Even if he finds this perfect system, chances are high that the control application that comes with it won't be what he wants: easy to use and to configure. He'll likely have to write a whole new control center application himself, from scratch. Oh, and if he also wants the system to be scalable, reliable, and secure, he can easily double—if not triple—the time he'll need to build it. Should we also talk about the mobile apps that will need to be built for the hotel guests? You get the idea.

Johnny's life may seem surreal. Sadly, it's pretty much what the IoT looks like today. We know this because we've had the chance to work with many Johnnies over the last decade, ranging from shop managers wanting to combine their existing security cameras with RFID gates to create smarter security systems, to LED manufacturers wanting their lights to be controlled from the web. We've experienced this scenario over and over.

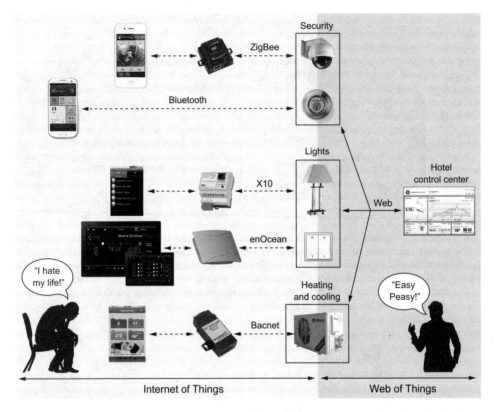

Figure 1.3   In the Internet of Things, hundreds of incompatible protocols coexist today. This makes the integration of data and services from various devices extremely complex and costly. In the Web of Things, any device can be accessed using standard web protocols. Connecting heterogeneous devices to the web makes the integration across systems and applications much simpler.

Wouldn't it be wonderful if any device could be easily integrated and consumed by any application, regardless of the networking protocols or standards they use? This is exactly what the Web of Things enables, as illustrated in figure 1.3.

1.2.2   *Comparing IoT and WoT*

Because more everyday objects will be digitally augmented, the next logical step is to use the World Wide Web ecosystem and infrastructure to build applications for the Internet of Things, effectively breaking this ongoing "one device, one protocol, one app" pattern. It would be particularly interesting to push down to each of those tiny devices the exact same technology that helped modern websites such as Facebook or Google scale to millions of concurrent users, without compromising on security or performance. The idea of maximizing existing and emerging tools and techniques used on the web and applying them to the development of Internet of Things scenarios is the ultimate goal of the Web of Things.

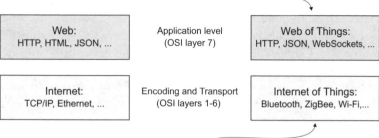

Easier to program, faster to integrate data and services, simpler to prototype, deploy, and maintain large systems.

Web: HTTP, HTML, JSON, ...	Application level (OSI layer 7)	Web of Things: HTTP, JSON, WebSockets, ...
Internet: TCP/IP, Ethernet, ...	Encoding and Transport (OSI layers 1-6)	Internet of Things: Bluetooth, ZigBee, Wi-Fi,...

More lightweight and optimized for embedded devices (reduced battery, processing, memory and bandwidth usage), more bespoke and hard-wired solutions.

Figure 1.4   The Web of Things is concerned with only the highest OSI layer (7), which handles applications, services, and data. Working with such a high level of abstraction makes it possible to connect data and services from many devices regardless of the actual transport protocols they use. In contrast, the Internet of Things doesn't advocate a single Application-level protocol and usually focuses on the lower layers of the OSI stack.

While the Internet of Things has been busy resolving networking problems, the Web of Things relies exclusively on Application-level protocols and tools (layer 7 of the Open Systems Interconnection (OSI) model described in chapter 5); see figure 1.4. Mapping any device into a web mindset makes the Web of Things agnostic to the Physical and Transport layer protocols used by devices. As you'll learn to do in the next chapters, the good news is that pretty much any custom IoT protocol or standard can be linked to the web thanks to software or hardware bridges called *gateways*.

Abstracting the complexity and variety of the lower-level protocols behind the simple model of the web offers many advantages. Just like the web has become the global integration platform for distributed applications over the internet, the Web of Things facilitates the integration of all sorts of devices and the applications that interact with them. In other words, by hiding the complexity and differences between various transport protocols used in the IoT, the Web of Things allows developers to focus on the logic of their applications without having to bother about how this or that protocol or device actually works.

Coming back to our smart hotel scenario, if all devices (regardless of their manufacturer) could offer a standard web API, integration of data across devices and applications will pretty much come out of the box because all devices would speak the same language. In this case, the hotel owner (or system integrator) will only need to worry about building the control center application that's likely going to be a web mashup—a single web application that combines data and services from various sources. He won't have to bother learning the specifics of each protocol used by the various devices he wants to use.[1] This will not only take significantly less time to build but will also minimize the effort required to maintain the system each time a device or service is added, removed, or updated.

Making this vision a reality has been the objective of the Web of Things community we started in 2007.[2] Using HTTP and other web standards or tools to interact with embedded devices made perfect sense to us. At the time, this idea seemed unrealistic and even pointless to some, and we got our fair share of criticism, mainly because embedded web servers in an Internet of Things generally have more limited resources than the clients who access them (such as browsers or mobile phones). But things have changed: recent embedded web servers with advanced features can be implemented with only 8 KB of memory. Thanks to efficient cross-layer TCP/HTTP optimizations, they can run on tiny embedded systems or even smart cards. Also, thanks to the massive developments in the JavaScript community, it has become increasingly easy to shift a lot of the workload from devices to client applications and even to the cloud.

In the Web of Things, devices and their services are fully integrated in the web because they use the same standards and techniques as traditional websites. This means that you can write applications that interact with embedded devices in exactly the same way as you would interact with any other web service that uses web APIs— in particular, RESTful architectures.

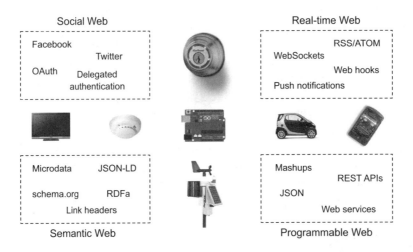

Figure 1.5 The Web of Things is the ability to use modern web standards on embedded devices. By using all these standards for Internet of Things scenarios, we both enable new types of interactive applications to be built and make sure that devices can be integrated with modern web applications and services with minimal effort.

---

[1] A not so short list of automation protocols: https://en.wikipedia.org/wiki/List_of_automation_protocols

[2] http://webofthings.org

As we'll describe in chapter 6, REST is an architectural style for developing distributed applications and is the basis upon which the modern web is built. The essence of REST is to focus on creating loosely coupled services that can be easily reused, which are implemented using URIs, HTTP, and standardized media types. Abstracting the services from their application-specific semantics thanks to a uniform interface (HTTP verbs and response codes) makes it easy to build loosely coupled services because it provides a simple mechanism for clients to select the best possible representations for interactions. This makes the web the ideal substrate to build a universal architecture and application programming interface (API) to interact with Things, as shown in figure 1.5.

In practice, this means you can start interacting with Things via web browsers and explore the Web of Things as you would surf the web (via links to other related Things). Real-time data collected from distributed sensors can then be easily retrieved, processed, and displayed on web pages using HTML, CSS, and JavaScript.

In contrast to many protocols and standards existing in the Internet of Things, the programming model behind the Web of Things is significantly easier to learn and to use. This is particularly interesting because it enables anyone with basic web programming skills to build websites and applications, not only around multimedia content but also with real-time data from the physical world, as figure 1.6 illustrates.

Although the Web of Things emphasizes the use of web standards to exchange data between devices, it doesn't imply anything about how the devices should be physically connected to each other. In other words, devices can (but don't have to) be

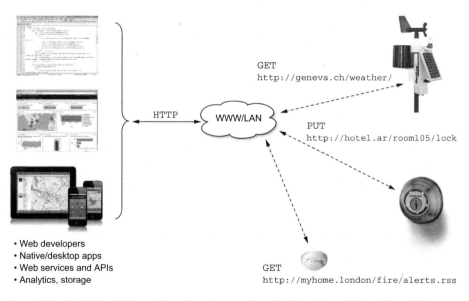

Figure 1.6 The Web of Things allows developers and applications to exchange data with any physical object or device using standard HTTP requests, regardless of how the device is connected.

openly connected to the web and publicly accessible by anyone just like websites. The Web of Things works equally well in a local network (for example, the intranet of your company or your Wi-Fi network at home).

In some cases, it makes sense for Things to have a public URL and be openly accessible over the web—for example, traffic or pollution sensors in a city operated by the public authorities. In this case, devices could also be crawled and indexed by search engines like any other web page and allow users to literally Google the physical world or bookmark the URL of a smart object and share it with friends. Web-connected objects can also become active and participate in the web just like other users by publishing their own blogs or talking to each other using the APIs of services such as Twitter.

Using services such as IFTTT,[3] users can create small, logical rules that mix real-world devices such as sensors in their home with virtual services in the cloud; for example, an SMS gateway or a weather forecast service. Such applications are called *physical mashups* and are the topic of chapter 10, where you'll learn the principles and tools that will allow you to create physical mashups on top of your Things.

To really understand why the Web of Things represents an interesting next stage in the evolution of the IoT, we first need to look at the history of this field up to today. Why did the idea of connected devices emerge in the first place? And if the vision of a global network of connected devices is so promising, why doesn't it exist yet? We attempt to answer these questions in the next section.

1.2.3   *The Internet of Things—a brief history*

To understand where the notion of the Internet of Things comes from, we have to look into a field of computer science research that goes by many names, most commonly *ubiquitous computing* or *pervasive computing*. One of the founding fathers of this discipline was Mark Weiser. While leading the Xerox PARC research lab in the early '90s, Weiser started to think about the next wave of computers:

> *The most profound technologies are those that disappear. They weave themselves into the fabric of everyday life until they are indistinguishable from it....Silicon-based information technology, in contrast, is far from having become part of the environment. More than 50 million personal computers have been sold, and nonetheless the computer remains largely in a world of its own. It is approachable only through complex jargon that has nothing to do with the tasks for which people actually use computers.*
>
> Mark Weiser, "The Computer for the Twenty-First Century," 1991

What Weiser understood before anyone else was that computers were clearly evolving from the big, bulky boxes on desktops and in offices toward smaller and smarter devices that would soon be seamlessly embedded everywhere in the world around us and become invisible.

---

[3] https://ifttt.com/

The years that followed 1991 were the early years of the internet we know today, which has grown into a massive public global network of computers, thanks to the invention, by Sir Tim Berners-Lee, and development of the web (HTTP and HTML)—the Application layer on top of the internet.

No wonder the stunning success of the internet had a strong impact on the ubiquitous computing research community. A number of researchers started to think about connecting physical objects to the internet. In particular, these included researchers from the Auto-ID Labs (an international cluster of research laboratories originally founded at MIT), such as Sanjay Sarma, Kevin Ashton, David Brock, and Daniel Engels at MIT and Friedemann Mattern and Elgar Fleisch at ETH Zurich. Their primary focus was on automatically identifying goods using radio frequency identification (RFID) tags in order to create a global network of electronically tagged products and to be able to optimize logistics and supply chains. Looking for a term to describe this global network, Kevin Ashton came up with the term *Internet of Things*.[4] The rest is history.

Although the term *Internet of Things* was coined in 1999, this concept has remained under the radar of the general public until the last few years, when people realized it was more than just a trendy term. According to Google Trends, since December 2013 the term *Internet of Things* clearly took over *Web 2.0* in news headlines (figure 1.7). Although Web 2.0 has been one of the most popular emerging web trends of the 2000s, in the last few years it has faded away from the spotlight as the popularity of the Internet of Things has grown exponentially.

When Google acquired NEST for a "modest" $3.3 billion USD in December 2013, a collective "Aha!" moment took place: *Hold on! There is actually money to be made with the Internet of Things.* And lots of it! In 2014, Gartner predicted a population of over 25 billion connected devices by 2020.[5] Cisco was a bit more optimistic and predicted that by 2020 there would be more than 50 billion Things connected to the internet.[6]

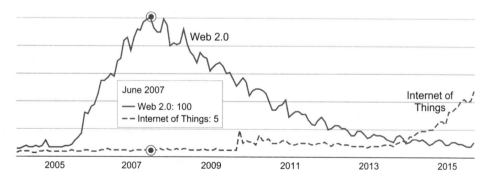

Figure 1.7 **Since December 2013, the term *Internet of Things* has become more popular in news headlines than *Web 2.0*. [Source: Google Trends, September 25, 2015]**

[4] http://www.rfidjournal.com/articles/view?4986
[5] http://www.gartner.com/newsroom/id/2905717
[6] https://www.cisco.com/web/about/ac79/docs/innov/IoT_IBSG_0411FINAL.pdf

It doesn't really matter who is right or wrong because one thing is certain: in the next decade, there will be a lot more internet-connected devices around us. A significant milestone was reached in 2008 when the number of Things connected to the Internet exceeded the number of people. In consequence, many of the largest companies in the world, from Cisco to Samsung to IBM, mentioned the IoT as a key strategic investment in 2014.[7]

We can learn two things from this sudden interest in the Internet of Things. First, regardless of whether you are a back-end guru, a front-end developer, or a hobbyist hacker, now is the ideal time to brush up on your Internet of Things skills. Second, the years of the Intranet of Things, where Things only ever communicate in their own little world, are numbered. But for the IoT to become a reality and unleash its potential, all those objects need to speak the same language. For devices and applications to interact with each other easily, securely, and in an ad hoc manner, we need a universal and open standard that promotes loose coupling, scalability, and flexibility.

1.3   *Use cases—why connected objects?*

It would be incorrect to ask when the IoT will be here because it already is. Countless examples can be found everywhere today. Your smart TV connects to the internet and records the shows you prefer to watch. The Nike+ sensor in your shoes uploads all your runs to the internet so you can compete with your friends. And your mobile phone streams your location so you can track it or disable it remotely if it gets stolen.

Nonetheless, the IoT is still in its early teenage years and will certainly influence our world in a much more profound way than these early use cases did. Let's look at the areas where the IoT will most likely have a big impact. This is an opportunity to see what benefits the Web of Things can bring to multiple areas. Hopefully, this will inspire you for your future weekend hacks or more serious product developments.

1.3.1   *Wireless sensor networks and distributed sensing*

The incredible progress in computing in the '80s and '90s, especially the miniaturization of embedded computers and radio networking chips, led to the emergence in the early 2000s of wireless sensor networks (WSNs). Those networks are composed of tiny, single-board computers such as the ones shown in figure 1.8.[8] Those devices, being cheap and battery-powered, could be deployed in large areas to continuously monitor various physical environments or structures using a multitude of sensors. For example, WSNs have been used to monitor the structure of historical buildings such as the Torre Aquila in Italy,[9] to understand the impact of humans on bird habitats,[10] and to monitor agricultural crops for food production.[11]

---

[7] http://postscapes.com/internet-of-things-investment
[8] http://en.wikipedia.org/wiki/List_of_wireless_sensor_nodes
[9] http://d3s.disi.unitn.it/projects/torreaquila
[10] http://www.cs.berkeley.edu/~culler/papers/wsna02.pdf
[11] http://www.mdpi.com/1424-8220/9/6/4728/htm

Mica Mote (~2004):
CPU: Atmel ATmega 128 @ 4 MHz
Flash: 128 KB RAM + 512 KB Flash
Radio: 868/916 MHz

Sun SPOT (~2010):
CPU: ARM ARM920T @ 180 MHz
Flash: 512 KB RAM + 4 MB Flash
Radio: 2.4 MHz IEEE 802.15.4

Intel Edison (~2014):
CPU: Atom dual core @ 500 MHz
Flash: 1 GB RAM + 4 GB Flash
Radio: Wi-Fi + Bluetooth

Figure 1.8 Three generations of wireless sensor nodes

Although early WSN deployments weren't connected to the internet, these systems influenced the IoT in many ways because this prolific research community gave birth to innovative ideas that shaped IoT technologies. The techniques, tools, and protocols developed for WSNs made it possible to use low-power platforms for large-scale distributed sensing applications in the real world.

The requirements and operating context of those devices also gave birth to a number of operating systems optimized for low-power sensing, such as TinyOS[12] or Contiki.[13] Indeed, when battery-powered devices are deployed in natural and unpredictable environments, it's essential to ensure robustness and minimal energy consumption because human intervention to debug or fix software and hardware problems—or even to change the batteries—is clearly impractical.

WSNS AND THE WEB OF THINGS

It's clear that the majority of WSN devices weren't designed for the public. Those platforms were intended to be mainly programmed by experts. Although web protocols are heavier (more verbose) than the optimized protocols used on embedded devices, there has been a lot of progress in optimized HTTP libraries that run on constrained devices.[14] Additionally, devices are becoming increasingly powerful and many come with Wi-Fi connectivity on board. The ability to interact with embedded sensors using standard web protocols makes the collection, storage, and analysis of data from heterogeneous sensors much simpler. Indeed, integrating data across several cloud services is much faster thanks to the simplicity and ubiquity of REST APIs.

---

[12] http://www.tinyos.net
[13] http://www.contiki-os.org
[14] http://research.microsoft.com/pubs/73067/tws.pdf

Figure 1.9   The Nike+ ecosystem was one of the pioneers in the quantified self or wearables trend. [Photo by ivyfield on Flickr licensed under CC BY 2.0]

1.3.2   *Wearables and quantified self*

Another interesting use case for the IoT is building tiny sensors that people can carry or wear to passively monitor their daily activities or even body factors such as heartbeats or chemicals in their blood or sweat. Heartbeat monitors have long been commercialized for long-distance runners to keep track of and regulate their heart activity. A major breakthrough in this domain was the Nike+, which was easy to use and could connect out of the box to an iPhone (see figure 1.9).

This trend has experiences a boom in the last few years with many more products ranging from activity trackers,[15] to smart scales connected to your phone helping you to control your weight and body fat,[16] to smart pedals tracking your rides and working as antitheft devices,[17] to smart pillows, smart pill boxes, alarm clocks, and smart watches giving you access to a whole new world of information about yourself.

WEARABLES AND THE WEB OF THINGS

Integrating wearable and quantified self devices on the web, so that the data is directly accessible by other devices and applications, will make it much easier to develop new classes of extensible applications for elder care, health and fitness, or fun and sports. It will also ensure you don't need a separate app for each of them (with interesting security and privacy challenges that we'll discuss in chapter 9).

---

[15] For example: http://misfit.com or https://jawbone.com/up
[16] http://www.withings.com/us/en/products/smart-body-analyzer
[17] http://connectedcycle.com

As illustrated by Nike's success story, early wearable devices focused on the social aspects of sports by sharing and comparing personal data such as race times, distances, and so on. Here again, the Web of Things helps because it allows a seamless connection between wearable devices and social networks on the web.

1.3.3 *Smart homes and buildings*

In the '60s and '70s, the house of the future was envisioned as an entirely automated and responsive system, like the ones you could see in *The Jetsons* or *Star Trek*. Doors would open automatically; food and coffee would be made by robots and readily served as soon as you pop out of your bed. Your environment would make your life easier and take care of everything you needed when you needed it.

Domotics—the technical term for smart and connected homes—became all the rage in the 2000s, and these systems included entertainment systems, lighting systems, heating, ventilation, air-conditioning systems (HVAC), and so on. But smart homes existed way before the Internet of Things was invented. The most important difference between the legacy systems and the second wave of smart homes is the use of internet or internet-friendly protocols, pushing home automation away from the world of proprietary systems by connecting devices directly to the internet or through residential gateways.

Interestingly enough, this trend toward digitalizing our homes went even further with the development of open-source hardware and software platforms such as Arduino.[18] Indeed, many amateurs started hacking around and connecting various bits in their houses. From energy and gas meters to lighting and presence detectors, amateur developers were suddenly interested and empowered to connect their houses to the internet.

SMART HOMES AND THE WEB OF THINGS

The smart home environment is probably symptomatic of the (too) vast number of standards and protocols that exist for connecting things to networks. Although all devices in your home should talk to each other, they can't because those protocols are incompatible and you end up with more apps and remote controls than ever before. The Web of Things offers an alternative approach where web languages are the baseline, the minimal API that devices should offer either directly or indirectly through gateways. In our own company—EVRYTHNG[19]—we used the Web of Things approach to connect, at scale, a number of home automation devices from different manufacturers.

The Web of Things allows interoperability between devices from different manufacturers and fosters cross-device applications. It also makes it possible for a larger group of amateurs to buy all sorts of devices, build rapidly their smart home systems, and especially reuse and customize these systems easily for their unique needs and desires.

---

[18] http://www.arduino.cc
[19] http://evrythng.com

1.3.4 *Smart cities and energy grids*

One of the most promising use cases for the Internet of Things might well be the emergence of smart cities. As more humans move from rural areas to cities each year, it becomes clear that changes are necessary to the way large cities are designed and operate to ensure the safety and well-being of their inhabitants. The ability to monitor urban environments in real time thanks to a plethora of sensors and computers is an incredibly promising substrate to make our cities smarter and more efficient.

Smart cities have always been at the heart of what WSN researchers do: getting more insights about our environment based on data gathered by tiny computers. But most of this work was based on an asynchronous and linear workflow:

1 Deploy wireless sensor nodes.
2 Collect data.
3 Analyze data in the lab.
4 Write reports.
5 Take actions based on these reports.

The Internet of Things gives new dimension to this domain by drastically short-circuiting the required steps. The data is now available on the internet as real-time streams upon which direct actions can be taken. These can be used to monitor safety, traffic, or utilities (water, waste disposal, and more) in real time and react rapidly when any anomaly is detected—ideally before a serious problem occurs.

The interest in smart cities has significantly increased in the past few years with a number of cities betting a lot on the potential of the Internet of Things, such as Milton Keynes in the UK,[20] Santander in Spain,[21] New York in the United States,[22] and Songdo in South Korea.[23]

As a stepping-stone to this vision of future cities, smart grids are using the Internet of Things to optimize the way we consume and distribute energy. Thanks to real-world services, home and industrial appliances can increasingly communicate their energy consumption in real time and raise consumers' energy awareness. Furthermore, appliances can communicate with each other to make whole buildings smarter by optimizing HVAC among other things. Even more important, through composite applications using real-world services, industrial machinery and citywide infrastructures will be able to negotiate energy consumption and limit consumption peaks.

SMART CITIES AND THE WEB OF THINGS

Using web standards in the context of smart cities is particularly interesting because they make it much easier to share sensor data with the public and make it easy for developers to consume real-time data about traffic, pollution, or public transportation in their own urban applications.

---

[20] http://www.mksmart.org
[21] htttp://www.smartsantander.eu
[22] https://nycopendata.socrata.com
[23] htttp://www.bbc.co.uk/news/technology-23757738

1.3.5 Smart manufacturing and Industry 4.0

Manufacturing went through three main cycles of evolution. First came the mechanization of production processes using water and steam power in the Industrial Era during the 19th century. Afterwards, mass production of goods was enabled thanks to electric power. The third revolution was the digital age, where electronics and computers made it possible to further automate production, distribution, and communication processes.

The IoT is enabling a fourth revolution in manufacturing and industrial systems commonly referred to as *Industry 4.0*. Germany has been at the forefront of this change driven by companies such as Bosch, Siemens, and SAP. The IoT can bring two main benefits to traditional industries. First is access to unparalleled amounts of data. Connecting machines to the internet and feeding them real-time data is one step toward more transparent and efficient industrial systems. Second, the IoT brings services to machines. Rather than being bound to a single set of operations, industrial machines can now offer services, making it possible to use and reuse these machines in combination with other machines by connecting their respective services. This ability will transform manufacturing machines and plants into flexible ecosystems of reconfigurable production lines that can rearrange themselves to perform any given tasks as efficiently as possible. Industry 4.0 is an ongoing revolution and most of the activities in this field are still taking place in research labs all over the world. But in the last two years, most large companies have actively engaged in IoT projects and products, showing that this isn't just a trend: it's a massive opportunity to reinvent any business. And it's here to stay.

INDUSTRY AND THE WEB OF THINGS

Using web standards to interconnect all the elements in a business process, such as the shop-floor machinery, enterprise software, employees in various departments, products, customer, and suppliers, will represent a significant change in how companies do business. Turning all the elements in a factory into easy-to-combine LEGO-like bricks will make it much easier and faster for companies to adapt to changing environments, get their products to market more quickly, optimize their business and manufacturing processes, and so on. When all the actors in those processes are able to automatically decide how best to perform their duty based on real-time data, there's no doubt that the way we design, manufacture, and distribute physical products will be profoundly changed.

1.3.6 Smart logistics and supply chains

As explained before, the first mention of the Internet of Things comes from the world of Auto-ID of the everyday consumer packaged goods (CPGs) or even the cheaper and short-lived fast-moving consumer goods (FMCGs). It's no wonder that the world of logistics and supply chains was the first to explore the connectivity between all kinds of real-world objects and the internet. Indeed, the Internet of Things isn't limited to devices but can include any physical object. Even if the object itself doesn't have any communication capabilities, one can use a mobile phone or an RFID reader to recognize the product and interact with it. In consequence, CPGs such as food products and also more expensive and long-lived items such as a luxury watch or a handbag only need a machine-readable tag to be part of the Internet of Things.

The EPCglobal network[24] was probably the first standardized system for applying the Internet of Things to logistics. The EPCglobal network is a set of standards that describe how to connect RFID-tagged objects to standard readers, which in turn are connected via the internet to RFID information systems and databases.

Passive RFID tags are tiny computers that harvest energy from the electromagnetic field generated by nearby RFID readers. RFID tags are certainly not the only way to identify FMCGs, but they present a key advantage over other technologies such as barcodes, image recognition, or QR codes: they can be read automatically, without human intervention or line of sight, and they're already widely deployed in live systems throughout the whole supply chain.

The biggest barrier of adoption for RFID in logistics and supply-chain operations has always been the relatively high cost of RFID, making it expensive to tag every object. But recent developments are producing radical changes in this space: a number of companies in the world have managed to print RFID tags, sensors, and batteries (see figure 1.10). In a few years, it will be easy and cheap to print embedded computers and sensors on products and/or their packaging.

Large-scale adoption of automated identification and tracking methods on products will have a massive impact on supply chains, allowing them to be much more efficient and also to offer better services to consumers.

SMART LOGISTICS AND THE WEB OF THINGS

Imagine a web-enabled supply chain that knows in real time the temperature of your strawberries and can send alerts as soon as the conditions change or even regulate automatically the temperature of trucks, ships, and warehouses according to the type of the products being stored and transported—all of that information accessible over web APIs. Sharing historical data about devices using web standards will make it much easier for multiple applications to work together across the whole lifecycle of products. This means much lower integration costs and high data integrity across the different systems that will process and handle those products.

Figure 1.10   A Thinfilm[25] printed NFC tag and temperature sensor. RFID tags, sensors, and batteries can now be printed, reducing the costs and allowing packages to become smart. [Source: Thinfilm, used with permission]

---

[24] http://www.gs1.org/epcglobal
[25] http://thinfilm.no/products-nfc-solutions/

1.3.7   Marketing 2.0

The ability to connect CPGs and FMCGs to the internet enables many interesting applications for product manufacturers and retailers, but beyond the supply chain, on the consumer side, it also allows new services, commonly referred to as Marketing 2.0. The ability to identify products with mobile phones using bar codes, QR codes, or image recognition makes it possible to launch personalized marketing campaigns by turning a product into a direct communication and service delivery channel between consumers and retailers. Typical applications in this field range from product personalization and gifting to customer loyalty, digital user guides and after-sales services, and personalized warranties and product recalls.

The use of IoT technologies for marketing purposes isn't limited to tagged products. Smart devices can be used to fuel the craziest and most creative (we'll let you be the judge of that.) marketing campaigns as well. Examples of those are the Evian Drop, a small device that lets you order water directly from your fridge for delivery to your doorstep,[26] the Dom Pérignon button (figure 1.11) that lets you order champagne at the push of a button in your hotel room at the prestigious Savoy Hotel in London,[27] and the Budweiser Red Light that glows bright red when your favorite team scores a goal.[28]

Figure 1.11   The Press for DP button manages the delivery of Dom Pérignon champagne in Savoy Hotel rooms within a few minutes. [Source: LVMH, used with permission]

---

[26] http://theinspirationroom.com/daily/2012/evian-smart-drop/
[27] http://www.altomagazine.com/newsdetails/travel/hotels/dom-prignon-at-the-press-of-a-button-4310934/
[28] http://www.wired.com/2013/02/budweiser-red-light/

MARKETING AND THE WEB OF THINGS

Mobile applications can retrieve data about CPG and FMCG products, interact with them to attach digital content, and share information about them on social networks much quicker and more easily over the web. If every product in the world had its own URL and web API, it would be easy for any application to recognize a product and access its data without much integration effort. At EVRYTHNG we used our Web of Things platform to connect products to the web and deliver such Marketing 2.0 applications. As an example, Diageo in Brazil printed unique QR codes on its whiskey bottles so that their customers could attach a personalized message to each bottle; in that case, it was a video created on the customer's smartphone for Father's Day.[29]

1.4   *The Web of Things—a supercharged Internet of Things*

As described previously, the majority of IoT systems paid little attention to the issues of an open and large-scale system of heterogeneous devices talking to each other. This is partially because the IoT focused strongly on the lower layers of the networking stack (how data can be transmitted between actors) and much less on how to facilitate the development of new applications (how data can be collected, visualized, or processed). In particular, limited effort has been devoted to enable ad hoc interoperability, and consequently it's still difficult to build scalable applications on top of heterogeneous devices.

The reason for that isn't as much technical as it is commercial. A plethora of protocols for the IoT have been proposed in the last decade by standardization bodies, industrial alliances, and vendors. In essence this is a good thing. But the crude reality is that none of those standards has reached sufficient traction to be "the one" universal protocol for the IoT (see figure 1.12).Today, if you want a smart house, at best you'll have to buy all components from the same manufacturer. Because of this, your only option to control that system will be through the application that comes with it. If that application has been designed mainly for iPhone and isn't available on Android, well, that's too bad. If that application is badly designed, is painfully slow, or doesn't have half the features you need, you're stuck with it.

Figure 1.12   The problem with Internet of Things. The Web of Things builds upon and extends existing and widely used web standards so that it can use the whole web ecosystem in place. [Source: http://xkcd.com/927/ used under Creative Commons 2.5 license]

---

[29] http://adage.com/article/global-news/diageo-personalizes-whiskeys-videos-gift-givers/238015/

Put simply, most IoT solutions on the market today have little in common with the Internet—a unique, open, global network where everything is interconnected. The Internet of Things of today should rather be called the *Intranets* of Things, because it's a set of isolated islands of functionality that weren't designed to talk to each other. Even though an increasing number of networked devices offer APIs to control and access data about them, a custom application still needs to be developed specifically for each of those APIs. This is the case not only because different devices have different functionalities, but also because each API is implemented using different application protocols and has a different data model without a shared and standardized language.

The simplicity and openness of the web and its standards (URL, HTTP, HTML, JavaScript, and so on) is likely what enabled the web we know today. This lingua franca enabled any user in the world to read any other web page without installing anything and has been a major factor in the success of the web. By enabling web pages, browsers, servers, and services to all speak the same application language, the integration of a large variety of content was incredibly simplified. The equivalent enabler has unfortunately not yet been found for devices and applications in the Internet of Things.

In this section, we describe the limitations and problems with the existing approaches to IoT that don't prioritize an open, universal, and simple Application layer protocol for devices. For each of those limitations, we show the benefits of using a Web of Things approach instead.

1.4.1 *Easier to program*

First, let's look at the way Things are programmed.

INTERNET OF THINGS

The first problem with existing solutions and products today is that many of those protocols are complex and difficult to use. Such a high barrier for adoption, like the internet had in the 70s, puts the IoT out of reach for most people. Learning to connect to various devices that use a variety of interfaces and protocols is an especially arduous task that will deter the most tenacious amateur who wants to get started with programming their smart house. If you have any doubt about this, we invite you to consult the specifications of the ZigBee[30] protocol or of the Devices Profile for Web Services (DPWS).[31]

WEB OF THINGS

Web protocols can easily be used to read and write data from/to devices, and are especially much simpler to use and faster to learn than the complex IoT protocols. In addition, if all devices could offer a Web API, developers could use the same programming model to interact with any of them. Once you get the basic skills needed to build simple web applications, you can rapidly talk to new devices with minimal effort.

---

[30] http://zigbee.org/zigbee-for-developers/zigbee3-0/
[31] http://docs.oasis-open.org/ws-dd/dpws/wsdd-dpws-1.1-spec.html

1.4.2   *Open and extensible standards*

Next, we look at how open the standards are in both worlds.

INTERNET OF THINGS

Another issue is that many of those protocols have been continually evolving as new use cases are made possible by new technological developments. Because some of those standards are funded and governed by one or a limited number of large corporations, they aren't as neutral as a community-led open-source project. Besides, these companies could decide to introduce breaking changes as they wish, thereby rendering existing devices and applications unable to talk to each other.

Moreover, some of those standards aren't publicly documented and can't be simply used and implemented without paying a significant annual fee. This automatically limits, which automatically limits their adoption to only large industrial organizations. Closed and proprietary protocols also lead to vendor lock-in. Ensuring that switching to a different vendor is time- and cost-intensive is a well-known business strategy for big software players—nothing new here. But in an IoT context the barriers are much higher because switching protocols sometimes also implies changing the hardware (e.g. using a different radio chip). Similarly, switching application protocols requires firmware updates, which are hard to apply in the real world.

WEB OF THINGS

The reason web standards have reached such popularity is that they're entirely open and free, so there's virtually zero risk that they would change overnight. They ensure that data can be rapidly and easily moved across systems, hence HTTP and REST are an obvious choice when one wants to offer public access to some data.

1.4.3   *Fast and easy to deploy, maintain, and integrate*

Let's look at the impact on deployment, maintenance, and integration for each approach.

INTERNET OF THINGS

Because entire systems would need to use a single protocol, significant effort is required to write custom convertors for each new device or application that needs to be integrated. Maintenance of such a delicate assemblage of custom code is a risky task and in business applications would mean significant investments.

WEB OF THINGS

There's no risk that the web will suddenly stop working and require an upgrade. Yet, the limits of what can be done on the web have not ceased to be redefined in a decade, such as the ability to capture images from a camera or share one's location. In contrast, there are always new devices and protocols in the IoT world, and each time one of the many protocols changes, all the other pieces of the puzzle that use the device need to be updated.

1.4.4 *Loose coupling between elements*

Next, we look at the dependencies of each approach, focusing on reusability.

INTERNET OF THINGS

The implication of the previous sections is most importantly a tight coupling between the devices and applications in the network. The system works well as long as all pieces behave as expected and are used as intended. Sadly, this doesn't leave much space for ad hoc, unplanned interactions and repurposing of services into new use cases, which are essential requirements in large-scale open networks of devices.

WEB OF THINGS

HTTP is loosely coupled by design because the contract (API specification) between actors on the web is both simple and well defined, which leaves little room for ambiguity. This allows any actor to change and evolve independently from each other (as long as the contract doesn't change). That's why you can still visit a web page that hasn't been updated since the early '90s (we'll skip any comments about its visual design). The ability for devices on the Internet of Things to talk to new devices as they get added without requiring any firmware updates is essential for a global Web of Things.

1.4.5 *Widely used security and privacy mechanisms*

The issue of personal data, privacy, and security of IoT/WoT systems has always been a major concern when building and deploying real-world applications. The two angles to consider are these:

- *Security*—How to ensure a system can't be easily accessed or used in a harmful way by unauthorized users or systems. In other words, this is about ensuring that no one can access data or a device they aren't supposed to have access to.
- *User privacy*—Assuming security is in place and only authorized and authenticated parties or applications can access some data, how do we ensure that no private information about users (for example, personal information or behavioral data—where the user is, what the user is doing, and the like) could be accessed or derived from it? This is particularly difficult because even if a piece of data available about a user is harmless on its own, when combined with another piece of data available from another sensor or system, it can be used to unambiguously identify a user and their behaviors.

The truth is that even though there have been many projects and efforts to improve the security of those systems, as of today, the Holy Grail of security and privacy in the IoT world remains to be found. The real challenge is that capabilities of the IoT are relatively new at this scale, and the risks associated with those technologies are both largely unknown and hard to identify or measure in real-world applications.

INTERNET OF THINGS

As explained earlier, because applications in the IoT are often developed individually, the security mechanisms for these deployments are too often written from scratch, not tested sufficiently in the real world, or simply non-existing. Even today, a number of IoT devices are being deployed without using a sufficient level of security, dangerously exposing their authentication keys to the world.[32] This is mainly because IoT-specific security systems have quite often been designed to work well in closed ecosystems, where every element is controlled.

WEB OF THINGS

The web can help here, too, and we'll look into this in chapter 9. Looking back at the history of the web, we can see that we've made tremendous progress in building usable and reliable security mechanisms and protocols. These methods are not bullet-proof—no security system is—but are a practical compromise of dependability, ease of use, performance, and availability.

The fact is that even today it isn't uncommon to hear that a large and famous online company has been hacked and the data about millions of its users has been leaked publicly. Even worse, protocols that have been viewed as secure and trusted might still suffer from tiny unknown problems, making them vulnerable when found (SSL Heartbleed[33] anyone?). With a few exceptions, as long as those systems are implemented correctly, the possibility of them being hacked remains minor, especially given that those systems are used daily by billions of users. The advantage of using web-based common standards, as opposed to custom and novel ones developed for the IoT, is that they have been and still are extensively used and tested. Many implementations of such systems are open source (for example, OpenSSL), which means the code is constantly used, tested, updated, and fixed by thousands of developers. Using such established methods reduced the risk of failures as opposed to the bleeding-edge (pun intended) techniques being developed from scratch for the IoT that have been tested and used in the wild only marginally.

1.4.6   WoT—the shortcomings

We realize that at this stage you might be thinking, "These guys got a little carried away with their WoT!" Maybe. But after using traditional IoT tools for over a decade, it's hard to describe the pleasure we feel after creating the same type of applications directly in our browser with a few lines of JavaScript and with much less effort, time, and suffering.

Nevertheless, the Web of Things isn't the "Answer to the Ultimate Question of Life, the Universe, and Everything" (aka 42).[34] As with every disruptive technology or approach, it comes with its own share of challenges. Security and general data privacy are some of these. Connecting all Things in our physical world to the internet and making them accessible on the web also means we potentially expose them to intrusive

---

[32] http://www.ioactive.com/news-events/IOActive_advisory_belkinwemo_2014.html
[33] The Heartbleed Bug is a serious vulnerability that was found in the popular OpenSSL cryptographic software library (see more at http://heartbleed.com/)
[34] http://goo.gl/l4rG1b

governments, viruses, or disreputable companies that could use this to run denial of service attacks or mine information about the real world. We should assume they will. Thinking about security is already a must for the IoT; the WoT adds a few more concerns, especially on the data privacy side of things. We'll cover these advanced topics in chapter 9, but the short answer is that a largely connected system will always be more vulnerable than an isolated one. But a system connected using open standards is usually better off than one based on custom security mechanisms. Moreover, this isn't the first time we've had to face such a dilemma: our computers could be isolated, but this would reduce their range of applications. The IoT and the WoT are no exceptions: we, as citizens, have a choice and should weigh each of these new technologies on the balance between risks and benefits. The WoT should be about making our lives easier and more enjoyable, not harder.

It's important to realize that pushing web standards on every single device isn't always the right thing to do, and in some cases it isn't practical or feasible. Under certain constraints (such as when a battery-powered device needs to operate for a very long time), you might be better off using an optimized IoT protocol. In chapter 5, we'll help you understand what these tradeoffs are and give you a framework to decide the best options for various situations. The good news is that the Web of Things is all about integration patterns: we'll show you how to integrate non-web or even non-IP devices to the web via proxies, gateways, or clouds. This type of hybrid solution sometimes makes deployments more complex but is more practical because it allows for optimizations where needed. We'll discuss these integration patterns in chapter 7.

1.5   *Summary*

- The Internet of Things has been around for much longer than you think and certainly before it was called this.
- Early IoT systems were designed to operate in isolation; therefore, the IoT today is a fragmented world—the Intranets of Things.
- The Web of Things is different because it doesn't care about underlying networking protocols or standards, only about how to weave various isolated systems and devices into a single, web-based ecosystem.
- Using simple and ubiquitous web standards such as HTTP, Web Socket, and JSON to integrate all sorts of devices and applications makes it much easier to rapidly prototype all sorts of applications and then scale them for enterprise-grade solutions.
- The IoT is still in its infancy, and there are many opportunities ahead for those who want to master the complexity of a world where the physical world becomes connected.
- This book will teach you how to use the Web of Things to build a new generation of IoT solutions that are more flexible, scalable, and interoperable by building upon and using the infrastructure, tools, and experience accumulated since the web was invented in the early 90s.

In the next chapter, we'll give you a first taste of what the Web of Things feels like. By working on a few hands-on exercises, you'll experience first-hand how easy it is to build Web of Things applications that read sensor data, send commands to devices, and merge information from various sources to create hybrid applications where the real world becomes accessible on the Web. We kept the next chapter simple by hiding the complexity of the devices behind web standards so that you are able to rapidly build and customize your first Web of Things application without having to deal with how to implement it directly on devices (yet!). In the chapters after that, you'll learn the details of how you can apply those principles to create elaborate applications and connectors for any device and scenario you might have in mind.

Hello, World Wide Web of Things

This chapter covers

- A sneak peek at the different levels of the Web of Things architecture
- Accessing devices with HTTP, URLs, WebSockets, and browsers
- Working with REST APIs to consume JSON data
- Learning about the notion of web semantics
- Creating your first physical mashup

Before we dive head first into the Web of Things architecture and show how to implement it from scratch, we want to give you a taste of what the Web of Things looks like. This chapter is structured as a set of exercises where you'll build tiny web applications that use data generated by a real device. Each exercise will be a smooth introduction to the many problems and technical issues that you'll face when building web-connected devices and applications that interact with them.

In this chapter, you'll have the opportunity to get your hands dirty and code some simple (and less simple) Web of Things applications. Oh, you don't have a device yet? No problem; just use ours! To make it possible for you to do those exercises without having to buy a real device, we connected our own device to the web so you can access it from your computer over the Web. Of course, if you already have a device, you can also download the source code used in this chapter and run it on your own device. How to run the code on the device will be detailed later, in chapter 7.

2.1   *Meet a Web of Things device*

This chapter is organized as a series of short and sweet exercises. Each exercise allows you to interact with an actual Web of Things device in our office that's live 24/7. This will allow you to do the exercises without having a real device next to you.

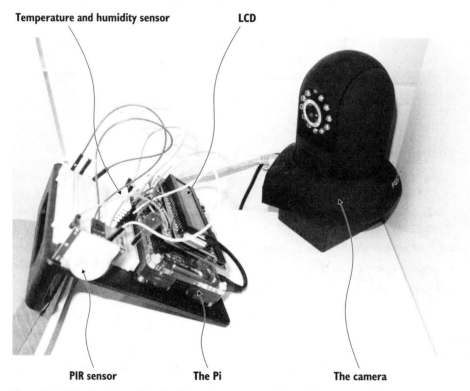

Figure 2.1   The Raspberry Pi and webcam you are accessing as they are set up in our London office

The device in our office is the Raspberry Pi 2 (or just Pi for friends and family) shown in figure 2.1, which we'll describe in detail in chapter 4. If you've never seen one, you can think of a credit card–sized computer board with a few sensors attached to it and connected to our local network and the web via an Ethernet cable. In our setup, the Pi acts as a gateway to various sensors or devices attached to it, so you can interact with those resources through the Web. Gateways are described in detail in chapter 7, but

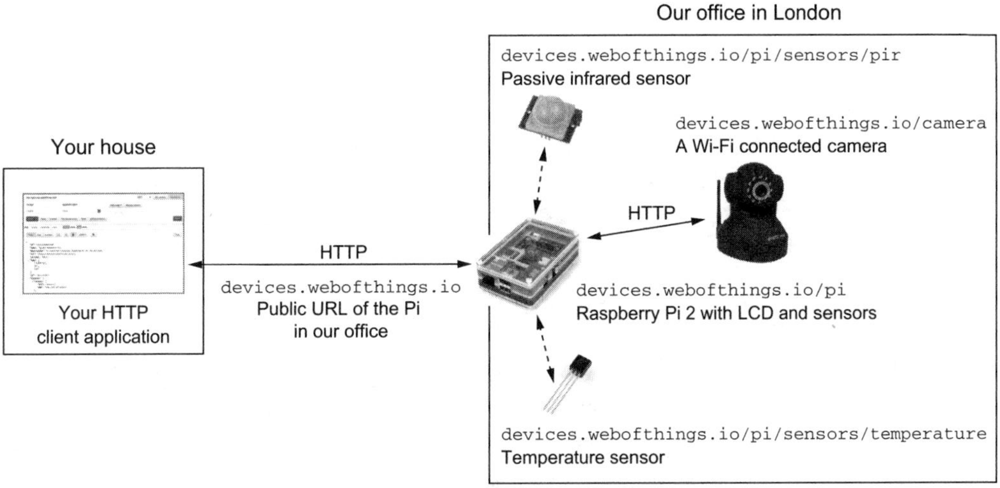

Figure 2.2 The setup of devices and sensors used in the examples of this chapter

for now just remember that the Pi runs a web server that allows you to access those resources over the Web, as shown in figure 2.2..

At the time of writing, we have a liquid crystal display (LCD), a camera, a temperature sensor, and a PIR sensor connected to our Raspberry Pi. We'll keep adding various sensors and actuators to it over time, so you're welcome to experiment and go well beyond the examples we provide here. You'll soon realize that the various techniques and patterns described in this book will allow you to quickly extend and customize the examples we provide to any device, sensor, or object you can think of.

2.1.1 *The suspect: Raspberry Pi*

We'll introduce the Raspberry Pi in greater detail in chapter 4, so all you need to understand for now is that a Pi is a small computer to which you can connect multiple sensors and accessories. It offers all the features you would expect from a desktop computer but with a lower power consumption and smaller form factor. Moreover, you can attach all sorts of digital sensors or actuators to it using the input/output (I/O) pins. *Actuator* is an umbrella term for any element attached to a device that has an effect on the real world, for example, turning on/off some LEDs, displaying a text on an LCD panel, rotating an electric motor, unlocking a door, playing some music, and so on. In the Web of Things, just as you send write requests to a web API using HTTP, you do the same to activate an actuator. Now back to our exercises. The first thing you need to do is to download the examples used in these pages from our repository here: http://book.webofthings.io.

You can check out the repository on your own computer, and in it you'll find a few folders—one for each chapter. The exercises in this chapter are located in the folder chapter2-hello-wot/client. If you're wondering about the code for the server, worry not! You'll learn how to build this in the rest of the book.

How to get the code examples in this chapter

We use the GitHub[a] service to synchronize code between our computer and our Pi. As an alternative, the Bitbucket[b] service works and is configured in a similar manner. Both services are based on the Git source version control system, and the source code for all the chapters is available from GitHub (here's the link: http://book .webofthings.io). The examples for this chapter are located in the chapter2-hello-wot folder.

If you're unfamiliar with Git and its commands, don't worry—there's plenty of information about this on the web, but here are the most vital commands to work with it:

- `git clone`—Fetches a version of a repository locally. For the book code you need to use the `recursive` option that will clone all the sub-projects as well: `git clone https://github.com/webofthings/wot-book --recursive`.
- `git commit -a -m "your message"`—Commits code changes locally.
- `git push origin master`—Pushes the last commits to the remote repository (origin) on the master branch.

---

[a] GitHub is a widely popular, web-based, source code management system. Many open source projects are hosted on GitHub, because, well, it's pretty awesome. Here's an excellent intro to GitHub: http://bit.ly/intro-git.

[b] https://bitbucket.com

2.2   *Exercise 1—Browse a device on the Web of Things*

We'll start our exploration of the Web of Things with a simple exercise where you have almost nothing to do but click on a few links in your browser. The first point we want to illustrate is that on the Web of Things, devices can offer simultaneously a visual user interface (web pages) to allow humans to control and interact with them and an application programming interface (API) to allow machines or applications to do the same.

2.2.1   *Part 1—The web as user interface*

In this first exercise, you'll use your browser to interact with some of the real Web of Things devices connected in our office. First, have a glimpse of what the setup in our office looks like through a webcam; see figure 2.3. Open the following link in your favorite browser to access the latest image taken by the web cam: http:// devices.webofthings.io/camera/sensors/picture. This link will always return the latest screenshot taken by our camera so you can see the devices you will play with (try it at night—at night it's even more fun!). You won't see the camera itself, though.

You probably noticed that the URL you typed had a certain path structure. Let's play a bit with this structure and go back to the root of this URL, where you'll see the homepage of the gateway that allows you to browse through the devices in our office (figure 2.4). Enter the following URL in your browser: http://devices.webofthings.io.

Sensor: Camera Sensor

Description: Takes a still picture with the camera.

1. Type: image
2. Recorded at: 2016-01-06T14:28:32.691Z
3. Value: http://devices.webofthings.io:9090/snapshot.cgi?user=snapshots&pwd=4MXfTSr0gH

Sensor Value

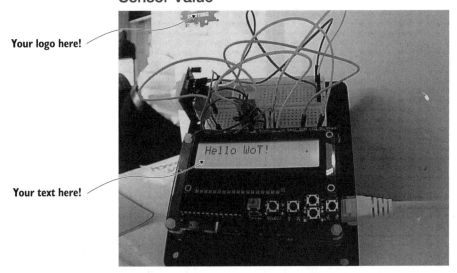

Your logo here!

Your text here!

Figure 2.3   The web page of the camera used in our setup. The image is a live screenshot taken by the camera.

Devices

The various **devices** connected to this gateway:

1. My WoT Raspberry PI: A simple WoT-connected Raspberry PI for the WoT book.
2. My WoT Camera: A simple WoT-connected camera.

The WoT Pi

Figure 2.4   The HTML homepage of the gateway of our WoT device. The two hyperlinks at the bottom of the page allow you to access the pages of the devices connected to the gateway.

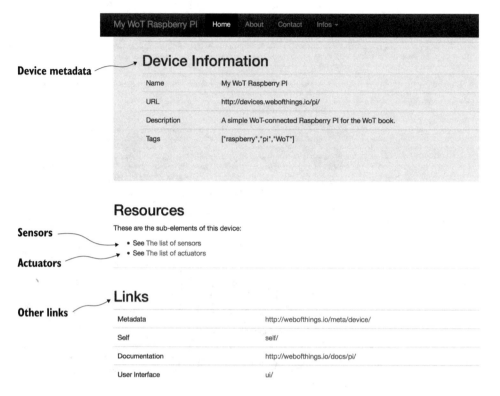

Figure 2.5   The homepage of the Raspberry Pi. Here, you can use the links at the bottom to browse and explore the various resources offered by this device; for example, its sensors and actuators.

This URL will always redirect you to the *root page* of the gateway running in our office, which shows the list of devices attached to it. Here, you can see that two devices are attached to the gateway:

- A Raspberry Pi with various sensors and actuators
- A webcam (the one you accessed earlier)

Note that this page is automatically generated based on which physical devices we have attached to it, so you might see a few more devices or sensors as we attach them. Yes, although it looks like any other web page, it's actually *real* data served in *real time* from *real* devices that are in a *real* office!

Now, click the My WoT Raspberry Pi link to access the root page of the device itself. Because you followed a link in your browser, you'll see that the URL has changed to http://devices.webofthings.io/pi, as shown in figure 2.5.

This is another root page—the one of the device this time. In this case, we just appended /pi to the root URL of the gateway.

Coming back to our device root page, hover with your mouse above the various links to see their structure, and then click The list of sensors link. You'll see the URL change again to this (figure 2.6): http://devices.webofthings.io/pi/sensors.

Sensors

Temperature sensor

The list of sensors available currently on the device.

1. **Temperature Sensor:** *A temperature sensor.*
2. **Humidity Sensor:** *A temperature sensor.*
3. **Passive Infrared:** *A passive infrared sensor. When true someone is present.*

Figure 2.6 The list of sensors on the Pi. You can click each of them and see the latest known value for each.

So far, it's pretty straightforward: your browser is asking for an HTML page that shows the list of /sensors of the device /pi connected to the devices.webofthings.io gateway. Remember that there's also a camera connected to this, so in your browser address bar replace /pi/ with /camera/ in the URL and you'll be taken directly to the Sensors page of the camera: http://devices.webofthings.io/camera/sensors; see figure 2.7.

Sensors

The list of sensors available currently on the device.

1. Camera Sensor: *Takes a still picture with the camera.* ◄—— **Link to the sensor**

Figure 2.7 The sensors on the camera. There's only one sensor here, which is the current image.

Now, go back to the list of sensors on your Pi and see the various sensors attached to the device. Currently, you can access three sensors: temperature, humidity, and passive infrared. Open the Temperature Sensor link and you'll see the temperature sensor page with the current value of the sensor. Finally, just like you did for the sensors, go to the actuators list of the Pi and open the Actuator Details page (see figure 2.13) at the following URL: http://devices.webofthings.io/pi/actuators/display.

The display is a simple LCD screen attached to the Pi that can display some text, which you'll use in exercise 2.4. You can see the information about this actuator—in particular the current value being displayed, the API description to send data to it, and a form to display new data. You won't use this form for now, but this is coming in section 2.4.

2.2.2   *Part 2—The web as an API*

In part 1, you started to interact with the Web of Things from your browser. You've seen how a human user can explore the resources of a device (sensors, actuators, and so on) and how to interact with that device from a web page. All of that is done by browsing the resources of a physical device, just as you'd browse the various pages of a website. But what if instead of a human user, you want a software application or another device to do the same thing, without having a human in the loop? How can you make it easy for any web client to find a device, understand what it does, see what its API looks like, determine what commands it can send, and so on?

Later in the book, we'll show you in detail how to do this. For now, we'll illustrate how the web makes it easy to support both humans and applications by showing you what another device or application sees when it browses your device.

For this exercise, you'll need to have Chrome installed and install one of our favorite browser extensions called Postman.[1] Or you could use cURL[2] if you'd rather use the command line. Postman is a handy little app that will help you a lot when working with a web API because it allows you to easily send HTTP requests and customize the various options of these requests, such as the headers, the payload, and much more. Postman will make your life easier throughout this book, so go ahead and install it.

In part 1, your browser is simply a web client requesting content from the server. The browser automatically asks for the content to be in HTML format, which is returned by the server and then displayed by the browser.

In part 2, you'll do almost the same exercise as in part 1 but this time by requesting the server to return JSON documents instead of an HTML page. JSON is pretty much the most successful data interchange format used on the internet. It has an easy-to-understand syntax and is lightweight, which makes it much more efficient to transmit

---

[1] Get it here: http://www.getpostman.com/

[2] cURL is a command-line tool that allows you to transfer data using various protocols, among which is HTTP. If it's not preinstalled on your machine, you can easily install it on Mac, Linux, or Windows. Website: http://curl.haxx.se/

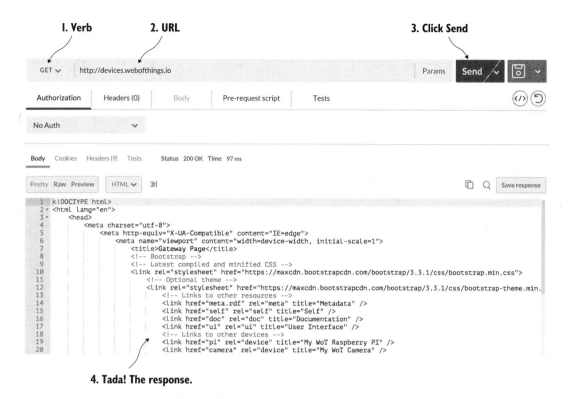

Figure 2.8 Getting the root page of the gateway using the Postman web client. The request is an HTTP GET (1) on the URL of the gateway (2). The response body will contain an HTML document (4).

when compared to its old parent, XML. In addition, JSON is easy for humans to read and write and also for machines to parse and generate, which makes it particularly suited to be *the* data exchange format of the Web of Things. The process of asking for a specific encoding is called *content negotiation* in the HTTP 1.1 specification and will be covered in detail in chapter 6.

STEP 1—GETTING THE LIST OF DEVICES FROM THE GATEWAY

Just as you did before, you'll send a GET request to the root page of the gateway to get the list of devices. For this you'll enter the URL of the gateway in Postman and click Send, as shown in figure 2.8.

Because most web servers return HTML by default, you'll see in the body area the HTML page content returned by the server (4). This is basically what happens behind the scenes each time you access a website from your browser. Now to get JSON instead of HTML, click the Headers button and add a header named `Accept` with `application/json` in the value, and click Send again, as shown in figure 2.9. Adding this header to your request is telling the HTTP server, "Hey, if you can, please return me

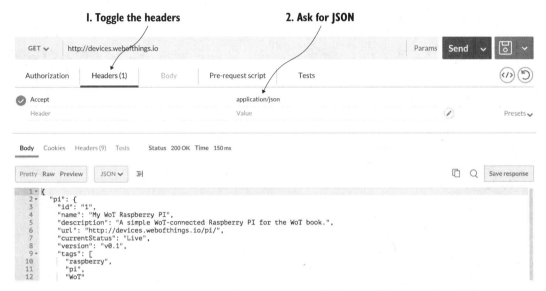

Figure 2.9   Getting the list of devices connected to the gateway via Postman. The `Accept` header is now set to `application/json` to ask for the results to be returned in JSON.

the results encoded in JSON." Because this is supported by the gateway, you'll now see the same content in JSON, which is the machine equivalent of the web page you've retrieved before, but this time with only the content and no visual elements (that is, the HTML code).

The JSON body returned contains a machine-readable description of the devices attached to the gateway and looks like this:

```
{
  "pi": {
    "id": "1",
    "name": "My WoT Raspberry Pi",
    "description": "A simple WoT-connected Raspberry Pi for the WoT book.",
    "url": "http://devices.webofthings.io/pi/",
    "currentStatus": "Live",
    "version": "v0.1",
    "tags": [
      "raspberry",
      "pi",
      "WoT"
    ],
    "resources": {
      "sensors": {
        "url": "sensors/",
        "name": "The list of sensors"
      },
      "actuators": {
        "url": "actuators/",
        "name": "The list of actuators"
```

```
        }
      },
      "links": {
        "meta": {
          "rel": "http://book.webofthings.io",
          "title": "Metadata"
        },
        "doc": {
          "rel": "https://www.raspberrypi.org/products/raspberry-pi-2-model-b/",
          "title": "Documentation"
        },
        "ui": {
          "rel": ".",
          "title": "User Interface"
        }
      }
    },
    "camera": {
      [ ... description of the camera object... ]
    }
}
```

In this JSON document, you can see two first-level elements (`pi` and `camera`) that represent the two devices attached to the gateway, as well as a few details about them, such as their URL, name, ID, and description. Don't worry for now if you don't understand everything here; all of this will become crystal clear to you in a few chapters.

STEP 2—GETTING A SINGLE DEVICE

Now change the URL of the request in Postman so it points back to the Pi device (which is exactly the same as the one you typed in your browser in part 1), and click Send again, as shown in figure 2.10.

Figure 2.10 Getting the JSON representation of the Raspberry Pi. The JSON payload contains metadata about the device as well as links to its sub-resources.

The body now contains the JSON object of the Pi except with the same information as shown previously, and you can see that the resources object has sensors, actuators, and so on:

```
"resources": {
  "sensors": {
    "url": "sensors/",
    "name": "The list of sensors"
  },
  "actuators": {
    "url": "actuators/",
    "name": "The list of actuators"
  }
}
```

STEP 3—GETTING THE LIST OF SENSORS ON THE DEVICE

To get to the list of sensors available on the device, just as you did before, append /sensors to the URL of the Pi in Postman and send the request again. An HTTP GET there will return this JSON document in the response:

```
{
  "temperature": {
    "name": "Temperature Sensor",
    "description": "A temperature sensor.",
    "type": "float",
    "unit": "celsius",
    "value": 23.4,
    "timestamp": "2015-10-04T14:39:17.240Z",
    "frequency": 5000
  },
  "humidity": {
    "name": "Humidity Sensor",
    "description": "A temperature sensor.",
    "type": "float",
    "unit": "percent",
    "value": 38.9,
    "timestamp": "2015-10-04T14:39:17.240Z",
    "frequency": 5000
  },
  "pir": {
    "name": "Passive Infrared",
    "description": "A passive infrared sensor. True when someone present.",
    "type": "boolean",
    "value": true,
    "timestamp": "2015-10-04T14:39:17.240Z",
    "gpio": 20
  }
}
```

You can see that the Pi has three sensors attached to it (respectively, temperature, humidity, and pir), along with details about each sensor and its latest value.

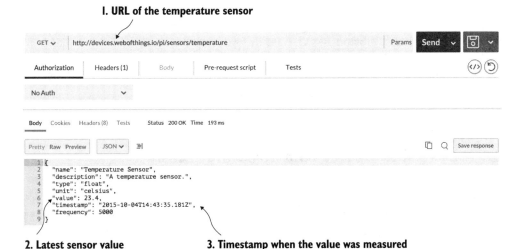

Figure 2.11   Retrieve the temperature sensor object from the Raspberry Pi. You can see the latest reading (23.4 degrees Celsius) and when it took place (at 14:43 on October 4, 2015).

STEP 4—GET DETAILS OF A SINGLE SENSOR

Finally, you'll get the details of a specific sensor, so append `/temperature` to the URL in Postman and click Send again. The URL should now be http://devices.webofthings.io/pi/sensors/temperature, as shown in figure 2.11.

You will get detailed information about the temperature sensor, in particular the latest value that was read (the value field). If you only want to retrieve the sensor value, you can append /value to the URL of the sensor to retrieve it, which also work for other sensors:

```
{
  "value":22.4
}
```

2.2.3   So what?

Now it's time for you to play around with the different URLs you've seen so far in this exercise. Look at how they differ and are structured, browse around the device, and try to understand what data each sensor has, its format, and so on. As an extension look at the electronic devices around you—the appliances in your kitchen or the TV or sound system in your living room, the ordering system in the café, or the train notification system, depending on where you're reading this book from. Now imagine how the services and data offered by all these devices could all have a similar structure: URLs, content, paths, and so on. Try to map this system using the same JSON structure you've just seen, and write the URLs and JSON object that would be returned.

What you have seen is that both humans and applications get data using exactly the same URL but using different encoding formats (HTML for humans, JSON for applications). Obviously, the data in both cases is identical, which makes it easy for application developers to go back and forth from one format to the other. This is one example of how simple—yet powerful—web technologies can be. Thanks to immensely popular web standards such as HTTP and URLs, it becomes straightforward to interact with the real world from any web browser. You'll learn much more about these concepts in chapter 6 onward.

2.3   Exercise 2—Polling data from a WoT sensor

In the first exercise you learned about the structure of a WoT device and how it works. In particular, you saw that every element of the device is simply a resource with a unique URL that can be used by both people and applications to read and write data. Now you're going to put a developer hat on and start coding your first web application that interacts with this Web of Things device.

2.3.1   Part 1—Polling the current sensor value

For this exercise, go to the folder you checked out from GitHub into the chapter2-hello-wot/client folder. Double-click the ex-2.1-polling-temp.html file to open it in a modern browser.[3] This page displays the value of the temperature sensor on the Pi in our office and updates this value every five seconds by retrieving it in JSON, exactly as you saw in figure 2.11.

This file uses jQuery[4] to poll data from the temperature sensor on our Pi. Now open this file in your favorite code editor and look at the source code. You'll see two things there:

- An <h2> tag showing where the current sensor value will be written.
- A JavaScript function called doPoll() that reads the value from the Pi, displays it, and calls itself again five seconds later. This function is shown in the following listing.

Listing 2.1   Polling for the temperature sensor

Use the AJAX helper to get the JSON payload from the temperature sensor.

Wait until the page is loaded and then call doPoll().

```
$(document).ready(
    function doPoll() {
        $.getJSON('http://devices.webofthings.io/pi/sensors/temperature',
        function (data) {
            console.log(data);
```

When the response arrives, this function is called.

---

[3] We fully tested our examples on Firefox (>41) and Chrome (>46) and suggest you install the latest version of these. Safari (>9) should also work. If you really want to use Internet Explorer, please be aware that you'll need version 10 onward; older versions won't work.

[4] jQuery is a handy JavaScript library that makes it easier to do lots of things, such as talk to REST APIs, manipulate HTML elements, handle events, and so on. Learn more here: http://jquery.com/.

```
    $('#temp').html(data.value + ' ' + data.unit);
  setTimeout(doPoll, 5000);
});
});
```

Select the "temp" HTML element and update its content using the data.value (the value) and data.unit (the unit) returned in the JSON payload.

The doPoll() function sets a timer to call itself again in 5 seconds (5000 milliseconds).

When developing (and especially debugging!) web applications, it might be useful to display content from JavaScript outside the page; for this you have a JavaScript console. To access it in Chrome, right-click somewhere on the page and select Inspect Element; then look for the console that appears below where you can see the HTML code of the current page. The `console.log(data)` statement displays the `data` JSON object received from the server in this console.

2.3.2   Part 2—Polling and graphing sensor values

This is great, but in some cases you'd like to display more than the current value of the sensor—for example, a graph of all readings in the last hour or week. Open the second HTML file in the exercises (ex-2.2-polling-temp-chart.html). This is a slightly more complex example that keeps track of the last 10 values of the temperature sensor and displays them in a graph. When you open this second file in your browser, you'll see the graph being updated every two seconds, as shown in figure 2.12.

We built this graph using Google Charts,[5] a nice and lightweight JavaScript library for displaying all sorts of charts and graphs. See our annotated code sample in the next listing.

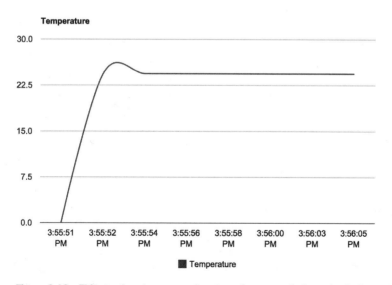

Figure 2.12   This graph gets a new value every few seconds from the device and is updated automatically.

---

[5] https://developers.google.com/chart/

Listing 2.2   Polling and displaying a sensor reading

Initialize the Google chart.

Create an array that will contain the data points.

Configure the parameters of the chart.

Add a data point to the chart data and remove the oldest one if needed (if there are already 10 points available).

Redraw the chart with the new data.

Poll the temperature sensor like before.

When the new readings are returned, use them to call the addDataPoint() function.

```javascript
$(document).ready(function () {
  var maxDataPoints = 10;
  var chart = new google.visualization.LineChart($('#chart')[0]);
  var data = google.visualization.arrayToDataTable([
    ['Time', 'Temperature'],
    [getTime(), 0]
  ]);

  var options = {
    title: 'Temperature',
    curveType: 'function',
    animation: {
      duration: 1000,
      easing: 'in'
    },
    legend: {position: 'bottom'}
  };

  function addDataPoint(dataPoint) {
    if (data.getNumberOfRows() > maxDataPoints) {
      data.removeRow(0);
    }
    data.addRow([getTime(), dataPoint.value]);
    chart.draw(data, options);
  }

  function getTime() {
    var d = new Date();
    return d.toLocaleTimeString();
  }

  function doPoll() {
    $.getJSON('http://devices.webofthings.io/pi/sensors/temperature/value',
      function (result) {
        addDataPoint(result);
        setTimeout(doPoll, 2000);
      });
  }

  doPoll();
});
```

2.3.3   *Part 3—Real-time data updates*

In the previous exercises, polling the temperature sensor of the Pi worked just fine. But this seems somewhat inefficient, doesn't it? Instead of having to fetch the temperature from the device every two seconds or so, wouldn't it be better if our script was *informed* of any change of temperature when it happens, and only if the value changes?

As we'll explore to a greater extent in chapter 6, this has been one of the major impedance mismatches between the model of the web and the event-driven model of wireless sensor applications. For now, we'll look at one way of resolving the problem using a relatively recent add-on to the web: *WebSockets*. In a nutshell, WebSockets are simple yet powerful mechanisms for web servers to push notifications to web clients introduced as part of the efforts around the HTML5 standards.

The WebSockets standard comprises two distinct parts: one for the server and one for the client. Since the server is already implemented for us, the only specification we'll use here is the client part. The client WebSockets API is based on JavaScript and is relatively simple and straightforward. The two lines of code in the following listing are all you need to connect to a WebSocket server and display in the console all messages received.

Listing 2.3   Connecting to a WebSocket and listening for messages

```
var socket = new WebSocket('ws://ws.webofthings.io');
socket.onmessage = function (event) {console.log(event);};
```

Let's get back to our examples. Go to the folder. Double-click the ex-2.3-websockets-temp-graph.html file to open it in your favorite browser. What you see on the page is exactly the same as in the previous exercise, but under the hood things are quite different. Have a look at the new code shown in the next listing.

Listing 2.4   Register to a WebSocket and get real-time temperature updates

```
var socket = new
    WebSocket('ws://devices.webofthings.io/pi/sensors/temperature');

socket.onmessage = function (event) {
  var result = JSON.parse(event.data);
  addDataPoint(result);
};

socket.onerror = function (error) {
  console.log('WebSocket error!');
  console.log(error);
};
```

Create a WebSocket subscription to the temperature sensor. Note that the URL uses the WebSocket protocol (ws://...).

Register this anonymous function to be called when a message arrives on the WebSocket.

Register this other anonymous function to be triggered when an error occurs on the WebSocket.

In this exercise, you don't poll periodically for new data but only register your interest in these updates by subscribing to the /sensors/temperature endpoint via Web-Sockets. When the server has new temperature data available, it will send it to your client (your web browser). This event will be picked up by the anonymous function you registered and will be given as a parameter the event object that contains the latest temperature value.

2.3.4   So what?

Let's take a step back and reflect on what you did in this exercise: you managed to communicate with an embedded device (the Raspberry Pi) that might be on the other side of the world (if you don't happen to be living in rainy and beautiful England). From a web page you were able to fetch, on a regular basis, data from a sensor connected to the device and display it on a graph. Not bad for a simple web page of 60 lines of HTML, JavaScript, and CSS code. You didn't stop there: with fewer than 10 lines of JavaScript you also subscribed to notifications from our Pi using WebSockets and then displayed the temperature in our office in real time. As an extension of this exercise, you could write a simple page that automatically fetches the image from the camera (ideally, you'd avoid doing this 25 times per second!).

If this was your first encounter with the Web of Things, what should strike you at this stage is the simplicity of these examples. Let's imagine for a second that our Pi wasn't actually providing its data through HTTP, JSON, or WebSockets but via a "vintage" XML-based machine-to-machine application stack such as DPWS (if you've never heard about it, don't worry; that's exactly our point!). Basically, you wouldn't be able to talk directly to the device from your browser without a lot more effort. You would have be forced to write your application using a lower-level and more complex language such as C or Java. You wouldn't have been able to use widespread concepts and languages such as URLs, HTML, CSS, and JavaScript. This is also what the Web of Things is about: making things from the real world programmable and universally accessible by bringing them closer to the masses of web developers, where a lot of today's innovations are happening.

As mentioned before, in this book you'll learn a lot more about the art of API crafting for physical things. In chapter 6 we'll look at HTTP, REST, and JSON as well as at the real-time web, and in chapter 7 we'll discover how to use gateways to bring other protocols and systems closer to the goodness of the web.

2.4   *Exercise 3—Act on the real world*

So far, you've seen various ways to read all sorts of sensor data from web devices. What about "writing" to a device? For example, you'd like to send a command to your device to change a configuration parameter. In other cases, you might want to control an actuator (for example, open the garage door or turn off all lights).

2.4.1   *Part 1—Use a form to update text to display*

To illustrate how you can send commands to an actuator, this exercise will show you how to build a simple page that allows you to send some text to the LCD connected to the Pi in our office. To test this functionality first, open the actuator page of the LCD: http://devices.webofthings.io/pi/actuators/display.

On this page (shown in figure 2.13), you now see the various *properties* of the LED actuator. First, you see brightness, which you could change (but can't, because we made it read-only). Then, you have content, which is the value you want to send, and finally there is the duration, which specifies how long the text will be displayed on our LCD. Use Postman to get the JSON object that describes the display actuator by entering the URL shown in the last paragraph, as you learned in the first exercise of this chapter:

```
{
  "name": "LCD Display screen",
  "description": "A simple display that can write commands.",
  "properties": {
    "brightness": {
      "name": "Brightness",
      "timestamp": "2015-02-01T21:06:02.913Z",
      "value": 80,
      "unit": "%",
      "type": "integer",
      "description": "Percentage of brightness of the display. Min is 0
        which is black, max is 100 which is white."
    },
    "content": {
      "name": "Content",
      "timestamp": "2015-02-01T21:06:32.933Z",
      "type": "string",
      "description": "The text to display on the LCD screen."
    },
    "duration": {
      "name": "Display Duration",
      "timestamp": "2015-02-01T21:06:02.913Z",
      "value": 5000,
      "unit": "milliseconds",
      "type": "integer",
      "read-only": true,
      "description": "The duration for how long text will be displayed
        on the LCD screen."
    }
  },
  "commands": [
    "write",
    "clear",
    "blink",
    "color",
    "brightness"
  ]
}
```

Obviously, it wouldn't be much fun to display something in our office if you couldn't see what was being displayed. For this reason, we've set up a webcam where you can see the LCD on our Pi, so you can always see what is displayed on it. Here's the URL: http://devices.webofthings.io/camera/sensors/picture. Go ahead; open this page, and you'll see the latest picture of the camera you saw in figure 2.3 (to see the latest image, refresh the page).

Now you'll send a new message to the Pi for it to be displayed by the LCD. The content property is always the current message displayed on the LCD, so to update it

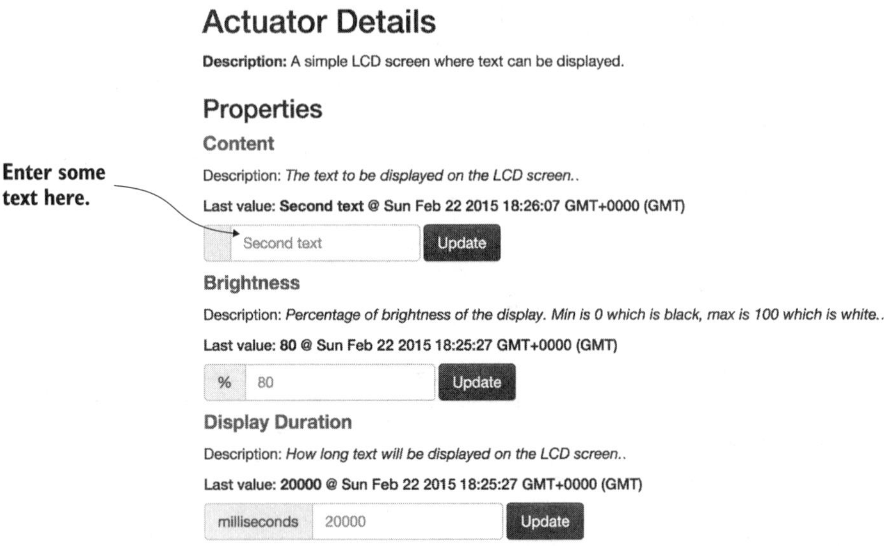

Actuator Details

Description: A simple LCD screen where text can be displayed.

Properties

Content

Enter some text here.

Description: *The text to be displayed on the LCD screen..*

Last value: **Second text @ Sun Feb 22 2015 18:26:07 GMT+0000 (GMT)**

Second text   Update

Brightness

Description: *Percentage of brightness of the display. Min is 0 which is black, max is 100 which is white..*

Last value: **80 @ Sun Feb 22 2015 18:25:27 GMT+0000 (GMT)**

%   80   Update

Display Duration

Description: *How long text will be displayed on the LCD screen..*

Last value: **20000 @ Sun Feb 22 2015 18:25:27 GMT+0000 (GMT)**

milliseconds   20000   Update

Figure 2.13   The details of the LCD actuator, with the various properties that you can set, for example, the text that should be displayed next on the device

you POST a new value for that property with the message to be displayed (for example, `{"value": "Hello World!"}`) as a body. You can go ahead and try this in Postman, but the simplest way to do it is through the page of the display actuator in your browser: http://devices.webofthings.io/pi/actuators/display. See figure 2.13 for the details of the LCD actuator.

On this page you can see the various properties of the LCD actuator. Some are editable, and some aren't. The `content` property is the one you want to edit, so enter the text you'd like to display and click Update. If all works fine, you'll see a JSON payload like this:

```
{
  "id":11,
  "messageReceived":"Make WoT, not war!",
  "displayInSeconds":20
}
```

The returned payload contains the message that will be displayed, a unique ID for your message, and an estimated delay for when your text will appear on the LCD screen (in seconds), so you know when to look at the camera image to see your text.

2.4.2   *Part 2—Create your own form to control devices*

Now let's build a simple HTML page that allows you to send all sorts of commands to a web device using a simple form. From your browser, open the file ex-3.1-actuator-form.html in the exercises folder and you'll see the screen shown in figure 2.14.

Display Message on WoT Pi

Enter a message: [Hello world!] [Send to Pi]

Figure 2.14   This simple client-side form allows you to send new text to be displayed by the Pi.

This page has an input text field and a Send to Pi button, as shown in the following listing. Whatever text you enter will be displayed on the LCD screen of the Pi in our office. Please keep it courteous, and because the API of our Pi is open to the public, we decline all responsibility for what people write there.

Listing 2.5   Simple HTML form to send a command to an actuator

```
<form action="http://devices.webofthings.io/pi/actuators/display/content/"
 method="post">
  <label>Enter a message:</label>
  <input type="text" name="value" placeholder="Hello world!">
  <button type="submit">Send to Pi</button>
</form>
```

This is a simple HTML form that sends an HTTP POST (value of method) to the URL of the display (the value of action). The input text bar is called *value* (name="value") so that the Pi knows what text to display. This method works well for a basic website. Unfortunately, what you don't see behind the scenes is that web browsers do not submit (nor do they make it possible to submit) data to the server using a JSON payload body (as you could easily do with Postman previously) but instead use a format called application/x-www-form-urlencoded. The Pi needs to be able to understand this format in addition to application/json in order to handle data input from HTML forms.

HTML forms can use only the verbs POST or GET, not DELETE or PUT. It's rather unfortunate that even modern browsers don't send the content of HTML forms as JSON objects because of some obscure legacy reasons, but hey, *c'est la vie!*

As you'll see later in this book, the ability for all entities on the Web of Things to receive and transmit JSON content is essential to guarantee a truly open ecosystem. For this reason, we'll show you how to send actual JSON from an HTML form page (by using AJAX and JavaScript), because doing so is an essential part of communicating with web devices.

Open the ex-3.2-actuator-ajax-json.html file to see a similar form but this time with a large piece of JavaScript, shown in the following listing.

Listing 2.6   Send an HTTP POST with JSON payload from a form

```
(function($){ function processForm(e){
  $.ajax({
    url: 'http://devices.webofthings.io/pi/actuators/display/content/',
    dataType: 'json',
    method: 'POST',
```

The URL the request will be sent to

The format of the data you expect to get

The HTTP verb this request will send

```
                        contentType: 'application/json',
The actual data         data: JSON.stringify({"value": $('#value').val()}),          The encoding of the
you are sending         processData: false,                                          data you are sending
  (the content          success: function( data, textStatus, jQxhr ){
   of the form)           $('#response pre').html( JSON.stringify( data ) );         The callback to
                        },                                                           invoke if the request
The callback to         error: function( jqXhr, textStatus, errorThrown ){           was successful
 invoke if the            console.log( errorThrown );
 request failed         }
                      });
                      e.preventDefault();                       Attach the processForm()
                    }                                           function to be called when
                    $('#message-form').submit(processForm);     someone clicks Submit.
                  })(jQuery);
```

In this code, a function called `processForm()` is defined, which takes the data from the form, packs it into a JSON object, POSTs it to the Pi, and displays the result if successful (or displays an error in the console otherwise). The `url` parameter specifies the end-point URL (the Pi display), the `method` is the HTTP method to use, and the `contentType` is the format of the content sent to the server (in this case `application/json`). The last line attaches the event generated by a click of the Submit button of the form `#message-form` to call the `processForm()` function.

There is a variation of this code, ex-3.2b-actuator-ajax-form.html, which encodes the data in the `application/x-www-form-urlencoded` format in place of JSON, as it's done with the simple form we showed in part 1 of exercise 3.

2.4.3   So what?

In this section you learned the basics of how to send data and commands to a device, both using a form on a web page and from an API. You had a crash course in the limitations, challenges, and problems of the modern web (don't worry; there are many more ahead!), in particular how different web browsers can interpret and implement the same web standards differently. Finally, you learned how to use AJAX to bypass these limitations and send JSON commands to a Raspberry Pi and control it remotely.

We hope that after doing this exercise you realize that it's straightforward to send actuator commands over the web to all sorts of devices—as long as these are connected to the web and offer a simple HTTP/JSON interface. But the last problem is how to find a device nearby, understand its API, determine what functions are offered by the device, and know what parameters you need to include in your command, along with their type, unit, limitations, and the like. The next section will show you how to solve this problem, so keep reading.

2.5   Exercise 4—Tell the world about your device

In the previous exercises you learned how devices can be easily exposed over the web and then explored and used by other client applications. But those examples assumed that you (as a human developer or as the application you wrote) *know* what the fields of the JSON objects (for example, sensor or actuator) mean and how to use them. But how is this possible? What if the only thing you know about a device is its URL and nothing else?

Imagine you'd like to build a web application that can control home automation devices present in your local network. How can you ensure this application will always work, even if you're in someone else's network and you don't know anything about the devices there?

First, you need to find the devices at a network level (the *device discovery* problem). In other words, how can your web application discover the root URL of all the devices around you?

Second, even if you happen to know (by some magic trick) the root URL of all Web of Things–compatible devices around you, how can your application "understand" what sensors or actuators these devices offer, what formats they use, and the meaning of those devices, properties, fields, and so on?

As you saw in exercise 2 (section 2.3.2), if you know the root URL of a device, you can easily browse the device and find data about it and its sensors, services, and more. This is easy because you're a human, but imagine if you had a JSON document with unintelligible words or characters and no documentation that explain what those words mean—how would you know what the device does? And how would you know it's a device, for that matter?

Open ex-4-parse-device.html in your browser and you'll see a form prepopulated with the URL of the Pi (figure 2.15). Click Browse This Device.

This JavaScript code of ex-4-parse-device.html will read the root document of the Raspberry Pi (as JSON) and generate a simple report about the device and its sensors,

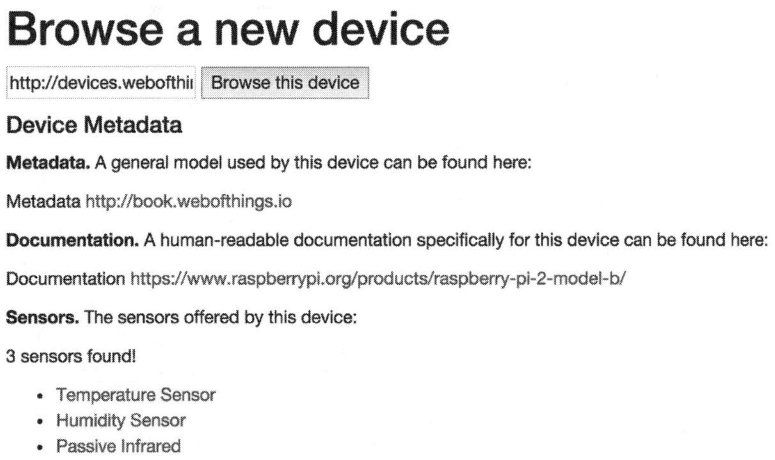

Browse a new device

| http://devices.webofthi | Browse this device |

Device Metadata

Metadata. A general model used by this device can be found here:

Metadata http://book.webofthings.io

Documentation. A human-readable documentation specifically for this device can be found here:

Documentation https://www.raspberrypi.org/products/raspberry-pi-2-model-b/

Sensors. The sensors offered by this device:

3 sensors found!

- Temperature Sensor
- Humidity Sensor
- Passive Infrared

Figure 2.15   A mini-browser that parses your device metadata and displays the results

along with link to the documentation for this device. First, let's look at the HTML code
to display the report, as shown in the next listing.

Listing 2.7   A basic device browser

```
<form id="message-form">
    <input type="text" id="host" name="host" value="http://devices.webofth-
    ings.io/pi"
placeholder="The URL of a WoT device" />
    <button type="submit">Browse this device</button>
</form>

<h4>Device Metadata</h4>
<p><b>Metadata.</b> A general model used by this device can be found here:
<div id="meta"></div></p>
<p><b>Documentation.</b> A human-readable documentation specifically for
this device can be found here: <div id="doc"></div></p>
<p><b>Sensors.</b> The sensors offered by this device:
    <div id="sensors"></div></p>
<ul id="sensors-list">
</ul>
```

The first thing you can see is a form where you can enter the root URL of a device with
a Browse button. Then, there are some HTML text elements that will act as placeholders (meta, doc, and so on). Now let's look at the AJAX calls in the following listing.

Listing 2.8   Retrieve and parse device metadata using AJAX JSON calls

```
(function ($) {
  function processForm(e) {

    var sensorsPath = '';                          GET the ROOT JSON of the device
                                                   and extract data from it.
    $.ajax({
      url: $('#host').val(),
      method: 'GET',
      dataType: 'json',
      success: function (data) {
        $('#meta').html(data.links.meta.title + " <a href=\"" +
        data.links.meta.rel + "\">" + data.links.meta.rel + "</a>");
        $('#doc').html(data.links.doc.title + " <a href=\"" +
        data.links.doc.rel + "\">" + data.links.doc.rel + "</a>");

        sensorsPath = data.url + data.resources.sensors.url;       Store the URL
                                                                   of the sensors
        $.ajax({                                                   resource.
          url: sensorsPath,
          method: 'GET',
          dataType: 'json',
          success: function (data) {
            var sensorList = "";
            $('#sensors').html(Object.keys(data).length + " sensors
            found!");
```

Update the "meta" and "doc" elements with the links found in the root JSON document.

GET the list of all sensors on the device.

Callback function that processes the sensors JSON document; 'data' contains the JSON object of the sensors.

Loop through all sensors.

```
                    for (var key in data) {
                        sensorList = sensorList + "<li><a href=\"" + sensorsPath +
                        key + "\">" + data[key].name + "</a></li>";
                    }
                    $('#sensors-list').html(sensorList);
                },
                error: function (data, textStatus, jqXHR) {
                    console.log(data);
                }
            });
        },
        error: function (data, textStatus, jqXHR) {
            console.log(data);
        }
    });
    e.preventDefault();
}

    $('#message-form').submit(processForm);
})(jQuery);
```

Display the list in the HTML.

Looking at this code, you can see that you first set the root JSON document of the device using the URL entered in the form (`$('#host').val()`). If the JSON file has been successfully retrieved, the `success` callback function will be triggered with the `data` variable containing the root JSON document of the device (which was shown in step 2 of section 2.2.2). Then you parse this JSON to extract the elements you're looking for; in this case the code is looking for a `links` element in the returned JSON object (hence the `data.links`), which contains various links to get more information about this device, which looks like the following code:

```
"links": {
  "meta": {
    "rel": "http://book.webofthings.io",
    "title": "Metadata"
  },
  "doc": {
    "rel":
"https://www.raspberrypi.org/products/raspberry-pi-2-model-b/",
    "title": "Documentation"
  },
  "ui": {
    "rel": ".",
    "title": "User Interface"
  }
}
```

In particular, the `meta` element contains a link (value of `rel`) to the general model used by this device (which describes the grammar used to describe the elements of this device) and then a `doc` that links to a human-readable documentation that describes the meaning (the semantics) and specific details of this particular device (that is, which sensors are present and what they measure).

The metadata document linked in the previous code is nothing more than a machine-readable JSON document model that allows users to describe WoT devices in a structured manner, along with a definition of the logic elements all WoT devices must have. If hundreds of device manufacturers would use this same data model to expose the services of their devices, it would mean that any application that can read and parse this file would be able to read the JSON file returned by the device and understand the components of the devices (how many sensors it has, their names or limitations, their type, and so on).

Now, what about the sensors or actuators themselves? The `links` element only defined metadata (such as documentation) about the device, not the device contents itself. To find the sensors contained in the device, you'll have to parse the `sensors` field of the `resources` element, which is what happens in the second AJAX call where you do a GET on the sensors resource of the device. Once you get the sensors JSON document, you iterate over each sensor and create a link to it using this pattern:

```
<li><a href=\""+sensorsPath+key+"\">"+data[key].name+"</a></li>
```

Here `sensorsPath` is the URL of the sensors resource (in this case http://devices .webofthings.io/pi/sensors) to which you add the sensor ID of each sensor (`key`), along with the name of the respective sensor (`data[key].name`).

2.5.1   So what?

If you didn't understand all the details of the previous exercises, it's perfectly fine—there's nothing wrong with you! What happened is that you got your first hands-on crash course on the Semantic Web, or rather, on the hard problems it tries to solve. The reason you've heard a lot about it yet never seen or used it (or understood it, for that matter) is that it's a complex problem for computers and people who program them: how the hell do you explain the real world—and its existential questions—to a computer? Well, it turns out you can't really teach philosophy to your machine yet. But as we've shown here and will detail in chapter 8, there are quite a few small tricks that you can apply successfully that make the web—and computers—just a little smarter.

You've seen how web devices can advertise their basic capabilities, data, and services in a machine-readable manner. The fact that we used well-known web patterns made it easy to build a web app interacting with our Things. Unfortunately, there's no single standard to define this information universally, and the JSON model we use is something born out of trial and error over the years. In order to unlock the full potential of the Web of Things, we must be able to define all the details about an object using a single data model with clear semantics that all machines and applications can understand without any room for ambiguity. We'll explore how to get there using web and lightweight Semantic Web technologies in much more detail in chapter 8.

2.6   *Exercise 5—Create your first physical mashup*

In the previous exercises, you learned how to access a web device, understand the service and data it offers, and read and write data from devices. In this exercise, we'll

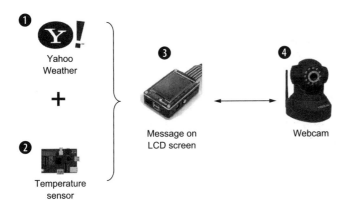

Figure 2.16   A physical mashup application. First (1), you retrieve the local temperature from Yahoo Weather and then the remote temperature from the sensor attached to our Pi (2). You compare it with the temperature in London and send the results to an LCD screen (3). When the screen displays the text you've sent, you retrieve a picture of the screen form the webcam (4) and display it on the mashup.

show you how to build your first mashup. The concept of mashups originates from the hip-hop scene to describe a song composed by taking samples of other songs. Similarly, a web mashup is a web application that gets data from various sources, processes it, and combines it to create a new application.

Here, you'll create not only a web mashup but a *physical mashup*—a web application that uses data from a real sensor connected to the web. In this exercise you're going to take local temperature data from the Yahoo! Weather service, compare it with the temperature sensor attached to the Pi in our office, and publish your results to the LCD screen attached to the Pi in London. Finally, to see what your message looks like, you'll use the web API of the webcam to take a picture and display it on our web page! See figure 2.16 for an illlustration of this process.

Go ahead and open the file ex-5-mashup.html in both your editor and your browser. This code is a little longer than what you've seen so far but not much more complicated, as shown in the following listing.

Listing 2.9   Mashup function

```
$(document).ready(function () {
  var rootUrl = 'http://devices.webofthings.io';

  function mashup(name, location) {
    var yahooUrl = "https://query.yahooapis.com/v1/public/yql?q=select item
    from weather.forecast where woeid in (select woeid from geo.places(1)
    where text='" + location + "') and u='c'&format=json";
    $.getJSON(yahooUrl, function (yahooResult) {
      var localTemp =
      yahooResult.query.results.channel.item.condition.temp;
      console.log('Local @ ' + location + ': ' + localTemp);
      $.getJSON(rootUrl + '/pi/sensors/temperature', function (piResult) {
        console.log('Pi @ London: ' + piResult.value);
        publishMessage(prepareMessage(name, location, localTemp,
        piResult.value));
      });
    });
  }
```

Get the temperature in the user location from Yahoo.

Get the temperature from the WoT Pi in London.

Prepare the text to publish and use it to update the content of the LCD screen.

Set a timer that
will call the
takePicture()
function in N
seconds (after the
LCD content has
been updated).

```
function publishMessage(message) {
    $.ajax(rootUrl + '/pi/actuators/display/content', {        ◄──┐ POST the message
        data: JSON.stringify({"value": message}),                   │ to the LCD actuator.
        contentType: 'application/json',
        type: 'POST',
        success: function (data) {
            $('#message').html('Published to LCD: ' + message);
            $('#wait').html('The Webcam image with your message will appear
            below in : ' + (data.displayInSeconds+2) + ' seconds.');
            console.log('We will take a picture in ' +
            (data.displayInSeconds+2) + ' seconds...');
            setTimeout(takePicture, (data.displayInSeconds+2) * 1000);
        }
    });
}

function prepareMessage(name, location, localTemp, piTemp) {      ◄──────────┐
    return name + '@' + location + ((localTemp < piTemp) ? ' < ' : ' > ')
    + piTemp;
}                                               Generate the text to display
                                                with the user name, location,
                                                       and Pi temperature.

function takePicture() {
    $.ajax({
        type: 'GET',
        url: rootUrl + '/camera/sensors/picture/',
        dataType: 'json',
        success: function (data) {
            console.log(data);
            $('#camImg').attr('src', data.value);          ◄──┐ Update the HTML <img>
        },                                                      │ tag with the image URL.
        error: function (err) {
            console.log(err);
        }
    });
}

    mashup('Rachel', 'Zurich, CH');
});
```

Retrieve the
current image
from the
webcam in
our office.

The mashup() function is responsible for running the different bits of the mashup. It takes two parameters: the first parameter is your name; the second one is the name of the city where you live formatted as city, country code (for example, Zurich, CH; London, UK; or New York, US). It's then essentially composed of two HTTP GET calls over AJAX requesting a response as application/json representations. The first call is to the Yahoo! Weather Service API, which given a location returns its current weather and temperature.

Once this call has returned (that is, the anonymous callback function has been invoked), the second function is called to fetch the latest value from the Pi temperature sensor, just as you did in section 2.3.1.

Next, you call prepareMessage(), which formats your message and passes the result to publishMessage(). This last function runs an HTTP POST call over AJAX with a JSON payload containing the message to push to the LCD screen, as done in Exercise 3—Act on the real world.

Because you need to wait in the queue for your message to be displayed, you set a timer that will trigger the takePicture() function. This last function runs a final HTTP GET request to fetch a picture of what the LCD screen shows, via the web-enabled camera. You then dynamically add the returned picture to the image container of your HTML page.

To start this chain of real-world and virtual-world events, all you need to do is edit the source code so it invokes the mashup(x,y) function using your own name and city. For example, Rachel from Zurich in Switzerland needs to call this function as follows:

```
mashup('Rachel', 'Zurich, CH')
```

Then open the file in your browser, and voilà! Within a few seconds, you'll see a live image from the webcam with your message appearing on the screen of the Pi in our office.

2.6.1 So what?

You've built your first web-based physical mashup using data from various sources, both physical and real-time, and run a simple algorithm to decide whether your weather is better than ours (although competing against London on the weather is somewhat unfair). Think about it for a second. This mashup involves a temperature sensor connected to an embedded device, a video camera, an LCD screen, and a virtual weather service, yet you were able to create a whole new application that fits into 80 lines of HTML and JavaScript, UI included! Isn't that nice? All this thanks to the fact that all the actors (devices and other services) expose their APIs on the web and therefore are directly accessible using JavaScript! You'll learn much more about physical mashups throughout the book and especially in chapter 10, where we'll survey the various tools and techniques available.

2.7 Summary

- You experienced your first hands-on encounter with web-connected devices across the world and could browse their metadata, content, sensors, actuators, and so on.
- Web-connected devices can be surfed just like any other website. Real-time data from sensors can be consumed via an HTTP or WebSocket API just like other content on the web.
- It's much easier and faster to understand the basics of HTTP APIs than the various and complex protocols commonly used in the IoT.
- In only a few minutes you were able to read and write data to a device across the world by sending HTTP requests with Postman.
- Connecting the physical world to the web enables rapid prototyping of interactive applications that require only a few lines of HTML/JavaScript code.

- As data and services from various devices are made available as web resources, it becomes easy to build physical mashups that integrate content from all sorts of sources with minimal integration effort.

We hope you enjoyed this first encounter with the Web of Things enough to read the ensuing chapters and learn how to implement these concepts on your own device. In the next chapters, we'll look at how to implement JavaScript on devices and we'll provide a short and sweet introduction to Node.js. Then, we'll look into configuring your own device and making it fit for the Web of Things. We'll show you how to create and deploy a Node.js application on a Raspberry Pi device, and you'll be able to create your first web-connected device and adapt these examples for your own use case.

Node.js for the Web of Things

The previous chapter provided a first encounter with web-connected devices. We hope it made you realize how easy it is to build applications that interact with various web-connected devices. But this was only the tip of the iceberg because we did all the hard work for you. In the rest of the book, we'll teach you all you need to know in order to implement your own web-connected devices and applications.

Before we jump straight to the code and other juicy bits, you have two important decisions to make. First, you have to pick an embedded platform on which your applications will run. This will be the subject of chapter 4. Second, you need to choose the programming language in which you'll write your code, and this is the topic of this chapter.

To choose a programming language for building your Web of Things prototypes you have two basic requirements: first, the language you pick should fully support web protocols and standards. Well, this doesn't help much because just about any serious language today (who said "whitespace"?[1]) provides tools and libraries to support HTTP. The second requirement is that you should be able to use a single language to build the client application, the cloud engine or gateways (which we'll present in chapter 6), and even the code running on the embedded device. It turns out that JavaScript can be The One.

In consequence, this chapter first looks into the recent developments around the JavaScript community and its massively growing importance for the internet and the Web of Things. Afterward, we'll introduce you to Node.js, an environment for writing server-side applications with JavaScript. This introduction won't make you a Node.js expert, but it will certainly give you all the elements you need to understand how Node.js works and to be able to build and deploy the examples of this book.

How to get the code

If you don't want to write the code samples we show from scratch, you can clone our GitHub repository (find the link here: http://book.webofthings.io). All code examples in this chapter are located in the chapter3-node-js folder.

3.1   *The rise of JavaScript: from clients to servers to things!*

JavaScript is a dynamic programming language where client-side scripts executed by web browsers can process data asynchronously and alter the page being displayed. Long gone are the days when JavaScript was solely used to animate banners on a web page! Thanks to its widespread support by virtually all web browsers, relative ease of use, and flexibility, JavaScript has become the de facto solution for writing dynamic, client-side applications. According to the number of public repositories on GitHub, it has also become one of the most popular programming languages ever,[2] with a community of developers growing faster than any other; see figure 3.1.

This ongoing JavaScript revolution aligns well with the core idea of the Web of Things, which is to integrate devices to the web so they become more accessible and easier to program. In other words, make it possible to interact with devices just like any other resource on the web by using well-known web standards. When the services exposed by physical objects can be accessed via simple HTTP requests, writing

---

[1] https://en.wikipedia.org/wiki/Whitespace_(programming_language)
[2] http://www.tiobe.com/tiobe_index

Rank of top languages on GitHub.com over time

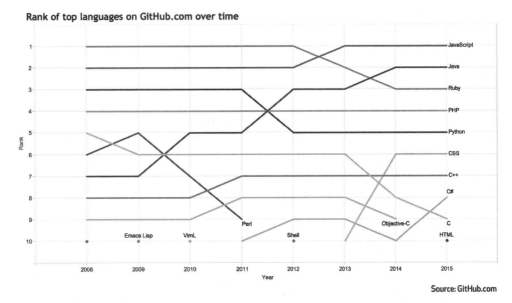

Source: GitHub.com

Figure 3.1   The ranking of the most popular languages on GitHub. Since 2008 JavaScript has experienced a steady growth that led it to outnumber all other languages in terms of available projects on GitHub. [Source: GitHub.com]

interactive applications for the physical world becomes as easy as creating any basic web application: by writing with HTML, CSS, and JavaScript!

On the server side, applications are often implemented using various languages such as PHP, Ruby, Python, or Java. But here JavaScript has recently become quite a popular option. Indeed, JavaScript is increasingly adopted for writing highly scalable server-side applications, particularly in runtime environments such as Node.js,[3] which we introduce shortly.

The convergence of all these platforms has a fortunate implication for this book: it means we can mainly focus on using JavaScript to write all the examples in this book. We'll use JavaScript and jQuery to build the client-side examples (as we did already in chapter 2), JavaScript with Node.js to build the servers offering the Things' services on the web, and even JavaScript and Node.js code to manage hardware resources of the Things themselves, as we explain next.

3.1.1   *Pushing JavaScript to things*

Interestingly enough, the JavaScript revolution fueled by Node.js didn't stop at the browser. Nor did it stop at the servers. In the last few years, it also infiltrated the world of devices themselves! In a world massively dominated by devices running low-level C programs, JavaScript and Node.js have managed to stand out as a viable and easy-to-use

---

[3]   Node.js isn't the only framework for server-side JavaScript. Another example is Vert.x: http://vertx.io.

alternative for powering all kinds of things from robots (for example, with the Cylon.js[4] library) to wireless sensor nodes. A number of embedded device platforms today directly support JavaScript and Node.js to write embedded code. This is the case for most Linux-based platforms that we'll introduce in the next chapter, such as the Raspberry Pi, the Intel Edison, and Beagle Board,[5] as well as some low-power platforms such as the Tessel[6] and Espruino.[7]

"When you have a hammer, everything looks like a nail!" we hear you say. Not exactly; we don't advocate using JavaScript and Node.js for every IoT implementation. We'd rather compare JavaScript and Node.js to the Swiss army knife of modern IoT and WoT development than to a hammer. It certainly isn't the optimal solution for every IoT project we can think of, but it's a great option for many of them.

An embedded application that requires absolutely predictable and real-time performance (for example, the code running in a high-speed train) is better off being written in a low-level language such as C. Moreover, JavaScript as a language is often criticized by its detractors for its lack of static typing and a plethora of different programming patterns and styles leading to code that's sometimes harder to maintain, typically in large projects involving a large number of people. Nevertheless, its ubiquity, portability, and asynchronous event-driven model, along with a large and vibrant online community, make it a solid candidate to consider seriously. This is certainly true when using Node.js to build scalable and real-time web systems, but is also increasingly true for the blazing-fast prototyping of hardware projects.

3.2   *Introduction to Node.js*

Node.js—or Node, as its aficionados call it—first emerged in 2009 when a brilliant developer named Ryan Dahl started to build it in "starving artist" mode in Germany. Later on, Ryan was hired by Joyent, a cloud provider company that was an early supporter of Node. In 2015, the Node.js foundation was formed, with key companies such as Joyent, IBM, Microsoft, and Intel getting on board, giving Node.js a great hope for a bright professional future.[8]

Node.js provides an event-driven architecture and a non-blocking I/O API (more details about that to follow) that optimizes an application's throughput and scalability. This model is commonly used to design high-performance real-time web applications.

The idea behind Node is to provide a framework in which high-performance server-side web applications can be written. Unlike other servers where you deploy your application in a running server instance, with Node your application *is* the server. Node builds on the highly efficient Google V8 JavaScript engine, which is at the heart of the Chrome browser. Node isn't JavaScript, but JavaScript is the language

---

[4] http://cylonjs.com/
[5] http://beagleboard.org/
[6] http://tessel.io/
[7] http://www.espruino.com
[8] https://nodejs.org/en/foundation/

you use to build Node applications, although other languages such as CoffeeScript can be used as well.

Although this book assumes you have some basic knowledge of client-side JavaScript, it will introduce you to server-side and device-side JavaScript. Node.js is the framework we'll use to build the servers running in the cloud or on the devices themselves. We'll also use Node.js to access the physical peripherals of the devices such as sensors or actuators.

This book is by no means a comprehensive Node.js manual: there are a number of great books dedicated to Node. See, for example, Mike Cantelo's *Node.js in Action, Second Edition* (Manning, 2015);[9] Alex Young and Marc Harter's *Node.js in Practice* (Manning, 2014);[10] or some good tutorials such as Manuel Kiessling's *The Node Beginner Book*.[11] But although we can assume that the basics of client-side JavaScript are known to most developers, Node is still fairly new and has some rather uncommon aspects that make it both powerful and, at times, tricky to grasp.

In the next sections we'll cover the basics of Node to make sure you're not too puzzled by the examples in the following chapters. First, we'll show you how to write your first Node web application (and, yes, Node HTTP server, too). Then, because we reuse many great libraries to build our examples, we'll look at the aspects of modularity and package management in Node. Then we'll dig a bit more into the way Node and other single-threaded web and networking frameworks work. Finally, we'll look at the core concepts of asynchronous programming in Node, providing you with the tools to build increasingly complex Node code.

3.2.1 *Installing Node.js on your machine*

If you don't have a Raspberry Pi, don't worry! Thanks to the awesomeness of Node.js, you can run all the examples in this chapter (and even in this book) without actually owning a device! It's just way nicer on a device.

You'll start by installing Node.js on your local machine.[12] Fortunately, this is as simple as installing any application on your favorite platform. Once it's installed, open a terminal window and type the following:

```
$ node --version
```

This should return the version of Node.js you installed (which should be at least 4.2.2 to ensure the code in this book runs). You're now ready to run your first example!

3.2.2 *Your first web server in Node.js*

Now that Node is installed on your computer, you can start using it. One thing Node is especially good at is building servers with only a few lines of code. You can use it to

---

[9] http://manning.com/cantelon2/?a_aid=wot&a_bid=9b654188

[10] http://www.manning.com/young/?a_aid=wot&a_bid=f45747b3

[11] http://www.nodebeginner.org/

[12] You can find the different installers on the official Node.js page at http://nodejs.org/en/download/.

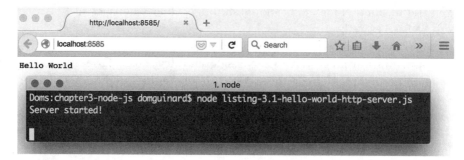

Figure 3.2 Starting your first web server with Node (bottom) and returning the traditional "Hello World" to your web browser (top)

build all kinds of servers accepting all kinds of protocols: from sockets, to TCP/IP, to HTTP, to WebSockets.

You'll use Node to build all kinds of servers in this book, but you'll get started with a web server based on HTTP because this is built into Node and doesn't require you to import any dependencies; see figure 3.2.

If you're used to PHP and Apache or Java and web servers like Tomcat, you're familiar with creating a web application and then deploying it to an existing server. In Node, things are different because your application is the server. Let's get started with building a simple web server that always returns "Hello World" to all incoming requests; see the following listing.

Listing 3.1 A Hello World HTTP server in Node.js

require() is used to import libraries.

Create an HTTP server and pass it a function to be called whenever a client sends a request.

```
var http = require("http");
http.createServer(function(req,res){
    res.writeHeader(200, {'Content-Type': 'text/plain'});
    res.end('Hello World!');
}).listen(8585);
console.log('Server started!');
```

Start the HTTP server on port 8585.

Write the response, beginning with the HTTP headers.

This is as small as it gets! First, you require the http module. This basically loads the HTTP module and makes it available to your application (we'll detail the way Node dependencies work in the next section). Afterward, you use the HTTP object to create a new server. You pass to this server a function that will be called whenever a client connects to your server. When a client actually connects, the function is called with two parameters:

- req represents the client request and offers a number of functions to retrieve information about it, such as the requested URL or the payload that was sent.
- res represents the response you'd like to send back to the client.

With `res.writeHeader()` you can write the HTTP headers. In this example you write the `Status` header with a value of `200` (meaning everything went well) and the `Content-Type` header to `text-plain`, meaning that you'll return plain text to the client. For now, don't panic if you don't understand exactly what this means because we'll cover this at length in chapter 6. You then start the server by invoking `listen(PORT)`, which will start the server on port 8585.

To run your first server, copy and paste listing 3.1 into a file[13] with a .js extension (for example, helloworld.js). Copy this file into a folder called hello-node, open a terminal window, go to this folder, and start your application with the command "node" followed by the name of your file, like this:

```
$ node helloworld.js
```

You should see the text Server Started! appearing in your terminal telling you that your Node application is running. Now go to http://localhost:8585 in your browser. You should see the "Hello World" message, as shown in figure 3.2. Not utterly impressive, but think about it: with only five lines of code you created a web application that talks to your browser. You didn't even need to install and configure an Apache server for your specific OS! You can now stop the server by pressing Ctrl-C in the terminal window.

3.2.3 Returning sensor data as JSON

Let's shift gears and build a server that actually delivers some values! You'll build a server that returns a temperature sensor value when browsing to `/temperature`, as shown in figure 3.3, and a light sensor value when browsing to `/light`. You'll connect real sensors to your Node code in the next chapter, but for now you'll return random

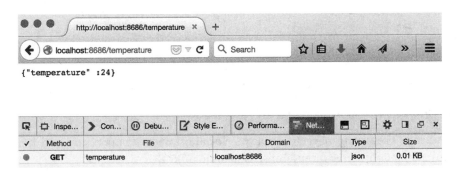

Figure 3.3   A simple Node web server returning temperature data with a JSON representation in Firefox

---

[13] You can create simple JavaScript files with any text editor, but for more serious projects you might need an advanced text editor such as Sublime Text (http://www.sublimetext.com), Atom (https://atom.io/), or Brackets (http://brackets.io/). You can also use a feature-rich IDE (Integrated Development Environment) such as WebStorm (https://www.jetbrains.com/webstorm/) or NetBeans (https://netbeans.org/).

data. You'll also change the data format that the browser returns to JSON, which you encountered in chapter 2.

Just as you did before, you first create an HTTP server, as shown in listing 3.2. But this time you inform the client that the response is in JSON using the {'Content-Type': 'application/json'} header. You then look into the request using req.url, which will contain the path, after the domain, that the client requested (for example, /temperature). You then create a switch that handles the requests to your different paths. For each path you generate the corresponding random value and return it as JSON.

Listing 3.2   A simple HTTP server returning JSON data

```
var http = require("http");
var port = 8686;

function randomInt (low, high) {
  return Math.floor(Math.random() * (high - low) + low);
}

http.createServer(function(req,res){
  console.log('New incoming client request for ' + req.url);
  res.writeHeader(200, {'Content-Type': 'application/json'});
  switch(req.url) {
    case '/temperature':
      res.write('{"temperature" :' + randomInt(1, 40) + '}');
      break;
    case '/light':
      res.write('{"light" :' + randomInt(1, 100) + '}');
      break;
    default:
      res.write('{"hello" : "world"}');
  }
  res.end();
}).listen(port);
console.log('Server listening on http://localhost:' + port);
```

Set the header to announce you'll return JSON representations.

Read the request URL and provide responses accordingly.

Write the temperature result as JSON.

Return the results to the client.

Now save this file and run your application like you did before:

```
$ node listing-3.2-webserver.js
```

Use your browser to navigate to http://localhost:8686/temperature and http://localhost:8686/light to see a random sensor value in JSON.

3.3   *Modularity in Node.js*

You've created your first server based on built-in Node modules. That worked well, but what if you'd like to benefit from the work of the growing and active community of Node developers by using third-party modules for specific tasks? This is what this section is about: first understanding the Node modules management system and then understanding the structure of the modules themselves.

3.3.1 *npm—the Node package manager*

Just as Java has Maven repositories, Ubuntu has apt-get, and Ruby has Gem, Node has its own package or module manager (and a great one!) called npm. As the npm team members put it,

> *"npm" doesn't stand for "Node Package Manager." It stands for "npm Is Not An Acronym." Why not "NINAA"? Because then it would be an acronym.*

Joke aside, the reason for not calling npm the Node Package Manager is that it is not only a package manager for Node, but also a package manager for client-side JavaScript.

If you installed Node the way we suggested in section Installing Node.js on your machine, you should be all set to use npm through the npm command-line utility. The first step is obviously choosing a module to install. This can be done in several ways, but a popular one is by searching for modules by keywords using the search engine of the main npm repository at https://www.npmjs.com/. As an exercise, look for the request module that you'll use later. All npm modules are identified by a unique name, so once you've found the one you want, write its name down.

Because of the popularity of Node.js, each search query will return a large number of options, and choosing the module you should use is sometimes overwhelming. Choosing the right module is especially relevant in a booming ecosystem such as Node where a lot of code is committed at a fast pace, sometimes at the cost of stability and quality. A good way to quickly evaluate the relevance and maturity of a project is to look at its GitHub page, which is accessible on the detail page of each module, as shown in figure 3.4. On this page you can find the number of people following the module (Watch), how many developers liked the module (Star), and how many created a new version of this module (Fork); these are good indicators of the popularity and stability of the module.

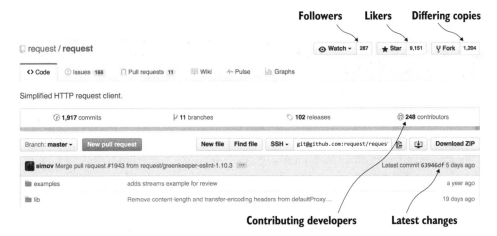

Figure 3.4   The GitHub page of a Node module. Look for the popularity metrics of the module when choosing it.

Now that you've picked a module, you can install it using the npm command-line tool with the unique name of the module. Let's install request, an intuitive module designed to make HTTP calls as simple and straightforward as possible. Create a new folder (here we name it hello-npm) and change the directory to this folder; then run the following command:

```
$ npm install request
```

This will communicate with the npm server and install the new module into a directory called node_modules/. Then you can use the module from any Node source file inside the hello-npm folder by using the require instruction, which loads the module into memory and makes it accessible to your source code. This is done with the following statement:

```
var request = require('request');
```

3.3.2   *Clean dependencies with package.json and npm*

The system we just illustrated works well, but adding more modules to your project and shifting it from one place to another requires a lot of manual runs of the npm command. Fortunately, npm solved this issue by allowing you to specify the modules your code depends on in a single JSON file called package.json. You can see the structure of a typical package.json file in the following listing.

Listing 3.3   A simple package.json file

```json
{
  "name": "hello-npm",
  "version": "0.0.1",
  "description": "Experimenting with npm modules",
  "author": "Me self <my@email.com>",
  "repository" : "https://github.com/...",
  "dependencies": {
    "request": "0.1.x"
  },
  "devDependencies": {
    "mocha": "2.x.x"
  },
  "engine": "node >= 4.2.2"
}
```

The name of your own module (your project name)

The version of your project

A short description of what your project does

A link to GitHub or another source control system where your code will live

The list of modules required for your project

The list of modules required for the development of your project (for example, test dependencies)

The version of Node required for your project

First, you give your project a name and a version. Note that if you ever decide to also publish your project as a module on npm, this name will be used. Then, you add a short description and an author, as well as a link to a source control system where the code of your project can be found (it can be private as well). Next comes the core of the file: the modules your project depends on. Here you have a single module:

request. Node modules usually follow the semantic versioning pattern,[14] `MAJOR.MINOR.PATCH`:

- `MAJOR` version when you make incompatible API changes
- `MINOR` version when you add functionality in a backward-compatible manner
- `PATCH` version when you make backward-compatible bug fixes

Wildcards are supported, so `2.x.x` means that npm will fetch the latest `MINOR` and `PATCH` versions of `request` `MAJOR` version 2. `devDependencies` is required for dependencies only when you build your project in a developer environment. A good example of such a dependency is a testing library that wouldn't need to be imported when deploying the final version of your code. Finally, with `engine` you can also specify the version of Node your project should run with. This is a minimal example of a package.json file because much more can be specified there. A great interactive guide to building your package.json files is provided online.[15]

Of course, you don't have to write your package.json file manually. Instead, you can use the `npm init` command, which will ask you for basic information about your application and generate a package.json file for you automatically.

Another useful feature of npm is that you don't have to manually add each new module to your package.json. Instead, you can install them with the `--save` flag as follows:

```
$ npm install request --save
```

This command will automatically add this dependency to your package.json file.

3.3.3 *Your first Node module*

Now that you've seen how to manage packaged modules in Node, we'll show how to organize your code by creating your own simple modules. Imagine you want to create a module that offers arithmetic operations to an application. The structure of the folders for your first module is shown in the following code. The module file (operations.js) is located in the /lib folder and accessed from the modules-client.js file:

```
hello-modules/
├── lib
│   └── operations.js
├── module-client.js
├── package.json
```

Begin by creating a folder for your project called hello-modules. To keep your code tidy and respect the Node conventions, create a lib folder inside hello-modules. You then write the module itself in a file called operations.js that you put into the lib folder; the code for operations.js is shown in the following listing.

---

[14] http://semver.org/

[15] http://browsenpm.org/package.json

Listing 3.4   operations.js: a mathematics module in Node.js

```
exports.add = function(a, b) {
  logOp(a, b, '+');
  return a + b;
}

exports.sub = function(a, b) {
  logOp(a, b, '-');
  return a - b;
}

exports.mul = function(a, b) {
  logOp(a, b, '*');
  return a * b;
}

function logOp(a, b, op) {
  console.log('Computing ' + a + op + b);
}
```

⟵ The exports object makes a
function of your module available
to the module users.

⟵ The logOp function is internal to
this module and won't be available
from outside this file.

This module contains three functions that you want to make available to module users: `add`, `sub`, and `mul`. You make them available by defining properties on the `exports` object. Note that you can also make any other object, string, or variable available through this mechanism. Other functions used only in your module file (for example, `logOp`) won't be available to files outside your module because you don't attach them to the `exports` object.

The last step is to create a client for your library. In the root folder of the project (that is, the hello-modules folder), create a new file called module-client.js (note that unlike the module name, the name of the client file doesn't matter). The code of this file is fairly straightforward, as shown in the next listing.

Listing 3.5   A simple Node application using the operations module

```
var ops = require('./lib/operations');

console.log(ops.add(42, 42));
console.log(ops.mul(42, 42));
console.log(ops.sub(42, 42));
```

⟵ Imports the
operations.js module

The key lies in `require`, where you import your new module. Essentially, you're telling Node to go fetch the module `operations` in the lib subdirectory and save it in the `ops` variable. Note that you don't need to specify the .js extension when using `require`.

That's it! Your first module is ready to be used. Run `node module-client.js` to test it. If everything works fine, you should see the following output in your console:

```
Computing 42+42
84
Computing 42*42
1764
Computing 42-42
0
```

There's much more to modules than what we covered here, but this will help you to get started and understand how we use modules in the rest of this book.

3.4 Understanding the Node.js event loop

Building server-side web applications such as the one you used in chapter 2—or generally any web server that needs to deal with more than a single client at a time—requires the ability to handle a large number of connections in a concurrent manner. If the connections couldn't be accepted concurrently, each new web client would have to wait until the clients that arrived earlier were served. This would be almost as slow as taking London's underground from Waterloo to Bank during rush hour! To use a more appropriate analogy, imagine a single gas station on a busy intersection, with a single pump used by a single attendant.

3.4.1 Multithreaded web servers

Two common patterns can be used to resolve this issue. As shown in figure 3.5, the first pattern is to create one process—or better, one thread—per request. A thread is essentially a lightweight process because it's able to share some of the process's resources (for example, some of the allocated memory) while executing largely independently.

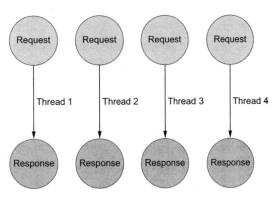

Consider this code snippet, which fetches data from a database and then displays it:

Figure 3.5 Dealing with a number of concurrent requests with a threading or process-forking approach: for each new client a new thread or process is created.

```
var result = database.query("SELECT things FROM deviceTable");
console.log(result);
```

If you ever worked with a server-side web language such as PHP running on Apache or Java on Tomcat, you most likely used code like this, working in a sequential manner white waiting for I/O operations to finish. This works fine in the PHP and Java worlds because while one client waits to be served, the underlying server (for example, Apache) serves the next clients. It does this by creating one thread for each incoming client.

3.4.2 Single-threaded, non-blocking web servers

Let's think about this example by applying it to our gas station: imagine each thread is a pump with an attendant, each web client is a customer, and the database is the central tank. We're better off than with a single pump and attendant, but each attendant is still idle some of the time, waiting for our tank to get filled. What if we had only one attendant managing several pumps in an efficient manner? Wouldn't this be more economical in terms of costs?

In a nutshell, this is what modern non-blocking web servers are all about: being able to handle more requests by minimizing the memory overhead required for each new client. This second pattern is an event-driven system often based on the idea of a single thread (or a limited number of threads) with an event loop and non-blocking or *asynchronous* I/O.

The Node.js runtime is built on these principles. It runs a single thread with an event loop, as shown on figure 3.6, and strongly favors asynchronous I/O operations. When the Node server accepts a client, it puts it on hold until the I/O operations it requested (for example, reading from the database, reading a value from a sensor, or uploading a file on a remote server) have returned and goes on serving other clients in the meanwhile.

A direct consequence of the event-loop pattern with a single

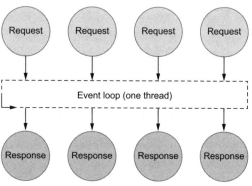

Figure 3.6   Dealing with a number of concurrent requests with a single-threaded event-driven approach. The event loop puts the clients on hold until the I/O operations have returned.

thread is that Node really doesn't like waiting actively because it completely blocks the Node server and prevents it from serving any subsequent request!

To better understand the difference between blocking and non-blocking calls, imagine that we run the synchronous code shown previously in a Node server. The Node runtime will fetch data from the database, wait until it gets it, and then execute the `console.log()` instruction. If there's a lot of data to fetch, you might have to wait for quite some time, during which the Node server wouldn't be able to serve or accept any other incoming request—not a good idea to scale your system! Let's rewrite the database function in a non-blocking way that fits the Node model, as shown in the next listing.

Listing 3.6   An asynchronous call to the database

```
database.query("SELECT things FROM deviceTable",
  function(results) {
    // do something with the results
  }
);
console.log(results);
```

> Here the content of the results variable will be undefined because the results will be accessible later on and only to the anonymous function.

The major difference with this version is that you pass a function as a parameter when calling the `database.query` function (we'll talk more about these functions, called *callbacks*, in the next section). The Node event loop will then put this call on hold until a response arrives from the database. This time, while waiting for the response, other instructions will be executed until the results have been fetched from the database and are ready to be consumed. When the results are retrieved, the event loop will call the callback `function(results)` with the results.

Interestingly enough, this means that the `database.query` instruction will return directly after it's called. As a consequence, the `console.log(results)` will execute right away, before the results are actually ready! Moreover, the results themselves will be available only to the anonymous function (injected in the callback by the event loop), and the variable will be undefined for the `console.log` instruction.

This way of serving requests on a single thread while not blocking all clients works only if all calls in the chain are asynchronous, so all the libraries you use and the code you write should be asynchronous unless there's a really good reason for them not to be. An example of a justified synchronous call occurs when loading configurations or dependencies at the startup of a Node program. As a convention, to make sure you keep track of your synchronous calls, Node functions that are synchronous end with the `Sync` suffix and do not usually take a function as a parameter. For example, `fs.readFileSync(filename)` reads a file synchronously (that is, blocking the single thread until the file is fully read) as opposed to `fs.readFile(filename, callback)`, which reads a file asynchronously (that is, releasing the thread to do other work while waiting for the file to be read).

Don't get us wrong: single-threaded servers with asynchronous I/O are not trivial to work with and aren't a silver bullet, either. But they've been shown to yield better performance and scaling in a number of situations, particularly for data-intensive real-time (DIRT) applications. Interestingly, the nature of real-world Things like sensors does perfectly fit into the DIRT type of applications, which partially explains the growing interest is these types of servers in the context of the Internet of Things. Reading data from the real world requires gathering a lot of sensor data (through I/O operations on physical sensors), and clients expect to be informed about changes of these sensors' state in a timely, event-driven, and almost real-time manner! This fits nicely the definition of DIRT applications and will be covered in chapter 6.

We hope we didn't lose you! If we did, don't worry, because you'll see many more examples of this throughout the book. For now, remember one thing: Node.js only has one thread, so you need to make sure your code isn't blocking waiting for I/O while reading files, fetching resources from the web, or reading data from onboard sensors. The simple way to ensure this doesn't happen is to pass callback functions that will be called by the event loop when the data becomes available.

3.5 *Getting started with asynchronous programming*

As demonstrated in the previous section, Node is largely based on the principle of asynchronous programming. Let's be honest: asynchronous programming is a good step toward scaling your server, but it isn't easy to master. The sequential model of PHP, where you can rely on the fact that instructions are executed one after the other, makes for clear and easily understandable code. But things that scale well rarely come without a cost. Having to deal with asynchronous programming is one of the prices we pay for using event-driven runtimes such as Node.

Node offers two main patterns for dealing with asynchronous calls: callbacks and event listeners. We'll use event listeners later in the book and will briefly talk about the concept when the time comes. Callbacks, on the other hand, are so important and ubiquitous in Node that we'll dig into them here.

3.5.1   *Anonymous callbacks*

Consider a function F that performs some asynchronous operation such as fetching some data from the network, as shown on figure 3.7. We need a way to express what to do next when F returns so we give F another function to call whenever F finishes with the message-sending operation. This is an example of a callback—that is, a function passed as a parameter to an asynchronous function describing what to do after the async function has completed.

As an example, the anonymous function passed as an argument of database.query() in listing 3.6 is a callback. Note that we call these

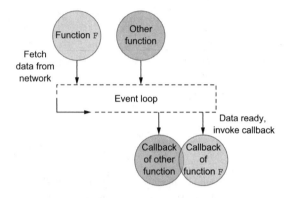

Figure 3.7   Callbacks and the event loop (simplification). F asynchronously fetches data from the network. Meanwhile, other functions are being served. When the data F requested is ready, the event loop calls the function specified by F for when the data is ready. This type of function is called a callback.

anonymous functions because they don't have a name, and hence, unlike named callbacks that we'll address shortly, they can't be called by any piece of code except for the function they're passed to in the first place. Another good example of using callbacks is the mashup of listing 2.9 in chapter 2; the mashup() function it contained had a number of client-side JavaScript callbacks, calling one physical thing after the other had responded.

Although you can use any function for your callbacks, it's a good practice to create your callback functions with two parameters; the first parameter, usually named err or error, will contain an error in case anything went wrong with the asynchronous function you called. The second parameter, usually named resp, response, or anything that reflects what you expect back, will contain the expected result if everything worked fine.

To better grasp how asynchronous calls and callbacks are used, let's create a mashup similar to the one in listing 2.9 but on the server side, as shown in figure 3.8. Our application will run the following operations when a request comes in for the /log resource:

1. Fetch a temperature value from the server.
2. Fetch a light value from the server.
3. Create a log entry for these two values and append it to a log.txt file.

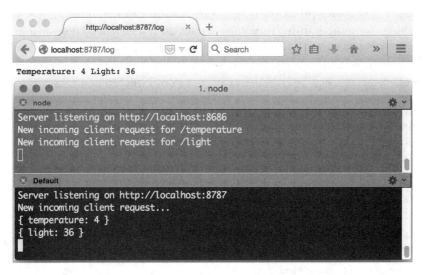

Figure 3.8 Running the server of listing 3.2 (terminal window, top) and consuming its data through a server-side mashup with callbacks called from a browser (bottom)

The crucial point here is that all three operations require I/O operations: 1 and 2 require fetching data from your HTTP server; 3 requires writing to the disk. Hence, if you were to run them in a blocking, synchronous manner, the whole Node event loop would be blocked for several CPU cycles, being unable to accept any connection from additional clients until these I/O operations return. You certainly wouldn't want that! The following code illustrates how to build this mashup in a non-blocking way using callbacks.

For this code you'll use the external module called `request` that you installed previously. Create a package.json file in a new directory and install the module using npm as shown earlier:

```
$ npm install request --save
```

Calling an HTTP resource with `request` is easy! The following listing will get the Web of Things homepage and return its HTML content.

Listing 3.7 Using the request library

```
var request = require('request');
request('http://webofthings.org',function(error,response,body){
  if (!error && response.statusCode === 200) {
    console.log(body)
  }
});
```

Displays the HTML code of the page →

An anonymous callback that will be invoked when the request library fetches the webofthings homepage from the web

---

You probably noticed that the call to `request` takes a callback as a parameter. This is expected because the call will be executed asynchronously. With the `request` library, your mashup becomes pretty straightforward, as you can see in listing 3.8. You begin by fetching the temperature from your server using `request`. Then, inside the callback of the temperature request, you fetch the light, and inside the callback of the light, you write to a file using the asynchronous built-in Node `fs.appendFile()` function and eventually reply to the client with the values you fetched.

Listing 3.8   A mashup with asynchronous calls leading to a "callback hell"

```
var http = require('http'),
  request = require('request'),
  fs = require('fs');

var port = 8787;
var serviceRootUrl = 'http://localhost:8686';

http.createServer(function (servReq, servResp) {
  console.log('New incoming client request...');

  if (servReq.url === '/log') {
    request({url: serviceRootUrl + '/temperature', json: true},
      function (err, resp, body) {
        if (err) throw err;
        if (resp.statusCode === 200) {
          console.log(body);
          var temperature = body.temperature;
          request({url: serviceRootUrl + '/light', json: true},
            function (err, resp, body) {
              if (err) throw err;
              if (resp.statusCode === 200) {
                console.log(body);
                var light = body.light;
                var logEntry = 'Temperature: '+ temperature + ' Light: '
                + light;
                fs.appendFile('log.txt', logEntry + '\n',
                  encoding = 'utf8', function (err) {
                    if (err) throw err;
                    servResp.writeHeader(200, {"Content-Type":
                     "text/plain"});
                    servResp.write(logEntry);
                    servResp.end();
                  });
              }
            });
        }
      });
  } else {
    servResp.writeHeader(200, {"Content-Type": "text/plain"});
    servResp.write('Please use /log');
    servResp.end();
  }

}).listen(port);
console.log('Server listening on http://localhost:' + port);
```

Annotations:
- **Fetch the JSON representation of the temperature sensor using request.** → (points to `request({url: serviceRootUrl + '/temperature', json: true},`)
- **Fetch the JSON representation of the light sensor.** → (points to `request({url: serviceRootUrl + '/light', json: true},`)
- **Log the result into a new log entry in the log.txt file.** → (points to `fs.appendFile('log.txt', logEntry + '\n',`)

Save this code and test it by first starting the server of listing 3.2:

```
$ node listing-3.2-webserver.js
Server listening on http://localhost:8686
```

Then, in a new terminal window run the mashup:

```
$ node listing-3.8-callbacks.js
Server listening on http://localhost:8787
```

Now point your browser to http://localhost:8787/log; if everything works as expected, you should see output similar to that of figure 3.8. This way of calling a callback inside another and so forth is known as *nesting callbacks*. Unfortunately, as you can see in the code of listing 3.8, nesting callbacks quickly pushes your code to the right, making it harder to read and manage with every additional callback. This unfortunate consequence of asynchronous programming with callbacks is known as *callback hell*. As you can see, this problem appears with a relatively low number of callbacks. A rule of thumb to keep your sanity is to not attempt to nest more than three callbacks like these.

3.5.2 Named callbacks

Don't lose hope just yet! There are number of ways to resolve your callback hell. The first one is to use actual named functions instead of anonymous functions. Using named functions leads to more readable code because it encapsulates the asynchronous calls. It reduces the callback hell to a chain of function calls, each first calling one asynchronous function and then calling the next function in the chain. If you were to rewrite your mashup with this strategy, it would look like the code listing that follows.

> **Listing 3.9 A mashup with asynchronous calls and named callbacks**

```
var http = require('http'),
    request = require('request'),
    fs = require('fs');

var serviceRootUrl = 'http://localhost:8686';

http.createServer(function (req, res) {
  console.log('New incoming client request...');

  if (req.url === '/log') {
    getTemperature(res);                                    ◀─┐ Get the temperature and
  } else {                                                     │ start the chain of calls.
    res.writeHeader(200, {"Content-Type": "text/plain"});
    res.write('Please use /log');
    res.end();
  }

}).listen(8787);
                                          ┌ A named temperature
                                          │ function
function getTemperature(res) {        ◀──┘
  request({url: serviceRootUrl + '/temperature', json: true}, function (err,
  resp, body) {
```

```
      if (err) throw err;
      if (resp.statusCode === 200) {
        console.log(body);
        var temp = body.temperature;
        getLight(res, temp);
      }
    });
}
```
◄──┐ **Once the callback for temperature
    │ has been called, proceed with
    │ calling the getLight function.**

```
function getLight(res, temp) {
  request({url: serviceRootUrl + '/light', json: true}, function (err, resp,
  body) {
    if (err) throw err;
    if (resp.statusCode === 200) {
      console.log(body);
      var light = body.light;
      logValuesReply(res, temp, light);
    }
  });
}
```
◄──┐ **Then call the named
    │ function to log values.**

```
function logValuesReply(res, temp, light) {
  var logEntry = 'Temperature: ' + temp + ' Light: ' + light;
  fs.appendFile('log.txt', logEntry + '\n', encoding = 'utf8', function (err)
  {
    if (err) throw err;
    res.writeHeader(200, {"Content-Type": "text/plain"});
    res.write(logEntry);
    res.end();
  });
}
```
◄──┐ **Return to
    │ the client.**

This code is essentially the same as listing 3.8, but this time the workflow is split across several functions. In the callback of the server you invoke getTemperature(); this function asynchronously gets the temperature and calls the getLight() function as soon as the temperature arrives. getLight() fetches the light from the server and invokes logValuesReply() as soon as the light value is ready. Finally, logValuesReply() asynchronously logs the value to a file and replies to the client.

The result is much more readable code with a manageable level of indentation. But on the flipside, you now have to pass the values manually across the chain of invocation as function parameters; these include the res argument, which contains a handle to the response object you need at the end of the chain. Furthermore, each function needs to know which function to call next. This means your functions are tightly coupled with each other and the code can't easily be reused for other workflows.

3.5.3 *Control flow libraries*

We clearly aren't the first developers to face the challenges of nested callbacks; as a consequence, a number of developers have contributed their methods of dealing with the problem to the community. This has led to a number of *control flow* modules. Essentially, these modules provide elegant solutions to the callback hell problem; they also address the shortcomings of using named callbacks in a clean, flexible, and reusable manner. We can't list all control flow libraries here, but we recommend using Async.[16] This library is probably the most comprehensive set of tools for dealing with asynchronous JavaScript in the browser and for Node.

Let's rewrite our mashup using the async control flow library that you install with the following command:

```
$ npm install async --save
```

You'll use the `async.series([])` construct, taking an array of functions as a parameter, as well as an optional final callback function to be invoked when all others have returned. The general structure of this construct is shown in the next listing.

Listing 3.10 Using `async.series` for serial control flow

```
async.series([
  function(callback){
    // some logic...                       First asynchronous
    callback(null, 'first result');        function call in the series
  },
  function(callback){
    // some logic...                       Second function
    callback(null, 'second result');       call in the series
  }
],
function(err, results){
  // some logic...                         Final function call; if all the calls in the series
});                                        worked so far, results will be equal to ['first
                                           result', 'second result'] inside this function.
```

Triggers a call to the next function in the series

Applying this construct to your mashup, you obtain the code in listing 3.11, which resembles your first attempt to solve the problem (using nested callbacks) except that the whole structure is much flatter and a lot more readable. To foster reusability, we also make use of the named functions we created before. The key in the control flow pattern is in calling in each function in the chain the `callback(err, result)` method, which calls the next function in the array (through the control flow library) and adds the result to an array of results made available to the last callback function. In this case the result array contains the temperature and light values in an ordered manner as expected in an array (note that an alternative with objects is also provided by Async).

Listing 3.11 Using a control flow library

```
[...] var async = require('async');

var port = 8787;
var serviceRootUrl = 'http://localhost:8686';

http.createServer(function (req, res) {
```

---

[16] https://github.com/caolan/async

```
        console.log('New incoming client request...');
        if (req.url === '/log') {
          async.series([
              getTemperature,
              getLight
          ],

            function (err, results) {
              console.log(results);
              var logEntry = 'Temperature: ' + results[0] + ' Light: ' +
                  results[1];
              fs.appendFile('log.txt', logEntry + '\n', encoding = 'utf8',
                function (err) {
                  if (err) throw err;
                  res.writeHeader(200, {"Content-Type": "text/plain"});
                  res.write(logEntry);
                  res.end();
                })
            }
          );
        } else {
          res.writeHeader(200, {"Content-Type": "text/plain"});
          res.write('Please use /log');
          res.end();
        }
}).listen(port);
console.log('Server listening on http://localhost:' + port);

function getTemperature(callback) {
  request({url: serviceRootUrl + '/temperature', json: true},
    function (err, res, body) {
      if (err) callback(err);
      if (res && res.statusCode === 200) {
        console.log(body);
        var temp = body.temperature;
        callback(null, temp);
      } else callback(null, null);
    });
}

function getLight(callback) {
  request({url: serviceRootUrl + '/light', json: true},
    function (err, res, body) {
      if (err) callback(err);
      if (res && res.statusCode === 200) {
        console.log(body);
        var light = body.light;
        callback(null, light);
      } else callback(null, null);
    });
}
```

Annotations:
- **Create an array of functions to be invoked in series.**
- **results is now equal to [light, temperature].**
- **This function is called when the last function in the series returns.**
- **This will call the next function in the series.**

Not only is this model much more readable, it's also much more flexible. As an example, although you executed the calls for temperature and light in series, there's nothing that forces you to do so; you just need the responses in any order. Now, using another construct of the `Async` library called `async.parallel`, you can speed up your mashup by running the calls in parallel. All you need for that is to change the initial call from `async.series([...])` to `async.parallel([...])`.

As you've seen in this section, asynchronous programming isn't always straightforward and there's a learning curve to master it. Luckily enough, there are a number of techniques and tools that can help you keep your code clean and structured despite this complexity. Moving forward in the book, we'll use simple anonymous and named callbacks for examples not requiring more than three levels of callbacks nesting. For all other examples we'll use the great `Async` library we just introduced.

The nerd corner—You promised me more!

The previous section is an introduction to patterns that help you work efficiently with asynchronous programming. There are a number of other popular patterns such as promises and events. Promises mainly come from the client-side JavaScript world, but you can also use this with Node with libraries such as Bluebird (https://www.npmjs .com/package/bluebird). The events pattern is used by many Node core modules and is a good way of implementing asynchronous libraries (https://nodejs.org/api/ events.html). Don't hesitate to go ahead and experiment with these patterns to find the one that best suits your needs!

3.6 Summary and beyond the book

- Embedded devices have become increasingly powerful over the last few years, which makes it possible and appealing to use JavaScript and Node.js directly on devices.
- Using only JavaScript end to end to build IoT prototypes offers considerable flexibility and makes it much easier to maintain your code.
- You can run Node.js applications on multiple platforms and environments without adapting your code, which makes it easy to develop and scale applications in heterogeneous deployments.
- The modularity of Node.js allows you to tap into thousands of community libraries to rapidly build complex applications.
- Single-threaded systems such as the Node runtime and the event loop call for a new way of designing applications. Code and libraries must be kept asynchronous.
- The basic idea of asynchronous programming is to pass callback functions that will be called later on when the results are available.
- Working with anonymous and named callbacks can lead you to experience callback hell! Control flow libraries such as the `async` module help you resolve it and better structure your code.

If we piqued your curiosity about Node, it's probably a good time for you to buy a Node.js book[17] and follow the official Node.js[18] blog.

Now that you have all the software foundations of your WoT toolbox in place, you're ready to learn about the hardware bits, in particular which devices to choose and how to configure them. In the next chapter, we'll first provide a high-level overview of the world of embedded devices and the existing types of platforms to consider. Afterward, we'll dig into setting up a Raspberry Pi device, connecting to it a number of sensors and actuators, and managing them with Node, and then you'll have everything ready to make your Pi part of the Web of Things.

---

[17] http://www.manning.com/catalog/by/subject/
[18] http://blog.nodejs.org/

Getting started with embedded systems 4

This chapter covers

- Understanding the various categories of embedded systems
- An introduction to working with the Raspberry Pi
- An introduction to setting up and using Node.js for IoT prototyping
- Learning to connect sensors and actuators using GPIOs

As we discussed before, there are two broad categories of physical objects on the Web of Things: *tagged* objects and *connected* objects. The first category comprises various *tagging* technologies that are attached to a product, such as barcodes, QR codes, NFC or RFID tags, and so on. In this case, objects aren't connected directly to the web, only passively, because there's a need for another device or application to interact with the product. Connected objects are directly connected to the Web of Things and are the world of embedded systems and embedded devices, which are essentially small, relatively inexpensive, low-power computers with limited resources and capabilities. You can apply the techniques and architecture you'll learn about in this book to both tagged and connected objects, but the focus of this book is mainly on connected objects.

In chapter 2, you learned how to consume services from a real embedded device—a Raspberry Pi located in our office—to get a first glimpse of the Web of Things. But this wasn't very physical because the device you interacted with was neither yours nor next to you.

In this chapter, we'll show you how to set up and configure your very own IoT device. By the end of this chapter, you'll have a real device connected to the Web of Things, and you'll have all the tools at hand to be able to program it and implement all the concepts presented in the next chapters of this book. You'll start by choosing a hardware platform. There are many options out there, so we'll make sure to help you. You'll then make your device fit for the Web of Things by installing various software packages and libraries. You'll also learn the basics of IoT prototyping with a hint of electronics by connecting real sensors and actuators directly to your Raspberry Pi.

If this is your first encounter with embedded devices and electronics, this chapter will be a gentle (yet challenging) and fun crash course!

4.1   The world of embedded devices

Literally thousands of embedded platforms types are available, ranging from small production runs of general-purpose sensor nodes built for researchers or hackers to cheap and mass-produced circuits built specifically for smoke alarms, microwave ovens, and alarm clocks. Obviously, we won't have time to get into a deep review of these platforms in this book. What you should remember is that there are two big leagues of embedded devices: those targeted at hobbyists (less specific and optimized but more reusable and flexible) and those meant to be built into real-world industrial products (more optimized for specific use cases, so harder to extend and use in other contexts).

4.1.1   Devices for hobbyists vs. industrial devices

The idea of embedding computers into everyday objects isn't so novel: our washing machines have contained integrated circuits for decades. But they didn't connect to the internet, nor were they designed to be easily accessible or reprogrammable by application developers or customers. The emergence of the Internet of Things changes the game quite a bit. First, IoT devices are connected to the internet, which can be challenging for low-power devices. This constraint gave birth to a number of industrial-grade embedded platforms that support various networking protocols out of the box, ready to be used for commercial applications. Second, the research community and hobbyists started to get increasingly interested in tiny computers that not only were easy to program but also could support all sorts of sensors or actuators.

These two trends gave birth to a myriad of platforms for both real-world and industrial use cases as well as for hobbyists and DIY projects. The main difference between these two categories is the focus of their users. For industrial platforms, the objective has been to reduce the costs so they could be embedded in all kinds of consumer products while maintaining a high level of stability (you wouldn't want to have to reboot your washing machine every now and then). Hobbyists, however, were less sensitive to industrial-grade performance and robustness and preferred platforms that were open and easier to use and extend and that also came with an elaborate and easy-to-use tool suite.

Having said that, the traction around the Internet of Things in the recent years blurred the line between the two worlds, and you can observe industrial platforms manufacturers working hard to make their devices more accessible with better tools. Likewise, hobbyist platforms are getting more robust and cheaper and hence are now also embedded in real-world products.

Providing a detailed overview of those platforms could easily consume the rest of this book, so we describe only some of the most popular ones in table 4.1. Note that this table is an oversimplification of the brands and their offerings and is provided as a high-level overview of some of the big players. Please refer to the respective sites of the platforms for more details.

Table 4.1   An overview of some IoT embedded platforms. Platforms targeting hobbyists usually cost more but also have more resources (RAM, CPU, and so on). Industrial platforms tend to offer lower specifications but the costs are usually lower.

Brand	Models	CPU	RAM	+	Price	Type	Connectivity
Arduino	20+ and many clones (Spark, Intel, and so on)	ATmega, 8–64 MHz, Intel Curie, Linino	16 KB– 64 MB	Largest community	~30 USD	RTOS, Linux, hobbyists	Pluggable extension boards (Wi-Fi, GPRS, BLE, ZigBee, and so on)
Raspberry Pi	A, A+, B, B+, 2, 3, Zero	ARMv6 or v7, 700 MHz -1.2 GHz	256–1 GB	Full Linux, GPU, large community	~5-35 USD	Linux, hobbyists	Ethernet, extension through USB, BLE (Pi3)
Intel	Edison	Intel Atom 500 MHz	1 GB	X86, full Linux	~50 USD	Linux, hobbyist to industrial	Wi-Fi, BLE
BeagleBoard	BeagleBone Black, X15, and so on	AM335x 1 GHz ARMv7	512 MB– 2 GB	Stability, full Linux, SDK	~50 USD	Linux, hobbyist to industrial	Ethernet, extension through USB and shields
Texas Instruments	CC3200, SoC IoT, and so on	ARM 80 MHz, etc.	from 256 KB	Cost, Wi-Fi	<10 USD	RTOS, industrial	Wi-Fi, BLE, ZigBee
Marvell	88MC200, SoC IoT, and so on	ARM 200 MHz, etc.	from 256 KB	Cost, Wi-Fi, SDK	<10 USD	RTOS, industrial	Wi-Fi, BLE, ZigBee
Broadcom	WICED, and so on (also at the heart of the Raspberry Pis)	ARM 120 MHz, and so on	from 256 KB	Cost, Wi-Fi, SDK	<10 USD	RTOS, industrial	Wi-Fi, BLE, ZigBee, Thread

4.1.2   *Real-time operating systems vs. Linux*

In table 4.1, you probably noticed the Type column showing RTOS and Linux devices. There are basically two categories of *operating system (OS)* used for embedded devices: *real-time OS (RTOS)* and, well, not so real-time OS!

In essence, what makes an OS real-time is its ability to respond quickly and predictably to data that comes in. Real-time OSs are necessary for applications that control "big and hairy things" such as nuclear power plants, manufacturing chains, and airplanes, where determinism and response time are more critical selection factors than anything else. They also usually lead to lower power consumption or at least quite predictable power consumption.

When it comes to embedded devices, the world of RTOS is dominated by FreeRTOS,[1] an open source real-time operating system, although some viable alternatives exist, such as Contiki,[2] TinyOS,[3] mbed OS,[4] and the commercial VxWorks.[5]

One of the drawbacks of a real-time OS is that it isn't very good at operating many tasks in parallel, which makes it hard to build complex layers offering simple abstractions. This is where a non-real-time OS can help. It becomes particularly helpful for things that are not so mission-critical where user experience and features are more important than a constant, very fast response time. In this world—even more than in the RTOS world—one operating system rules them all: Linux.[6]

Because of its large community, plethora of tools, abstractions, and supported architectures, Linux is the ideal environment in which to start tinkering and innovating with IoT devices. But don't get it wrong; it's also increasingly a solid candidate for real-world and robust IoT applications such as for home automation or for building application gateways as described in chapter 5.

The nerd corner—I want more operating systems!

Over the past few years, Linux has become such a popular operating system used on embedded devices that a project from the Linux Foundation called Yocto[a] is now dedicated to creating custom Linux distributions for embedded devices. Similarly, Google is working on Brillo,[b] an extension of Android (which is built on Linux as well) for the IoT, and Ubuntu launched Ubuntu Core for the IoT.[c] Although Linux is massively dominating, there are a few alternatives to Linux in this space, such as Windows 10 for IoT.[d] We'll be using Linux Raspbian on the Pi, but you can also try Yocto, Ubuntu Core, or Windows 10, all of which run on the Pi (from the Pi 2 onward).

[a] https://www.yoctoproject.org/
[b] https://developers.google.com/brillo/?hl=en
[c] http://www.ubuntu.com/internet-of-things
[d] https://dev.windows.com/en-us/iot

---

[1] http://www.freertos.org/
[2] http://www.contiki-os.org/
[3] http://www.tinyos.net/
[4] https://www.mbed.com/en/development/software/mbed-os/
[5] http://www.windriver.com/products/vxworks/
[6] Note that a number of projects offer modified versions of the Linux kernel to transform it into a real-time OS; see, for instance, http://www.osadl.org/Realtime-Linux.projects-realtime-linux.0.html.

4.1.3 *Summary and beyond the Pi*

In this section, we offer a condensed introduction to the world of embedded devices. Obviously, entire books have been written on this topic, so we didn't try to be exhaustive in our search, but rather tried to give you a general understanding of the options and elements to consider when choosing a hardware platform for your project.[7]

We decided to use the Raspberry Pi as the reference platform for the remainder of this book. Why the Raspberry Pi? First, because it's arguably the most popular embedded platform along with the Arduino. But unlike the Arduino,[8] it was built for Linux and was designed from the beginning to be a powerful and accessible platform for automation and the Internet of Things. Basically it will let you dig into the web and the Internet of Things without having to deal with all the challenges (for example, C programming, limited RAM, and rough tools) that come with RTOS platforms.

Moreover, as you'll see in the next section, it's inexpensive and is available in many countries, and it comes with several USB ports for accessories and an HDMI output to connect it to your TV or screen. Because it's based on Linux and offers direct access to the OS and therefore Node.js, all the required dependencies can be easily installed on it as you would install things on your PC.

This does not mean the Pi is the only option to run the code provided in this book or to learn the Web of Things. As long as you pick a device that can run Node.js, you're pretty much good to go.

FROM PROOF OF CONCEPT TO INDUSTRIAL PROTOTYPE

The Pi is definitely one of the easiest ways to get started with the WoT and to build all sorts of prototypes. But for anything more serious, such as industrial and commercial-grade prototypes or actual products, the classic version of the Pi isn't the best choice. There are a number of reasons for this, but the two main ones are the use of an SD card as storage and the form factor of the Pi.

Relying on an SD card doesn't work well in the real world. SD cards have a limited lifespan. They also occasionally break, get corrupted, or could be easily dislodged. A more practical way to store the operating system and the data you need is to rely on on-board flash memory. Like SD cards, flash memories are persistent, meaning that the data will be kept even if the device isn't powered. They're soldered to the boards and are also faster and more stable than SD cards.

Furthermore, the Pi wasn't primarily designed to be used in commercial applications and therefore has more components and connectors that might not be required for most use cases.

Does that mean you won't be able to apply what you learn here to building a commercial-strength prototype? Not at all! Real-world-ready platforms are available that are compatible with what you'll learn in this book and with the code you'll write.

---

[7] A good roundup of popular hardware platforms can be found here: http://postscapes.com/internet-of-things-hardware.

[8] It's worth noting that there are also a number of new Linux-based Arduinos; for example, the Arduino Yun.

First, there's a version of the Pi that's much more realistic for the real world: the Pi Compute Module.[9] The Compute Module is an embedded platform similar to the classic Pi, but with a much smaller form factor and an on-board flash memory. Also, the Pi Zero is the latest addition to the Pi family and the smallest (65mm x 30mm). Add to that a shocking $5 price tag and it also becomes a viable candidate to be embedded within a commercial solution, although it lacks network connectivity or on-board flash memory. Similarly to the Pi Zero, the C.H.I.P[10] has a small form factor and for $9 also offers Wi-Fi and Bluetooth connectivity.

Other very good (but slightly more expensive) alternatives exist, such as the Intel Edison,[11] which, like the Pi 3, also supports Bluetooth Low Energy (see chapter 5) and Wi-Fi out of the box but is much smaller and has an onboard flash.

If you're looking for a device to build more mechanically stable prototypes without having to solder too much, you should consider the BeagleBoard[12] platform from BeagleBone, a platform similar to the Pi but known for its robustness and stability. Moreover, the BeagleBone offers both SD card and flash-based storage, making it easy to move your prototype from a concept to a real-world trial.

Plenty of other platforms are available, but what's interesting with the Pi, Beagle-Bone, and Edison is that they all run on Linux and support Node.js. This means that most of the examples will run out of the box on these three platforms (and many others), but some more advanced examples, such as those using GPIOs, might need a slightly different setup or alternative libraries. The appendix gives you a number of pointers on using the architecture, concepts, and code examples of this book with other devices such as the BeagleBone Black, the Intel Edison, and the Arduino boards.

4.2   Set up your first WoT device—Raspberry Pi

So far, this chapter has described the world of embedded systems and the various aspects to consider when choosing the most appropriate hardware platform for your own project. Next, we briefly cover the software layer running on top of your hardware platform by discussing the operating system on the device and describing how Java-Script and particularly Node.js are a very interesting application-development ecosystem for building Web of Things devices.

4.2.1   Meet the Raspberry Pi

The Raspberry Pi is a popular series of single-board computers: think of an entire computer not much larger than the credit card you used to buy it (see figure 4.1). These devices were developed by the Raspberry Pi foundation primarily as educational tools for more people to learn about basic computer science and physical computing.

---

[9] https://www.raspberrypi.org/products/compute-module/
[10] http://getchip.com
[11] http://www.intel.com/content/www/us/en/do-it-yourself/edison.html
[12] http://beagleboard.org/BLACK

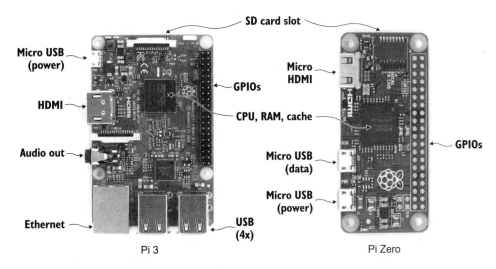

Figure 4.1   The Raspberry Pi 3 and the Pi Zero and their different ports and interfaces

The most disruptive model to date is the Raspberry Pi Zero. This device kicked off a little revolution: a full Linux computer for $5, a price tag usually reserved to the resource limited, low-cost RTOS devices out there. The Pi Foundation went so far as to give it away for free, attached to the December 2015 issue of *The MagPi* magazine,[13] showing that the days when computers will be attached to any object for a ridiculously low cost aren't that far away!

In terms of performance, the Pi Zero is pretty similar to the Pi A, but its ARMv6 CPU is overclocked at 1 GHz and it boasts twice as much RAM. For only 9 grams, it also features a micro-SD card slot, a mini-HDMI socket, and two micro USB ports (one for power, the other for data).

The latest Pi model at the time of writing is the Pi 3. It's more expensive than the Pi Zero, but it also has significantly more to offer. The Pi 3 boasts a quad-core 1.2 GHz CPU, 1 GB RAM, a micro-SD slot, and a Broadcom VideoCore IV graphic unit. In terms of connectivity, the Pi 3 has four USB ports (and a Micro USB, which is used to power it), an HDMI port, a 3.5mm jack, an Ethernet connector, and 40 general-purpose input/output ports (GPIO). Finally, unlike its predecessors, the Pi 3 also offers out-of-the-box Wi-Fi and Bluetooth connectivity, making a fully WoT-ready device. All of that for a mere 45 grams in total weight!

4.2.2   Choosing your Pi

All the examples in this book were tested on the Pi B+, Pi 2, Pi 3 and Pi Zero. Which one should you grab?

---

[13] https://www.raspberrypi.org/magpi/raspberry-pi-zero-out-today-get-it-free-with-the-magpi-40/

If you're just beginning with the IoT and embedded devices, the Pi 3 (or any successor) is a safe choice: it offers all the required connectivity out of the box and doesn't require any soldering to connect sensors and actuators to the GPIOs. But the Pi 3 is significantly larger and also more power hungry (4 watts for the Pi 2 or 3 versus 0.8 watts for the Pi Zero).

If size matters to you or if you plan on battery-powering your WoT device, then the Pi Zero is an interesting option. But it will require a bit more soldering and tinkering.

Ideally, by now we've convinced you to go ahead and buy a Pi. If we didn't, all hope is not lost! Most of the examples can run on any platform supporting client-side JavaScript and Node.js (like, hmm, your laptop!). For those who require a Pi—essentially the examples interfacing directly with sensors and actuators connected to the embedded device—we've created a small library that simulates them. Finally, the beauty of using JavaScript and Node for the Physical Web is that these examples will work on pretty much any device out of the box. The only significant exception is the last mile of code that actually talks to your sensors, which you'll likely have to customize for each device.

It goes without saying that you'll have much more fun with this book if you actually do have a real device next to you to implement the examples. After all, discovering the Web of Things without a Thing to work with sounds like skiing in the summer without any snow: a tad frustrating.

4.2.3 Shopping list

If you do decide to acquire a Raspberry Pi, you might as well get the other items on our shopping list. Again, they're not mandatory to follow the book, but they will add a physical touch to the virtual examples of the book. Table 4.2 lists all the things you should buy or gather to be able to create all the prototypes of the book.

Table 4.2 The components needed to create the physical prototypes described later in this section and the rest of this book

Description	Price
Raspberry Pi (any model from the B+ onward, Pi 3 recommended)	~35 USD
A 4–16 GB SD card (e.g., SanDisk Ultra Class 10 MicroSDHC, 16 GB)	~10 USD
HCSR501 PIR sensor for Raspberry Pi	~5 USD
DHT22 humidity and temperature sensor	~5 USD
Small breadboard or protoboard	~2 USD
Jumper wires for Raspberry Pi (4 M/M and 4 M/F)	~2 USD
330 Ohm resistor	<1 USD
LEDs	<1 USD

Table 4.2 The components needed to create the physical prototypes described later in this section and the rest of this book *(continued)*

Description	Price
Wi-Fi USB dongle (optional, for Pi Zero)	~ 10 USD
Pi Zero cables bundle (optional, for Pi Zero)	~ 5 USD

To know where to buy those items and your Pi, have a look on the book's official website, http://book.webofthings.io, where you'll find a list of our partner retailers, along with special offers or bundles they provide to readers of this book.

4.2.4   Setting up your Raspberry Pi

A detailed tutorial on how to use a Raspberry Pi is beyond the scope of this book, and its usage has been widely documented on the web.[14] Nevertheless, we'll help you set up your Pi to make it fit for the WoT.

Start by installing the right operating system. A number of operating systems can run on a Raspberry Pi. For practical reasons, in this book we'll focus on Raspbian, which is essentially a port of the Debian Linux system tailored to fit the needs of the Pi and its users. The advantage of Raspbian is that it has been widely used and tested on the Pi and is easy to install and customize; therefore, it provides a stable and popular operating system to build on.

The easiest way to get Raspbian installed on your Pi is to use a tool called NOOBS (New Out Of the Box Software). NOOBS is an OS manager that will assist you with the installation, and we'll show you how to use it in this section.

Should you want to take the fastest possible route, we also created a WoT version of Raspbian that contains everything you need to get started already set up. You can find it on http://book.webofthings.io and jump directly to section 4.3. Taking the manual route will let you learn more and will ensure you have a custom and up-to-date system at hand, so it's your call.

The nerd corner—Let's have a word about current

The Pi gets all the power it needs from the Micro USB connector (shown in figure 4.1); this means that the current provided on this cable should be high enough. Under stress, a Pi B+ or Zero will draw about 500 mA. A Pi 2 will need about 1000 mA and a Pi 3 about 1.5 mA. Exactly how much current you'll need depends on what you connect to the Pi, especially to the male USB ports of the Pi. We won't connect power-hungry accessories in this book, so you can consider the power requirements for a bare-bones Pi but a good compromise is a USB power source that provides 2000 mA (check the back of the USB adapter or the specs of your computer's USB ports to find this out).

---

[14] A good place to start is the Pi portal at http://www.raspberrypi.org/.

INSTALLING RASPBIAN WITH NOOBS

First, you'll need to format your micro SD card as FAT32. Make sure your card is large enough because it's the primary storage space of the Pi. It should be at least 4 GB, but we recommend using a larger one to ensure you have plenty of space for the software you'll install.

> **ATTENTION!** According to the SD specification, a card with more than 32 GB will be formatted using exFAT instead of FAT. This means it might not work on the Raspberry Pi using NOOBS. You can use a formatting tool such as GParted on Linux or Disk Utility on a Mac OS to transform it to FAT32, but some users reported problems with this as well. To avoid any hassle, choose an SD card between 4 GB and 32 GB, ideally a fast one from a trusted brand. We had good success with SanDisk Ultra Class 10 16 GB cards.

To install Linux on your SD card so that you can plug it in your Pi and use it, follow these instructions:

1   Format the micro SD card where Raspbian will be installed.

    On Linux, open GParted[15] and use the Devices menu to select the device corresponding to your SD card (make sure you're formatting the SD card and not your computer). Then, right-click the biggest partition to format it to FAT32.

    On Mac OSX, use Disk Utility. Select the SD card reader and click Erase. Select MS-DOS (FAT) as the format, give it a name (for example, WOT_PI), and select Erase to proceed with formatting the card; see figure 4.2. Alternatively, you can install the free ApplePi-Baker[16] utility—a nice little tool that also lets you backup and restore your Pi images.

    On Windows, download and use the SD Card Formatter tool.[17] Select the Overwrite Format option; note, however, that this tool won't work on cards bigger than 32 GB because it will format them in exFAT.

2   Download the latest NOOBS software from the download page of the Raspberry Pi community[18] (select NOOBS). The fastest way to download the distribution is usually using a Torrent file (before you ask: yes, it's absolutely legal in this case).

3   Unzip the content of the NOOBS archive and transfer it to the freshly formatted SD card. Don't put the content in a subfolder; copy all the content to the root folder of the SD card. Eject (or unmount) the card once you've copied the files.

4   Plug the SD card into the slot on the side of your Pi and plug the HDMI cable into a screen, a USB mouse and keyboard into the USB slots, and finally the micro USB cable to power (see figure 4.1 to find the right ports).

---

[15] http://gparted.org/

[16] http://www.tweaking4all.com/hardware/raspberry-pi/macosx-apple-pi-baker/

[17] https://www.sdcard.org/downloads/formatter_4/

[18] http://www.raspberrypi.org/downloads/

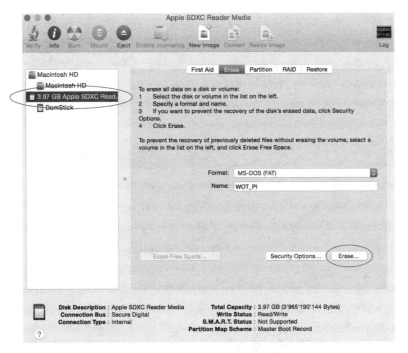

Figure 4.2   Formatting an SD card for the NOOBS installer using Disk Utility on Mac OS. Make sure you format the card using the MS-DOS (FAT) format.

5 NOOBS should now boot. After about a minute you'll see a splash screen allowing you to install the different OSs supported by the Pi. Select Raspbian (a special version of the Linux Debian operating system tailored for the Pi) and click Install. This will start installing the OS, which may take up to 30 minutes.

The OS should now be ready. When you start it for the first time, the Pi boots up with the X Window graphical environment. If you want to disable this graphical user interface, select Menu > Preferences > Raspberry Configuration, and in the System tab select To CLI as Boot option. Now restart your Pi; choose Menu > Shutdown > Reboot. The Pi should restart, and you'll soon see a terminal. Should any of these steps turn sour, please read the complete install manual online[19] or post a message on the book forum.[20]

CONNECTING THE PI TO A NETWORK

Next, you need to connect the Pi to a network. We'll discuss a range of networking protocols in chapter 5, but for now we'll use Ethernet or Wi-Fi. If you opted for a Pi B, B+, or 2, this step is straightforward: plug an Ethernet cable from your router into the Pi (see figure 4.1).

---

[19] https://www.raspberrypi.org/help/noobs-setup/
[20] http://book.webofthings.io

If you chose a Pi Zero or Pi 3 and don't have the option of connecting a cable to your router, you'll need a little more work to add Wi-Fi connectivity to your Pi. This extra work also brings the advantage of portability: your Pi becomes wireless and can be placed wherever you want as long as it's within range of your wireless router.

The software to support Wi-Fi connectivity is already present in Raspbian, but you need to enable this feature by modifying the Wi-Fi network configuration file, as shown in the next listing.

Listing 4.1   Modifying the Wi-Fi configuration file

```
$ sudo nano /etc/wpa_supplicant/wpa_supplicant.conf        ◀── Open the Wi-Fi network's
                                                                configuration file.
network={
  ssid="YOUR NETWORK NAME"          ◀── Add these lines;
  psk="YOUR WIFI PASSWORD"              replace with the values
}                                       for your network.
$
```

You can now save and close this file by pressing CTRL+X, then Y, and then ENTER. Once this is done, perform a clean shutdown with sudo shutdown -h now. Then, if you use a Pi Zero, insert a compatible Wi-Fi USB dongle into any free USB port (no need to do this on a Pi 3 because the Wi-Fi is onboard). Note that when using the Pi Zero you'll need to unplug any other device (for example, your keyboard) and use a USB-to–Micro USB converter. Check the shopping list in table 4.2 for more details about these components.

Once your Pi restarts, it should connect to your Wi-Fi network. This process can take up to a minute on some networks. In the next section we'll verify that this all worked by remotely accessing the Pi.

The nerd corner—I want more Wi-Fi

The method described here works to connect your Pi to a WPA (Wireless Protected Access) or the more secure WPA2. It may not work if your Wi-Fi is set up using a different security protocol such as (the not-so-secure) WEP or WPA2 Enterprise. All hope is not lost, however, and you'll find a number of good tutorials on the web on how to connect a Pi to different Wi-Fi networks. A good place to start is https://www.raspberrypi.org/documentation/configuration/wireless.

REMOTELY ACCESSING YOUR PI

Your Pi should now be up, running, and connected. Although you can write and run all exercises directly on the Pi using a keyboard, mouse, and screen, a more practical option is to run it "headless" (that is, without a display/keyboard attached to it) and remotely connect to it via SSH. The only problem in this mode is finding your Pi in the first place. This is actually a well-known problem in the Internet of Things known as the bootstrap or discovery problem: *given a device connecting the very first time to a network, how do you find its address?*

To resolve this problem, use the Avahi mDNS server of your Pi. mDNS is a discovery protocol that we'll cover in chapter 8, but for now it's enough to understand that it gives your Pi an address that nearby computers can use to find it. Avahi is installed by default on the latest versions of Raspbian, so you can go ahead and use it.[21] By default, Avahi will set up the Pi to respond to the `raspberrypi.local` domain. You can check this by running the command shown in listing 4.2 from a terminal on Linux/Mac OS. Windows users should try the ping command shown in the following listing with the command prompt (`cmd.exe`). Unfortunately, you might not find your Pi, because mDNS isn't supported out of the box on Windows machines. It will work if you installed an application bundling an mDNS service such as iTunes. But if you didn't, you'll need to install an mDNS service such as Bonjour Print Services for Windows.[22]

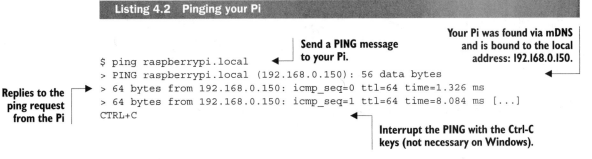

Listing 4.2   Pinging your Pi

Send a PING message to your Pi.

Your Pi was found via mDNS and is bound to the local address: 192.168.0.150.

```
$ ping raspberrypi.local
> PING raspberrypi.local (192.168.0.150): 56 data bytes
> 64 bytes from 192.168.0.150: icmp_seq=0 ttl=64 time=1.326 ms
> 64 bytes from 192.168.0.150: icmp_seq=1 ttl=64 time=8.084 ms [...]
CTRL+C
```

Replies to the ping request from the Pi

Interrupt the PING with the Ctrl-C keys (not necessary on Windows).

If everything worked well, you should now be able to access your Pi via its local DNS address: `raspberrypi.local`. Note that you can change this address should you need to; for example, if you have more than one Pi at home.[23]

CREATING A NETWORK FOR YOUR PI

The method just described works well if you have access to a nearby router with an Ethernet port available or have added a Wi-Fi dongle to your Pi. If that's not the case—for example, if you're in a hotel room—there's another nice and easy way of working with your Pi: creating a wired network between your Pi and your desktop/laptop computer.

This process is supported on Windows, Mac OS, and Linux and is well-documented on the internet.[24] As an example, we'll describe how to do this on a Mac OS machine.

---

[21] If it isn't installed on your Pi, run `sudo apt-get install avahi-daemon` to install it.

[22] You can download it for free from http://www.apple.com/support/bonjour.

[23] See http://www.howtogeek.com/167195/how-to-change-your-raspberry-pi-or-other-linux-devices-hostname/.

[24] https://pihw.wordpress.com/guides/direct-network-connection/

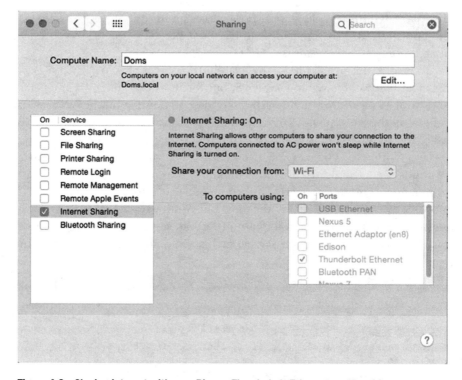

Figure 4.3   Sharing internet with your Pi over Thunderbolt Ethernet on Mac OS

If your machine doesn't have an Ethernet port, you'll need an Ethernet-to-USB or Thunderbolt adapter. To get started, plug your Pi into the Ethernet port on your machine. Then, open your System Preferences and select Sharing. Enable Internet Sharing from Wi-Fi to Thunderbolt Ethernet, as shown on figure 4.3. This will effectively share the internet connection that your machine gets through Wi-Fi with the Pi.

If you didn't change the configuration of the Ethernet port, this should work out of the box. If it doesn't, go to System Preferences again and check that the Ethernet connection (for example, USB Ethernet or Thunderbolt Ethernet) is set to Using DHCP.

4.2.5   *Connecting to your device*

Once the Pi has started successfully, you'll be able connect to it using SSH (Secure Shell).

SSH TO YOUR PI ON LINUX OR MAC OS

On a Linux or Mac OS machine, an SSH client is already installed, so all you need to do is open your terminal with the command (the default password is "raspberry") in the following listing.

> **Listing 4.3 Connecting to the Pi using `ssh`**

> **Connects (using the SSH protocol) to your Pi using the pi user**

```
$ ssh pi@raspberrypi.local
The authenticity of host '192.168.0.150 (192.168.0.150)' can't be
established.
RSA key fingerprint is 7c:4e:ad:4f:42:cf:d2:a4:0f:75:38:83:a7:03:63:58.
Are you sure you want to continue connecting (yes/no)? yes
Warning: Permanently added '192.168.0.150' (RSA) to the list of known
hosts.
pi@192.168.0.174's password:
[...]
Last login: Sat Jan 17 12:05:36 2015

pi@raspberrypi ~ $
```

> **You're connected to your Pi via SSH, ready to enter commands.**

SSH YOUR PI ON WINDOWS

To use SSH on Windows you can download the PuTTy SSH client.[25] This client is lightweight and doesn't even require an installation: download it and double-click to start it. Write the address of your Pi (`raspberrypi.local` or the IP address) in the Host Name field and click Open. Your Pi should then prompt you for a username (the default is "pi") and a password (the default is "raspberry").

> **ATTENTION!** Once you're logged in, use the `passwd` command to change your password. Provided you'll connect your device to the world *wild* web, this is probably a good idea unless you're ready to literally open source your home!

4.3 *Installing Node.js on the Raspberry Pi*

As explained in the previous chapter, Node is slowly but steadily making its way in the world of embedded systems, providing a nice alternative to the traditional C environments of the embedded world, so let's see how to use Node on a Raspberry Pi.

The Node.js framework is installed by default on the most recent versions of Raspbian, but you need to install the latest version on your Pi. The installation is pretty straightforward, but you need a special version of Node. "Why can't I just use the standard Node.js version?" we hear you say. Well, as mentioned before, the Pi—and most of the embedded devices out there—run on CPU architectures that aren't compatible with the ones your PCs run on (x86 or x64). More precisely, a lot of embedded devices run on ARM[26] processors, which is what's on your Pi. As a consequence, the node binaries that you need on your Pi are not the same as the ones you need on your PC. Fortunately, since Node version 4.0.0, ARM binaries are also available from the official Node website.

To install the ARM version of Node.js, go to the Node download page at https://nodejs.org/en/download/ and select the right version for your Pi or other embedded

---

[25] http://www.chiark.greenend.org.uk/~sgtatham/putty/

[26] If you decide to use a non-ARM-based platform, you'll need to find a compiled version of Node.js for the system you have or compile it from the source on your target platform.

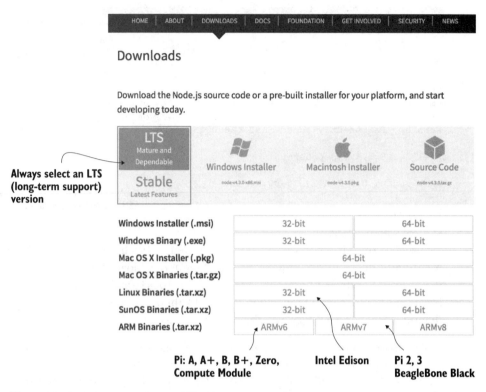

Always select an LTS (long-term support) version

Pi: A, A+, B, B+, Zero, Compute Module — Intel Edison — Pi 2, 3 BeagleBone Black

Figure 4.4   Node.js download page: ARM CPUs are supported, but you need to select the right architecture for your embedded device model. As an example, the Pi 2 and 3 are built on an ARMv7 CPU architecture whereas the Pi Zero uses an ARMv6 architecture.

device. As shown in figure 4.4, the archive to download depends on the version of the ARM architecture your device uses. As an example, the Pi 3 runs on an ARMv7 architecture.

Once you locate the right link, copy it (right-click Copy Link Location) and run the commands shown in the following listing. This will install Node on your Pi.

Listing 4.4   Installing Node.js on your Pi

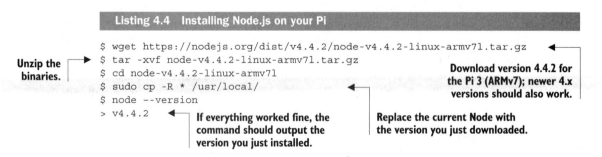

```
$ wget https://nodejs.org/dist/v4.4.2/node-v4.4.2-linux-armv7l.tar.gz
$ tar -xvf node-v4.4.2-linux-armv7l.tar.gz
$ cd node-v4.4.2-linux-armv7l
$ sudo cp -R * /usr/local/
$ node --version
> v4.4.2
```

Unzip the binaries.

Download version 4.4.2 for the Pi 3 (ARMv7); newer 4.x versions should also work.

If everything worked fine, the command should output the version you just installed.

Replace the current Node with the version you just downloaded.

If the installation was successful (of course it was!), this command should give you the version of Node.js installed on the Pi. At the time of writing, 4.x is the latest long-term support (LTS) version of Node.js and the code has been tested with this version.

4.3.1 Using Git and GitHub on the Pi

Now that Node.js is installed on the Pi, you need a way to write code to work with it. Although you could use an editor like Nano/Pico or Vi, you should find it much more efficient and comfortable to write code on your desktop or laptop machine using your favorite text editor or integrated development environment (IDE) and sync it with the Pi whenever you want to test the code.

Start by forking our project on GitHub. In case you're not familiar with Git, *forking* means creating your own copy of the WoT-Book code repository, which will allow you to modify the code as you fancy. This is especially useful because it lets you write code on your desktop machine or Pi, commit it locally, push it to your fork on GitHub, and then pull it back on your Pi. To fork the project, go to our GitHub repository at https://github.com/webofthings/wot-book and click the Fork button. This creates a copy of the WoT-Book repository in your own GitHub space. Then you can install Git on your Pi and clone the project, as shown in the next listing.

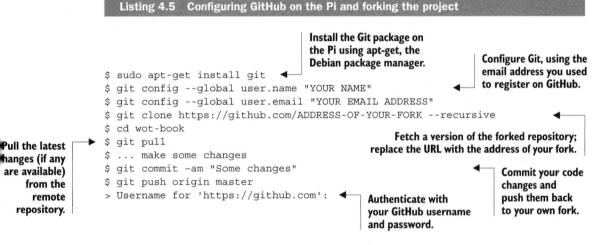

Listing 4.5   Configuring GitHub on the Pi and forking the project

Install the Git package on the Pi using apt-get, the Debian package manager.

Configure Git, using the email address you used to register on GitHub.

```
$ sudo apt-get install git
$ git config --global user.name "YOUR NAME"
$ git config --global user.email "YOUR EMAIL ADDRESS"
$ git clone https://github.com/ADDRESS-OF-YOUR-FORK --recursive
$ cd wot-book
$ git pull
$ ... make some changes
$ git commit -am "Some changes"
$ git push origin master
> Username for 'https://github.com':
```

Fetch a version of the forked repository; replace the URL with the address of your fork.

Pull the latest changes (if any are available) from the remote repository.

Commit your code changes and push them back to your own fork.

Authenticate with your GitHub username and password.

4.3.2 So what?

Hopefully, you've made it this far without too many scars and you've been able to do everything as described. If that's the case, you're doing absolutely great and can pat yourself on the back. You now have a fully functional and WoT-ready Raspberry Pi on which you'll be able to connect not only your first sensors and actuators, as shown in the next section, but also run all the code examples waiting for you in the upcoming chapters.

4.4   Connecting sensors and actuators to your Pi

Your Pi is now ready to conquer the World Wide Web of Things, but it doesn't have much to work with in the real world yet. To make it more real-world-connected you'll need to connect some sensors (for example, a humidity sensor) and actuators (an LED) to the Pi.

4.4.1   Understanding GPIO ports

The way to do this on most platforms, Pi included, is to connect the sensors and actuators using the general-purpose input/output (GPIO) ports. Essentially, a GPIO is a pin on which current can be read or output. GPIOs have two modes: an input mode and an output mode. When the output mode is selected, the pin can be set to HIGH, which means it outputs 3.3 volts; when the pin is set to LOW, it is off and doesn't output any voltage. With the input mode, you essentially can read a value on the pin. Unlike other embedded platforms (such as Arduino), the Pi supports only digital input. This means that you can work only with components that supply series of 0s (LOW, ~0 volts) or 1s (HIGH, 3.3 volts) to the input pins—that is, with digital components. As an example, an LED is a digital actuator and a button is a digital sensor.

Analog components, on the other hand, are those that do not provide or consume only LOWs and HIGHs but also supply or consume variable voltages on the pins. As an example, a cheap, light-dependent resistor is an analog light sensor and a potentiometer button is an analog actuator. If you'd like to experiment with analog sensors and actuators, there are a number of extensions boards you can connect to your Pi to make it analog-friendly.[27]

Back to our GPIOs: their numbering differs depending on the model of the Pi. Unfortunately, the numbering is anything but intuitive! Figure 4.5 helps you to understand what each GPIO pin corresponds to for the Raspberry Pi 3, 2, and B+. The GPIO pins have had exactly the same layout since the Pi A+.

In this book when we refer to, for example, pin 12, we mean pin 12 in figure 4.5, not GPIO12, which would be pin 32.

In the following section, you'll get your hands dirty and connect a passive infrared sensor, temperature sensor, and humidity sensor to the Pi through the GPIOs.

4.4.2   Working with breadboards and electronic components

Let's begin with the hardware part. For this you'll need a breadboard, but not the kind you're likely to find in your kitchen. As shown on figure 4.6, a breadboard is a board made of plastic and metal that prevents you from having to solder components when creating a prototype. Basically, the exterior blue row is the one that gets connected to the ground (GND, -). All holes in this row are connected through a metal plate. The exterior red row is the one that will receive the power (VCC, +). All rows are connected. The inner columns are meant to hold components like LEDs and sensors or resistors.

---

[27] Here's a simple tutorial for how to read analog sensors from your Pi: https://learn.adafruit.com/reading-a-analog-in-and-controlling-audio-volume-with-the-raspberry-pi/overview.

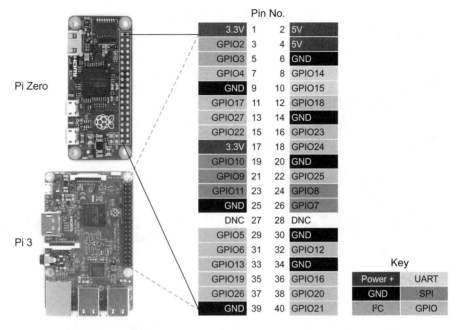

Figure 4.5   Layout of the GPIO, power, and ground pins on the Raspberry Pi Zero and Pi 3

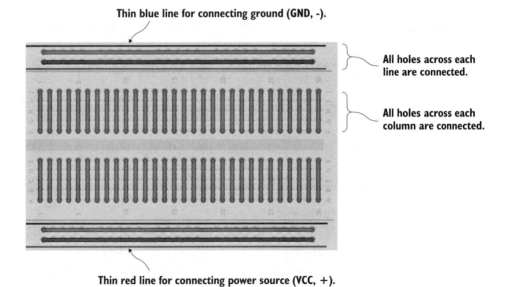

Figure 4.6   A typical breadboard where the outer rows as well as the inner columns are connected. The line marked with a thin blue line is usually used for connecting to the ground, and the line marked with a thin red line is for connecting to the power source.

GND (black)   Short leg (GND)

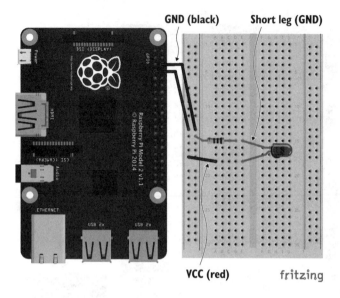

Figure 4.7 **Wiring an LED to the GPIO ports of the Pi through a resistor. The resistor and the LED are plugged into the holes of the breadboard. No need to solder anything!**

VCC (red)   fritzing

For our "Hello World" blinking LED example, we'll start by placing the elements on the breadboard, as shown in figure 4.7.[28] If it's the first time you've worked with electronics, we recommend you use an antistatic mat or a grounding strap to avoid damaging your Pi.[29]

Place the LED and the 330 Ohm resistor (color code: orange, orange, brown, gold/silver) on the breadboard according to the schematics shown in the figure. Note that resistors don't have a direction; they must simply be plugged in, so you can connect them in any manner. In case you're wondering what's the purpose of the resistor, it prevents the LED from melting by limiting the current going through it. It also makes sure that the LED doesn't blow if you invert the connection of the VCC and GND pins. Note that you can also use resistors with a greater resistance; for example, 1K Ohm—brown, black, red, gold/silver. This will reduce the brightness of the LED. Then connect the column with the short leg of the LED to the GND (-, blue) line using the resistor and the one with the long leg to the VCC (+, red) line using a cable. Finally, connect a cable (ideally a black one to signify ground) to pin 6 (GND) and one (ideally a red one to signify power) to pin 7 (GPIO4).

4.4.3 *Accessing GPIOs from Node.js*

The hardware is now ready, so you can start working with GPIOs. On Linux, GPIOs aren't that mysterious. The values that are being read or written to the pins are available through files, so you could theoretically read these virtual files directly from your

---

[28] This was created with Fritzing, a very cool tool for creating electronic schematics: http://fritzing.org/.

[29] Learn more about antistatic products here: http://www.explainthatstuff.com/howantistaticcoatingswork .html.

Node code. Doing this correctly is not the easiest thing for a beginner, so we won't cover this method in this book but we'll use a library that others have made. You can find a dozen Node GPIO libraries for the Pi, offering different abstraction layers and functionality. We decided to use one we like called onoff.[30] For more advanced users, pi-gpio[31] would be an excellent alternative.

To do the next exercises in this chapter, you can either fork them from our GitHub repository and go to the folder chapter4-gpios or create a new folder from scratch. Go to that folder and install onoff with NPM (npm install onoff --save).

Note that the following examples that use the onoff library won't work on your PC because it doesn't have accessible GPIOs; they will only run on your Pi.

BLINK.JS—THE HELLO WORLD FOR THE IOT

You're now ready to interface the Pi with sensors and actuators. In software engineering, the simplest piece of code one can write—the famous Hello World—displays "Hello World" in the console. The Hello World equivalent of the IoT is to make a real LED blink, so let's build exactly that, as shown in listing 4.6.

As mentioned before, you'll use pin 7, corresponding to GPIO4 (see figure 4.5). You'll then create a function that opens the pin in output mode, which means you'll "push" current on it. It then either activates or deactivates the pin, depending on the result of the modulo function, and launches itself again at a specified interval.

Finally, you listen for SIGINT, which corresponds to pressing Ctrl-C, and ensure that you release the pin and turn the LED off before exiting.

Listing 4.6 blink.js: the Hello World of the IoT

```
var onoff = require('onoff');                          ◄─┐ Import the
                                                          │ onoff library.
var Gpio = onoff.Gpio,
  led = new Gpio(4, 'out'),          ◄─┐ Initialize GPIO 4
  interval;                            │ to be an output pin.

interval = setInterval(function () {
  var value = (led.readSync() + 1) % 2;      ◄─┐ Synchronously read the
  led.write(value, function() {                 │ value of pin 4 and
    console.log("Changed LED state to: " + value);   transform 1 to 0 or 0 to 1.
  });                                       ◄── Asynchronously write
}, 2000);                                       the new value to pin 4.

process.on('SIGINT', function () {
  clearInterval(interval);                    ◄─┐ Listen to the event
  led.writeSync(0);                              │ triggered by Ctrl-C.
  led.unexport();
  console.log('Bye, bye!');       ◄─┐ Cleanly close the GPIO
  process.exit();                    │ pin before exiting.
});
```

This interval will be called every two seconds.

---

[30] https://github.com/fivdi/onoff
[31] https://github.com/rakeshpai/pi-gpio

Save this file and run it by typing node blink.js. If everything works as expected, you should now see your LED blinking. Well done if this is your first physical prototype!

PIR.JS—CONNECTING A PROXIMITY SENSOR

Let's now move to a slightly more interesting use case by adding a sensor to your Pi. The sensor you'll add is known as a passive infrared (PIR) sensor. A PIR is sensitive to infrared light and captures the beams emitted by warm bodies like humans—or your cat, for that matter, but not zombies. This makes it a cheap and ideal sensor to detect movements and intrusions somewhere, so these sensors are commonly used in simple burglar alarms or automatic light switches to turn on/off lights when needed.

Again, let's begin with the hardware part of the project. You'll need a digital PIR sensor such as the ones we mentioned on the shopping list of section Meet the Raspberry Pi, as well as five cables and a breadboard.

As you can see in figure 4.8, the PIR sensor has three pins: one marked VCC (which is its 5-volt power source), one marked OUT (which will contain a digital value of sensor status at any point in time: 1 if a warm body is detected, 0 otherwise), and the last marked GND (for ground). The pin marked OUT needs to be connected to a data pin (GPIO 17 in our example).

Connect the components as shown in figure 4.8. First, connect the GND pin to a ground GPIO on the Pi (for example, pin 39) either directly if you have a female-female cable (a cable that can plug into a pin on each side) or through the breadboard.

Then, connect the OUT pin of the PIR to the GPIO 17 (pin 11) on the Pi; this is the pin you'll read the results from. Finally, connect the VCC pin to a GPIO (for example, pin 4), providing 5 volts on the Pi, again either directly or through the breadboard.

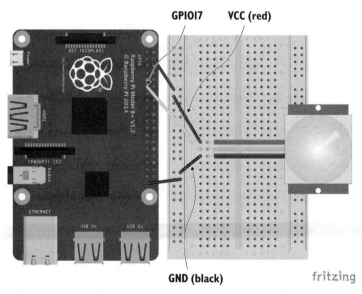

Figure 4.8 Connecting a passive infrared sensor to the Pi. The big sensor on the breadboard is the PIR, which is connected to a 5-volt power source, a GPIO pin, and the ground.

You're now ready to move to the coding part. To make this work, you could regularly poll the PIR sensor with the onoff readSync() function. But instead of constantly polling the sensor for its state and reading the same state several times, it would be much better to have your code called whenever the state of the physical world changes. This is precisely the level of abstraction that the onoff library offers; see listing 4.7. The watch(callback) function lets you enable your code to listen for state changes on a GPIO port. The library then automatically calls the callback function you pass it whenever the state changes. This is a good example of *event-driven programming*, where your code reacts only to events that you're interested in, in which case your code doesn't need to continuously check a certain value but only do something when it changes. It allows your code to be simpler, which also reduces the chance of obscure bugs occurring. The event-driven approach fits a number of real-world things quite well, and this is somewhat of a challenge for the web, as you'll see in chapter 6.

> **Listing 4.7   pir.js: reading a PIR sensor using the onoff library**

```
var Gpio = require('onoff').Gpio,
  sensor = new Gpio(17, 'in', 'both');        ◄── Initialize pin 17 in input mode; 'both'
                                                  means you want to handle both
                                                  rising and falling interrupt edges.

sensor.watch(function (err, value) {                              ◄─┐
  if (err) exit(err);
  console.log(value ? 'there is some one!' : 'not anymore!');
});
                                                  Listen for state changes on
                                                  pin 17; if a change is
function exit(err) {                              detected, the anonymous
  if (err) console.log('An error occurred: ' + err);  callback function will be
  sensor.unexport();                            called with the new value.
  console.log('Bye, bye!')
  process.exit();
}
process.on('SIGINT', exit);
```

As you can see in this listing, the onoff library will listen to both rising and falling hardware interrupts, and each time the state of the GPIO pin changes, it will call the callback function that was registered with the watch() function.

DHT.JS—CONNECTING A TEMPERATURE AND HUMIDITY SENSOR

Finally, you'll make your Pi sense the environment by connecting it to a sensor combining temperature and humidity readings. The sensor we'll use is a DHT22 (aka AM2302).[32] Begin by connecting it to your Pi, as shown in figure 4.9. The DHT22 has four pins. Working from right to left, follow these steps:

❶ Connect the first DH22 pin to a ground (GND) pin; for example, pin 39. You don't connect anything to the second pin.

---

[32] This can also work with a DHT11 sensor.

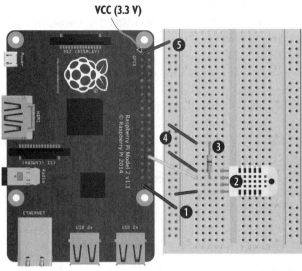

VCC (3.3 V)

fritzing

Figure 4.9   Connecting a DHT22 temperature and humidity sensor to the Pi

❷ Connect the third DH22 pin to the GPIO12 of your Pi (pin 32) and place a 4.7K Ohm resistor (yellow, violet, red, gold/silver)[33] between the DH22 pin and the connection to the pin of the Pi.

❸ Connect this resistor to the VCC line on the breadboard, the red line.

❹ Connect the fourth DH22 pin to the VCC line on the breadboard.

❺ Connect the 3.3-volt power source to the VCC line on the breadboard.

Because the DHT22 uses a special protocol, you'll first need to install an additional driver on the Pi called the BCM 2835 C Library.[34] The next listing shows how to install it.

Listing 4.8   Installing the BCM2835 driver

Unzip the code.

```
$ cd chapter4-gpios/drivers
$ tar zxvf bcm2835-1.50.tar.gz
$ cd bcm2835-1.50
$ ./configure
$ make
$ sudo make check
$ sudo make install
```

We packaged a version of the driver for you.

This driver is written in C, so you need to compile it yourself.

You're now ready to interact with the sensor using Node code. To do this, you'll use a Node library called `node-dht-sensor` that you first need to install with `npm install --save node-dht-sensor`. The code to run on the Pi is shown in the following listing.

Listing 4.9   dht.js: communicating with the DHT22 sensor

```
var sensorLib = require('node-dht-sensor');
sensorLib.initialize(22, 12);
var interval = setInterval(function () {
  read();
}, 2000);
```

22 is for DHT22/AM2302; 12 is the GPIO you connect to on the Pi.

Create an interval to read the values every two seconds.

---

[33] You can use resistances from 4.7K to 10K Ohms.
[34] See http://www.airspayce.com/mikem/bcm2835/index.html.

```
function read() {                              ◀───  Read the sensor values.
  var readout = sensorLib.read();
  console.log('Temperature: ' + readout.temperature.toFixed(2) + 'C, ' +  ◀─┐
    'humidity: ' + readout.humidity.toFixed(2) + '%');                       │
};                                                    Readout contains two values:
[...]                                                 temperature and humidity.
```

Save this file and run it as superuser with the `sudo` command because accessing the BCM 2835 driver requires it: `sudo node dht.js`. If everything works fine, you should see temperature and humidity values appearing every two seconds.

This concludes your first encounter with GPIOs, which are a great way to add functionality to your Pi—or any other embedded device, really!—so that it can sense or actuate the real world. Now that you have the basics, nothing prevents you from adding other sensors and actuators to your Pi; you'll find plenty of tutorials on the web.

The nerd corner—I want to see bits!

Libraries like `onoff` or `node-dht-sensor` prevent you from having to deal with the nitty-gritty details of interacting with low-level hardware sensors and actuators. This is also what the Web of Things is about: abstracting these (complex) details so that you can focus on your creative applications and build them using web tools. You might still want to know roughly how these libraries work. Basically, `onoff` puts watches on virtual files that Linux uses to update the values of GPIOs (1 or 0) using a library called `epoll`. `node-dht-sensor` needs to retrieve more complex binary data and uses a C library that communicates over the GPIOs using two popular protocols in the low-level embedded world of bits: I2C (Inter-Integrated Circuit) and SPI (Serial Peripheral Interface). If you want to dig deeper, reading about these protocols is a good start.

4.4.4   Beyond the book

If you want to learn more about embedded platforms, sensors, and hardware prototyping, there are many excellent resources and books that can help. A good source of information for emerging embedded platforms is Postscapes[35] and their IoT Toolkit.[36] For the more industrial side of things, you can use the Embedded portal.[37] For resources about hardware prototyping and electronics, make sure you check the Make[38] blog posts, books, and magazines. You might also look into the Instructables,[39] Element 14,[40] and Sparkfun communities,[41] where you'll find many step-by-step tutorials and lots of good advice.

---

[35] http://postscapes.com
[36] http://postscapes.com/internet-of-things-resources/
[37] http://www.embedded.com/
[38] http://makezine.com/
[39] http://www.instructables.com/
[40] http://www.element14.com/community/welcome
[41] https://learn.sparkfun.com/

No doubt this chapter was a challenging one! Covering so many different technologies and concrete skills in a single chapter isn't easy, so you've done a great job making it so far. But getting your Pi ready for the Web of Things is only the beginning.

4.5   Summary

- Many types of embedded platforms are commonly used in the Internet of Things, and you learned how to pick the right one for your use case.
- There are two main categories of operating systems for devices: RTOS and Linux.
- By installing Linux on a Raspberry Pi, you can easily access it remotely over SSH and configure it to be ready for the Web of Things.
- Embedded devices allow you to use breadboard, wires, and resistors to wire various sensors and actuators to the GPIO pins.
- Using Node.js on your Pi makes it easy to write simple applications that read data from your sensors and control the LED using the `onoff` library asynchronously over the GPIO ports.

Now that you have a real embedded device at home, it's time to connect it to the Web of Things. The next chapters will be about making sure it seamlessly integrates with the World Wide Web of Things. The first step comes with the next chapter: architecting an API for your Pi, its sensors, and actuators and using REST, HTTP, WebSockets, and JSON. In the following chapters you'll see how to make these sensors and actuators accessible through web APIs.

*Building networks
of Things*

5

This chapter covers

- An introduction to network classification models and layered architectures
- An overview of the various protocols for networking Things
- A review of the difference between the Transport and Application layers
- A systematic approach to pick the right communication method for your use case
- An overview of the Web of Things layered architecture

In the previous chapter you learned how to configure a single device—your Pi—and how it can interact with the real world using various sensors and actuators. But your Pi is still very lonely: it's not part of any large network and it can't talk (yet!) with other Things. Nor is it able to communicate with other applications and services over the internet. Obviously, the real value of the IoT is realized when devices become social and are able to talk to other devices or applications. Today, hundreds of different and incompatible networking protocols are being used in IoT systems, and sadly, we're still far from the Internet of Things, where all apps and devices can easily talk to each other. How did we end up here and why isn't there a single official protocol for the IoT? Which one is "The" best networking protocol I should use for my device? Should I use Bluetooth or Wi-Fi for my smart bird feeder? Those are all valid questions, and the goal of this chapter is to give you a broad overview of the most common protocols and which one is best for a given scenario. Although the beauty of the Web of Things is that it doesn't really matter which one you choose because the WoT is a level of abstraction above, you'll benefit greatly from understanding the nuts and bolts of how devices can be connected to form large networks of things.

The truth is that if you only want to write client applications and services for the Web of Things, you don't need to worry about the underlying protocols and you could jump directly to section 5.4. But to really understand how the Internet of Things works, or if you're building a connected product, the next sections will provide a crash course in the underlying protocols and technologies that are used for building networked devices.

Figure 5.1 shows the three types of connectivity (stages) we consider in this book. First, we have a lonely device that can sense and interact with its surroundings but doesn't have any connectivity. Second, the device supports at least one communication protocol and can talk to other devices to form a small network of devices. Third, these devices can be connected to the wider web ecosystem so that any application or service can talk to these devices over the internet. You had a glimpse of this last stage in chapter 2, where you interacted with some real web devices across the globe.

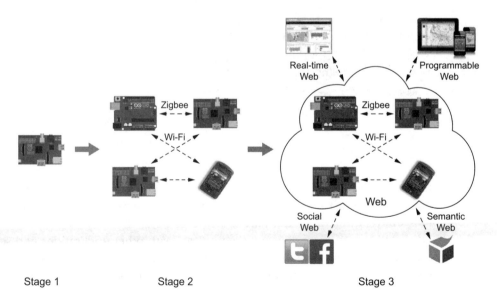

Stage 1   Stage 2   Stage 3

Figure 5.1   From one Pi to a network of embedded devices to a network of embedded devices interacting with the web and its ecosystem

In this chapter, we explore how an isolated device can move to stages 2 and 3. First, we look at various networking protocols for devices, such as ZigBee and Bluetooth, and explain their respective benefits and drawbacks. We don't expect you to become an IoT networking protocol specialist overnight, but you'll have enough understanding of these protocols to know the differences between them and which one is better suited for which usage scenario. Next, we'll introduce you to the application layers for Things and describe the most common protocols by looking at their strengths and weaknesses. Finally, we'll show how to go beyond that and integrate Things to the web in a systematic manner thanks to the Web of Things architecture that the following chapters are based on.

5.1 Connecting Things

You probably already know that computers talk to each other by using a networking protocol. Let's set the stage for a deeper dive into some of the most common networking protocols for the IoT so that you know which one is best for your next IoT project. Before diving into the protocols, we have to present two important networking concepts: topologies and classification models.

5.1.1 Network topologies

One way to understand how a network of devices differs from another is to look at its *topology*, which is a fancy word for the structure of the connections between the devices. Members of a network are often called *nodes*, and the topology is the spatial organization of the nodes to form a network. Let's look at the different topologies of a network and which topology to use in which situation.

POINT-TO-POINT

The simplest network topology occurs when any two devices establish a direct connection and start talking to each other. This model is called *point-to-point* and is particularly used in the context of wearable devices: you synchronize your fitness tracker with your mobile phone over Bluetooth by pairing the two devices. This model can also be used for the initial configuration of a Wi-Fi device. For example, a thermostat can create a point-to-point network called *Wi-Fi ad hoc mode*, where you can connect with your mobile phone and send to your thermostat the credentials and configuration of your home network.

STAR NETWORKS

In a *star network* topology, shown in figure 5.2, several nodes communicate with a single *central node* and might not be aware of other nodes in the network. This model is also often used as a *star of stars*, where each central node is in turn connected to another nearby central node.

In the IoT, cellular phone networks commonly use the star topology, where your phone (a node) connects to the nearest cell phone antenna (the central node). The star of stars topology can also be used for home automation systems, such as smart lighting systems. For example, light bulbs (nodes) can talk to several gateways using a

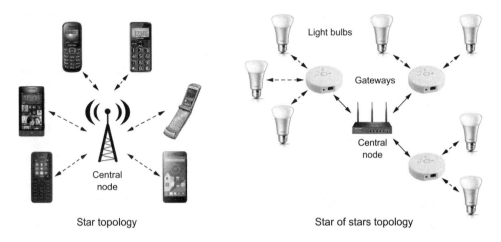

Star topology   Star of stars topology

Figure 5.2   Star topology: all nodes communicate with a single central node. Star of stars topology: nodes connect to intermediate nodes (gateways), which are in turn connected to a central node using a star topology.

wireless radio protocol such as ZigBee. Those gateways are in turn connected to your internet router (the central node) using Ethernet.

MESH NETWORKS

The last network topology that you might encounter in the IoT is also the most complex: *mesh networks.* In a mesh network, there are no central nodes because any node in the network is able to forward messages from one node to another. As an example, consider the devices shown in figure 5.3. The Pi on the left is too far from the Intel Edison on the right to communicate with it directly. In a mesh network, the Pi can use the nearby devices as intermediate hops, called *relays,* to forward the message to its destination. In this particular case, the Pi can use the Arduino, which is connected to the Edison, to relay the message. In short, a mesh network means that you can extend the range of each device by adding more nodes. You can also make the network more

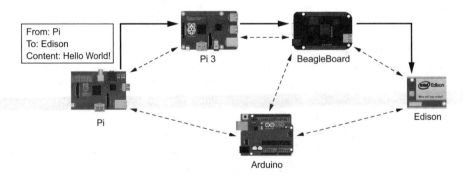

Figure 5.3   Mesh topology: messages are forwarded across several devices to reach their destination.

robust against individual node failures. For instance, if the Arduino fails, the Pi could still communicate with the Edison by going through all the other devices.

The internet is the best and largest example of a mesh network: you don't have a direct communication (point-to-point) with the server you want to talk to. Instead, messages travel across the internet by hopping from one router to another until they reach their final destination.

You'll see that mesh networking plays an important role in the IoT. This is particularly useful where no fixed network infrastructure—for example, Ethernet or Wi-Fi—is available. Take the example of monitoring the pollution level in a remote forest. There's no Wi-Fi infrastructure in place, so the best way to form a network is to drop nodes in the forest and have them communicate with each other by forming a mesh network. Only a few nodes need to be connected to the internet, using 3/4/5G or even a satellite link. The mesh topology is supported by a number of specialized IoT protocols that we'll cover shortly, such as ZigBee and 6LoWPAN.

5.1.2 *Network classification models*

Computer networking is a vast and complex topic where one can easily get lost. To make it easier to navigate the complexity of communication system, network classification models have been proposed to organize the variety of existing protocols in different layers, each having a specific purpose and knowing about only the one directly below it. After reading the brief introduction to networking models we provide in this section, you'll have a decent understanding of where each protocol fits on the map and especially how all these protocols relate to each other. Once you understand the difference between Application-level protocols and those at lower levels (Network/Transport-level protocols), you'll quickly realize why the Web of Things proposes an approach to the IoT that's fundamentally different, yet not necessarily incompatible, and is complementary in many other cases. Let's now look at the two most common models in use today: OSI (Open Systems Interconnection) and TCP/IP.

OSI AND TCP/IP MODELS

If you're an IT professional, you've surely heard about the OSI model or the widespread alternative model known as the internet protocol suite (IPS) or TCP/IP model. The basic concept of these models is to define *layers*, which are essentially abstractions. Each layer builds on the next; a layer serves the layer above and is served by the layer below. This means that a protocol in a particular layer can only make assumptions as to what the layer directly below will offer. As a consequence, each layer focuses on a particular set of problems and abstracts this problem for the layers above.

The OSI defines seven layers, and the IPS lists only four layers, as shown in figure 5.4. We'll focus on the IPS model here because it's the model of the internet. Teaching in detail each layer of the IPS model is beyond the scope of this book,[1] so here we'll only summarize what they are and what they do.

---

[1] *Computer Networks* (5th Edition) by Andrew S. Tanenbaum (Pearson, 2010) is a fantastic book to help you better grasp the details of the core concepts of computer networking, including the layered models.

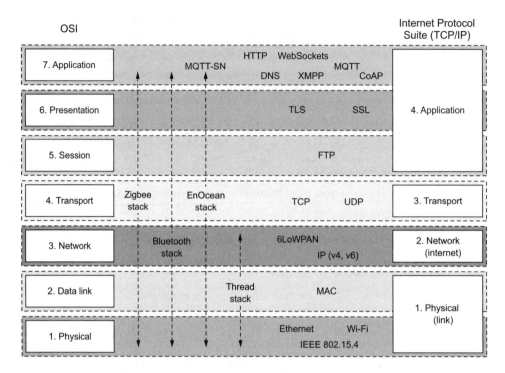

Figure 5.4   The OSI model (left) compared with the Internet Protocol Suite (aka TCP/IP, right), along with examples of some of the most relevant protocols and protocol stacks for the IoT (center)

- The *Physical layer* (also called the Link layer) cares about the communication technologies for a single segment of the network as well as the interfaces required to transmit the information. The key actors here are the bits transformed to packets. This is where the Ethernet or Wi-Fi (IEEE 802.11) protocols live.

- The *Network layer* (also called the Internet layer) looks into connecting hosts across independent networks. Common actors here are IP addresses; hence, this is where the Internet Protocol (IP) lives.

- The *Transport layer* handles the communication of information between two hosts. This is where the two well-known internet protocols TCP and UDP live.

- The *Application layer* looks at data exchange between two applications. This is the layer most software developers are usually exposed to. Because this is where HTTP lives, web browsers or mobile applications use it to let us do all kinds of things, from managing our online calendars to reading emails to retrieving Wikipedia content.

As you'll see later in the chapter, the Application layer is where the Web of Things architecture lives. Obviously, this means that the Web of Things can't exist without the networking layers below the Application layer. In order to consume real-world data from applications on mobile phones and in browsers, we first need to somehow get this data from the lower layers of model. The good news here is that if you abstract the layers below the Application layer, it doesn't matter which protocols or interfaces are used underneath.

When you combine the protocols of these different layers with each other, layer-by-layer you form a *protocol stack*. As you'll see later on, many different protocol stacks exist; for example, Bluetooth or ZigBee, some of which are shown in figure 5.4.

5.2 *Networking protocols for Things*

In chapter 1, we defined the Internet of Things as "a system of physical objects that can be discovered, monitored, controlled, or interacted with by electronic devices that communicate over various networking interfaces and eventually can be connected to the wider internet." But what does it mean for a Thing to be "connected to the internet?" It means that you can interact with it using the communication protocols of the Internet Protocol Stack shown in figure 5.4.

More concretely, this means that the Thing should use the IP on layer 2 and TCP or UDP on layer 3. If that's the case, then the Thing "speaks" internet-ese!

5.2.1 *Spatial considerations*

The last factor we consider when classifying networks is the distance between two nodes (range). Protocols can be classified according to how far or near nodes need to be from each other and also if they can be wired or if they must use radio signals. The various spatial scopes for IoT applications are shown in table 5.1.

Table 5.1   Spatial scope and range of various IoT networking protocols

Spatial Scope	Typical Range	Examples
Near field (NFC)	< 10 cm	NFC Forum
Personal area network (PAN)	1 m–50 m	Bluetooth, ZigBee, Thread, IEEE 802.4.15
Local area network (LAN)	50 m–1 km	Wi-Fi, Ethernet
Wide area network (WAN)	1 km–50 km	SigFox, LoRa, 5G, 4G, GSM

This well illustrates a harsh reality: the IoT isn't running off one single network protocol and probably never will because of different needs in terms of ranges of different devices. Why don't they all run on WAN protocols? Because the larger the distance, the more power you need, which is a no-go for battery-operated devices. As you'll see later in this chapter, some protocols allow low-power devices to transmit data over long distances, but the tradeoff is that you can transmit only very small amounts of data, also referred to as a low bandwidth.

5.2.2   *Internet protocols and the IoT*

To help you understand the difference between IoT protocols, let's review the basics of the IP, TCP, and UDP protocols. If you're familiar with those, you're welcome to skip this section.

INTERNET PROTOCOL: IPV4 AND IPV6

It's not accidental that the Internet Protocol shares the same name as what we commonly call the internet: this protocol is used for any byte of data that's sent over the internet. IP provides any node of a network with a unique IP address and is responsible for routing packets of information between any nodes using their IP addresses. When you type a URL in your browser, IP will find the address of the site you want to visit and retrieve the page across many subnetworks—for example, your local network, the network of your country, and so on.

Currently, IP version 4 (IPv4) is the most widely used version of the protocol. IPv4 addresses have a size of 32 bits (see figure 5.5), which means there are 2^{32} unique IP addresses, or approximately 4.3 billion. When IPv4 was invented back in 1974, this seemed more than enough to cater to all the machines that would be connected to the internet. Back then no one imagined how popular the internet would be 40 years later. Today, Cisco estimates that there are more than 15 billion things connected to the internet.[2] In other words, we've been running short of IPv4 address for quite some time.

Figure 5.5   Comparing the size and addressing space in IPv4 and IPv6

With the Internet of Things, this shortage has become a major hurdle. The first countermeasure was the idea of *Network Address Translation (NAT)*. NAT enables several hosts in a local network to share a single public IP address. Most routers and firewalls can perform NAT, and it has become a cornerstone of today's Internet of Things. But NAT is merely a patch because it adds lots of complexity to the network. This led to the design of a longer-term solution: IPv6.

IPv6 is based on 128-bit addresses represented as a series of eight groups of four hexadecimal (base 16) characters separated by colons (see figure 5.5), which allows

---

[2]   See http://blogs.cisco.com/news/cisco-connections-counter.

2^{128} unique addresses—that is, 340,282,366,920,938,463,463,374,607,431,768,211,456 different IPv6 addresses, in case you didn't do the mental math. Will that cover IoT's hunger for IP addresses? To put things in perspective, this number means that we could assign an IPv6 to every single atom on earth, and we'd still have enough IP addresses for every atom on another 100 earths!

IPv6 will be instrumental to IoT's success at scale. But upgrading the whole internet to IPv6 is no mean feat because this requires upgrading pretty much anything that's connected to the internet. From the operating system of your laptop or mobile phone to the firmware of any router or firewall connected to the internet, all will have to support IPv6.

Your Raspberry Pi isn't IPv6-enabled out of the box, but adding IPv6 support is quite straightforward, as shown in the following listing. Simply connect to your Pi via SSH and run this code.

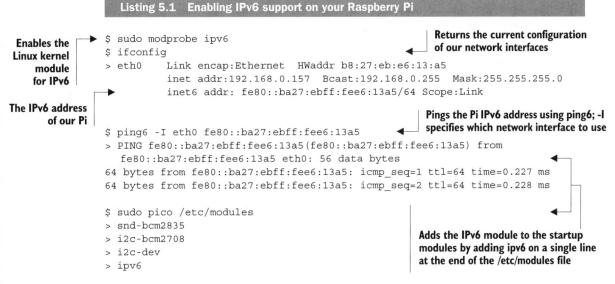

Listing 5.1 Enabling IPv6 support on your Raspberry Pi

Enables the Linux kernel module for IPv6

The IPv6 address of our Pi

Returns the current configuration of our network interfaces

Pings the Pi IPv6 address using ping6; -I specifies which network interface to use

Adds the IPv6 module to the startup modules by adding ipv6 on a single line at the end of the /etc/modules file

```
$ sudo modprobe ipv6
$ ifconfig
> eth0    Link encap:Ethernet  HWaddr b8:27:eb:e6:13:a5
          inet addr:192.168.0.157  Bcast:192.168.0.255  Mask:255.255.255.0
          inet6 addr: fe80::ba27:ebff:fee6:13a5/64 Scope:Link

$ ping6 -I eth0 fe80::ba27:ebff:fee6:13a5
> PING fe80::ba27:ebff:fee6:13a5(fe80::ba27:ebff:fee6:13a5) from
   fe80::ba27:ebff:fee6:13a5 eth0: 56 data bytes
64 bytes from fe80::ba27:ebff:fee6:13a5: icmp_seq=1 ttl=64 time=0.227 ms
64 bytes from fe80::ba27:ebff:fee6:13a5: icmp_seq=2 ttl=64 time=0.228 ms

$ sudo pico /etc/modules
> snd-bcm2835
> i2c-bcm2708
> i2c-dev
> ipv6
```

If this is your first encounter with IPv6, then welcome to the future!

TRANSPORT PROTOCOLS OF THE INTERNET

As you've just seen, the Network layer is only responsible for how packets are routed between two hosts on the Internet, not how to deliver data to applications, which is the responsibility of the layer above—the Transport layer. This layer introduces the notion of source and destination ports that identify applications. For instance, it gives one port to a web server and a different one to a mail server. You can think of a port as a mailbox that an application such as a web server can rent to receive packets. The combination of source and destination IP addresses along with a port number forms what's commonly called a network socket or just a socket.

Figure 5.6   A good UDP/TCP joke! [Source: http://pcp-comics.com/, used with permission]

On the internet, there are two protocols at this layer: the Transmission Control Protocol and the User Datagram Protocol. The best way to learn about TCP and UDP and their differences is by starting with a joke; see figure 5.6.

Joking aside, this emphasizes the fundamental difference between UDP and TCP: UDP does not offer reliability and sequenced delivery, which is why you might never get the joke, whereas TCP does. On the downside, TCP is more complex and hence heavier, and it requires synchronization and acknowledgment messages to guarantee data delivery, as we'll detail in a moment.

Ideally, we should stop here and ignore the details. But some IoT protocols are based on TCP and others on UDP, so to understand the difference between IoT protocols—and the joke—we'll now dive into a brief introduction to these two protocols.

USER DATAGRAM PROTOCOL

We'll start with UDP, which is simpler to understand. UDP is a *connectionless protocol*, which means that you don't need to establish a connection (a handshake) between the sender and recipient of a message. You send the message and cross your fingers hoping it will arrive, because delivery is not guaranteed. It usually will be delivered, but sometimes it won't, hence the joke!

Let's see a concrete example. A Thing wants to send a temperature update to a server using UDP. It needs to send a UDP message with the temperature value as content, along with the IP address and port of the receiver. The Thing also provides its own IP address and port in case the receiver wants to reply. This is just like when you send a letter with economy postage and hope it arrives. It's good enough to send items of little value. This model is called *unicast*, because the message is sent to a unique receiver by providing the address. Because UDP is connectionless, it can also be used to *multicast* messages. This means it can also be used to send a message to several receivers within a range of IP addresses—that is, a subnet.[3] Multicast relies on routers to send the messages to multiple receivers, so it works well in local networks but not so

---

[3] https://en.wikipedia.org/wiki/Subnetwork

much across the global internet because multicast messages are generally blocked by routers and gateways.

TRANSMISSION CONTROL PROTOCOL

The simplicity of UDP comes at the cost of some features that are important for some applications, such as guaranteed delivery of messages. To send a valuable item to someone across the globe, economy postage won't work—you'll want to use a trusted service, which will not only require a lot of paperwork but also flatten your wallet. This is the price you pay for guaranteed delivery.

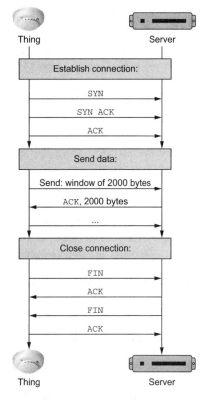

TCP is the FedEx of the internet. It also deals with sockets but ensures the communication is reliable and ordered by adding acknowledgement messages, sequence numbers, retransmission of missed packets, and also congestion and flow control, which we'll explain shortly.

Figure 5.7 gives you a simplified overview of a TCP connection. Imagine a Thing wants to send a super-important message to an application server on the internet; for example, your smoke detector wants to tell you that your house is on fire. Unlike UDP, TCP is a *connection-oriented protocol*, and the first thing it does is establish a connection to the server. Also note the numerous ACK messages used, which are confirmations that a message was received. Once the connection is established, the client can send messages cut into chunks (called *TCP packets*). The size of these packets will vary depending on how congested the network is, which is known as the *control flow* mechanism of TCP. Sequence numbers

Figure 5.7 TCP communication: a client establishes a connection (SYN) to a server and starts pushing data to it. Once the data has been reliably transmitted, the client closes the connection to the server (FIN).

are also added to packets so that when the sender doesn't receive an ACK for a given packet, it will send it again, ensuring that the entire message has been received. Finally, the Thing terminates the connection.

TCP VS. UDP FOR THE IOT

As you've seen, TCP is a necessity when delivery must be guaranteed. Thus, the majority of the traffic on the internet relies on TCP. But this reliability comes at a price: the protocol is heavier because it requires many more messages to be sent, and the packets are also significantly larger because they contain more information to guarantee reliability and ordering. This means additional overhead on both the client and the server sides and delays due to messages being retransmitted, which makes TCP generally slower than UDP. For this reason, UDP fits better with time-sensitive applications where dropped packets are preferable to delayed packets. For example, UDP is commonly used for Voice over IP applications or to stream music or video over the internet.

In the IoT, both protocols are interesting and there's no clear winner. Some widespread application protocols such as HTTP or MQTT (Message Queue Telemetry Transport; see section 5.3.2) use TCP, whereas others such as CoAP (Constrained Application Protocol; see section 5.3.3) are based on UDP.

Being lighter and faster, UDP seems more appropriate for embedded devices with limited resources. But some IoT applications might need guaranteed delivery; therefore, some application protocols on top of UDP are trying to reproduce some of the guarantees TCP provides. More important, unlike with TCP, routers often reject UDP traffic coming from the internet to the local network, unless the message was requested within the last few seconds. This means that if you try to control your connected thermostat with your mobile phone across the internet, your thermostat might never get the joke. Ahem, we mean the message.

This will significantly change when IPv6 dominates the internet because all Things will be able to have an IP address and NAT won't be needed anymore. But until then, TCP remains significantly easier to deploy in large heterogeneous networks, hence the battle for the transport protocol of the IoT goes on.

5.2.3   *IoT personal area networks*

Personal area network (PAN) protocols are used to communicate with Things located nearby, from wearable fitness trackers to a smart thermostat in your home to the connected garage door in your building. PAN protocols are hugely popular in the IoT because they offer an attractive tradeoff between communication range and power consumption. Let's start by describing and comparing the most common PAN protocols.

IEEE 802.15.4 AND 6LOWPAN

As you make new friends in the IoT community, you'll certainly hear them talk about "15.4." What they really mean is IEEE 802.15.4, which is a low-power, low-cost, and low-rate wireless protocol for communication between devices close to each other. These characteristics made it an excellent candidate for the IoT, especially when considering home automation devices with limited resources that are used indoors. As a consequence, 15.4 is the basis of many IoT PAN protocols.

One drawback of the IEEE 802.15.4 protocol is that it can't communicate directly with other devices via the internet—that is, via TCP/IP or UDP. This limitation has been addressed by the creation of 6LoWPAN, which allows bridging the two worlds. 6LoWPAN stands for "IPv6 over low-power wireless personal area networks." It gives you the ability to send and receive IPv6 packets over IEEE 802.15.4-based networks. It not only uses IPv6 addresses but also optimizes the size of IPv6 headers to be used on devices with constrained resources.

ZIGBEE

ZigBee has become one of the most popular protocols based on IEEE 802.15.4. ZigBee has two interesting characteristics: first, it supports mesh networking. Second, ZigBee is much more than a Physical layer protocol. As shown in figure 5.4, it spans from the Physical layer to the Application layer. Unfortunately, ZigBee is a proprietary standard controlled by a group of companies and requires a paid membership in order to build and ship products that use this protocol. Although some industrial and hobbyists platforms (for example, Arduino) do support ZigBee, your Pi does not directly support it. Adding ZigBee support to your Pi is possible using a special shield[4] or by adding a ZigBee dongle, such as Telegesis USB, to your Pi.

THREAD

Thread[5] is one of the most recent IoT networking protocols. Like ZigBee, Thread is based on IEEE 802.15.4 and supports mesh networks. The difference is that Thread reuses open protocols where possible and implements IP via 6LoWPAN so it can directly communicate with devices on the internet. Furthermore, at the Transport layer it uses UDP. Unlike ZigBee or Bluetooth, Thread doesn't provide an explicit Application layer and supports the various internet Application layer protocols (web standards, anyone?).

Thread allows creating large mesh networks with 250–300 devices that can be deployed in a house or building. The latency, while not real-time, is fairly low, with less than 100 milliseconds for typical interactions. It's also power-efficient and allows battery-operated devices running Thread to last for several years.

Although a paid membership is needed to create and sell products that use Thread, the protocol is built on open standards, which makes it easier to integrate than other protocols. Adding Thread support to your Pi is not trivial, mainly because the Thread protocol specification is fairly new. Once the protocol is adopted, you'll simply need to add an IEEE 802.15.4 or ZigBee dongle to your device because the Thread protocol requires only a software (firmware) update of ZigBee controllers to work.

BLUETOOTH

Bluetooth is another interesting IoT protocol and, unlike the other PAN protocols we've examined so far, it isn't based on the 802.15.4. What makes Bluetooth so appealing is its popularity: pretty much any mobile phone (and many other devices) supports Bluetooth out of the box. This makes Bluetooth the ideal candidate for wearables because most of these IoT devices use mobile phones as a gateway to other devices and to the web.

Bluetooth is managed by a nonprofit consortium of several technology partners and therefore requires a membership to build certified Bluetooth hardware and software stacks. But many of the standards and documentation are freely accessible.[6] Similarly to ZigBee, the Bluetooth protocol stack also spans several layers from the Physical to the Application layer (see figure 5.4), which we'll discuss in more detail in section 5.3.

---

[4] For example, http://www.cooking-hacks.com/documentation/tutorials/raspberry-pi-xbee.
[5] Official site: http://threadgroup.org
[6] http://bluetooth.com

Since it was first introduced as a protocol for connecting wireless headsets to your mobile phone, it has evolved significantly to support many other devices. Bluetooth 4.0, also known as Bluetooth Smart or Bluetooth Low Energy (BLE), has positioned Bluetooth as an excellent candidate for many IoT applications. BLE focuses on lowering energy consumption, which makes it ideal for battery-powered devices.

At the time of writing, the Bluetooth standard doesn't include support for mesh networking, although many researchers have shown how it could be done. Nevertheless, the Bluetooth consortium announced that it's working on adding mesh support to the standard,[7] making it likely that Bluetooth-based mesh networks will appear in the near future.

A number of devices come with out-of-the-box Bluetooth connectivity. For example, the Intel Edison we talked about in chapter 4 offers both Wi-Fi and Bluetooth 4.0 connectivity. The Pi 3 also comes with Bluetooth 4.0 BLE support; for other versions of the Pi you can add BLE support via USB dongles.[8] The following listing shows how to scan for Bluetooth devices from your Pi.

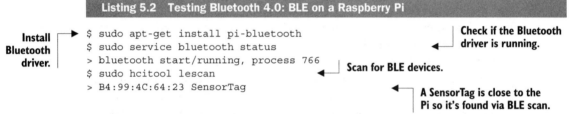

Listing 5.2   Testing Bluetooth 4.0: BLE on a Raspberry Pi

Install Bluetooth driver.

```
$ sudo apt-get install pi-bluetooth
$ sudo service bluetooth status
> bluetooth start/running, process 766
$ sudo hcitool lescan
> B4:99:4C:64:23 SensorTag
```

Check if the Bluetooth driver is running.

Scan for BLE devices.

A SensorTag is close to the Pi so it's found via BLE scan.

WI-FI AND LOW-POWER WI-FI

Wi-Fi, technically called IEEE 802.11, is the first protocol that comes to mind when talking about wireless connectivity. Because of its ubiquity, Wi-Fi seems like the perfect match for the Physical layer of the IoT, and that's why an increasing number of consumer electronics such as TV, microwaves, music players, and many more, support Wi-Fi.

But the Wi-Fi protocols (802.11a–n) are limited for some IoT applications. The biggest problem is energy usage. The second problem of Wi-Fi is its range. In a Wi-Fi network, all nodes must be within range of the access point: there's no mesh networking with Wi-Fi. Yes, the internet is the greatest example of a mesh network, but at the level of routers, not at the level of single Wi-Fi nodes acting as clients. These problems are being worked on, and a new Wi-Fi standard optimized for the IoT (IEEE 802.11ah[9]) is in the works and will have a better range and much lower power consumption.

Since the Pi 3, Wi-Fi is supported onboard. For other Pis, adding Wi-Fi is easy because the Raspbian Linux OS supports most Wi-Fi USB dongles out of the box.[10] We explained how to set up Wi-Fi on your Pi in chapter 4, section 4.2.3.

---

[7] Read more: http://blog.bluetooth.com/range-limitation-what-range-limitation-introducing-mesh-networks/.

[8] http://www.raspberrypi.org/learning/robo-butler/bluetooth-setup/

[9] http://en.wikipedia.org/wiki/IEEE_802.11ah

[10] More details: http://elinux.org/RPi_USB_Wi-Fi_Adapters.

ENOCEAN

Another lesser-known protocol worth mentioning here is EnOcean,[11] which is an energy-harvesting wireless technology mainly used in buildings and other industrial solutions. Although you may have never heard about it, EnOcean is particularly relevant for the IoT because it solves the energy problem elegantly. The technology allows devices to gather the energy they need from their environments. As an example, the kinetic energy produced when you flick a light switch is captured by the switch and used to transmit a message. Other products also use electromagnetic, solar, or thermoelectric energy converters.

The EnOcean specification spans the Physical and Networking layers, but additional specifications are also provided for the Application layer. The protocol is proprietary and requires a dedicated wireless transceiver module on a gateway to receive messages from various EnOcean devices. This technology saves time and materials because it allows battery-less devices to be installed rapidly in a building without having any wires in place. Interestingly, element14 offers an EnOcean extension board for the Raspberry Pi so you can turn it into an EnOcean gateway.[12]

SUMMING UP PAN

The various PAN protocols we've discussed are summarized in table 5.2, which compares their characteristics based on IoT-relevant criteria. In the Observed Range column we consider the range between two nodes when operating indoors. Note that the range of these protocols strongly depends on environmental variables such as the presence of thick walls or interferences. Furthermore, if the protocol supports mesh networking—for example, ZigBee—the maximal range can be much larger because messages can be relayed across multiple nodes.

The *ease of use* is a subjective evaluation based on our real-world experience with these different protocols. It merely expresses the pain we went through when using these different protocols both in lab and real-world settings.

Finally, if your device will be plugged into the power grid, then you should use Wi-Fi (great), Ethernet (even better), or both (ideally). If devices will be deployed in a fixed location rather than mobile and you can install a wired infrastructure, then you should use Ethernet, ideally with Power over Ethernet, so you only need the network cable.

Table 5.2 Comparison of the most common PAN protocols

Name	Battery Usage	Observed Max Range (Indoors)	Mesh Networking	Openness	Ease of Use	Internet Integration
EnOcean	Very low	<30 m	No	Low	Medium	No
ZigBee	Low	<50 m	Yes	Low	Hard	No
Thread	Low	<50 m	Yes	Medium	Medium	Yes

---

[11] Online: https://www.enocean.com/.
[12] Online: http://www.element14.com/community/community/raspberry-pi/raspberry-pi-accessories/enocean_pi/.

Table 5.2   Comparison of the most common PAN protocols (*continued*)

Name	Battery Usage	Observed Max Range (Indoors)	Mesh Networking	Openness	Ease of Use	Internet Integration
Bluetooth	Low[a]	<50 m	Coming in 2016	Medium	Medium	No (upcoming)
Wi-Fi	High (low upcoming)	<30 m	No (internet)	High	Easy	Yes

[a] With Bluetooth version 4 (Bluetooth Low Energy).

There are clearly many more PAN protocols than those, ranging from the wireless Z-Wave[13] to the wired KNX.[14] A good place to hunt them all down is Wikipedia[15] or Postscapes.[16]

5.2.4   *IoT wide area networks*

For some IoT applications, the PAN protocols presented in the previous section are not appropriate. If you want to deploy thousands of nodes to monitor large areas, such as a field, a forest, or a city, in theory you could use ZigBee. In practice, however, deploying and maintaining long-lived (months or years) and large-scale PAN mesh networks turn out to be extremely complex and costly. You'd have to deploy gateways, replicators, and amplifiers. Batteries would need to be changed. PANs are mainly suited for small distances between nodes, hence for smaller-scale deployments.

This limitation has led to the emergence of a different type of IoT network: wide area networks. The typical common denominator of IoT WANs is that they involve low-power nodes communicating directly with very high-power gateways called base stations or antennas. A good example of a WAN is the mobile phone network. Let's take a closer look at the most relevant WAN networks that are relevant for the IoT.

MOBILE NETWORKS: FROM GPRS TO 5G

The most common way to connect Things to the IP network without wires is to use the mobile phone network if available. You can use the data channel of mobile networks—for example, GPRS, 3G, or 4G—or use SMS. All you need is a cellular modem on your device and you're good to go—at least, as long as you don't forget to pay your phone bill!

The drawback of cellular connectivity is that it wasn't designed for the IoT. Nodes need a lot of energy—how often do you charge your cell phone, again?—so using the data channel to send data regularly isn't viable for battery-powered devices. For less data-intensive scenarios, you could also send SMS periodically and put the device into

---

[13] http://z-wavealliance.org
[14] http://www.knx.org/
[15] http://en.wikipedia.org/wiki/Personal_area_network
[16] http://postscapes.com/internet-of-things-protocols

sleep mode most of the time. This will work for sensing use cases where devices only send data, but it won't work when you need to send commands to your device because you'll have to wait until the device wakes up to process your request. Another limitation is that mobile phone networks weren't meant for billions of things. Only a limited number of devices can connect at any given time to a gateway, so you'll need to deploy a lot more antennas. Finally, the cost of using mobile networks is relatively high because pricing was set with a one-person, one-device business model that doesn't fit the requirements of the IoT. These limitations imply that current mobile phone networks are merely a provisory solution for the IoT.

A viable long-term solution will be needed for the many billions of Things that will want to connect to the internet in the coming years. With this in mind, the NGMN (Next Generation Mobile Networks) Alliance,[17] a mobile telecommunications association of powerful mobile operators, vendors, manufacturers, and research institutions, is working on a mobile network specifically geared for the IoT, code-named 5G. This network should be rolled out by 2020 and will have several improvements. First, it will be much more energy-efficient. Second, it will allow a significantly higher number of simultaneously connected clients per gateway. Third, it will support mesh networking, which will improve coverage and energy usage. Finally, the cost of 5G subscriptions will be better suited to the IoT model.

The use of mobile networks for the IoT is definitely not uncommon, so there are a number of embedded device platforms that support this mode of communication either natively or through simple extension shields. Your Pi is no exception; several shields or Wi-Fi dongles can connect it to mobile networks whether via SMS or data networks.[18]

IOT WIDE AREA NETWORKS: LOW-POWER WANS

Because current cellular mobile networks are ill-suited for most IoT applications, the number of IoT-dedicated WANs mushroomed over the past few years under the umbrella term *low-power wide area networks (LPWANs)*. The result is a number of technically compelling solutions, competing with similar offers. Most of these networks are organized with a star model: a number of low-power nodes communicate directly with powerful base stations directly attached to the power grid and to IP networks. Because of this architecture, LPWAN operators also face a major challenge: deploying their infrastructure. These dedicated networks require deploying additional communication antennas in the wild, just as mobile operators had to dot the landscape with antennas.

The leading network in this field is SigFox.[19] Being the first large-scale LPWAN operator dedicated to the IoT, SigFox has broad coverage in several European countries. But competition there is fierce and other networks (for example, LoRa[20] or nwave and the Weightless Alliance[21]) are catching up quickly.

---

[17] https://www.ngmn.org

[18] http://postscapes.com/raspberry-pi-wireless-options

[19] http://www.sigfox.com/en/

[20] https://www.lora-alliance.org/

[21] http://www.nwave.io and http://www.weightless.org

These networks have a number of advantages. First, deploying the infrastructure is the operator's business, not yours. Then, the range of the base station is quite high, in the order of several kilometers. In addition, each base station can handle a significant amount of parallel traffic coming from potentially millions of devices connected to a single base station. Finally, their power consumption is much lower than that of networks using WAN or PAN protocols. Let's consider a smart meter[22] powered by a standard battery (2.5 Ah) and sending a few messages per day. With most WAN or PAN protocols, the battery would barely last several months. With LPWAN, that same battery could last up to 20 years!

These advantages make the deployment of LPWAN-based devices straightforward—in theory, at least, because LPWAN coverage remains sparse in comparison with mobile phone networks. Besides, these networks are often proprietary and closed ecosystems where your Things will be locked forever and beyond.

Where's the catch? Well, LPWAN is perfect for low-bandwidth sensing scenarios such as sending data from a smart meter, but it won't work for actuation, like opening your garage door, because sending commands to devices is challenging and extremely slow.

Because of their industrial focus, connecting off-the-shelf embedded devices to LPWAN IoT is still more complex than with PANs. Fortunately, as LPWAN gains traction, various modules for embedded devices have appeared.[23]

SUMMING UP WAN

Most of the WAN protocols we described in this section share more or less the same capabilities. The only exception is mobile phone networks, which requires much more power than other IoT WAN protocols. This will likely change with the arrival of 5G networks, but we still have a few years to wait for that. For the other protocols, the main differentiator is their coverage. Because they're still far from having the coverage of mobile phone networks, deploying IoT use cases with these protocols requires careful planning with the network providers to ensure the target zones are sufficiently covered. Coverage of LPWANs will likely improve significantly in the near future, but it's still hard to predict which protocol will prevail and dominate the world of IoT WANs. See table 5.3 for a comparison of WAN protocols.

Table 5.3 A comparison between most common WAN protocols .

Name	Battery Usage	Max Range	Downlink	Openness	Coverage
Weightless	Very low	20+ km	Limited	Medium	Medium
SigFox	Very low	30+ km	Limited	Low	Medium-high
LoRa	Very low	30+ km	Limited	Medium	Medium
GPRS/3G/4G	High	50+ km	Yes	High	High
5G	Very low	?	? (probable)	High	Not deployed yet

---

[22] A smart meter is a connected device that measures electricity consumption.

[23] http://www.cooking-hacks.com/sx1272-lora-module-for-arduino-raspberry-pi-intel-galileo-900-mhz

5.2.5   *So, which one should I choose?*

Selecting the right network protocol stack for your next IoT project can be a daunting task. There are literally hundreds of possibilities for every layer of the stack, and these choices will be harder to revert. Unlike computers, Things will likely have a longer lifetime because consumers won't change the hardware of their fridge just to support a new Physical layer protocol. The CEO of a major home appliance manufacturer once told us that his top concern with the IoT was the ongoing war of standards and the implications of choosing the wrong one: "People don't want to upgrade the protocol stacks of their ovens, do they?"

There's no secret recipe for picking the right networking protocol stack because all protocols we've presented have their respective strengths and weaknesses. In this section, we'll provide some considerations and tradeoffs that will help you choose the right protocols for your application or device.

POWER SOURCE

The first thing you need to consider is how your device will be powered. Your options are battery, wired power source, and energy harvesting. This decision will depend on the context where the device will be used; for example, a power cord is ideal for fixed devices such as a lamp or a fridge. If wired power isn't an option in a remote environment such as a forest, a battery or solar panel will be a better choice, unless you're in Scotland. Likewise, a mobile device (for example, a portable Geiger counter) will have to use a battery or energy-harvesting technique.

If your device doesn't have the luxury of wired power, you'll need to use low-power protocols such as those based on IEEE 802.15.4 or LPWAN. Bluetooth LE, Thread, or SigFox would be a good choice in this case. At the Transport layer, if some data loss is acceptable, you could use UDP instead of TCP to further reduce power consumption.

If your device can connect to a power socket, Wi-Fi is the obvious choice, especially within a building where Wi-Fi can be easily installed. You might also consider Ethernet or Power Line Communication (PLC). If you have only an Ethernet socket, you might want to use Power over Ethernet (PoE) because this protocol tends to be more stable. At the Transport layer, you should use the reliability and good overall support of TCP.

COST

Cost is an important factor because together with power consumption, it determines which type of embedded device you can build into your Thing. If your budget per embedded device is less than 10 USD, you'll have to look into resource-constrained SoC (system on chip) platforms such as the ones we looked at in chapter 2—for example, Marvell, Broadcom, TI, and NXP. These platforms usually have limited RAM, storage, and processing power, which directly impacts the networking protocol stack you can use. If every single byte counts, you might be better off with protocols that were designed for resource-constrained devices at their core, such as IEEE 802.15.4, ZigBee, and Bluetooth LE. In terms of a Transport protocol, UDP is known to use fewer resources (RAM, CPU, and bandwidth) than TCP. If your target cost is above $10–$20 per device, you can start thinking about Linux-based platforms, giving you total free-dom in terms of the IoT networking protocols you can use.

RANGE AND NETWORK TOPOLOGY

Another aspect to consider is how far a Thing will be from a gateway or from other Things. This is tightly coupled with how much power your device can use. Roughly speaking, the more power your device has, the farther away it will be reachable—with the exception of LPWAN. We described the ranges of the different protocols before, so you should be able to make a decision. Don't forget that mesh networking can help. It lets you use low-power PAN networks like Thread or ZigBee while extending their range using multi-hop communication.

The infrastructure already in place is also an important consideration. For instance, if a star topology is available, you might as well use it. This is the case in a home environment where a Wi-Fi router is likely to be present, or outdoors in an area covered by LPWAN, making deployments a lot easier.

BANDWIDTH, LATENCY, ACTUATION, AND SENSING

You need to clearly know the interaction types and the bandwidth your Things will require. First, is this a sensing application where devices only need to send data to other devices or to the cloud? How often will you send messages; that is, will the device send data a few times per minute? Or will it sleep most of the time and send messages only a few times per day? Also, will you require sending commands to the device (actu-ation), and if so, how much latency can your application tolerate? Finally, how large will those messages be? A few bytes? Much more?

Some protocols like LPWAN—with the exception of mobile phone networks—don't work well with actuation or with use cases requiring large bandwidth. For these, Wi-Fi and Ethernet are probably the most suitable physical protocols. Other PAN pro-tocol stacks, like ZigBee, Bluetooth, and Thread, are somewhere in between in terms of available bandwidth and offer decent communication, so they're suitable for send-ing and actuation, although end-to-end latency may increase with the number of hops messages have to travel through.

INTERNET INTEGRATION AND OPENNESS

Finally, the openness of the protocol stack you choose can be an important factor. Is it an open or proprietary standard? How open and accessible are the specifications? How well supported is the protocol in the real world? How integrated with the inter-net protocols stack is that protocol? If a protocol stack doesn't provide ways of translat-ing to internet protocols (IP, TCP, or UDP) easily, it might be fine in closed networks (industrial machines in a factory, for example), but not if those devices need to be accessible through the internet.

Because of the pressure the IoT exerts on protocol stacks to be internet-compati-ble, all the protocol stacks we described previously can be integrated to the internet in one way or another. But the question really is this: at what layer and what deployment effort? The higher in the layers the integration takes place, the harder it is to reuse the internet infrastructure already in place. For instance, an implementation at only the Transport layer (such as by implementing TCP) means that you won't be able to use the infrastructure already in place for the layers below, such as internet access points, bridges, hubs, routers, and switches, and these will need to be replaced by other actors playing similar roles.

Basically, if the internet integration takes place at layer 3, someone will need to deploy hardware and software that covers the services offered by the layers below, leading to more complex deployments. The key underlying question here is this: who will deploy these additional components? In the case of a system based on an existing infrastructure like, say, SigFox, they do this for you so the burden is minimal but you have a dependency on a single company (SigFox, in this case). In the case of a home environment, for example, things are quite different, because you'll need to put in place the infrastructure if you don't plan to rely on the existing internet infrastructure.

Let's look at a concrete example, as shown in figure 5.8. Imagine you'd like to build a smart lamp that users can control from their mobile phone. You decide to choose a ZigBee protocol stack for your lamps. Because mobile phones can't speak ZigBee directly, you could decide to use HTTP as an application protocol. Communication goes down the layer from HTTP to Wi-Fi. Your lamps, on the other hand, use IEEE 802.15.4, which is the physical protocol of the ZigBee stack. Because it's unlikely that your customers have access points that support 802.15.4 and this protocol is physically incompatible with Wi-Fi, you need new hardware to support the 802.15.4, so you need to package your lamps with a ZigBee access point, too. Then, you need to bridge Wi-Fi to ZigBee and translate IP to ZigBee addressing, TCP to the transport protocol of ZigBee, and finally, HTTP to the application protocol of ZigBee. Then you need to translate this back to HTTP, TCP, IP, and Wi-Fi to respond to the mobile phone application.

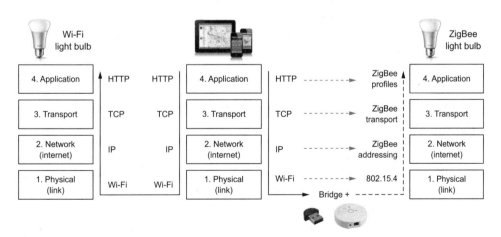

Figure 5.8 Two smart lamps communicating with web applications. Left: a smart lamp with Wi-Fi on board and implementing the IP stack. Right: a smart lamp implemented with ZigBee on board and implementing a ZigBee stack. In this second case, translators are required between the application and the lamp.

Of course, a number of these translations are standardized; nevertheless, it adds complexity to the deployment of your system and this complexity even reaches your customer, who needs to install additional hardware in their house for your system to work. Now imagine deploying this system in several buildings or in an entire city: you thought you were deploying smart lamps, but suddenly you're deploying an entirely new network! ZigBee isn't a bad choice per se, but if your main goal is to build a large-scale network where interoperability is prime, other options will make your life easier.

Choosing a protocol stack based on open standards or large alliances will help here. Popular and/or open protocol stacks—think Wi-Fi, Thread, Bluetooth, and the like—are far more likely to be supported by future generations of access points, routers, and mobile phones. In contrast, proprietary technologies like EnOcean and ZigBee will likely continue to require additional hardware and gateways to connect to the internet.

5.3   *Application protocols for Things*

So far, we've only looked at the lower layers of the networking stacks: the Physical, Network, and Transport layers. These protocols give a voice to Things that can be heard on the internet. Although those Things can now speak internet, no one else can understand what these Things are saying—unless they can speak a common language. What's the *universal language* of the internet? Well, just like there isn't only a single language on earth, there are many languages for different purposes. The *languages of the internet* are the protocols of the Application layer (layer 4 of figure 5.8). As you'll see in this section, many Application layer protocols have been designed for the IoT; unfortunately, few of them integrate seamlessly with the web.

Let's begin by looking at Application layers that aren't based on internet protocols. This space is filled with standards that have been used in fields such as home automation, building management, and manufacturing, so we could easily write another book just on these. Instead, let's focus on two built on top of two PAN protocol stacks we've looked at before: ZigBee and Bluetooth.

5.3.1   *ZigBee and Bluetooth application stacks*

Both ZigBee and Bluetooth offer a conceptually similar stack for the Application layer. The key idea is to provide a set of specifications for domain-specific applications; these are very specific use cases, such as managing security systems or controlling industrial machines. These specifications are called *application profiles* in the case of ZigBee or just *profiles* in the Bluetooth case. For example, Bluetooth defines a custom profile for health monitoring devices called the Health Device Profile (HDP). For building accessories (such as your car) that can read messages on a mobile phone, it defines a profile called the Message Access Profile (MAP). For ZigBee there are profiles for building lighting systems, fans, HVAC systems, or shades. Profiles define the protocol, operations, and payloads that can be used to interact with a device that uses a certain profile.

You don't have to use these profiles to build applications using Things built on top of ZigBee or Bluetooth; you can also build your own application protocol. But these profiles ensure that a client application understands what a ZigBee or Bluetooth device has to offer, so they're important for facilitating interoperability between services running on Things and applications.

Bluetooth and ZigBee Application layers also address other Application layer issues. For instance, both standards provide a way to uniquely identify devices as well as ways to perform network discovery. That is, they provide a way for several devices or several applications and devices to discover each other without knowing of their existence in the first place. In Bluetooth, for example, this is achieved by broadcasting a Bluetooth identifier and a reference to a profile to all listening devices. A similar system is in place for ZigBee.

All in all, Bluetooth and ZigBee have a lot to teach us in terms of what's needed at the Application layer. But as you've seen before, Bluetooth and ZigBee don't natively speak internet or web protocols. Moreover, there's a lack of SDK support for common languages: while you have web client libraries available for virtually any programming language, this isn't the case of Zigbee or Bluetooth.[24] In consequence, the application protocols of ZigBee and Bluetooth make them largely incompatible with devices that use other protocol stacks.

To deal with this, a number of bridges (gateways) have been built. As an example, a number of Bluetooth vendors have proposed integrations of Bluetooth devices to 6LoWPAN,[25] where every Bluetooth device gets an IPv6 address via special Bluetooth smart gateways. Similar initiatives exist for ZigBee, and the respective working groups are busy standardizing these bridges.

There's a good likelihood that ZigBee and Bluetooth will systematically implement the Internet Protocol Stack in the near future. This puts them on the internet resolving the networking of these Things but not their Application layer. Although the Application layer of Bluetooth or ZigBee is not built on top of IP-based protocols, a number of IP-based application protocols are available. Some of them, such as XMPP[26] (Extensible Messaging and Presence Protocol) and AMQP[27] (Advanced Message Queuing Protocol), were not meant for IoT use cases in the first place, yet people started adapting them over the years. Others, such as CoAP (Constrained Application Protocol) and MQTT (Message Queuing Telemetry Transport), were specifically created for the Internet of Things and are built on top of internet protocols, so we need to take a more detailed look at these two. But first, let's look at two other protocols pushed by today's most notorious tech giants: Apple and Google.

---

[24] Although Bluetooth is in a slightly better place in terms of SDKs with standard SDKs for Android and iOS or Linux (see http://www.bluez.org/)

[25] A good example is the Bluetooth IoT SDK for NordicSemic: https://www.nordicsemi.com/eng/Products/Bluetooth-Smart-Bluetooth-low-energy/nRF51-IoT-SDK.

[26] http://xmpp.org

[27] https://www.amqp.org

5.3.2   *Apple HomeKit and Google Weave*

In June 2014, Apple announced it was entering the IoT and in particular the home automation market with a protocol called HomeKit,[28] to be supported on all iOS-based devices. The HomeKit protocol stack covers several options, as shown in figure 5.9. There's an option for Bluetooth devices that uses the Bluetooth protocols stack and an option for internet-ready devices that uses IP, TCP, HTTP, and JSON. Finally, a bridge specification allows other devices to be integrated to the HomeKit Accessory Protocol. Regardless of the stack you choose to use, the Things you connect are eventually available for applications through iOS SDK interfaces.

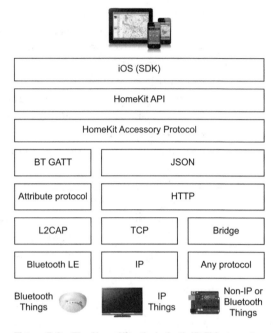

Figure 5.9   The HomeKit stack: both IP Things and Bluetooth Things are supported. Things based on other stacks are integrated via a HomeKit bridge. At the Application layer, HomeKit enables direct access to Things through iOS.

Although HomeKit is still in its early days, the presence of Apple devices in many homes means that it's likely to play an important role. Because it's based on a number of open standards, integration between HomeKit and other devices won't be a major technical challenge. But the HomeKit Protocol itself isn't open, so implementing a HomeKit Thing or an application requires being part of Apple's MFi (Made for iPhone) program.

Not surprisingly, Google decided to strike back and announced Google Weave in 2015. Conceptually, Weave is similar to HomeKit because it provides a protocol for an application (for example, a mobile app) to talk to an IoT device built on web technologies. But unlike HomeKit, it also specifies a set of cloud APIs and supports both Android and iOS devices. At the time of writing, Google Weave hasn't been publicly released but is likely to also play an important role, especially in home automation.[29]

5.3.3   *Message Queuing Telemetry Transport*

The Message Queuing Telemetry Transport (MQTT) Application layer protocol was invented in 1999 by Andy Stanford-Clark and Arlen Nipper. It was meant as a lightweight messaging protocol built on top of TCP/IP that allowed constrained devices

---

[28] https://developer.apple.com/homekit/
[29] https://developers.google.com/weave/

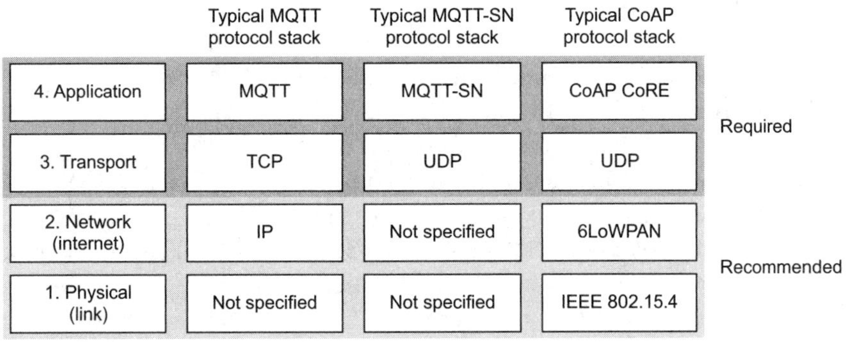

	Typical MQTT protocol stack	Typical MQTT-SN protocol stack	Typical CoAP protocol stack	
4. Application	MQTT	MQTT-SN	CoAP CoRE	Required
3. Transport	TCP	UDP	UDP	
2. Network (internet)	IP	Not specified	6LoWPAN	Recommended
1. Physical (link)	Not specified	Not specified	IEEE 802.15.4	

Figure 5.10 Typical protocol stacks for MQTT, MQTT-SN, and CoAP. MQTT is built on top of TCP. CoAP is built on top of UDP and usually IPv6 (6LoWPAN). MQTT-SN is usually built on top of UDP.

with limited bandwidth to talk to each other. MQTT did this very well, with implementations fitting the constraints of most embedded devices. Over the years, MQTT has become an important Application layer protocol for machine-to-machine (M2M) communication. See figure 5.10.

As you'll learn in the next chapter, MQTT is a publish-subscribe protocol. For now, all you need to know is that with MQTT clients *subscribe* to a topic of interest and receive notifications whenever a new message for this topic is *published*. The publisher and subscribers of messages don't speak to each other directly but through an intermediate called a *broker*. The broker can be deployed locally if you only require local communication, or on the internet if the publishers and subscribers are not in the same local network.

QUALITY OF SERVICE

An interesting feature of MQTT is that it offers three levels of quality of service (QoS) to guarantee what a client application can expect when it comes to the delivery of messages. Note that this is complementary to the Transport layer delivery guarantee of TCP you saw before because it relates to delivery between subscribers and publishers at the Application layer. Clients can request the following QoS levels from brokers that support them:

- *QoS 0: fire and forget*—A published message might be delivered to the subscribers, but this is not guaranteed. Receivers won't acknowledge a message and brokers won't store or redeliver them.
- *QoS 1: deliver at least once*—A published message will be delivered at least once to the subscribers. This means that if a subscriber temporarily disconnects, it will receive the message as soon as it reconnects. An example of the messages required for such a connection is shown in figure 5.11.
- *QoS 2: deliver exactly once*—A published message will be delivered once—and only once—to each subscriber.

PERSISTENT CONNECTIONS

As shown in figure 5.10, MQTT is built on top of TCP and IP. This means that all the publication and subscription happens via TPC/IP. But one interesting aspect of MQTT is that it keeps the connection between a client and a broker open for as long as it can. To maintain this open connection, the client sends regular ping requests (PINGREQ) to the server, as shown in figure 5.11, where a client is connected to a broker with QoS 1.

SECURITY AND ENCRYPTION

Security in MQTT works via Transport Layer Security (TLS), the successor of SSL that's used to encrypt traffic on the web. On top of encryption, the broker can request a username and password to identify the clients.

MQTT FOR TINY DEVICES—MQTT-SN

Even if it was designed to be lightweight, the fact that MQTT maintains permanent connections over TCP can be problematic for some devices. This isn't an issue for your Pi, but it could be problematic for resource-constrained devices such as the RTOS platforms we talked about in chapter 4. In particular, this is clearly a problem for battery-powered devices, because keeping a TCP connection open permanently will rapidly drain the battery.

The MQTT world has a protocol with a similar objective: MQTT for Sensor Networks (MQTT-SN). MQTT-SN is conceptually similar to MQTT but with two major differences, as shown previously in figure 5.10. First, it doesn't require a permanent connection and is built on top of UDP and not TCP, which saves some bandwidth—and introduces some limitations, as you've seen before. Then, an MQTT-SN broker indexes topic names, which are sometimes too long for very-low-bandwidth networks. Even though it's an interesting protocol, MQTT-SN isn't as popular as MQTT or CoAP, and the only full-featured broker freely available to date is the Really Small Message Broker provided via the Eclipse foundation.[30]

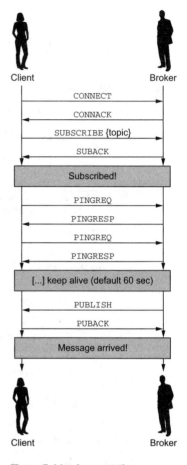

Figure 5.11   A connection between a client and a broker with QoS 1. The connection is kept open by sending regular PINGREQ requests. The frequency of these requests depends on a keepalive parameter set by the client. Because MQTT is a protocol working on connections that should be kept open, this parameter ensures that both the broker and client are connected. If the broker doesn't receive a PINGREQ or any other message in 1.5x the keepalive interval, it will close the connection.

[30] http://git.eclipse.org/c/mosquitto/org.eclipse.mosquitto.rsmb.git/

5.3.4 *Constrained Application Protocol*

Focusing on a footprint acceptable for very limited embedded devices as well as saving battery power are among the raisons d'être of the next Application level protocol we look at: the Constrained Application Protocol (CoAP).[31] CoAP is a set of protocol specifications designed to work on embedded devices with as little as 10 KB of RAM, and it yields a code footprint of about 100 KB. CoAP is also the youngest application protocol we looked at here; it was officially released in June 2014.

UDP FOR NON-PERSISTENT CONNECTIONS

The typical stack CoAP, often referred to as "IP for Smart Objects," differs from MQTT in three ways. first, as shown in figure 5.10, CoAP is usually used alongside 6LoWPAN at the Network layer. Then, at the Transport layer, it uses UDP (just like MQTT-SN), not TCP. This means that CoAP doesn't maintain an open TCP connection and thus requires less power. In practice, though, this also means that CoAP is harder to deploy in certain environments. As you've seen before, UDP poses a number of challenges when combined with Network Address Translation, and this won't likely change until IPv6 is fully deployed; see section 5.2.1.

REQUEST/RESPONSE AND OBSERVE

CoAP is a request/response protocol implemented on the principles of REST. These principles are at the core of the web and the Web of Things and will be discussed in great detail in the next chapter. In that respect, CoAP is a very interesting protocol, and the concepts you'll learn in the following chapters will be really useful for you to understand both HTTP for Things and CoAP.

In a separate specification called CoAP Observe,[32] the request/response paradigm is extended with support for "observing" resources. In short, this means you can subscribe to a resource in a similar way to what the pub/sub of MQTT offers. But unlike in MQTT, there's no broker and the Things themselves push the updates to the clients. Not relying on an external broker means that every Thing becomes both a client and a server, which allows devices to easily and directly communicate with each other.

5.3.5 *So, which one should I use?*

HomeKit is a promising protocol that will likely evolve a lot over the next few years. But it has the clear limitation of working only within the boundaries of the Apple ecosystem. Google Weave has yet to prove what it can do for the IoT. MQTT and CoAP are interesting alternatives, but they have two main challenges in the context of the Web of Things.

First, they don't integrate directly with the web (of browsers). You can't build client-side JavaScript that directly interacts out of the box with CoAP or MQTT. That doesn't mean it's the end of the story just yet. There are ways to integrate both these protocols to the web of browsers directly in the browser by channeling MQTT requests

---

[31] http://coap.technology/
[32] https://datatracker.ietf.org/doc/draft-ietf-core-observe/

over WebSockets or via an HTTP proxy for CoAP. This topic will be covered in more detail in chapter 7.

Second, MQTT and CoAP both propose a way to implement an Application level protocol for the Internet of Things, but they don't address the idea of a data model with fixed semantics and syntax and the possible interactions. In other words, even if you use MQTT, you'll still need to create your own model for your Things or applications. Because this isn't based on a clearly defined standard, MQTT clients need to know in advance the custom model of a given device, which limits ad hoc interaction.

Bridging this gap is precisely the objective of the Web of Things: creating an application protocol for Things using and reusing Web standards and tools. This is what the Web of Things architecture is all about, and the good news is that what you'll learn in the next chapters will also be applicable to other popular Application layer protocols such as MQTT and CoAP.

5.4   *The Web of Things architecture*

As you've seen, existing IoT Application layer protocols offer a variety of features that are useful for embedded device deployment, from device and service discovery to reliable messaging, to ad hoc secure pairing, and so on. Unlike those protocols, HTTP and WebSockets alone don't support these features because they weren't designed for embedded devices. To be truly useful, the Web of Things will require those capabilities and also the ability to be easily extended to support additional features when needed. In this section, we propose a structured architecture for the Web of Things that will form the basis for the rest of the book. This architecture will show in practice how web protocols can be extended to support all the features we need for building any type of WoT application, while remaining truly integrated into the web.

Unlike the OSI or the Internet Protocol Stack, the WoT architecture stack is not composed of layers in the strict sense but rather of levels that add functionality, as shown in figure 5.12. Each layer helps to integrate Things to the web even more and hence makes them more accessible for applications and humans. The WoT architecture stack starts where the OSI and Internet Protocol Stack ends: it looks into all protocols and tools that live at the Application layer and above (layer 7 and upward). The powerful implication of this is that you don't have to worry about the underlying layers (1–6), because the Web of Things is concerned only with Application layer protocols and what you do with them—not which underlying protocols are used.

The following chapters of this book will describe each layer in detail so you'll have all the tools you need to use those device-specific features for your WoT products and applications in a way that maximizes reuse and interoperability. Let's now review the various layers of the WoT architecture and describe their purpose; see figure 5.12.

5.4.1   *Layer 1: Access*

The Access layer is also the most fundamental because it looks into the way Things can be connected to the web by offering a web API. This layer is responsible for turning any Thing into a programmable web Thing that other devices and applications can easily talk to.

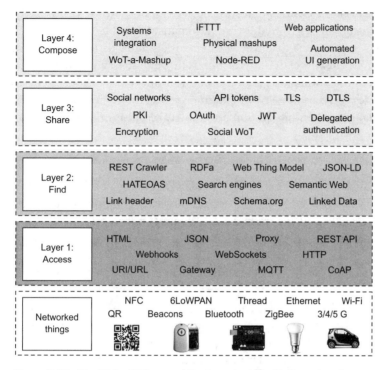

Figure 5.12   The Web of Things architecture stack[33] with its various layers

The core idea of this level is simple: Things can be smoothly integrated to the web by exposing their services through a RESTful API using HTTP, built on top of TCP/IP as well as the JSON data format. The Access level also describes how to use WebSockets to accommodate the fact that a number of IoT use cases are real-time or event-driven. We'll look into these aspects in chapter 6.

Not all Things will be able to speak web protocols or even be connected to the internet, but that doesn't mean those things won't be part of the Web of Things. Thus, we'll look into the web integration of non-web and non-internet Things using several integration patterns such as gateways. These aspects of the Access layer are covered in chapter 7.

5.4.2   Layer 2: Find

Marking things accessible via a web API doesn't mean a client can "understand" what the Thing is, what data or services it offers, and so on. This is the goal of the second layer: Find. In this layer we propose an HTTP-based protocol with a set of resources, data models, payload syntax, and semantic extensions that web Things and applications

---

[33] This Web of Things architecture was proposed in Dominique Guinard's PhD thesis: http://webofthings.org/2011/12/01/phd-web-of-things-app-archi/.

should follow. This layer ensures that your device can not only be easily used by other HTTP clients butcan also be findable and automatically usable by other WoT applications. The approach here is to reuse web semantic standards to describe things and their services. This enables searching for things through search engines and other web indexes as well as the automatic generation of user interfaces or tools to interact with Things. At this level, we also describe Semantic Web technologies such as JSON-LD and HTML5 microdata and their integration into the API of Things. These topics will be covered in chapter 8.

5.4.3   *Layer 3: Share*

The Web of Things is largely based on the idea of Things pushing data to the web, where more intelligence and big-data techniques can be applied—for example, to help us manage our health or optimize our energy consumption. But this can only happen in a large-scale way if some of the data can be efficiently—and securely—shared across services. This is the responsibility of the Share layer, which specifies how the data generated by Things can be shared in an efficient and secure manner over the web.

At this level, we look into applying fine-grained sharing mechanisms on top of RESTful APIs. We also look at delegated web authentication mechanisms and integrate OAuth to our Things' APIs. Finally, we discuss implementing the Social Web of Things by using social networks to share Things and their resources. We cover these topics in chapter 9.

5.4.4   *Layer 4: Compose*

Finally, once Things are on the web (layer 1) where they can be found by humans and machines (layer 2) and their resources can be shared securely with others (layer 3), it's time to look at how to build large-scale, meaningful applications for the Web of Things. In other words, we need to understand the integration of data and services from heterogeneous Things into an immense ecosystem of web tools such as analytics software and mashup platforms. The goal of the Compose layer is to make it even simpler to create applications involving Things and virtual web services.

Tools at the Compose layer range from web toolkits—for example, JavaScript SDKs offering higher-level abstractions—to dashboards with programmable widgets, and finally to physical mashup tools such as Node-RED. Inspired by Web 2.0 participatory services and in particular web mashups, the physical mashups offer a unified view of the classical web and Web of Things and empower people to build applications using Web of Things services without requiring programming skills. We'll look at this level in chapter 10.

5.4.5   *Why does the WoT matter?*

The good news is that on the Web of Things you needn't care about how various devices talk to each other physically, or at the Network layer. Just like on the web, you don't need to worry about whether your phone uses 4G or Wi-Fi to fetch a web page. All you need to care about in the Web of Things is that those devices share a common set of languages that allows them to communicate at the Application level regardless of the way they're networked. By layering the well-known web standards on top of the myriad of networking protocols in use, you're enabling any device and application across any network to talk to each other and exchange data in a standard and meaningful way. In short, the Web of Things is agnostic to anything below the Application layer, so that any device can be part of the universal Web of Things regardless of what protocol(s) it uses connects to the internet.

As you've also learned, a number of Application layer protocols have been proposed for the IoT, but none can be considered "The One." The premise of the WoT is different: instead of creating yet another protocol from scratch, why not reuse and adapt something widely popular and universally supported, like the web? The architecture we proposed for the Web of Things in section 5.4 puts this exact idea in practice: have a single uniform architecture for the Web of Things that any WoT device, service, or application can use to talk to each other. How this can be done is what the remainder of this book will teach you.

5.4.6 Beyond the book

What you've certainly realized is that a single universal protocol stack to rule them all is both unrealistic and impractical. Certain protocol stacks are much better suited for some scenarios than others, and compromising on those doesn't make sense, especially for commercial use cases. If you were to remember one thing about this chapter, it would be to ensure that you choose protocols that play well with the internet. It seems like a pretty obvious statement when working on building the Internet of Things, but the more straightforward the integration, the easier it will be to develop and deploy your product.

The arena of IoT protocols is likely to remain a hodgepodge of old, new, and incompatible protocols for many years to come—the battle is far from being over! You should follow the upcoming developments in this field. A good place to start is the IPSO (Internet Protocol for Smart Objects) Alliance,[34] a consortium of powerful players promoting the use of internet protocols on embedded devices. Also make sure you follow the Thread Group,[35] which is actively looking at creating a clean and operational IoT protocol stack up to the Network layer. You should also take a closer look at the AllSeen Alliance[36] and the OIC (Open Interconnect Consortium),[37] which are becoming increasingly popular.

---

[34] http://www.ipso-alliance.org/
[35] http://threadgroup.org/
[36] https://allseenalliance.org/
[37] http://openinterconnect.org/

5.5   *Summary*

- There are various models for classifying network topologies and protocols, and they help us compare and contrast various tools and use cases commonly used in the IoT.
- The IoT today is a hodgepodge of protocols, and few of them are based on the Internet Protocol suite.
- Some popular IoT protocols have been designed specifically for the constraints of embedded devices—low power or bandwidth, for example—and therefore require specifically designed gateways to be connected to the internet.
- There are also various Applications layer protocols for the IoT that can't be easily integrated with one another. These protocols offer additional capabilities that are desirable for IoT applications, such as real-time push, device discovery, and so on.
- The Web of Things helps maximize interoperability across various physical networks.
- Web technologies are widely popular and offer all the flexibility and features needed for the majority of IoT applications, including discovery, security, and real-time push.
- The WoT architecture stack organizes the variety of tools, techniques, and standards commonly used on the web so they form a complete framework on which to build IoT systems that are natively part of the web.

If you're new to IoT and networking, no doubt this chapter was a tough one. It certainly didn't turn you into an IoT networking protocol expert, but at least it equipped you with a solid overview of the variety of technologies that can be used to build networked devices. If you have to deal with hardware and/or infrastructure, knowing which protocol is good for which use case will definitely help you choose the right tools for your next project.

Part 2

Building the WoT

In part 2 we describe how to build the Web of Things, and we show how to implement the various layers of the Web of Things architecture that was introduced in part 1.

Chapter 6 is a quick introduction to the modern web architecture and describes how it can be applied to embedded devices and the Web of Things.

Chapter 7 shows how to implement the concepts presented in the previous chapter on various devices.

Chapter 8 introduces the issues of discoverability and findability and shows how to use the web techniques to expose and share metadata about the services and capabilities of web-connected devices.

Chapter 9 offers a quick introduction to web security and how to connect devices to the web and share their data in a secure manner.

Chapter 10 shows how to use the techniques and methods presented in the previous chapters in order to rapidly build hybrid Web of Things applications called physical mashups.

Access: Web APIs for Things

This chapter covers

- Designing APIs for Things based on the REST principles
- Implementing RESTful Things with HTTP and WebSockets
- Representing resources with JSON and MessagePack
- Allowing cross-site requests using CORS
- Using WebSockets and web hooks to implement real-time communication with Things
- Looking at HTTP/2, the future of HTTP

By now, it should be clear that the central idea behind the Web of Things is to make it easy for devices, services, and applications to talk to each other by using patterns and standards that are similar to anything else on the web.

In this chapter, we'll describe in detail what those patterns are and will show you how to use them to implement web APIs for physical objects. Before jumping head-first into code, a little bit of theory is needed, so we'll start by exploring the fundamentals of the modern web architecture. First, we'll introduce REST, which defines the core architecture of the web. Afterward, we'll propose a set of guidelines and a methodology to design RESTful APIs for physical devices so that HTTP clients can easily read data from their sensors or send control commands to them. Finally, we'll expose the limitations of REST APIs over HTTP when it comes to real-time sensor data and notifications, and we'll describe how the latest developments in web technologies such as WebSockets can be used to provide push notifications for the Web of Things.

6.1   Devices, resources, and web Things

Let's start our discovery of the first layer of the Web of Things architecture we presented in the previous chapter. This layer is aptly named Access because it covers the most fundamental piece of the WoT puzzle: how to connect a Thing to the web so that it can be accessed using standard web tools and libraries. By the end of this chapter, you'll have gained a sound understanding of HTTP and WebSockets and how to use them for physical objects. This will allow you to model the services and data offered by your Things with a clean, RESTful API that other developers and devices can easily understand and use. Figure 6.1 illustrates the Access layer of the Web of Things.

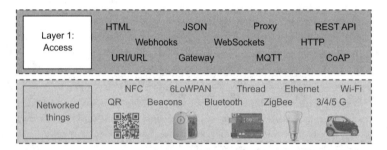

Figure 6.1   The Access layer of the Web of Things. This layer assumes that Things are connected in some way to the internet and focuses on how devices and their resources (properties, services, data, sensors, and so on) can be exposed as web APIs.

6.1.1   Representational State Transfer

If you've ever used web APIs, you've certainly come across the term REST or RESTful. Representational State Transfer (REST) is a set of architectural principles that any distributed system can adopt and that was formalized in Roy Fielding's PhD thesis:[1]

> *REST provides a set of architectural constraints that, when applied as a whole, emphasizes scalability of component interactions, generality of interfaces, independent deployment of components, and intermediary components to reduce interaction latency, enforce security, and encapsulate legacy systems.*

---

[1]   Source: http://www.ics.uci.edu/~fielding/pubs/dissertation/top.htm.

In short, if the architecture of any distributed system follows the REST constraints, that system is said to be RESTful. The idea is that when each component of the system (servers and clients) complies with those constraints, the interactions between the components are well defined and thus fairly predictable. This maximizes interoperability and scalability of the system, which is essential for a global system such as the web. These properties are what made the web so successful, and that's becauseHTTP— the Application layer protocol at the heart of the World Wide Web—is based on REST! Another RESTful protocol is CoAP, which we introduced in chapter 5 and which will be discussed further in chapter 7. REST was designed to enable a large-scale distributed system for multimedia content (aka hypermedia), and as the success of the web can attest, it's been working pretty well. Let's see what those constraints are.

CONSTRAINT #1—CLIENT-SERVER

Interactions between components are based on the *request-response* pattern, where a client sends a request to a server and gets back a response. This maximizes decoupling-between components because clients don't need to know anything about the implementation of the server, only how to send the request to get the data they want. Likewise, servers don't need to know about the state of clients or how that data will be used. Such a separation of concerns between data, control logic, and presentation improves scalability and portability because loose coupling means each component can exist and evolve independently.

CONSTRAINT #2—UNIFORM INTERFACES

Loose coupling between components can be achieved only when using a uniform interface that all components in the system respect. Unambiguous, simple, and standard interfaces that can be easily extended for all sorts of content and scenarios have largely contributed to the success of the web as an open and participatory system. This is also essential for the Web of Things because new, unknown devices can be added to and removed from the system at any time, and interacting with them will require minimal effort.

CONSTRAINT #3—STATELESS

The client context and state should be kept only on the client, not on the server. Because each request to the server should contain the client state, visibility (monitoring and debugging of the server), robustness (recovering from network or application failures), and scalability are improved. Of course, servers and applications can be stateful because this constraint simply requires that interactions between clients and servers contain information about each other's state.

CONSTRAINT #4—CACHEABLE

Caching is a key element in the performance (loading time) of the web today and therefore its usability. Clients and intermediaries can store some data locally, which boosts their loading time, because that data doesn't need to be fetched from the actual server for each request. Servers can define policies as when data expires and when updates must be reloaded from the server. This leads to better performance because fewer client-server interactions improve server scalability and also reduce latency.

CONSTRAINT #5—LAYERED SYSTEM

Uniform interfaces make it easy to design a layered system, which means that several intermediate components can hide what's behind them. Layered systems make it possible to use intermediary servers to further improve scalability and response times. For example, distributed caches or content delivery networks (CDNs) such as Akamai[2] can cache data in various locations throughout the globe to allow clients to retrieve some data faster. This is possible because clients rarely need to know if they interact with the target server or some other proxy along the way. Another benefit of layered systems is that it enables encapsulation of legacy protocols and systems–for example, gateways to proprietary protocols–which makes it simpler to enforce various security policies.

6.1.2   *Why do we need a uniform interface?*

As you can tell, these constraints are largely responsible for making the web work. Without them, the web wouldn't be as open, scalable, flexible, and efficient as it is today, and it would have become another ghost in the closed and proprietary systems paradise. Remember CompuServe?[3] Exactly!

The most important of these constraints is the uniform interface because limiting all possible interactions to a subset of generic and well-defined operations offers several advantages. First, using a uniform interface such as that defined by HTTP minimizes the coupling between components, which helps us design more scalable and robust applications. Second, we can use a web-like mindset to design applications: markup languages, event-based browser interactions, scripting languages, URLs, and the like. Third, HTTP traffic on port 80 is the only protocol that's always permitted by most firewalls. Fourth, it makes it easy to hide low-level protocol details behind simple, high-level abstractions, which promotes openness, programmability, and reusability of services and data regardless of how they're actually stored or encoded.

Our point here is that what REST and HTTP have done for the web, they can also do for the Web of Things. As long as a Thing follows the same rules as the rest of the web—that is, shares this uniform interface—that Thing is truly part of the web. In the end, the goal of the Web of Things is this: make it possible for any physical object to be accessed via the same uniform interface as the rest of the web. This is exactly what the Access layer enables and, as we'll describe in the rest of this section, the uniform interface of the web is based on these four principles:

- *Addressable resources*—A *resource* is any concept or piece of data in an application that needs to be referenced or used. Every resource must have a unique identifier and should be addressable using a unique referencing mechanism. On the web, this is done by assigning every resource a unique URL.

---

[2] http://www.akamai.com

[3] CompuServe was the first major commercial online service in the United States. It implemented services on top of the internet (and other networks) using mainly proprietary protocols. The service competed with the open World Wide Web for several years but lost the game and was completely shut down in 2011: https://en.wikipedia.org/wiki/CompuServe.

- *Manipulation of resources through representations*—Clients interact with services using multiple representations of their resources. Those representations include HTML, which is used for browsing and viewing content on the web, and JSON, which is better for machine-readable content.
- *Self-descriptive messages*—Clients must use only the methods provided by the protocol—GET, POST, PUT, DELETE, and HEAD among others—and stick to their meaning as closely as possible. Responses to those operations must use only well-known response codes—HTTP status codes, such as 200, 302, 404, and 500.
- *Hypermedia as the engine of the application state (HATEOAS)*—Servers shouldn't keep track of each client's state because stateless applications are easier to scale. Instead, application state should be addressable via its own URL, and each resource should contain links and information about what operations are possible in each state and how to navigate across states. HATEOAS is particularly useful at the Find layer, so we'll discuss it in more detail in chapter 8.

Thanks to such a simple, uniform interface and to the wide availability of HTTP clients and libraries, RESTful services can be reused and recombined easily, without requiring prior knowledge about the specifics of any resource, because those can be discovered and understood on the fly, as will be shown in section Principle 4: Hypermedia as the Engine of Application State. In the rest of this section, we describe in more detail how those four principles are put into practice with HTTP, and then we'll show how to use them when designing RESTful APIs for Things. Finally, for each of those principles, we'll propose a set of rules to help you build web-friendly APIs for your Things.

6.1.3 *Principle 1: addressable resources*

REST is a *resource-oriented architecture (ROA)*, where every component of a system or an application (a sensor, its sampling frequency, a variable, and so on) is called a *resource*. A resource is explicitly identified and can be individually addressed. With HTTP, this is done using the well-known *Uniform Resource Identifier (URI)* standard scheme defined in RFC 3986.[4] Using the exact same standard naming scheme as all other web resources allows you to seamlessly integrate Things and their properties into the web because their functions, data, or sensors can be linked to, shared, bookmarked, and used just like anything else on the web.

A URI is a sequence of characters that unambiguously identifies an abstract or physical resource. There are many possible types of URIs, but the ones we care about here are those used by HTTP to both identify and locate on a network a resource on the web, which is called the *URL (Uniform Resource Locator)* for that resource. From this, we generalize that any URL of resources in the Web of Things must follow the following syntax:

```
<scheme> ":" <authority><path> [ "?" query ] [ "#" fragment ]
```

- In the Web of Things, <scheme> is always either http or https.
- <authority> is a host with optional port or access credentials.

---

[4] See https://tools.ietf.org/html/rfc3986.

- <path> is any hierarchical path to the resource, which must start with /.
- Last come optional query parameters and/or fragments.

An important and powerful consequence of this is the addressability and portability of resource identifiers: they become unique (internet- or intranet-wide) and can be resolved by any HTTP library or tool (for example, a browser) and they can be bookmarked, exchanged in emails, used in instant messaging tools, encoded in QR codes, used in RFID tags, and broadcasted by beacons, as you'll see in in chapter 7.

The nerd corner: URL vs. URI

A URL is a type of URI that identifies a resource via a representation of its primary access mechanism—for example, its network location—rather than by some other attributes it may have. On the web, a URL is a URI beginning with the http:// scheme and resolvable through HTTP. Also, note that the root URL of a device doesn't require the device to be connected and accessible publicly over the web. The URL works equally well inside a local area network.

Every device on the Web of Things must have a root URL that corresponds to its network address, and here are a few examples of root URLs for various devices:

```
http://gateway.api.com/devices/TV/
http://kitchen-raspberry.device-lab.co.uk/
https://192.168.10.10:9002/
https://kitchen:3000/fridge/
```

In the Web of Things we can have several types of resources. Although some of them represent Things and their actual properties, others can be entirely virtual (a mashup, a data processing service, and so on):

```
# User with the ID No. 12
https://webofthings.org/users/12

# Sample No. 77654 from october 2009
https://webofthings.org/samples/2009/10/77654

# Device called lamp14
https://devices.webofthings.io/lamp14
```

Resources on the web are often organized in a hierarchy defined by a path. This hierarchical way of organizing and linking resources is particularly relevant in the physical world because it can be used to identify not only the resources of a Thing and how Things relate to each other but also the relationship between Things and their physical location. We can also identify collections of resources, which are resources themselves:

```
# a list of sensors on a device (all the sensors on device ID 24)
http://devices.webofthings.io/24/sensors

# a list of devices in an area (building 4)
http://192.168.44.12/building4/devices/
```

```
# a list of sensor readings
https://webofthings.org/devices/4554/samples
```

It's interesting to step back for a second and think about what these URLs mean in the grand scheme of internet protocols we looked at before. As shown in figure 6.2, there's a lot to learn from a Thing URL!

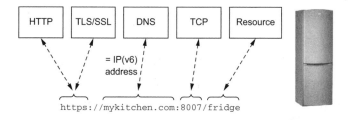

Figure 6.2 A Thing URL and the protocols each bit of the URL refers to. The first part specifies the protocol we use, here HTTP+TLS/SSL (HTTPS); then the domain is resolved by DNS to an IP address, the port is used by TCP to know what process to redirect to, and finally the REST resource is shown.

Let's make this more concrete by taking the example of our Raspberry Pi. You can see in figure 6.3 how the different resources are related to each other and how you can construct the URL for any element of your Pi. From this hierarchy, you can see first

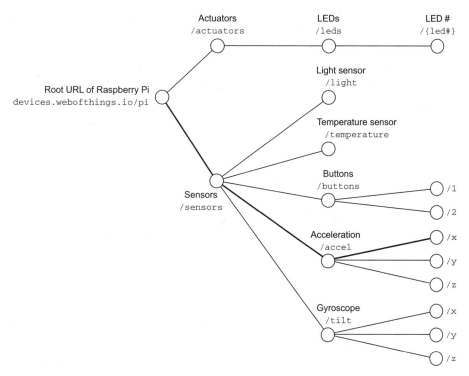

Figure 6.3 An example of URL structure of the various resources on a Raspberry Pi. The full URL of the X-axis reading of the acceleration sensor of the Pi highlighted in bold is http://devices.webofthings.io/pi/sensors/accel/x.

that any device must have a root URL (http://devices.webofthings.io/pi). Then, it has various sensors (light, temperature, and so on) and actuators (such as LEDs). The URL of each element is constructed by appending its name to the path of its predecessor in the hierarchy. For instance, the light sensor will have the following URL:

All the components of a device can be mapped into a similar resource tree, where each sensor, actuator, or system property of the device is assigned its own URL. This way, every component of your device fully blends into the web and becomes a distinct web resource that anyone on the web can address and interact with.

In chapter 8 we'll look at semantics and will propose a naming scheme for resources. For now, it's worth noting that there are no official rules about the semantics of resources' identifiers. Nevertheless, you should adhere to the following guidelines for all your resources:

- *Use descriptive names.* Because the resource names appear in the URLs, using names with some semantic value can be of great help to developers and users.
- *Don't use verbs in URLs.* Avoid using verbs—for example, lock or start—and use names where you can: /garagedoor/openDoor is bad; /garagedoor/status is much better. Verbs are for HTTP methods, not for URLs!
- *Use the plural form for aggregate resources.* If a Thing has several sensors, they should be accessible via a parent resource called /sensors. But you would use /accel for the accelerometer because there's only one such sensor, although it provides values for three dimensions.

DESIGN RULES #1—ADDRESSABLE RESOURCES

The first principle we looked at emphasizes that every element in your web Thing, service, or application becomes an addressable web resource. From this, we propose the following set of design rules to follow when implementing web Things:

- *Web Things must be an HTTP server.* Simply put, if you can't send an HTTP request to a device, then it's not part of the Web of Things. To ensure maximal compatibility, web Things must always support HTTP version 1.1—ideally v2 as well, but not only v2—because it's currently the most widely used version of the protocol. Thanks to the layered architecture of REST, the HTTP server doesn't need to be actually hosted on the device itself. We'll describe the various integration patterns in chapter 7.
- *Web Things should use secure* HTTP *connections (HTTPS).* When possible, a Thing should offer only secure connections. This is essential if the Thing is accessible from the outside world.

- *Web Things must have a root resource accessible via an HTTP URL.* A client application must have a URL to send the HTTP request to. The URL doesn't need to be externally accessible or public; it can be the IP address of a device on your LAN.
- *Web Things must expose their properties using a hierarchical structure.* Things must expose their properties using a hierarchical structure to facilitate discovery of their resources. A specific model and resource structure will be proposed in chapter 8.

6.1.4 *Principle 2: manipulation of resources through representations*

A challenge in computer-based communication is how to encode information so that it can be universally decoded and understood. On the web, *Multipurpose Internet Mail Extensions (MIME)* types have been introduced as standards to describe various data formats transmitted over the internet, such as images, video, or audio. The MIME type for an image encoded as PNG is expressed with image/png and an MP3 audio file with audio/mp3. The Internet Assigned Numbers Authority (IANA) maintains the list of the all the official MIME media types.[5]

A resource as defined previously is only a concept—an abstract idea of a thing—and not the thing itself. The tangible instance of a resource is called a *representation*, which is a standard encoding of a resource using a MIME type. Web browsers typically support quite a few representations, such as (HTML, GIF, and MPEG; or can use plugins or external applications to render them, such as PDF, vCards, or Flash).

HTTP defines a simple mechanism called *content negotiation* that allows clients to request a preferred data format they want to receive from a specific service. Using the Accept header, clients can specify the format of the representation they want to receive as a response. Likewise, servers specify the format of the data they return using the Content-Type header. To illustrate this principle, let's look at what happens when you enter the URL of the Pi in your browser. The following listing shows the request and the response messages.

Listing 6.1 A simple HTTP request and response

Request:

```
GET /pi
Host: devices.webofthings.io        Request headers
Accept: text/html
```

Response:

```
200 OK HTTP/1.1
Content-Type: text/html            Response headers

<html>
...                                ◀── Response body
```

---

[5] Online: http://www.iana.org/assignments/media-types/.

As you can see, the request, which is a simplified version of what your browser actually sends, contains the following header: `Accept: text/html`, which instructs the server to return an HTML representation of the Pi, the Pi root page you saw in chapter 2. By default, browsers request HTML files they can render and allow human users to interact with the resource. But in some cases, HTTP clients don't want HTML and would prefer a machine-readable format such as JSON OR XML—for example, when the client is an application and not a web browser. This can be done by using another value for the `Accept:` header, as shown in the next two listings.

Listing 6.2   Requesting an XML return payload using the `Accept` header

Request:

```
GET /pi
Host: devices.webofthings.io
Accept: application/xml
```

Response:

```
200 OK
Content-Type: application/xml

<device>
  <name>Pi</name>
  ...
</device>
```

Listing 6.3   Requesting a JSON return payload using the `Accept` header

Request:

```
GET /pi
Host: devices.webofthings.io
Accept: application/json
```

Response:

```
200 OK
Content-Type: application/json

{
  "name" : "Pi"
  ...
}
```

You can use various encoding formats to describe sensor data so that it can be understood and processed by other applications, and obviously not all servers will support all of them.

The `Accept:` header of an HTTP request can also contain not just one but a weighted list of media types the client understands—for example, application/

json;q=1, application/xml;q=0.5. The server then tries to serve the best possible format (as requested by the client using the parameter q as a quality factor) it knows about and specifies it in the Content-Type of the HTTP response. In our case the Pi can't offer XML and hence would return a JSON representation and set the HTTP header to Content-Type: application/json.

JSON AND BEYOND FOR THE WEB OF THINGS

The format we suggest for web Things is JSON. JSON is particularly suited for web applications because it's lightweight, portable, and self-contained and can be easily parsed in browsers using JavaScript, as well as by every programming language out there! It's a lighter alternative to XML because it requires less processing power and bandwidth and is also easier on the eyes of a developer. But even if JSON is lightweight, it isn't a binary format because it's still text. Alternative representation formats make sense when a more efficient format is needed—for instance, because of the memory limitations of a device or the fact that it runs on batteries. A number of formats can translate JSON into a binary format.

MessagePack[6] is one of our favorite alternatives. It's supported by libraries for all popular programming languages, including client-side JavaScript, Node.js, and C. MessagePack isn't an official MIME media type, but you can still ask for it in a content-negotiation process. A common way of dealing with unofficial MIME types is to use the x- extension, so if you want your client to ask for MessagePack, use Content-Type: application/x-msgpack.

DESIGN RULES #2–CONTENT NEGOTIATION

Based on what you've just learned, we propose the following rules to follow when implementing your web Things:

- *Web Things must support JSON as their default representation.* Your Thing can support as many representations as it wants, as long as it accepts at the minimum JSON in requests and can return a JSON representation when requested. Always use CamelCase; for example, lastValue instead of Last-Value or last_value, for object names in JSON payloads.

- *Web Things support UTF8 encoding for requests and responses.* A web Thing can support many other encoding formats (for example, it can describe the services it offers in Chinese or Russian), but it has to support UTF8 for any resource at the very least.

- *Web Things may offer an HTML interface/representation (UI).* In addition to a computer-friendly API, devices should also offer a human-friendly user interface that's accessible from a web browser. This is especially useful for consumer products to make it easy for users to access, control, and troubleshoot their devices.

---

[6] http://msgpack.org/

6.1.5 *Principle 3: self-descriptive messages*

REST emphasizes a uniform interface between components to reduce coupling between operations and their implementation. This requires every resource to support a standard, common set of operations with clearly defined semantics and behavior. HTTP defines a fixed set of operations that every resource can support, also called verbs or methods. The most commonly used among them are GET, POST, PUT, DELETE, and HEAD. Although it seems that you could do everything with just GET and POST, it's important to correctly use all four verbs to avoid bad surprises in your applications or introducing security risks.

Constraining operations to these methods is one of the keys to enabling loose coupling of services because clients only need to support mechanisms to handle these methods. In the Web of Things, these operations map rather naturally because Things usually offer quite simple and atomic services that can usually be reduced to the four basic CRUD operation types: create, read, update, and delete.

GET

GET is a read-only operation, as shown in listing 6.4. It's both a safe and idempotent operation. *Safe* means that invoking a GET doesn't change the state of the server at all (read-only). *Idempotent* means that no matter how many times you apply the operation, it won't have an effect on the resource state. Reading an HTML document with an HTTP GET request once or 10 times won't change the resource state.

> **Listing 6.4   GET to read a resource (the temperature sensor of our Pi)**

Request:

```
GET /pi/sensors/temperature/value
Accept: application/json
Host: devices.webofthings.io
```

Response:

```
200 OK HTTP/1.1
Content-Type: application/json

{"temperature" : 37}
```

In this listing, we want to know the latest value of the temperature sensor; therefore, this is a read-only operation. Because we specify the encoding to be JSON, the response payload contains a JSON message with the value 37. You might be thinking "37 what?" The answer to this will be provided in chapter 8, when we discuss semantics.

In some cases, an HTTP client might not need the full response payload, such as when the client wants only to verify if a resource is available or has been updated recently. In this situation, the client might use the HEAD verb instead of the GET, which does essentially the same thing but returns only the headers and not the payload. This is particularly useful when the request is sent to a resource-constrained device, where every byte counts.

POST

POST is both a non-idempotent and unsafe operation of HTTP, which means it not only will change the server status but also will have a different result each time it's called. POST should be used only to create a new instance of something that doesn't have its own URL yet, such as a new user in a system or bank account. The request in the following listing creates a message to be shown on the LCD display for 30 seconds.

Listing 6.5   POST to create a new resource

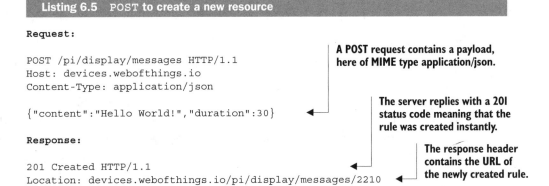

```
Request:

POST /pi/display/messages HTTP/1.1
Host: devices.webofthings.io
Content-Type: application/json

{"content":"Hello World!","duration":30}
```

A POST request contains a payload, here of MIME type application/json.

The server replies with a 201 status code meaning that the rule was created instantly.

```
Response:

201 Created HTTP/1.1
Location: devices.webofthings.io/pi/display/messages/2210
```

The response header contains the URL of the newly created rule.

The URL of the resource you've just created, the message to be displayed, should always be returned in the answer via the Location header. This URL now allows you to interact with the resource you just created, which you can update or delete later on.

As you'll see in the next chapters, in some cases the result of a POST might not be instantaneous. For example, when you'd like to control an actuator, such as to move the arm of a robot, it may take a few seconds or minutes for the operation to be executed. Likewise, if your request gets buffered (for example, when messages are queued instead of being displayed right away), your request will be treated asynchronously. For synchronous requests processed instantly, such as resource creation, you should return a 201 Created. For all asynchronous operations, you should return a 202 Accepted, which means that the resource will eventually be created.[7]

PUT

PUT is usually modeled as an idempotent but unsafe update method. You should use PUT to update something that already exists and has its own URL, such as when you change the name of a user or add a deposit to their bank account, but not to create a new resource. Unlike POST, it's idempotent because sending the same PUT message once or 10 times will have the same effect, whereas a POST would create 10 different resources. In the next example we change the color of LED 4 with its new RGB value as a parameter encoded as a JSON object.

---

[7]   RFC 2616, section 10.2.3: https://www.ietf.org/rfc/rfc2616.

Listing 6.6   PUT to update an existing resource (change the colors of the LEDs)

`Request:`

```
PUT /pi/actuators/leds/4 HTTP/1.1
Host: devices.webofthings.io
Content-Type: application/json

{"red" : 0, "green" : 128, "blue" : 128}
```

`Response:`

```
200 OK HTTP/1.1
```

You should use PUT only to change something that already exists, not to create a new resource—use POST for that. In the Web of Things, this means PUT should be used to change the status of something (LED 4), to open/close the door of the garage, and the like. As you'll see later, there's a thin line when choosing whether to send commands to a device via PUT or POST. As a rule of thumb, if the command will be executed immediately without being buffered, then you should use PUT. But if you need to buffer the requests, typically when several users will access the same resource at the same time (for example, the LCD screen of our Pi in chapter 2), then you're creating a resource (an item in a waitlist) that will change the status at a later stage, so you should use POST.

DELETE

DELETE is an idempotent, unsafe method that should be used only to delete a resource. Typically, you'd use this verb to permanently remove a resource from a Thing, such as when you delete a subscription to a topic or a rule on the device, as the next listing shows.

Listing 6.7   DELETE to remove an existing resource

`Request:`

```
DELETE /rules/24 HTTP/1.1
Host: devices.webofthings.io
```

`Response:`

```
200 OK HTTP/1.1
```

Because you use DELETE to remove a resource from an object, the URL of the resource you're sending the request to will no longer be accessible once the request has been executed. If you want to remove a device from a gateway, you should use a DELETE. But if you want to disable a sensor, it would be a state change; therefore you should use a PUT.

ERROR CODES

HTTP also offers a way of expressing errors and exceptions. The status of an HTTP response is represented by standardized status codes sent back as part of the header in the HTTP response message. There are several dozen codes, each of which has well-known meanings for HTTP clients; these codes and their meanings are listed in the specification of HTTP 1.1.[8]

In the Web of Things, these codes are valuable because they provide a lightweight but powerful way of notifying abnormal and successful request execution. As an example, a `POST` request on `/pi/sensors/humidity/` in the previous example will return a `405 Method Not Allowed` status code. The client understands from that status code that it can't send the `POST` verb to this resource, so there's no point in trying again in the future.

HTTP defines a list of standard status codes to be returned by the server upon reception of every request. The most commonly used are these:

- `200 Ok`—Returned upon successful completion of a request. Another common flavor of this code is `204 No Content`.
- `201 Created`—Returned when a new resource has been successfully created. The header `Location` contains the URI of the resource that has been created.
- `202 Accepted`—Returned for asynchronous operations when the request has been accepted but the resource not yet created.
- `401 Unauthorized`—Either the request requires user authentication or the authorization failed using the given credentials.
- `404 Not Found`—The requested resource or document has not been found on the server.
- `500 Internal Server Error`—The server encountered an error that prevented it from fulfilling the request.
- `501 Service Unavailable`—The server can't handle the request at this time due to maintenance or temporary overload.

CORS—ENABLING CLIENT-SIDE JAVASCRIPT TO ACCESS RESOURCES

Although accessing web resources from different origins located on various servers in any server-side application doesn't pose any problem, JavaScript applications running in web browsers can't easily access resources across origins for security reasons. What we mean by this is that a bit of client-side JavaScript code loaded from the domain apples.com won't be allowed by the browser to retrieve particular representations of resources from the domain oranges.com using particular verbs.

Generally speaking, browsers can do only simple cross-site requests, such as loading images from another site, but can't request other types of representations such as JSON or JavaScript. For example, the `PUT /pi/actuators/leds/4` request of listing 6.6 wouldn't be authorized by the browser. This security mechanism is known as the *same-origin policy* and is there to ensure that a site can't load any scripts from another domain. In particular, it ensures that a site can't misuse cookies to use your credentials to log onto another site. Let's look at an example to illustrate this. You log into facebook.com, which creates a cookie that your browser will send alongside each request to facebook.com. If the browser would allow cross-site requests, a script loaded from

---

[8] Section 10 of RFC2616.

apples.com could send a request to facebook.com using your Facebook cookie, thus pretending to be you on Facebook!

Clearly, this security mechanism is a good thing, but it also means that interacting with the API of web Things directly from JavaScript code in the browser is not allowed by default. Hold on! Then how did you manage to access http://devices.webofthings.io to talk to our WoT Pi in chapter 2? Fortunately for us, a new standard mechanism called *cross-origin resource sharing (CORS)*[9] has been developed and is well supported by most modern browsers and web servers.

When a script in the browser wants to make a cross-site request, it needs to include an `Origin` header containing the origin domain. The server replies with an `Access-Control-Allow-Origin` header that contains the list of allowed origin domains (or `*` to allow all origin domains). The next listing provides an example of CORS in action for the request and response corresponding to exercise 2.1 of chapter 2.

Listing 6.8   GET request to a resource using CORS

`Request:`

```
GET /pi/sensors/temperature HTTP/1.1
Host: devices.webofthings.io
Origin: http://localhost:8090
```

If you directly opened the file in your browser, the Origin would be null.

`Response:`

* means "allow all origins"; alternatively it could have replied with a domain like http://localhost:8090.

```
200 OK HTTP/1.1
Access-Control-Allow-Origin: "*"
```

When the browser receives the reply, it will check to see if the `Access-Control-Allow-Origin` corresponds to the origin, and if it does, it will allow the cross-site request.

For verbs other than `GET/HEAD`, or when using `POST` with representations other than `application/x-www-form-urlencoded`, `multipart/form-data`, or `text/plain`, an additional request called *preflight* is needed. A preflight request is an HTTP request with the verb `OPTIONS` that's used by a browser to ask the target server whether it's safe to send the cross-origin request. An example of a preflight request is shown in figure 6.4.

Although there are a number of additional options in the CORS specification, we won't go into more detail because that would require an entire book.[10] But this should provide you enough understanding of why it's important to know what CORS is and how to apply it in the WoT.

---

[9]   See http://enable-cors.org/ and http://www.w3.org/TR/cors/.

[10] There's a really good book on the subject called *CORS in Action* by Monsur Hossain (Manning Publications, 2014).

Preflight
OPTIONS
request

Allowed headers

Allowed verbs

Allowed origins

Client origin

The client wants
to send a POST
request with the
Content-Type
header

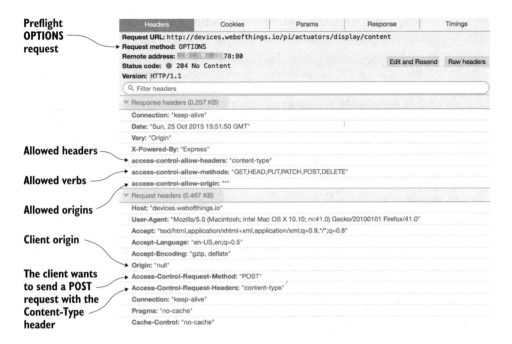

Headers	Cookies	Params	Response	Timings

Request URL: http://devices.webofthings.io/pi/actuators/display/content
Request method: OPTIONS
Remote address:　　　　　:78:80
Status code: ● 204 No Content　　　　　　　Edit and Resend　Raw headers
Version: HTTP/1.1

Filter headers

▼ Response headers (0.257 KB)

Connection: "keep-alive"
Date: "Sun, 25 Oct 2015 15:51:50 GMT"
Vary: "Origin"
X-Powered-By: "Express"
access-control-allow-headers: "content-type"
access-control-allow-methods: "GET,HEAD,PUT,PATCH,POST,DELETE"
access-control-allow-origin: "*"

▼ Request headers (0.467 KB)

Host: "devices.webofthings.io"
User-Agent: "Mozilla/5.0 (Macintosh; Intel Mac OS X 10.10; rv:41.0) Gecko/20100101 Firefox/41.0"
Accept: "text/html,application/xhtml+xml,application/xml;q=0.9,*/*;q=0.8"
Accept-Language: "en-US,en;q=0.5"
Accept-Encoding: "gzip, deflate"
Origin: "null"
Access-Control-Request-Method: "POST"
Access-Control-Request-Headers: "content-type"
Connection: "keep-alive"
Pragma: "no-cache"
Cache-Control: "no-cache"

Figure 6.4　A preflight request corresponding to exercise 5 of chapter 2. The JavaScript needs to send a `POST` to another server with a `Content-Type` header. The server replies with the allowed origin, methods, and headers. Because they match what the script wanted, the call will be authorized.

DESIGN RULES #3–SELF-DESCRIPTIVE MESSAGES

To summarize, we can define four simple design rules based on the self-descriptive messages principle of REST:

- *Web Things must support the GET, POST, PUT, and DELETE HTTP verbs.* To benefit from the advantages offered by RESTful architectures, the uniform interface constraint is instrumental. In a Web of Things context, GET is used to retrieve a sensor resource, such as a temperature reading; POST is used to create a new resource that will get a new URL—for example, to create a rule; PUT to update an actuator resource given its URL—for example, updating an LED; and DELETE to remove a resource, such as a rule.

- *Web Things must implement HTTP status codes 20x, 40x, 50x.* As mentioned, it's important to use HTTP verbs as intended. Of course, it's unrealistic for every web Thing to support all of them, but the device should at least support one of each group—for example, 200 if the request was successful; 400 for client errors, meaning the request was invalid; and 500 for server error, meaning the request was valid but couldn't be fulfilled because of the server.

- *Web Things must support a GET on their root URL.* Ideally, every resource should support the GET verb, so that clients can always retrieve its representations. But at the very least, the root URL must support GET so that a client is always able to access information about the device.

- *Web Things should support CORS.* Both simple and preflight CORS requests should be supported to allow direct access by applications in web browsers.

6.1.6   *Principle 4: Hypermedia as the Engine of Application State*

The fourth principle of REST is known as *Hypermedia as the Engine of Application State (HATEOAS).* Although this might be the worst acronym in the history of computer science, this principle isn't as bad as it sounds. It contains two subconcepts: hypermedia and application state.

HYPERMEDIA

This fourth principle is centered on the notion of *hypermedia,* the idea of using links as connections between related ideas. Hypermedia was proposed in the early 1960s by Ted Nelson as a generalization of hypertext that includes various media formats in addition to text, such as video, images, or sounds. Links have become highly popular thanks to web browsers yet are by no means limited to human use. For example, UUIDs used to identify RFID tags are also links. Consider the abridged HTML fragment in the following listing.

Listing 6.9   HTML representation of the Raspberry Pi root resource

```
<html><body>
  <h1 class="device-name">Raspberry Pi</h1>
  <a href="http://devices.webofthings.io/pi" class="self">Root URL</a> of
  this device.
  View the list of <a href="sensors/" class="wot-sensors">sensors</a> and <a
  href="actuators/" class="actuators">actuators</a> on this device.

  You can also view all <a href="links/" class="links">links</a> available on
  this device.

  Or read the <a href="about/" class="help">documentation</a>.
</body></html>
```

Based on this representation of the device, you can easily follow these links to retrieve additional information about the subresources of the device, such as where to find its documentation. Instead of describing the entire structure of a web Thing and all its subresources into a single document that has to be maintained separately, such a tree-based model maps conveniently to the Things' resource tree shown in figure 6.3 because every layer in the tree acts as a proxy that hides the layer underneath. Conveniently, this also enables us to retrieve and parse such a large file every time the structure changes because we only need to retrieve the resources we're interested in.

HATEOAS

The *application state*—the *AS* in HATEOAS—refers to a step in a process or workflow, similar to a state machine, and REST requires the *engine* of application state to be hypermedia driven.[11] Okay, great, but what does this mean? Simply that each possible state of your device or application needs to be a RESTful resource with its own unique URL, where any client can retrieve a representation of the current state and also the possible transitions to other states. Resource state, such as the status of an LED, is kept on the server and each request is answered with a representation of the current state and with the necessary information on how to change the resource state, such as turn off the LED or open the garage door.

In other words, applications can be stateful as long as client state is not kept on the server and state changes within an application happen by following links, which meets the self-contained-messages constraint. Links are very important in the Web of Things because they enable clients to *discover* related resources, either by browsing in the case of a human user following links on pages, or by crawling in the case of a machine.

In short, linking resources allows them to be dynamically discovered and rearranged without having to keep a sitemap somewhere. We'll explain this in detail and experiment with it in chapter 8, but for now let's use the example shown in listing 6.9. From the HTML representation you can see that there's a link to a resource called "links." As we'll detail later, you could send a GET request to that resource to retrieve a JSON object with all the resources offered by the device, which is shown in the next listing.

Listing 6.10　JSON representation of the "links" resource of a Raspberry Pi

```
"links":{
  "sensors": {
    "link": "http://devices.webofthings.io/pi/sensors/",
    "title": "List of Sensors"
  },
  "actions": {
    "link": " http://devices.webofthings.io/pi/actions/",
    "title": "List of actions"
  },
  "meta": {
    "link": "http://w3c.org/schemas/webofthings/",
    "title": "Metadata"
  },
  "self": {
    "link": " http://devices.webofthings.io/pi/",
    "title": "Self"
  },
  "help": {
    "link": "http://webofthings.io/docs/pi/",
    "title": "Documentation"
  },
  "ui": {
    "link": " http://devices.webofthings.io/pi/",
    "title": "User Interface"
  }
}
```

[11] http://roy.gbiv.com/untangled/2008/rest-apis-must-be-hypertext-driven

Thanks to this document, any HTTP client will be able to use the methods described in chapter 8 to find the various resources and services offered by this device, what they mean, and how to interact with them. When a client requests an HTML representation of that same resource, such as your browser, you'll see this same content but with actual links you can click on.

OPTIONS

In the previous section we looked at HTTP verbs. A less-known HTTP verb implemented by most HTTP servers is quite helpful in terms of discovering what can be performed on resources. The OPTIONS verb can be used to retrieve the list of operations permitted by a resource, as well as metadata about invocations on this resource. This is a very useful feature in a programmable Web of Things, because it allows applications to find out what operations are allowed by a resource at runtime, simply by knowing the resource's URL; see the next listing.

Listing 6.11   Using OPTIONS to retrieve the verbs supported by a resource

Request:

```
OPTIONS pi/sensors/humidity/ HTTP/1.1
Host: devices.webofthings.io
```

Response:

```
204 No Content HTTP/1.1
Content-Length: 0
Allow: GET, OPTIONS
Accept-Ranges: bytes
```

As an example, listing 6.10 is an OPTIONS request on pi/sensors/humidity/ returning GET, OPTIONS to tell the client that the resource supports only those two verbs. Combining links with the OPTIONS verb means that clients can discover the resources available for a Thing but also what operations can be performed on a newly discovered resource.

DESIGN RULES #4–HATEOAS

The fourth set of design rules emphasizes the ability to link resources logically so that clients can discover the resources of Things and the links between them, their operations, and parameters:

- *Web Things should support browsability with links.* This means that web Things should always offer links to the resources related to them in the resource hierarchy, particularly to parent and children resources. This enables discovering all the resources of a Thing by browsing the ones that can be used by both humans and applications (crawlers). Ideally, links should be present in all representations.

- *Web Things may support* OPTIONS *for each of its resources.* When possible, sending an HTTP request to any resource should return the list of verbs supported by that resource. This is a useful piece of the HATEOAS puzzle because clients can automatically determine what they can do with a resource just by knowing its URL.

6.1.7 *Summary—web Things design process*

In this section, we've shown that APIs for Things can be built by reusing patterns from the architecture of the web. Instead of using the web solely as a transport protocol, we make Things an integral part of the web and its infrastructure by using HTTP for what it was intended: as an Application layer protocol.

FIVE-STEP DESIGN PROCESS FOR WEB THINGS APIS

We described how a RESTful architecture makes it possible to use HTTP as a universal protocol for web-connected devices. We described the process of web-enabling Things, which are summarized in the five main steps of the web Things design process:

1 *Integration strategy*—Choose a pattern to integrate Things to the internet and the web, either directly or through a proxy or gateway. This will be covered in chapter 7, so we'll skip this step for now.

2 *Resource design*—Identify the functionality or services of a Thing and organize the hierarchy of these services. This is where we apply design rule #1: addressable resources.

3 *Representation design*—Decide which representations will be served for each resource. The right representation will be selected by the clients, thanks to design rule #2: content negotiation.

4 *Interface design*—Decide which commands are possible for each service, along with which error codes. Here we apply design rule #3: self-descriptive messages.

5 *Resource linking design*—Decide how the different resources are linked to each other and especially how to expose those resources and links, along with the operations and parameters they can use. In this final step we use design rule #4: Hypermedia as the Engine of Application State.

6.2 *Beyond REST: the real-time Web of Things*

Until now, our interface has offered access only through HTTP. With this protocol, clients always initiate the communication with a server by sending requests and expecting a response in return; this is known as *request-response* communication.

In the Web of Things this pattern works well when the clients only need to send requests to a Thing. This is the case, for example, when a mobile application wants to retrieve the value of a sensor reading or when a web application is used to unlock a door. Unfortunately, the request-response model is insufficient for a number of IoT use cases. More precisely, it doesn't match event-driven use cases where events must be communicated (pushed) to the clients as they happen. In this section we look at this issue in more detail and propose how to extend the request-response model of HTTP by using another web-friendly application protocol: WebSocket!

6.2.1   *The WoT needs events!*

A client-initiated model isn't practical for applications where notifications need to be sent asynchronously by a device to clients as soon as they're produced. For example, a security camera or smoke alarm must be able to send an alert immediately when any anomaly has been detected and shouldn't have to wait a until a client asks for this information. Consider the PIR sensor that we added to our Pi in chapter 4. As a recap, a PIR sensor can detect when a person passes by. Using a request-response pattern with REST over HTTP isn't efficient because we have to constantly poll the Pi for the latest value of the PIR sensor. Not only is this inefficient, but we might also miss an intruder if we don't poll at the right moment. As shown in figure 6.5, *polling* is one way of circumventing the problem.

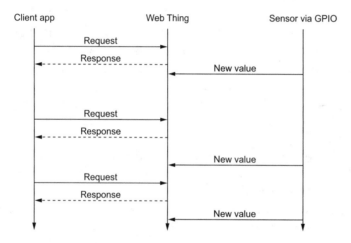

Figure 6.5   Basic polling: a client app sends requests to a web Thing at regular intervals. The results the client app gets are not synchronized with new values available from the sensor.

The idea is that clients can request updates periodically from a web Thing by sending a GET request to the Thing on a regular basis. Although near real-time behavior can be simulated by a client sending the same request continuously—for example, every second—this approach is inefficient for most applications because it consumes unnecessary bandwidth and processor time. Most of the requests will end up with empty responses (304 Not Modified) or with the same response as long as the value observed remains unchanged. This is suboptimal for two reasons. First, it generates a great number of HTTP calls, and a large part of these calls are void. Because reducing the number of HTTP calls to the minimum is key in scaling web applications, this model doesn't scale well when the number of clients increases. Second, a large amount of HTTP calls is a problem for battery-powered devices where only strictly necessary data should be sent.

6.2.2 *Publish/subscribe*

Interactive and reactive applications for the Web of Things require a simple and flexible mechanism to send events or receive notifications. What's really needed on top of the request-response pattern is a model called publish/subscribe (*pub/sub*) that allows further decoupling between data consumers (*subscribers*) and producers (*publishers*). Publishers send messages to a central server, called a *broker*, that handles the routing and distribution of the messages to the various subscribers, depending on the type or content of messages. The simplest analogy is a chat room—some are public, and some are private. Sometimes you chat with only one person, and sometimes thousands. For devices, it would be the same thing. A publisher can send notifications into a *topic* (think chat room). Interested consumers can subscribe to one or several channels to receive all the notifications pushed by producers in that channel. Topics in pub/sub protocols are usually specified as arbitrary strings so it's easy for us to map the REST resources of our web Things to pub/sub topics.

Let's look at a practical example of how this would work for our Pi. As shown in figure 6.6, a number of clients subscribe to a topic managed by a broker. Whenever a client wants to update a topic, it sends a message to the broker—that is, it publishes the message via the broker. The broker in turn sends it to all the topic's subscribers. Note that the broker could be the Thing itself or an external broker somewhere on the web. In the left side of figure 6.6, Client A subscribes to the following topic: http://devices.webofthings.io/pi/sensors/temperature.

We'll shorten the topic here to `/temperature` for readability. Clients B and C subscribe to `/pir` via the broker. The right part of figure 6.6 shows the publication mechanism. Someone passed by the sensor, so the Thing generates a PIR sensor update

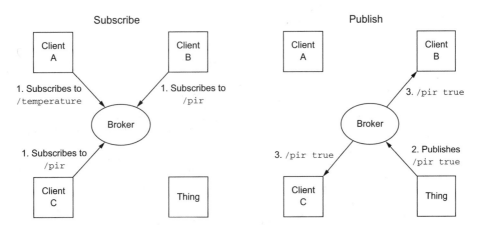

Figure 6.6 Left: subscription pattern in a pub/sub. Client A subscribes to temperature updates, clients B and C to PIR updates. They all subscribe via the broker, which maintains a list of who has subscribed to what topic. Right: publication pattern. An intruder is detected, so the Thing publishes a PIR update to the broker. The broker delivers the update to clients B and C.

notification to inform all the listeners. The broker knows which clients are currently listening for the /pir topic, so it immediately sends this update to clients B and C.

Now that we have the pattern we needed on top of request-response interactions, the question is how to implement it with technologies supported on the web—and hopefully also by common web browsers. Speaking in terms of layers, we need a web application protocol that can support the implementation of a pub/sub system. There are a number of candidates to achieve that, and we'll look at three techniques: webhooks, Comet, and WebSockets.

6.2.3   *Webhooks—HTTP callbacks*

The simplest way to implement a publish-subscribe system over HTTP without breaking the REST model is to treat every entity as both a client and a server. This way, both web Things and web applications can act as HTTP clients by initiating requests to other servers, and they can host a server that can respond to other requests at the same time. This pattern is called *webhooks* or *HTTP callbacks* and has become popular on the web for enabling different servers to talk to each other. For example, this is the mechanism used by PayPal to confirm to eBay—or any other shopping site—that your payment has been accepted.

The implementation of this model is fairly simple. All we need is to implement a REST API on both the Thing and on the client, which then becomes a server as well. This means that when the Thing has an update, it POSTs it via HTTP to the client, as shown in figure 6.7. This implies that the client must implement an HTTP server with a REST API that can be accessed by the Thing—for example, by having a public URL. The detail of the necessary calls is shown in the following listing.

Listing 6.12   Subscription via a webhook

```
Client Request:

POST /pi/sensors/humidity/subs HTTP/1.1
Host: devices.webofthings.io
Content-Type: application/json

{"callback" : "https://url-of-client-a.com/pubs"}


Thing Response:

201 Created HTTP/1.1
Content-Type: application/json
Location: devices.webofthings.io/pi/sensors/humidity/subs/1234

{"humidity": 37}
```

The client subscribes via a POST request on the Thing to the humidity events.

The client provides a callback URL that will be used by the Thing to push the event. Note that sometimes the Referer header is used to specify the callback, but because the header was intended for a very different purpose, we recommend not using it in another way than intended.

The Thing responds with a reference to the newly created subscription.

As a good practice, the Thing also sends the current humidity value to spare another request.

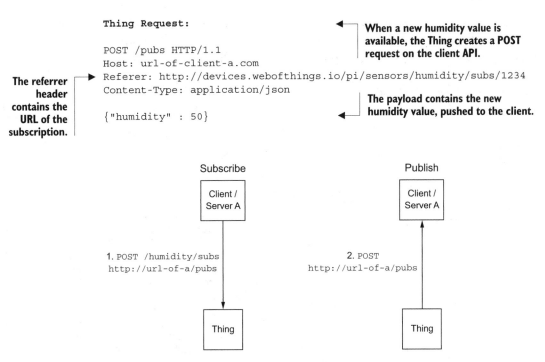

Thing Request:

```
POST /pubs HTTP/1.1
Host: url-of-client-a.com
Referer: http://devices.webofthings.io/pi/sensors/humidity/subs/1234
Content-Type: application/json

{"humidity" : 50}
```

When a new humidity value is available, the Thing creates a POST request on the client API.

The referrer header contains the URL of the subscription.

The payload contains the new humidity value, pushed to the client.

Subscribe

Client / Server A

1. POST /humidity/subs
http://url-of-a/pubs

Thing

Publish

Client / Server A

2. POST
http://url-of-a/pubs

Thing

Figure 6.7   A webhook mechanism implemented between a Thing and a client. The client subscribes to the humidity resource via a POST on the Thing API. The Thing then informs the server of humidity changes via a POST on the client API.

Webhooks are a conceptually simple way to implement bidirectional communication between clients and servers by turning everything into a server. As you've just seen, webhooks can also be used to implement a pub/sub for the Web of Things. But webhooks have one big drawback: because they need the subscriber to have an HTTP server to push the notification, this works only when the subscriber has a publicly accessible URL or IP address. In the real world this is very limiting because it will rarely be the case outside server-to-server (or Thing-to-Thing!) communication. Consider the case of a JavaScript application running in your browser that wants to get notifications from a Thing: even if there was a hacky way for the application to start an HTTP server inside your web browser,[12] it's unlikely that the firewall of your network would allow incoming requests from the internet to your machine.

6.2.4   Comet—hacking HTTP for a real-time web

The limitations of webhooks when it comes to browser applications led to a number of workarounds to deal with the problem of real-time events on the web. *Comet* is an

---

[12] Note that this can be done by writing a custom plugin for your browser that will allow it to interact with Things. But using such non-standard extensions is a no-go in the real world because it severely limits the vision of a seamlessly accessible Web of Things.

umbrella term that refers to a range of techniques for circumventing the limitations of HTTP polling and webhooks by introducing event-based communication over HTTP. This model enables web servers to push data back to the browser without the client requesting it explicitly. Since browsers were initially not designed with server-sent events in mind, web application developers have exploited several specification loop-holes to implement Comet-like behavior, each with different benefits and drawbacks.

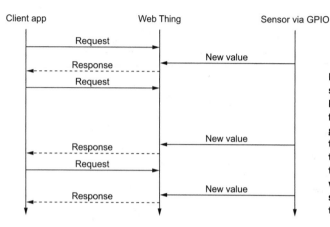

Figure 6.8   Long polling: a client sends a request, which is kept on hold until an event is received from the sensor, at which point it gets forwarded by the web Thing to the client as the response of their initial request. After that, they reinitiate a new request, which will be kept open in the same way until a new value from the sensor is retrieved.

Among them is a technique called *long polling*, illustrated in figure 6.8. With long poll-ing, a client sends a standard HTTP request to the server, but instead of receiving the response right away, the server holds the request until an event is received from the sensor, which is then injected into the response returned to the client's request that was held idle. As soon as the client receives the response, it immediately sends a new request for an update, which will be held until the next update comes from the sensor, and so on. The latency for events to reach the client is thus minimized. But the client must be put on hold with an open HTTP request that's waiting for an answer and must send a request after each response. This increases the load on the server and forces the clients to send unnecessary messages.

6.2.5   *WebSockets*

Although workarounds like Comet helped move things forward, they are patches, not solutions. Comet and other long polling solutions are inefficient. Webhooks are impractical in the case of web browsers.

But not all hope is lost! A more recent, true web protocol for push communica-tions has emerged: WebSocket! WebSocket[13] is part of the HTML5 specification. The increasing support for HTML5 in most recent web and mobile web browsers means WebSocket is becoming ubiquitously available to all web apps. Just like for REST over

---

[13] Reference: http://www.websocket.org/.

HTTP, this ubiquitous support makes WebSocket a fairly good candidate to implement pub/sub support in the Web of Things.

In chapter 2, you experimented with building a WebSockets client and were exposed to the simple client API of WebSockets giving access to the protocol directly via JavaScript running in your browser. Here, we'll focus in more detail on the WebSockets protocol and how to use it to implement a pub/sub mechanism for web Things.

WEBSOCKET PROTOCOL HANDSHAKE

WebSockets enables a full-duplex communication channel over a single TCP connection. In plain English, this means that it creates a permanent link between the client and the server that both the client and the server can use to send messages to each other. Unlike techniques we've seen before, such as Comet, WebSocket is standard and opens a TCP socket. This means it doesn't need to encapsulate custom, non-web content in HTTP messages or keep the connection artificially alive as is needed with Comet implementations.

A WebSocket connection is initialized, creating a *handshake*, as networking nerds would put it, in three steps, as shown in figure 6.9. The first step is to send an HTTP call to the server with a special header asking for the protocol to be upgraded to WebSockets. If the web server supports WebSockets, it will reply with a `101 Switching Protocols` status code, acknowledging the opening of a full-duplex TCP socket.

Let's look at a concrete example using the PIR sensor we set up in chapter 4, which runs on our Pi at http://devices.webofthings.io/pi/sensors/pir. If you access this address with your browser,

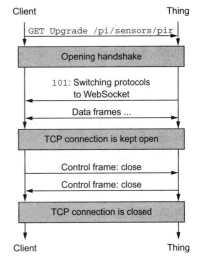

Figure 6.9 **A WebSockets protocol handshake. First, the connection is opened via a GET request for a protocol upgrade. Then the persistent TCP connection is opened, and the client and server can exchange data frames. One of the parties (server or client) eventually sends a control frame to signal that the communication is over and can be closed.**

you'll get the HTML representation of the PIR sensor. Similarly, if you access it and ask for it using the `Content-Type: application/json` header shown previously, you'll get the value of the PIR sensor in JSON; this is REST over HTTP, implemented as you've seen before. Now, using the same resource, you can also ask for WebSockets content by asking for a protocol upgrade, as shown in the next listing.

Listing 6.13 Client request in a WebSockets handshake

```
GET /pi/sensors/pir HTTP/1.1
Origin: http://localhost:63342
Host: devices.webofthings.io
```

◀—— **Begin by specifying the URL (host + resource) you want to access via WebSockets; note that this is an HTTP call.**
◀—— **The host + resource form the subscription topic.**

The browser appends the Origin header because WebSockets requests are subject to the same-origin policy (see CORS, section 6.1.5)

```
Upgrade: websocket
Connection: Upgrade
[...]
```

Special headers asking to upgrade the protocol to "websocket"

What's really interesting here is that the call to upgrade the protocol is issued via HTTP. This means that a client wanting real-time data can always ask for a REST resource to be delivered via WebSockets and fall back to pure HTTP in case the server doesn't support WebSockets. In the case of our `devices.webofthings.io` server, it does support WebSockets and will reply with an acknowledgement of the protocol upgrade, as shown in the following listing.

Listing 6.14   Server response in a WebSockets handshake

```
HTTP/1.1 101 Switching Protocols
Connection: Upgrade
[...]
Upgrade: websocket
Access-Control-Allow-Origin: http://localhost:63342
```

The connection was upgraded to a WebSockets connection.

The server replies with status code 101, meaning that it's okay to switch the protocol.

The cross-origin connection (CORS) for localhost:63342 is authorized.

The full handshake between the client and the server offering values for the PIR sensor via WebSockets is shown in figure 6.10.

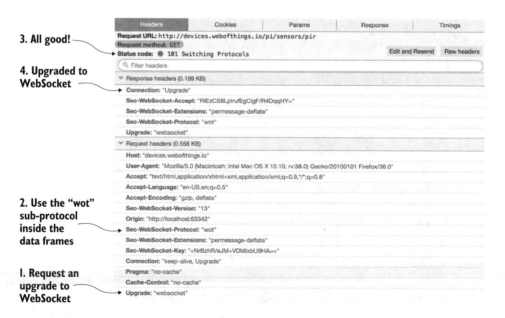

3. All good!

4. Upgraded to WebSocket

2. Use the "wot" sub-protocol inside the data frames

1. Request an upgrade to WebSocket

Figure 6.10   A WebSocket protocol handshake in action as seen in the Network tool of Firefox. The client requests a protocol upgrade that the server accepts. From then on, the client and the server can send each other messages over the TCP connection, which will be kept open until the client or server decides to close it.

Once the initial handshake takes place, the client and the server will be able to send messages back and forth over the open TCP connection; these messages are not HTTP messages but WebSockets data frames. Text and binary data frames can be sent in either direction and simultaneously. The overhead of each WebSockets data frame is 2 bytes, which is small compared to the 871-byte overhead of an HTTP message meta-data (headers and the like). Add to this the overhead of IP, TCP, and TLS (see chapter 9), and you have an additional 60–100 bytes per message! This makes WebSockets communication a lot less bandwidth-consuming than HTTP.

The syntax and semantics of the messages they exchange are open, but the Sec-WebSocket-Protocol request header can be used to specify a protocol to use inside the data frames (in this example, we use "wot," which is a fictive sub-protocol). The registered sub-protocols are managed by the Internet Assigned Numbers Authority (IANA).[14]

WEBSOCKETS FOR THE WOT

What's really interesting with WebSockets for the Web of Things is that they use standard internet and web technologies. Because they open a TCP connection over port 80, WebSockets aren't blocked by firewalls and can traverse proxies. Then, because they work in the browser and are bootstrapped via HTTP, they let us use a lot of the principles we looked at when exploring HTTP and REST. First, the hierarchical structure of Things and their resources as URLs can be reused as-is for WebSockets. As you saw in listing 6.14, we can subscribe to events for a Thing's resource by using its corresponding URL and asking for a protocol upgrade to WebSockets. Moreover, WebSockets do not dictate the format of messages that are sent back and forth. This means we can happily use JSON and give messages the structure and semantics we'll work on in chapter 8.

Moreover, because WebSockets consist of an initial handshake followed by basic message framing layered over TCP, they can be directly implemented on many platforms supporting TCP/IP—not just web browsers. They can also be used to wrap several other internet-compatible protocols to make them web-compatible. One example is MQTT, a well-known pub/sub protocol for the IoT that can be integrated to the web of browsers via WebSockets. You'll see that in more detail in the next chapter.

The permanent link created by WebSocket communication is interesting in an Internet of Things context, especially when considering applications wanting to observe—or subscribe to—real-world properties such as environmental sensors. Finally, WebSockets offer all of these benefits with significantly reduced bandwidth consumption when compared to HTTP polling, for example. The drawback, however, is that keeping a TCP connection permanently open can lead to an increase in battery consumption and is harder to scale than HTTP on the server side.

---

[14] http://www.iana.org/assignments/websocket/websocket.xml

6.2.6   *The future: from HTTP/1.1 to HTTP/2*

When used correctly, HTTP/1.1 is a great protocol to build web services, as you saw in this chapter. But it dates back to 1999. Remember that time? Back then, we were using Windows 95 and using wired phones to call each other, and the IoT term had just been coined! We also mainly used HTTP to display hit counters, sitemaps, and animated "under construction" gifs, but not to display much real-time data and certainly not to interact with devices.

Clearly, the web has evolved tremendously since then, and the need for scalability, performance, real-time messaging, and security has increased significantly. As a result, the internet is about to fully embrace a revolution called IPv6 (see chapter 5) and another called HTTP/2.[15] The new protocol wasn't designed specifically for the IoT, but the creators of this new protocol clearly took into account some of the needs of the IoT. HTTP/2 focuses on a number of improvements over HTTP/1.1 and can easily run on your Pi![16]

PERFORMANCE IMPROVEMENTS

This new version of HTTP allows multiplexing responses—that is, sending responses in parallel. This fixes the head-of-line blocking problem of HTTP/1.x where only one request can be outstanding on a TCP/IP connection at a time[17]. Furthermore, it fosters clients and servers to use a single TCP connection on which requests and responses are sent in streams.

This is an interesting feature for the WoT because it leads to a more efficient use of connections, which reduces the overhead of HTTP. It also leads to faster transmissions and hence potential savings in terms of battery power required to communicate.[18]

MORE EFFICIENT FORMATS

HTTP/2 also introduces compressed headers using an efficient and low-memory compression format,[19] unlike GZIP, the most common compression format used on top of HTTP. This reduces the size of each HTTP request and response. In addition, whereas HTTP/1.1 was an ASCII protocol—that is, a protocol transmitting ASCII characters—HTTP/2 uses binary framing, meaning that it transmits binary streams of data. Binary protocols are more efficient to parse and more compact.

All of this is particularly interesting for the "Web of resource-limited Things" because it means the size of packets is significantly smaller, allowing for devices with limited RAM to happily deal with HTTP/2.

---

[15] http://http2.github.io

[16] There are already several implementations of HTTP/2 for Node.js. Should you want to experiment with HTTP/2 on your Pi, you should try the `node-http2` module available on https://github.com/molnarg/node-http2.

[17] In HTTP/1.1 pipelining was proposed to fix this problem but it did not completely address the problem and is hard to deploy; see https://devcentral.f5.com/articles/http-pipelining-a-security-risk-without-real-performance-benefits.

[18] Akamai developed a simple page that lets you experiment with these improvements: https://http2.akamai.com/demo.

[19] Called HPACK: Header Compression for HTTP/2. See: https://datatracker.ietf.org/doc/rfc7541/.

SERVER PUSH

Finally, HTTP/2 introduces the notion of *server push*. Concretely, this means that the server can provide content to clients without having to wait for them to send a request. In the long run, widespread adoption of server push over HTTP/2 might even remove the need for an additional protocol for push like WebSocket or webhooks.

HTTP/2 AND THE WEB OF THINGS

This overview of the features of HTTP/2 and what they mean for the Web of Things is by no means complete, but it shows that the future of the web will make an even better Web of Things. Interestingly enough, you won't have to change your approach very much: the implementation of HTTP will change, but not the API you build on top of it, because the semantics of HTTP remain unchanged with HTTP/2. Thus, anything you'll learn in the reminder of this book will be applicable to HTTP/2 as well!

The HTTP/2 specification was officially accepted in February 2015, and several browsers such as Chrome, Firefox, and Opera have started supporting it. This means that the standard is about to be globally deployed and will soon make the Web of Things a lot more efficient!

6.3 Summary

- When applied correctly, the REST architecture is an excellent substrate on which to create large-scale and flexible distributed systems.
- REST APIs are interesting and easily applicable to enable access to data and services of physical objects and other devices.
- Various mechanisms, such as content negotiation and caching of Hypermedia as the Engine of Application State (HATEOAS), can help in creating great APIs for Things.
- A five-step design process (integration strategy, resource design, representation design, interface design, and resource linking) allows anyone to create a meaningful REST API for Things based on industry best practices.
- The latest developments in the real-time web, such as WebSockets, allow creating highly scalable, distributed, and heterogeneous real-time data processing applications. Devices that speak directly to the web can easily use web-based push messaging to stream their sensor data efficiently.
- HTTP/2 will bring a number of interesting optimizations for Things, such as multiplexing and compression.

You've had an in-depth look at REST and HTTP, but if you're hungry for more you might want to have a look at the very good *RESTful Web Services* by Leonard Richardson and Sam Ruby (O'Reilly Media, 2007)[20] or browse to the WoT Publications page,[21] where you'll find a number of resources about using REST for real-world devices.

---

[20] http://shop.oreilly.com/product/9780596529260.do
[21] http://webofthings.org/publications/

After being introduced to so much theory about REST, HTTP, and WebSockets, you might be wondering how to actually implement all of this on your Things. Get ready— this is what the next chapter will focus on. You'll learn how to implement the patterns you've learned about in this chapter so that you can access any device, regardless of whether it's internet-connected or not. Get your coding fingers ready; in the next chapter you'll need them a lot more!

Implementing web Things

7

This chapter covers

- Exploring the three possible patterns to implement web Things
- Giving access to sensors and actuators via web protocols
- Building REST and WebSockets APIs on your Pi with Node.js and Express
- Building CoAP devices and connecting them to the web
- Using MQTT on your Pi to connect to the EVRYTHNG API

In the previous chapter, we focused on how to design a clean web API for physical Things. This chapter builds on the principles you learned and describes how to actually implement those APIs for real Things.

The next sections detail the three different ways to implement a web Thing API so it deals with the implementation strategy. Here, we focus on the integration patterns of Things to the web, answering the question, "Where do we actually implement the API of the Thing to integrate it to the web?" This question is important because not all Things are equal! As you saw in chapter 5, some Things can have internet access and implement web protocols natively. But for other Things that are more computationally or power-constrained, web protocols might be challenging.

7.1   *Connecting devices to the web*

The most straightforward integration pattern is the *direct integration pattern*. It can be used for devices that support HTTP and TCP/IP and can therefore expose a web API directly. This pattern is particularly useful when a device can directly connect to the internet; for example, it uses Wi-Fi or Ethernet. Second, we explore the *gateway integration pattern*, where resource-constrained devices can use non-web protocols to talk to a more powerful device (the gateway), which then exposes a REST API for those non-web devices. This pattern is particularly useful for devices that can't connect directly to the internet; for example, they support only Bluetooth or ZigBee or they have limited resources and can't serve HTTP requests directly. Third, the *cloud integration pattern* allows a powerful and scalable web platform to act as a gateway. This is useful for any device that can connect to a cloud server over the internet, regardless of whether it uses HTTP or not, and that needs more capability than it would be able to offer alone.

Choosing one of these patterns is the first step in the web Things design process presented in chapter 6. After that, we can apply steps 2–4 of the design process. Step 5 will be covered in greater detail in chapter 8:

1   *Integration strategy*—Choose a pattern to integrate Things to the internet and the web. The patterns are presented in this chapter.
2   *Resource design*—Identify the functionality or services of a Thing, and organize the hierarchy of these services.
3   *Representation design*—Decide which representations will be served for each resource.
4   *Interface design*—Decide which commands are possible for each service, along with which error codes.
5   *Resource linking design*—Decide how the different resources are linked to each other.

The reference WoT server—webofthings.js

Over the next few chapters, you'll learn how to implement a full-featured Web of Things server that allows connecting any device to the web based on the WoT architecture and concepts presented throughout this book. Each chapter will extend the code written in the previous one, so you'll get the most out of this book by reading the next chapters in order. By doing so, at the end of the book you will have built from scratch a complete, extensible, and secure framework to implement web Things.

If you can't wait, you could also download the latest version of the reference implementation of the Web of Things: webofthings.js. You can find it on our GitHub[a] or directly

---

[a] https://github.com/webofthings/webofthings.js

7.2 Direct integration pattern—REST on devices

The first and easiest way to implement a web Thing API is directly on a Thing, as shown in figure 7.1. This requires the Thing to be accessible via internet protocols (TCP/IP) and be able to host an HTTP server directly. Crazy idea, we hear you say? Well, web servers aren't that big and can easily fit on the smallest devices out there. Some of the smallest HTTP servers can work with less than 50 bytes of RAM,[1] TCP/IP stack included, which makes it possible for even tiny and cheap 8-bit devices to speak HTTP. This also means that your Pi—or any other Linux device you use—can definitely implement a web server to provide access to its resources through a REST API.

Although it's possible to implement web protocols on the vast majority of embedded devices, the direct integration pattern is the perfect choice when the device isn't battery powered and when direct access from clients such as mobile web apps is required. A good example is home automation, where power is usually available and

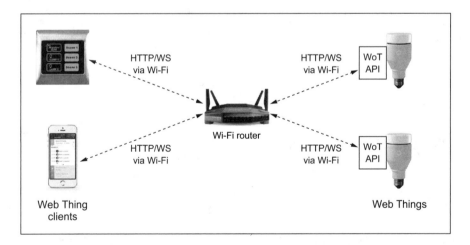

Figure 7.1 Direct integration pattern. In this pattern the web Things are Wi-Fi–connected lamps that run an embedded HTTP server and therefore offer a Web of Things API directly. This allows web Thing clients, such as mobile applications or other web Things, to communicate with the lamps directly over HTTP. Image used with permission from http://model.webofthings.io.

---

[1] MiniWeb is an example of an extremely small web server; see http://miniweb.sourceforge.net/.

low-latency local interactions are important—for instance, turning lights on/off. In the rest of this section, we'll show how to implement a WoT server directly on your Pi so that it can directly speak web protocols and join the Web of Things club.

7.2.1   Creating a WoT server

Let's begin by setting up a web server on your Pi. Node.js is primarily meant for building web applications, so you could easily build one from scratch just as you did in chapter 3. But because we're switching gears and want to implement a full-blown REST API, a large number of Node.js frameworks can help us.[2] For simplicity's sake, we'll use the most popular: Express.[3]

The architecture of the server you'll build is shown in figure 7.2. It revolves around a central model that plugins can update and observe. Furthermore, all the sensors and actuators are available as web resources thanks to the use of the Express framework.

We'll deploy this code on the Pi, but if you don't yet own a Pi, don't worry; with a few exceptions, you'll be able to run all the examples in this chapter on your computer. But it'll be more fun on a Pi. Just saying![4]

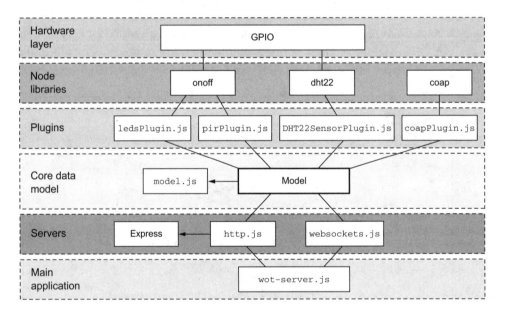

Figure 7.2   The components architecture of our WoT server: The servers use the Express framework. The rest of the system is built around a model that plugins can observe and change. The plugins are built on other Node libraries, providing access to physical resources via GPIOs.

---

[2] A number of the most popular web/REST frameworks for Node.js are listed here: http://nodeframework.com/.

[3] http://expressjs.com/

[4] Check out the special deals offered by our partners: http://book.webofthings.io.

EXPRESS: A NODE.JS WEB FRAMEWORK

Express is much more than a web server; it's a complete framework that handles pretty much everything modern web applications need, from RESTful APIs to HTML and CSS templating engines, database connectors, cookie management, and even social network integration. Express also has a large developer community and a variety of plugins.

Although Express will run smoothly on the Pi and most other Linux devices, it's worth pointing out that Express isn't the lightest way to implement web APIs for IoT devices. But as you'll see on numerous occasions, such a flexible framework allows us to quickly extend our web Thing APIs and implement the various patterns we'll encounter.

We'll now show how to create a WoT server based on Express.[5] The project's structure is shown in the following listing. You could reproduce this structure and install Express via NPM. Alternatively, you could clone the project from the book's GitHub repository,[6] which is available in the folder chapter7-implementation/part1-2-direct-gateway/.

Listing 7.1   WoT server for Pi project directory structure

```
wot-pi
├─── middleware
│    └─── converter.js
├─── plugins
│    ├─── external
│    │    └─── coapPlugin.js
│    └─── internal
│         ├─── DHT22SensorPlugin.js
│         ├─── ledsPlugin.js
│         └─── pirPlugin.js
├─── public
│    └─── websocketsClient.html
├─── resources
│    ├─── model.js
│    └─── resources.json
├─── routes
│    ├─── actuators.js
│    ├─── sensors.js
│    └─── things.js
├─── servers
│    ├─── coap.js
│    ├─── http.js
│    └─── websockets.js
├─── utils
│    └─── utils.js
├─── package.json
└─── wot-server.js
```

---

[5] Although you can certainly run these commands directly on the Pi, it's easier and more practical to develop applications on your laptop or desktop computer and then pull the code via Git on the Pi, as explained in chapter 4.

[6] See http://book.webofthings.io.

7.2.2   *Resource design*

You now have all the elements in place to implement your API, so let's start with the first step of our process: the *resource design*. You first need to consider the physical resources on your device and map them into REST resources. Starting from the Pi you configured in chapter 4, your device should have at least an LED, a passive infrared (PIR) sensor and possibly a temperature sensor, and a humidity sensor. If you don't have all these sensors, don't worry. We'll show you how to simulate them as well! These sensors and actuators can be mapped into the resource tree shown in figure 7.3.

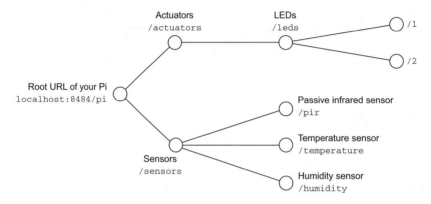

Figure 7.3   The resource tree of your Pi with a number of sensors and actuators and their hierarchy. Each resource gets a URL formed by following the path to this resource. As an example, the URL of the passive infrared sensor would be http://localhost:8484/pi/sensors/pir.

STEP 1: CREATE THE RESOURCE MODEL

You can now map this tree into a JSON file that your application will use to expose your desired URL structure. Create or open the resources/resources.json file that contains the object shown in the next listing.

Listing 7.2   /resources/resources.json: JSON model of the Pi resources

```
{
  "pi": {
    "name": "WoT Pi",
    "description": "A simple WoT-connected Raspberry PI for the WoT book.",
    "port": 8484,
    "sensors": {
      "temperature": {
        "name": "Temperature Sensor",
        "description": "An ambient temperature sensor.",
        "unit": "celsius",
        "value": 0,
        "gpio": 12
      },
```

```
      "humidity": {
        "name": "Humidity Sensor",
        "description": "An ambient humidity sensor.",
        "unit": "%",
        "value": 0,
        "gpio": 12
      },
      "pir": {
        "name": "Passive Infrared",
        "description": "A passive infrared sensor.
           When 'true' someone is present.",
        "value": true,
        "gpio": 17
      }
    },
    "actuators": {
      "leds": {
        "1": {
          "name": "LED 1",
          "value": false,
          "gpio": 4
        },
        "2": {
          "name": "LED 2",
          "value": false,
          "gpio": 9
        }
      }
    }
  }
}
```

Next, you create the resources/model.js file, which imports our JSON model as follows:

```
var resources = require('./resources.json');
module.exports = resources;
```

This file loads the JSON model of our Pi from the resources.json file, and `exports` will make this object available as a node module that you can use in your application.

STEP 2: CREATE THE EXPRESS ROUTES

You can now bind these resources to URLs that your web server will reply to. In Express and many other web frameworks, the URL of a resource is defined by a *route*. You define those routes in two files available in the routes/ folder (actuators.js and sensors.js), which are shown in the next two listings.

Listing 7.3   /routes/sensors.js: routes for sensors

```
var express = require('express'),
  router = express.Router(),
  resources = require('./../resources/model');
```
◄─ **Require and instantiate an Express router to define the path to our resources.**

Reply with the sensor model when this route is selected.

```
router.route('/').get(function (req, res, next) {
  res.send(resources.pi.sensors);
});
```

Create a new route for a GET request on all sensors and attach a callback function.

```
router.route('/pir').get(function (req, res, next) {
  res.send(resources.pi.sensors.pir);
});
```

This route serves the passive infrared sensor.

```
router.route('/temperature').get(function (req, res, next) {
  res.send(resources.pi.sensors.temperature);
});
```

These routes serve the temperature and humidity sensors.

```
router.route('/humidity').get(function (req, res, next) {
  res.send(resources.pi.sensors.humidity);
});
```

```
module.exports = router;
```

Export router to make it accessible for "requires" of this file.

STEP 3: CREATE AN EXPRESS APPLICATION

Now that the routes are ready, you need to load them inside an HTTP server, which is done in the servers/http.js file. The content of this file is shown in the following listing and is in essence an HTTP server wrapped inside the Express framework.

> **Listing 7.4   /servers/http.js: Express application**

```
var express = require('express'),
  actuatorsRoutes = require('./../routes/actuators'),
  sensorRoutes = require('./../routes/sensors'),
  resources = require('./../resources/model'),
  cors = require('cors');
```

Requires the Express framework, your routes, and the model

```
var app = express();
```

Creates an application with the Express framework; this wraps an HTTP server.

Enable CORS support (see section 6.1.5).

```
app.use(cors());
```

```
app.use('/pi/actuators', actuatorsRoutes);
app.use('/pi/sensors', sensorRoutes);
```

Binds your routes to the Express application; bind them to /pi/ actuators/... and /pi/sensors/...

```
app.get('/pi', function (req, res) {
  res.send('This is the WoT-Pi!')
});
```

Creates a default route for /pi

```
module.exports = app;
```

You need one more file before you can test your implementation: wot-server.js, shown in the next listing. This is the entry point of your WoT Pi server and is in charge of starting the servers with the right configuration.

> **Listing 7.5   /wot-server.js: application entry point**

```
var httpServer = require('./servers/http'),
  resources = require('./resources/model');
```

Load the HTTP server and the model.

```
var server = httpServer.listen(resources.pi.port, function () {
  console.info('Your WoT Pi is up and running on port %s',
    resources.pi.port);
});
```

Start the HTTP server by invoking listen() on the Express application.

Once the server is started, the callback is invoked.

You can now test your server from your PC by starting the app via your terminal as usual.[7] Once it's started, you'll be able to access the resources with your browser—for example, the temperature sensor at http://localhost:8484/pi/sensors/temperature or the list of actuators at http://localhost:8484/pi/actuators. In both cases, you'll get the JSON payload corresponding to your request. Obviously, if you run the code on your Pi, replace localhost with the IP address or name (raspberrypi.local) of your Pi.

STEP 4: BIND THE SENSORS TO THE SERVER

This is all nice, but currently all we return are bits of the JSON model in listing 7.2, and the real-world data—the actual temperature—is missing! You need to put some sensor data from your Pi into the server. You'll do this by creating a number of plugins, one per sensor or actuator. Each sensor plugin should update the model each time new data is read from the sensor. A sensor plugin should at least have the functions shown in the following listing. All plugins are inside the plugins/ directory. The implementation of the PIR sensor plugin is shown in the next listing and is essentially an extension of the pir.js code you wrote in chapter 4.

Listing 7.6 /plugins/internal/pirPlugin.js: PIR sensor plugin

```
var resources = require('./../../resources/model');

var interval, sensor;
var model = resources.pi.sensors.pir;
var pluginName = resources.pi.sensors.pir.name;
var localParams = {'simulate': false, 'frequency': 2000};

exports.start = function (params) {
  localParams = params;
  if (localParams.simulate) {
    simulate();
  } else {
    connectHardware();
  }
};

exports.stop = function () {
  if (localParams.simulate) {
    clearInterval(interval);
  } else {
    sensor.unexport();
  }
  console.info('%s plugin stopped!', pluginName);
};
```

Starts and stops the plugin, which should be accessible from other Node.js files, so you export them

---

[7] After you run an `npm install` in the `wot-pi/` folder, run `node wot-server.js` or `nodemon wot-server.js`, as shown in chapter 3.

Configure the GPIO pin to which the PIR sensor is connected.

```
function connectHardware() {
  var Gpio = require('onoff').Gpio;
  sensor = new Gpio(model.gpio, 'in', 'both');
  sensor.watch(function (err, value) {
    if (err) exit(err);
    model.value = !!value;
    showValue();
  });
  console.info('Hardware %s sensor started!', pluginName);
};

function simulate() {
  interval = setInterval(function () {
    model.value = !model.value;
    showValue();
  }, localParams.frequency);
  console.info('Simulated %s sensor started!', pluginName);
};

function showValue() {
  console.info(model.value ? 'there is someone!' : 'not anymore!');
};
```

Require and connect the actual hardware driver and configure it.

Start listening for GPIO events; the callback will be invoked on events.

Allows the plugin to be in simulation mode, which is useful when developing or when you want to test your code on a device with no sensors connected, such as your laptop

The code for the temperature and humidity sensor is shown in the next listing, except for one new function: connectHardware(), which uses the node-dht-sensor library introduced in chapter 4.

Listing 7.7   /plugins/internal/DHT22SensorPlugin.js: temperature and humidity sensor plugin

```
[...]
function connectHardware() {
 var sensorDriver = require('node-dht-sensor');
 var sensor = {
   initialize: function () {
     return sensorDriver.initialize(22, model.temperature.gpio);
   },
   read: function () {
     var readout = sensorDriver.read();
     model.temperature.value = parseFloat(readout.temperature.toFixed(2));
     model.humidity.value = parseFloat(readout.humidity.toFixed(2));
     showValue();

     setTimeout(function () {
       sensor.read();
     }, localParams.frequency);
   }
 };
[...]
```

Initialize the driver for DHT22 on GPIO I2 (as specified in the model).

Fetch the values from the sensors.

Update the model with the new temperature and humidity values; note that all observers will be notified.

Because the driver doesn't provide interrupts, you poll the sensors for new values on a regular basis with a regular timeout function and set sensor.read() as a callback.

The code for the two plugins clearly shares a number of common functions, so as an exercise you might want to extract the common features into a JavaScript prototype. If you don't know how to do that, don't worry; we'll illustrate this when we improve the code in chapter 8.

You can now install your plugins on your server by requiring them from the wot-server.js file and starting each plugin with the right parameters, as shown in the following listing.

Listing 7.8 Integrating the plugins to wot-server.js

```
[...]
var ledsPlugin = require('./plugins/ledsPlugin'),
  pirPlugin = require('./plugins/pirPlugin'),
  dhtPlugin = require('./plugins/DHT22SensorPlugin');

pirPlugin.start({'simulate': true, 'frequency': 2000});
dhtPlugin.start({'simulate': true, 'frequency': 10000});
[...]
```

> Require all the sensor plugins you need.

> Start them with a parameter object; here you start them on a laptop so you activate the simulation function.

Run your server again and open the humidity sensor page at http://localhost:8484/pi/sensors/humidity. Refresh the page several times; this should give you different values each time.

TEST IT WITH REAL HARDWARE ON YOUR PI

Simulating sensors is nice, but using real ones is way nicer! To use real sensors on your Pi, you first need to install the libraries that connect the sensors. The problem is that these libraries aren't supported on non-IoT platforms like your laptop, so if you add the dependencies via `npm install --save`, you won't be able to install your code on your PC anymore. Don't worry: there's a way out! NPM allows you to set an `optional-Dependencies` object for the package.json file. The idea is that `npm install` won't fail if a dependency in `optionalDependencies` can't be installed. Go ahead and add the following code in your package.json file; the first dependency supports the PIR sensor and LEDs, and the second one supports the temperature and humidity sensor (if you have one):

```
"optionalDependencies": {
  "onoff": "^1.0.4",
  "node-dht-sensor": "^0.0.8"
}
```

Finally, run `npm install` on your Pi to install these dependencies. Now modify the parameters of the plugins you want to enable with `{'simulate': false}` and run your application on the Pi;[8] this will connect to physical drivers. Your Pi is now exposing its real sensor data and actuators to the world via a web API. You can access them

---

[8] If you did set up the temperature and humidity sensor, you'll need to run the code with sudo: `sudo node wot-server.js`.

via REST using the address of your Pi, for example, http://raspberrypi.local:8484/pi/sensors/pir.

7.2.3   *Representation design*

The next step of the design process is the *representation design*. REST is agnostic of a particular format or representation of the data. We mentioned that JSON is a must to guarantee interoperability, but it isn't the only interesting data representation available. In this section you'll add support for two more. You'll add HTML support because this allows you to browse your Pi and discover its resources in a human-friendly way. For this first step, you'll use a simple JSON-to-HTML library called json2html.

While you're at it, let's also add support for MessagePack, a more compressed and binary alternative to JSON that was briefly introduced in chapter 6. MessagePack can easily be mapped to JSON but is more compact than JSON, which makes it interesting for resource-constrained Things that communicate over low-bandwidth networks. There are libraries for encoding and decoding MessagePack in most popular programming languages, so adding support for it in your server is merely a matter of installing the msgpack5 module for Node.

IMPLEMENTING A REPRESENTATION CONVERTER MIDDLEWARE

There are several ways of supporting other representations in Express, but we propose a modular way based on the middleware pattern. Many Node libraries, including Express, support the idea of chaining functions that have access to the request (req) response (res) objects in a request-response cycle. This pattern allows for extensibility while keeping the code clean and modular. In essence, a middleware can execute code that changes the request or response objects and can then decide to respond to the client or call the next middleware in the stack using the next() function. The chain of middleware we'll implement here is shown in figure 7.4.

The stub of a typical middleware looks like this:

```
function myMiddleware(req, res, next) {
  // do something with the request
  // AND/OR add something to the response
  res.send("something");
  next();
}
```

We use this pattern to implement a representation converter supporting MessagePack and HTML representations. First, install the two libraries via NPM (npm install node-json2html msgpack5). The middleware code is located in middleware/converter.js, as shown in listing 7.9. Essentially, our representation converter middleware will implement the content negotiation pattern described in chapter 6, where it looks for the Accept header in a request and tries to deliver a representation in the format the client asked for. If it doesn't recognize the format, it will return JSON by default.

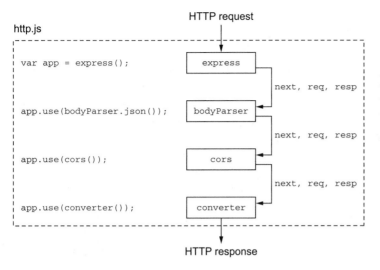

Figure 7.4 **The middleware chain implemented for the WoT server: each middleware is added to the Express application with the `app.use()` function. Then, each middleware gets a reference to the request object, the response object, and the next middleware in the chain.**

Listing 7.9 /middleware/converter.js: implementing representation middleware

```
var msgpack = require('msgpack5')(),
  encode = msgpack.encode,
  json2html = require('node-json2html');
```
◄── **Require the two modules and instantiate a MessagePack encoder.**

In Express, a middleware is usually a function returning a function.
```
module.exports = function() {
  return function (req, res, next) {
    console.info('Representation converter middleware called!');

    if (req.result) {
```
◄── **Check if the previous middleware left a result for you in req.result.**

Read the request header and check if the client requested JSON.
```
      if (req.accepts('json')) {
        console.info('JSON representation selected!');
        res.send(req.result);
        return;
      }

      if (req.accepts('html')) {
        console.info('HTML representation selected!');
        var transform = {'tag': 'div', 'html': '${name} : ${value}'};
```
If HTML was requested, use json2html to transform the JSON into simple HTML.
```
        res.send(json2html.transform(req.result, transform));
        return;
      }

      if (req.accepts('application/x-msgpack')) {
        console.info('MessagePack representation selected!');
        res.type('application/x-msgpack');
        res.send(encode(req.result));
```
◄── **Encode the JSON result into MessagePack using the encoder and return the result to the client.**
```
        return;
      }
```

For all other formats, default to JSON.
```
      console.info('Defaulting to JSON representation!');
      res.send(req.result);
      return;
```

```
    }
  else {
    next();
  }
 }
};
```

> If no result was present in req.result,
> there's not much you can do,
> so call the next middleware.

Now that the middleware is ready, you need to modify the routes of your server so they call the next middleware in the chain, the representation converter, rather than answering the request directly. You can easily implement this inside the two route files, sensors.js and actuators.js, by replacing every `res.send(resource)` with `req.result = resource` and `next()`. The following listing shows the changes for the sensor's routes, so make sure you apply those changes to the actuator's routes as well.

Listing 7.10   Calling the next middleware in sensors.js

> Assign the results to a new
> property of the req object that
> you pass along from
> middleware to middleware.

```
[...]
router.route('/').get(function (req, res, next) {
  req.result = resources.pi.sensors;
  next();
});

router.route('/pir').get(function (req, res, next) {
  req.result = resources.pi.sensors.pir;
  next();
});

router.route('/temperature').get(function (req, res, next) {
  req.result = resources.pi.sensors.temperature;
  next();
});
[...]
```

> Call the next middleware;
> the framework will ensure
> the next middleware gets
> access to req (including the
> req.result) and res.

Finally, you need to add the middleware to the Express application so that it gets called in the middleware chain. In http.js, first require the middleware with `converter = require('./../middleware/converter')` and add it to the chain by calling `app.use(converter())`. Because your converter middleware responds to the client, make sure you add it last, after `app.get('pi')`, or it will bypass any other middleware. Test your new server on your Pi (or PC) from your browser: http://raspberrypi .local:8484/pi/sensors/pir. You should now see a minimalist HTML representation of the PIR sensor. Now use cURL to request other types of representations by setting the Accept header to the desired MIME type (`application/json` for JSON and `application/x-msgpack` for MessagePack) as shown here:

```
curl -i -H "Accept: application/json" \
-X GET 'http://raspberrypi.local:8484/pi/sensors/pir'

curl -i -H "Accept: application/x-msgpack" \
-X GET 'http://raspberrypi.local:8484/pi/sensors/pir'
```

Your server is now capable of serving three different representations—JSON, HTML, and MessagePack—for all the resources it offers. All this thanks to a middleware that's 20 lines long! How's that for an illustration of the power of open web standards and Node.js?

7.2.4 *Interface design*

So far so good, but you're only able to GET resources from your Pi over HTTP. What about the other verbs like PUT and POST? What about HTTP status codes? What about using WebSockets to subscribe to sensor data? This is the goal of the *interface design* step.

ADDING A BODY PARSER

The GET verb is enough for sensors because you only read them, but what if you want to change the actuators—for example, turning on/off an LED or changing its color? The first step is to inform Express that you're happy to receive JSON payloads from clients. Adding an HTTP body parser to the middleware chain does just this. In http.js require the body-parser module: bodyParser = require('body-parser'). Also add the middleware at the beginning of the chain. Why the beginning? You want to parse the body of the HTTP message first to make it available to all other middleware: app.use(bodyParser.json()).

SUPPORTING OTHER HTTP VERBS

Your server can now handle incoming JSON messages as well, so let's add support to update the state of the Pi LED using a PUT request. To add support for PUT, you need to extend again the routes in actuators.js. Transform the route for /leds/:id as shown in the next listing.

> **Listing 7.11 Adding PUT support for LEDs in /routes/actuators.js**

Callback for a GET request on an LED

Update the value of the selected LED in the model.

Callback for a PUT request on an LED

```
[...]
router.route('/leds/:id').get(function (req, res, next) {
    req.result = resources.pi.actuators.leds[req.params.id];
    next();
}).put(function(req, res, next) {
    var selectedLed = resources.pi.actuators.leds[req.params.id];
    selectedLed.value = req.body.value;
    console.info('Changed LED %s value to %s', req.params.id, selectedLed.value);
    req.result = selectedLed;
    next();
});
```

You can now update the state of the LED by running a PUT request on the LED resource with the appropriate JSON payload. In cURL this looks like the following:

```
curl -i -H "Content-Type: application/json" \
  -H "Accept: application/json" \
  -X PUT 'http://localhost:8484/pi/actuators/leds/1' \
  -d '{"value":true}'
```

If you're successful, you'll see the following in the Node console: Changed LED 1 value to true.

BINDING ACTUATORS TO THE SERVER

This is all nice but it actually only updates your model; it doesn't actuate the real world! To change this behavior you need to write an LED plugin that has a similar structure to the sensor plugins but with a notable exception: it has an observe() function. observe() is needed for actuator plugins, and its goal is to observe changes in the model and report them to the physical world.

The core of this implementation is using the Object.observe() function.[9] This allows you to asynchronously observe the changes happening to an object by registering a callback to be invoked whenever a change in the observed object is detected:

```
Object.observe(obj, function(changes) {
  console.log(changes);
});
```

Let's use this feature to implement your LED plugin. It uses the on/off library to change the state of the GPIO the LED is connected to. Note that to keep things simple, this code supports only one LED (LED #1), but feel free to extend it to support more as an exercise. Inside observe you register a callback to be triggered whenever the model of your LEDs changes. It is inside this callback that you actually change the state of the GPIO, as shown in the next listing.

Listing 7.12   /plugins/internal/ledsPlugin.js: LED plugin

```
[...]
exports.start = function (params) {
  localParams = params;              Observe the model
  observe(model);                    for the LEDs.

  if (localParams.simulate) {
    simulate();
  } else {
    connectHardware();
  }
};

exports.stop = function () {
  if (localParams.simulate) {
    clearInterval(interval);
  } else {
    actuator.unexport();
```

---

[9]   Note that this function has been supported by Node since version 0.11.13 and is available in the current Node LTS v4.X we use for this book, but it could be removed in the future LTS, so make sure you use node 4.X LTS for this to work. See http://www.infoq.com/news/2015/11/object-observe-withdrawn.

```
  }
  console.info('%s plugin stopped!', pluginName);
};

function observe(what) {
  Object.observe(what, function (changes) {
    console.info('Change detected by plugin for %s...', pluginName);
    switchOnOff(model.value);
  });
};
```

Listen for model
changes; on changes
call switchOnOff.

```
function switchOnOff(value) {
  if (!localParams.simulate) {
    actuator.write(value === true ? 1 : 0, function () {
      console.info('Changed value of %s to %s', pluginName, value);
    });
  }
};
```

Change the
LED state by
changing the
GPIO state.

```
function connectHardware() {
  var Gpio = require('onoff').Gpio;
  actuator = new Gpio(model.gpio, 'out');
  console.info('Hardware %s actuator started!', pluginName);
};
[...]
```

Connect the GPIO in
write (output) mode.

Add this plugin to the list of initialized plugins in wot-server.js and set the simulation to false: `ledsPlugin.start({'simulate': false})`. Run it on your Pi and try the last cURL request again against the URL of your Pi; this time the LED should turn on! Yeah, we know. It's *just* an LED, but, oh my, this feels so good. Welcome to the IoT!

7.2.5 *Pub/sub interface via WebSockets*

The last part in our interface design step is to support publish/subscribe via WebSockets. Our goal is to offer the ability to subscribe via WebSockets on all our resources by a simple protocol upgrade to WebSockets.

There are several implementations of WebSockets for Node. The most complete and best-known one is probably Socket.io, which is more than a WebSocket server. It also supports fallbacks for clients that don't support WebSockets; for example, long polling as shown in chapter 6. We suggest you have a closer look at Socket.io, but for the server of our Pi we'll choose a pure and high-performing WebSockets implementation called WS.

The implementation of the WS integration is illustrated in figure 7.5. You create a WebSocket server and attach a listener to the main HTTP server of Express to listen for protocol upgrade requests to WebSockets; see chapter 5. You then take these upgrade requests and use the URL of the request to observe the corresponding resource in the model. Whenever a change is detected, you propagate the change to the client via the open WebSockets connection.

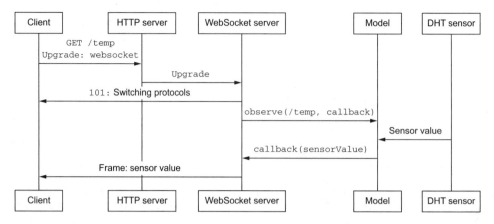

Figure 7.5 Sequence diagram of the WebSockets implementation of the WoT server: the WebSocket server is reacting to clients opening a WebSocket connection via an HTTP upgrade request by observing the corresponding resource;, for example, /temp. Whenever a new value for the resource is available, the WebSocket server sends it over the TCP connection it maintains open with the client.

To integrate this into your WoT server on the Pi, first install the WS module (npm install --save ws). Then implement the WebSocket server as shown in the next listing.

Listing 7.13   /server/websockets.js: WebSockets server

```
[...]
exports.listen = function(server) {
  var wss = new WebSocketServer({server: server});       ◀── Create a WebSockets server by
  console.info('WebSocket server started...');                passing it the Express server.
  wss.on('connection', function (ws) {
    var url = ws.upgradeReq.url;
    console.info(url);
    try {
      Object.observe(selectResouce(url), function (changes) {    ◀──
        ws.send(JSON.stringify(changes[0].object), function () {
        });                                              Register an observer
      })                                      corresponding to the resource in
    }                                          the protocol upgrade URL.
    catch (e) {
      console.log('Unable to observe %s resource!', url);
    };
  });
};

function selectResouce(url) {                ◀── Take a request URL and return
  var parts = url.split('/');                    the corresponding resource.
  parts.shift();
  var result = resources;
  for (var i = 0; i < parts.length; i++) {
    result = result[parts[i]];
  }
  return result;
}
```

Triggered after a protocol upgrade when the client connected

Use a try/ catch to catch to intercept errors; for example, malformed/ unsupported URLs.

The last step to enable the support for WebSockets is to initialize the WebSockets server after starting the HTTP server in wot-server.js. Modify the call to `listen()` to include a callback that starts the WebSockets server, as shown in the following listing.

Listing 7.14   Enabling the WebSockets server in wot-server.js

```
var httpServer = require('./servers/http'),
  wsServer = require('./servers/websockets'),
  resources = require('./resources/model');
[...]
var server = httpServer.listen(resources.pi.port, function () {
  console.log('HTTP server started...');
  wsServer.listen(server);
  console.info('Your WoT Pi is up and running on port %s',
  resources.pi.port);
})
```

That's it! You can now subscribe to all the resources on the web Thing with WebSockets and be informed whenever the state of a resource changes. You can use any WebSockets client—for example, a web page, such as the example you saw in chapter 2. Try adapting it to subscribe to your WoT Pi, or you can use the /public/websockets-Client.html file in any recent browser. When you open this file in your browser, you'll see the WebSockets messages in the JavaScript console of your developer tools, as shown in figure 7.6.

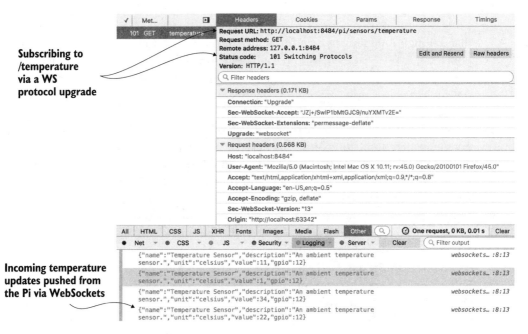

Figure 7.6   Subscribing to temperature updates via WebSockets using a simple WebSockets client in Firefox. The upper part shows the protocol upgrade process and the lower part the incoming messages pushed from the Thing (a Pi here) directly to the browser-based client.

> ### The nerd corner—I want better JavaScript!
>
> The WoT server we built in this section was kept extremely simple in terms of the code to ensure everyone could follow along. The code could be made a lot cleaner and more reusable by applying a number of JavaScript good practices and patterns. If you know JavaScript, a good exercise is to modularize the code; for instance, by starting with prototypes to factorize a large chunk of plugin code. In chapter 8 you'll see an improved version of the framework we presented here, but don't hesitate to build your own right now!

7.2.6 *Summary—direct integration pattern*

In this section, we showed how to rapidly build a complete Web of Things API that not only can run on actual devices and talk to actual sensors and actuators, but also can support many advanced capabilities, such as content negotiation and push support via WebSockets. But there's a whole range of devices where you won't have the luxury of running Node natively. A solution for these cases is described in the next section, where we provide another pattern for non-HTTP/WebSockets devices: the gateway integration pattern.

7.3 *Gateway integration pattern—CoAP example*

In the previous section, you transformed your Pi into a web Thing by creating an HTTP and WebSockets API for its sensors. This worked well because your Pi was not battery powered, had access to a decent bandwidth (Wi-Fi/Ethernet), and had more than enough RAM and storage for Node. But not all devices are so lucky. Native support for HTTP/WS or even TCP/IP isn't always possible or even desirable. For battery-powered devices, Wi-Fi or Ethernet is often too much of a power drag, so they need to rely on low-power protocols such as ZigBee or Bluetooth instead. Does it mean those devices can't be part of the Web of Things? Certainly not, as illustrated in figure 7.7.

Such devices can also be part of the Web of Things as long as there' s an intermediary somewhere that can expose the device's functionality through a WoT API like the one we described previously. These intermediaries are called *application gateways* (we'll call them WoT gateways hereafter), and they can talk to Things using any non-web application protocols and then translate those into a clean REST WoT API that any HTTP client can use. Some gateways can also do more than simply translate across protocols. They can add a layer of security or authentication, aggregate and store data temporarily, expose semantic descriptions for Things that don't have any, and so on.

To better understand what a WoT gateway is and what it can do for non-web devices, let's look at a concrete example where we expose a CoAP device using an HTTP and WebSockets API. As you've seen before, CoAP is an interesting protocol based on REST, but because it isn't HTTP and uses UDP instead of TCP, a gateway that translates CoAP messages from/to HTTP is needed. It's therefore ideal for device-to-device communication over low-power radio communication, but you can't talk to a CoAP device from

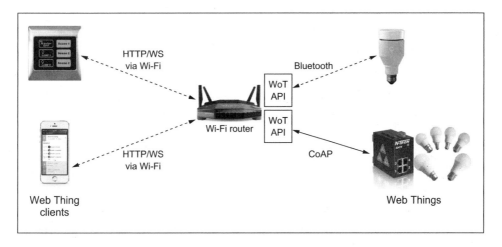

Figure 7.7 Gateway integration pattern. In this case, the web Thing can't directly offer a web API because the device might not support HTTP directly. An application gateway is working as a proxy for the Thing by offering a web API in the Thing's name. This API could be hosted on the router in the case of Bluetooth or on another device that exposes the web Thing API; for example, via CoAP.

a JavaScript application in your browser without installing a special plugin or browser extension. Let's fix this by using your Pi as a WoT gateway to CoAP devices.

7.3.1 Running a CoAP server

Start by creating a simple CoAP resource. For the sake of simplicity—and to keep your budget in check—you'll simulate a CoAP device on your computer. Of course, you could also buy a resource-constrained device such as an Arduino Uno and install CoAP on it.[10]

There are a number of libraries for CoAP on Node but our favorite is `coap` (run `npm install coap` to install it). An implementation of a minimal CoAP server is provided in /servers/coap.js, shown in the following listing.

Listing 7.15 coap.js: a simple CoAP server

```
var coap = require('coap'),                          ◀─┐ Require the Node.js CoAP
  utils = require('./../utils/utils');                 │ module you installed.

var port = 5683;
coap.createServer(function (req, res) {
  console.info('CoAP device got a request for %s', req.url);
  if (req.headers['Accept'] != 'application/json') {
    res.code = '4.06';            ◀─┐ You only serve JSON, so you reply with
    return res.end();               │ a 4.06 (= HTTP 406: Not acceptable).
  }
```

---

[10] For instance, using the microcoap implementation available here: https://github.com/1248/microcoap.

Handle the different resources requested. →

```
switch (req.url) {
  case "/co2":
    respond(res, {'co2': utils.randomInt(0, 1000)});
    break;
  case "/temp":
    respond(res, {'temp': utils.randomInt(0, 40)});
    break;
  default:
    respond(res);
  }
}).listen(port, function () {
  console.log("CoAP server started on port %s", port)
});

function respond(res, content) {
  if (content) {
    res.setOption('Content-Format', 'application/json');
    res.code = '2.05';
    res.end(JSON.stringify(content));
  } else {
    res.code = '4.04';
    res.end();
  }
};
```

← **The CO2 resource; generate a random value for it and respond.**

← **Start the CoAP server on port 5683 (CoAP's default port).**

← **Send the JSON content back or reply with a 4.04 (= HTTP 404: Not found).**

You'll likely realize that this code isn't very different from what you've learned in the last two chapters. That's because CoAP is heavily inspired by HTTP and REST but adapted for the requirements of low-power embedded systems. Because CoAP is using UDP and not HTTP/TCP, you can't access these resources directly from your browser via a CoAP URI: coap://localhost:5683/co2.

But you can use an excellent plugin for Firefox called Copper.[11] Once the plugin is installed, start the CoAP server (node coap.js in the servers directory) and you'll be able to access the resources you just created by typing the CoAP URI; for example, coap://localhost:5683/co2, in Firefox's address bar.

7.3.2 *Proxying CoAP via a gateway*

The next step is to proxy CoAP requests to HTTP so that you can access CoAP devices from web browsers. Here you'll extend your WoT gateway to provide access to CoAP devices via your Pi.

Transforming your Pi into a WoT gateway requires two simple steps. First, you create a CoAP plugin, which is essentially a CoAP client creating a new device in our model. Second, you create routes for the resources the CoAP device has to offer. The code for the CoAP plugin is shown in the next listing. Because most of the code is just like the other temperature/humidity sensor plugins, we focus on what's different.

---

[11] https://addons.mozilla.org/en-US/firefox/addon/copper-270430/

Listing 7.16 /plugins/external/coapPlugin.js: a simple CoAP plugin

```
[...]
function connectHardware() {
  var coap = require('coap'),                    Require the CoAP
    bl = require('bl');                          and BL library,
                                                 a Buffer helper.

  var sensor = {
    read: function () {                          Create a sensor object and
      coap.request({                             give it a read function.
        host: 'localhost',
        port: 5683,
        pathname: '/co2',
        options: {'Accept': 'application/json'}  When CoAP device sends
      })                                         the result, the on response
      .on('response', function (res) {           event is triggered.
        console.info('CoAP response code', res.code);
        if (res.code !== '2.05')
          console.log("Error while contacting CoAP service: %s",
            res.code);
        res.pipe(bl(function (err, data) {       Fetch the results and
          var json = JSON.parse(data);           update the model.
          me.value = json.co2;
          showValue();
        }));
      })
      .end();
    }
  };
  pollInterval = setInterval(function () {       Poll the CoAP device for new CO2
    sensor.read();                               readings on a regular basis.
  }, localParams.frequency);
};

function configure() {
  utils.addDevice('coapDevice', 'A CoAP Device',  Add the resources managed
    'A CoAP Device',                              by this plugin to the model.
    {
      'co2': {
        'name': 'CO2 Sensor',
        'description' : 'An ambient CO2 sensor',
        'unit': 'ppm',
        'value': 0
      }
    });
  me = resources.things.coapDevice.sensors.co2;
  pluginName = resources.things.coapDevice.name;
}; [...]
```

The read function wraps a coap over UDP request with the enclosed parameters; replace localhost with the IP of the machine you're simulating the CoAP device from, such as your laptop.

Then you need to add the routes for the resources for your CoAP device. To keep it simple, you connect only a CO2 sensor, but feel free to extend this to support any other resources you want. You need to add these routes in /routes/things.js:

```
router.route('/coapDevice/sensors/co2').get(function (req, res, next) {
  req.result = resources.things.coapDevice.sensors.co2
  next();
});
```

You load the router as a middleware in /servers/http.js, binding it to /things. This means the CoAP device will be accessible on /things/coapDevice/sensors/co2, which makes sense because it's a Thing managed by the Pi, which acts as a proxy, not the Pi itself. Finally, you require and start the CoAP plugin in wot-server.js:

```
var coapPlugin = require('./plugins/external/coapPlugin');
coapPlugin.start({'simulate': false, 'frequency': 10000});
```

If everything works, you should be able to access the simulated CoAP device through the Pi gateway using HTTP. First, start the CoAP server on your PC (node coap.js) and then the gateway on your Pi (node wot-server.js), and finally, try to run the following cURL:

```
curl -i -H "Accept: application/x-msgpack" \
  -X GET 'http://raspberrypi.local:8484/things/coapDevice/sensors/co2'
```

You should get the sensor readings as a MessagePack representation. You can also try to use a snippet of JavaScript that connects to the CoAP CO2 sensor via WebSockets (for example, use the file /public/websocketsClient.html) or even point your browser at http://raspberrypi.local:8484/things/coapDevice/sensors/co2. All of these will work, even if the CoAP device can't serve MessagePack or HTML representations and can't speak WebSockets. This is the *gateway pattern in action*: it seamlessly integrates the CoAP device to the web of browsers!

This was a very short introduction to CoAP. If you want to learn more about this young and growing web-inspired protocol, start by exploring the CoAP technology portal.[12]

The nerd corner—I want a generic CoAP proxy

Even though CoAP isn't supported by the web of browsers, it offers an interesting trade-off for resource- or battery-constrained devices, especially when considering device-to-device communication. It's similar to HTTP, so the translation is easier because we don't need to map between different data models and could use the same JSON model over both HTTP and CoAP. The translation we illustrated here was simple but not generic: we needed to manually map a CoAP resource to HTTP routes. Building a generic HTTP proxy for CoAP devices is possible and not overly complex. Should you want to try, you'll find a number of examples on the web.[a]

---

[a] For instance, here: https://github.com/morkai/h5.coap/blob/master/example/http-proxy.js.

7.3.3   *Summary—gateway integration pattern*

For some devices, it might not make sense to support HTTP or WebSockets directly, or it might not even be possible, such as when they have very limited resources like

---

[12] http://coap.technology/

memory or processing, when they can't connect to the internet directly (such as your Bluetooth activity tracker), or when they're battery-powered. Those devices will use more optimized communication or application protocols and thus will need to rely on a more powerful gateway that connects them to the Web of Things, such as your mobile phone to upload the data from your Bluetooth bracelet, by bridging/translating various protocols. Here we implemented a simple gateway from scratch using Express, but you could also use other open source alternatives such as OpenHab[13] or The Thing System.[14]

7.4 *Cloud integration pattern—MQTT over EVRYTHNG*

As you saw in the previous sections, it's possible to implement WoT servers directly on devices or via gateways. This is sufficient in many situations, but as soon as you need to manage large quantities of devices and data, you'll need to have a much more powerful and scalable platform to store and process the data. The cloud integration pattern, shown in figure 7.8, is an extension of the gateway pattern where the gateway is a remote server that devices and applications access via the internet.

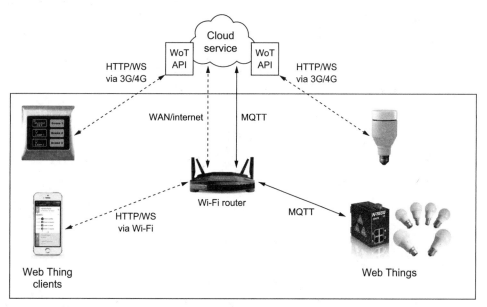

Your local network at home

Figure 7.8   Cloud integration pattern. In this pattern, the Thing can't directly offer a Web API. But a cloud service acts as a powerful application gateway, offering many more features in the name of the Thing. In this particular example, the web Thing connects via MQTT to a cloud service, which exposes the web Thing API via HTTP and the WebSockets API. Cloud services can also offer many additional features such as unlimited data storage, user management, data visualization, stream processing, support for many concurrent requests, and more.

---

[13] http://www.openhab.org/
[14] https://github.com/TheThingSystem/steward

Using a cloud server has several advantages. First, because it doesn't have the physical constraints of devices and gateways, it's much more scalable and can process and store a virtually unlimited amount of data. This also allows a cloud platform to support many protocols at the same time, handle protocol translation efficiently, and act as a scalable intermediary that can support many more concurrent clients than an IoT device could. Second, those platforms can have many features that might take considerable time to build from scratch, from industry-grade security, to specialized analytics capabilities, to flexible data visualization tools and user and access management. This means you can get started building complex applications in a fraction of time. Third, because those platforms are natively connected to the web, data and services from your devices can be easily integrated into third-party systems to extend your devices.

Over the years, many cloud platforms have appeared, and they usually share similar characteristics: creating virtual devices in the cloud that can permanently talk to their physical counterparts, storing all the data generated by the devices, and visualizing that data in multiple ways. Xively[15] (ex-Cosm, ex-Pachube) was one of the earliest ones; its simple API allowed developers throughout the world to quickly connect devices to the cloud. There are many other ones you can use for your projects, such as ThingWorx,[16] ThingSpeak,[17] Carriots,[18] and thethings.io.[19]

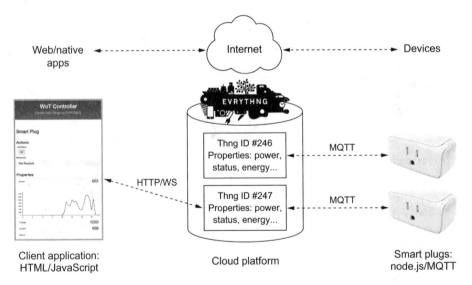

Figure 7.9   **A physical device connects to a cloud platform using MQTT over TCP/IP and talks to its proxy on the web—called Thng. An external application can then talk to the Thng using a simple HTTP client.**

[15] https://xively.com/

[16] http://www.thingworx.com/

[17] https://thingspeak.com/

[18] https://www.carriots.com/

[19] https://thethings.io/

In this section, we'll teach you how to connect to our favorite IoT platform ever: EVRYTHNG. Okay, we might be biased because we built it! But at least it will help you learn quickly about the advantages of the cloud integration pattern. Started in 2011, EVRYTHNG was also the first IoT platform to apply the Web of Things principles, so it should feel familiar! In this section, you'll learn how to implement a basic web-connected power plug, as shown in figure 7.9. The plug monitors the energy consumption of the device attached to it and permanently sends this data to the cloud. These readings will be permanently stored in the cloud. In addition, the plug is permanently connected to the cloud using MQTT (which we described in chapter 5), which means that the cloud can send commands to it at any time with minimal latency.

Afterward, we'll implement a simple web application using HTML and JavaScript that subscribes to the plug using WebSockets, displays the current consumption in real time, and also allows you to turn the plug on and off. You'll find all the source code you need in the folder chapter7-implementation/part3-cloud of the book's GitHub repository.

7.4.1 Set up your EVRYTHNG account

The first thing you need to do is create an EVRYTHNG account and log into it.[20] Don't worry; it's quick and it won't cost you a dime to implement this exercise. EVRYTHNG services are completely free for non-commercial projects! To get you up to speed, you can check out our quick tutorial for how to use it.[21]

Once you've created your account, you'll need your account API key (called *operator API key*[22]). This key will allow you to create and manage the digital identities for your device in the cloud and interact with them. It's critical that you don't share it with anyone because this API key is so powerful that it can delete every Thng—this is not a typo; EVRYTHNG likes to drop vowels—in your account. Don't even share it with your girlfriend/boyfriend or best buddy! Unless he's really a great guy, in which case it might be okay—or not!

In this section you set up your account so that you can connect your devices and applications to the engine. You could also do all the following steps from the EVRYTHNG dashboard or via POSTman. In this section, we'll show you how to use cURL so that you can easily run those requests from your terminal and also see the details of the various HTTP requests. You can append the `--verbose` flag to the request to see more details about your request.

Set up your account data automatically

You'll have to manually create a few entities in your EVRYTHNG account by running various HTTP requests against our cloud, as described in steps 1–4. If you run into any problems or you don't want to do this all manually, we've prepared a cool script

---

[20] You can do it here: https://dashboard.evrythng.com/signup.
[21] Quick introduction to EVRYTHNG: https://developers.evrythng.com
[22] Find it here: https://dashboard.evrythng.com/account.

(continued)

for you that does steps 1–4 automatically, which is described at the end of this section. The script is called setup.sh and you can run it from the terminal of your Pi with

```
$ sh setup.sh XXX
```

where XXX is your operator API key. You'll see a matrix-like effect that not only runs all the commands you've seen to create those entities for you but also saves them into a config.json file that you'll need in the next section. You're now ready to experience the full power of the cloud implementation pattern.

STEP 1—CREATE A PROJECT AND AN APPLICATION

Before we start, you must copy and paste these two lines in your terminal, which will define two shell *environment variables* that the cURL requests in this section will use:

```
SERVER="https://api.evrythng.com"
EVRYTHNG_API_KEY="YOUR-API-KEY"
```

Obviously, replace YOUR-API-KEY with your own operator API key before you run it. You'll have to define quite a few other environment variables in the same way in this section.

The first thing you'll do is to create a project inside your account. A *project* is a placeholder (a scope) that allows you to separate the various elements you'll generate (Thngs and data). Also, you'll need a project to create applications that can access some of your data because you don't want to use your operator API key in client applications. Paste the following request into your terminal:

```
curl -X POST "$SERVER/projects" \
    -H "Authorization: $EVRYTHNG_API_KEY" \
    -H "Content-Type: application/json" \
    -d '{ "name": "Web of Things Book", "description": "My First WoT
    Project" }' --verbose
```

If this request wasn't successful make sure the SERVER and EVRYTHNG_API_KEY environment variables are correct, which you can test by running echo $SERVER in your terminal. If it was successful, you should receive a 201 Created response that looks like this:

```
HTTP/1.1 201 Created
Access-Control-Allow-Origin: *
Access-Control-Expose-Headers: Link, X-Result-Count
Content-type: application/json
Date: Sun, 14 Jun 2015 18:41:52 GMT
location: https://api.evrythng.com/projects/UCkWEEKnPe5wWhgbdhSfwnGc
Content-Length: 150
Connection: keep-alive
{
  "id":"UCkWEEKnPe5wWhgbdhSfwnGc",
  "createdAt":1434810298365,
  "updatedAt":1434810298365,
  "name":"Web of Things Book",
  "description":"My First WoT Project"
}
```

Note that there's now an `id` field in the object, which contains the EVRYTHNG ID of the project you created. Go ahead and save this value into the environment variable `$PROJECT_ID` as you did when you pasted the `EVRYTHNG_API_KEY="XXX"` earlier, by pasting `PROJECT_ID=YYY` into your terminal, where YYY is the ID of the project you just created—`PROJECT_ID=UCkWEEKnPe5wWhgbdhSfwnGc`, in this example.

Once you've created your first project, you can create an application in it. An application will give you another API key (an *App API key*) that you can use in the client application we'll build later. This one isn't so dangerous, because what it can do is very limited; basically it only allows you to create users. To create an application, send the following cURL request in your terminal:

```
curl -X POST "$SERVER/projects/$PROJECT_ID/applications" \
    -H "Authorization: $EVRYTHNG_API_KEY" \
    -H "Content-Type: application/json" \
    -d '{ "name": "My Awesome WoT App", "description": "My First WoT Client
    Application","tags":["WoT","device","plug","energy"], "socialNetworks":
    {} }'
```

Again, just like you did for projects, store the ID returned in the response inside the `$APP_ID` environment variable. Also, note the API key in the response; you'll use it to build your web application later on. Now you're ready to create a web Thing in our cloud.

STEP 2—CREATE YOUR FIRST PRODUCTS AND THNGS

A *product* is a *class* of physical objects (think TV model or car type) but not a unique *instance* (think serial number). You shouldn't use products to store data about physical objects. They're a conceptual entity, a model of a physical object, and should only contain information that many physical objects of this class share—attributes such as size, image, weight, and color—but no real-time information such as location, sensor readings, or current state. Create a product using the following request:

```
curl -X POST "$SERVER/products?project=$PROJECT_ID" \
    -H "Authorization: $EVRYTHNG_API_KEY" \
    -H "Content-Type: application/json" \
    -d '{ "fn": "WoT Smart Plug", "description": "A Web-connected Smart
    Plug","tags":["WoT","device","energy"],"photos":["https://
    webofthings.github.io/files/plug.jpg"] }'
```

Note the `?project=$PROJECT_ID` query parameter, which tells EVRYTHNG to store this product inside the project we created earlier. Store the product ID in the `$PRODUCT_ID` variable.

Thngs, on the other hand, are the digital representation of unique instances of physical objects: the Thing you hold in your hands! For each unique device or object you want to web-enable, you'll need to create a unique Thng. You can do it like this:

```
curl -X POST "$SERVER/thngs?project=$PROJECT_ID" \
    -H "Authorization: $EVRYTHNG_API_KEY" \
    -H "Content-Type: application/json" \
    -d '{ "name": "My WoT Plug", "product":"'$PRODUCT_ID'", "description":
    "My own Smart Plug","tags":["WoT","device","plug","energy"] }'
```

You can see that we're also sending the product ID in this request. Keep track of the ID of the Thng returned in the payload in the $THNG_ID variable.

STEP 3—CREATE A DEVICE API KEY

Technically, you could use your operator API key to update the property of your Thng, but it's unwise to use this on a production device for various security reasons. Instead, you can easily generate a *Thng API key* that allows your device to see and edit only itself. Send a POST (using your operator API key) to the end point https://api.evrythng.com/auth/evrythng/thngs with the ID of your Thng, as follows:

```
curl -X POST "$SERVER/auth/evrythng/thngs" \
    -H "Authorization: $EVRYTHNG_API_KEY" \
    -H "Content-Type: application/json" \
    -d '{ "thngId": "'$THNG_ID'" }'
```

You'll get this in return:

```
{
  "thngId": "UCE7qfbK8VKwdt8kAfqtbwmd",
  "thngApiKey": "M1ST3RP0TAT0H3ADROCKS"
}
```

The thngApiKey field contains an API key that allows the device to see and update itself. Store its value in the $THNG_API_KEY environment variable.

STEP 4—CHANGE PROPERTIES

If you've successfully completed the previous lines, you'll now have a project, an application, a product, and an instance of this product in your account. You can see them in your dashboard. Now you're going to update the properties of your smart plug. A *property* is an array of data that you can update any time and that's stored permanently inside the engine. You can continuously update each property individually and retrieve it anytime.

To update one or more properties, use the device API key and send a POST request to the thngs/$THNG_ID/properties endpoint, using this request:

```
curl -X POST "$SERVER/thngs/$THNG_ID/properties" \
    -H "Authorization: $THNG_API_KEY" \
    -H "Content-Type: application/json" \
    -d '[{"key": "status","value": true},
        {"key": "energyConsumption","value": 71}]'
```

Now you can navigate to the page of your Thng in the EVRYTHNG dashboard, which is shown in figure 7.10. There you'll see the information about this plug and its properties changing in real time as you run this request several times with different values.

7.4.2   *Create your MQTT client application*

In the previous section, you learned how to set up your EVRYTHNG account to create web Things for any physical object you want to connect to the web. You did this using cURL commands to learn about the endpoints and how they work, but obviously this is not how your device will talk to the engine.

For this project, you'll write a simple Node application that simulates a smart plug and that you can run from your Pi or on your PC. The application uses the Thng API key (created in step 3 of the previous exercise) to open a permanent connection to the EVRYTHNG engine over MQTT and update its properties every five seconds.

Open the file simple-plug.js and look at the code. Before you can execute it, you'll need a config.json file with the IDs and API keys of your EVRYTHNG account. If you ran the setup.sh bash script instead of going through the four manual steps, it will have generated this file for you. Otherwise, create a copy of the file config-sample.json named config.json and put the Thng ID (step 2 of previous section) and the Thng API key (step 3) in it, as shown in the following listing.

Listing 7.17 simple-plug.js: simulated power plug that connects to EVRYTHNG via MQTT

```
var mqtt = require('mqtt');

var config = require('./config.json');          Load configuration from file
var thngId = config.thngId;                      (Thng ID and Thng API key).
var thngUrl = '/thngs/'+thngId;
var thngApiKey = config.thngApiKey;
var interval;

console.log('Using Thng #'+thngId+' with API Key: '+ thngApiKey);

var client = mqtt.connect("mqtts://mqtt.evrythng.com:8883", {   Connect to the secure MQTT server on EVRYTHNG.
  username: 'authorization',
  password: thngApiKey
});
                                                 Callback called once
client.on('connect', function () {               when the MQTT
  client.subscribe(thngUrl+'/properties/');      connection suceeds
  updateProperty('livenow', true);               Set the property
                                                 livenow to true.
  interval = setInterval(updateProperties, 5000);   Call the function
});                                                  updateProperties()
                                                     in five seconds.
client.on('message', function (topic, message) {   Called every time an MQTT message is received from the broker
  console.log(message.toString());
});

function updateProperties () {                     Measures voltage
  var voltage = (219.5 + Math.random()).toFixed(3);  (fluctuates around ~220 volts)
  updateProperty ('voltage',voltage);

  var current = (Math.random()*10).toFixed(3);     Measures current
  updateProperty ('current',current);             (fluctuates 0–10 amps)

  var power = (voltage * current *
(0.6+Math.random()/10)).toFixed(3);               Measures power using P=U*I*PF
  updateProperty ('power',power);                 (PF=power factor fluctuates 60–70%)
}
```

Subscribe to all properties.

```
function updateProperty (property,value) {
  client.publish(thngUrl+'/properties/'+property, '[{"value":
  '+value+'}]');
}

process.on('SIGINT', function() {
  clearInterval(interval);
  updateProperty ('livenow', false);
  client.end();
  process.exit();
});
```

◀— **Cleanly exit this code and set the livenow property to false.**

You can see that this example connects to EVRYTHNG via secure MQTT (MQTTS) and subscribes to all property updates. It then calls the function `updateProperties()` every five seconds, which simulates typical current and voltage readings a real plug might measure, and finally sends the readings to the cloud by updating the properties of the Thng, as you did in the step 4 of the previous section.

You can then go back to the Thngs page in the dashboard and start the simulated device by running the Node code: `npm install` and `node simple-plug.js`. You can now go back to the Dashboard tab to see the properties of the plug being updated in real time, as shown in figure 7.10.

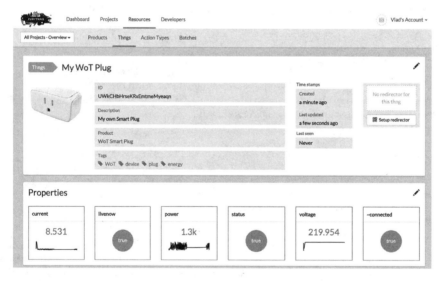

Figure 7.10   See the smart plug directly from the dashboard and the properties being updated in real time.

7.4.3   *Use actions to control the power plug*

You've built a device that's permanently connected to the internet and that pushes its updates to a service via MQTT. This illustrates how using a cloud engine can allow you to rapidly build web-connected devices without implementing a local gateway.

At this point, you're probably thinking, "Okay, great, but how do I send commands to the plug to turn it on or off?" Fair enough! The simplest answer is this: because the device has subscribed to all properties using MQTT, it will receive a message each time any property in the EVRYTHNG cloud changes. Indeed, the text you see in the terminal is displayed by the `console.log()` statement in that callback function. With the Node application running, go to the dashboard, click the property `status` of the Thng, and set it to `false`. You'll see this change immediately in your terminal:

```
[{"timestamp":1434823136116,"key":"voltage","value":220.259}]
[{"timestamp":1434823136116,"key":"current","value":0.839}]
[{"timestamp":1434823136898,"key":"status","value":false}]
[{"timestamp":1434823137065,"key":"voltage","value":219.919}]
[{"timestamp":1434823138184,"key":"power","value":913.355}]
```

You could then modify that callback handler to trigger something else in your code when this happens, and this will work fine.

But this isn't the best option because you must carefully keep track of which properties the device should set and which ones should only be changed by applications. Besides, a property is only a single value; therefore, you'd have to use several properties if you wanted to send commands to your device that have multiple input parameters; for example, setting the RGB value of several LEDs.

For this reason, you'll use *actions* to send more complex commands with several input parameters. For this, you can look at the more advanced plug-with-control.js. If you've run the bash script in section 7.4.1, it will have created an *action type* called `_setStatus` for you. If not, you'll have to create it yourself using this command:

```
curl -X POST "$SERVER/actions?project=$PROJECT_ID" \
    -H "Authorization: $EVRYTHNG_API_KEY" \
    -H "Content-Type: application/json" \
    -d '{ "name": "_setStatus", "description": "Changes the Status of the
    Thng","tags":["WoT","device"] }'
```

Before you create actions, you need to change your device application so that it also subscribes to the `actions/` resource and does something each time it receives a specific action. You can open the file plug-with-control.js where the callback functions have been modified, as shown in the next listing.

Listing 7.18　plug-with-control.js: subscribe and handle actions pushed from the server

```
[...]
client.on('connect', function () {
  client.subscribe(thngUrl+'/properties/');
  client.subscribe(thngUrl+'/actions/all');          ◄── Subscribe to all actions
  updateProperty('livenow',true);                        on this thing.
  updateInterval = setInterval(updateProperties, 5000);
});

client.on('message', function(topic, message) {
  var resources = topic.split('/');                  ◄── Verify if the MQTT
  if (resources[1] && resources[1] === "thngs"){         message is on a Thng.
```

Check if a
property was
changed; if so,
display it.

Verify if the
message is for
the current Thng.

Was it an action?
If so, call
handleAction().

```
      if (resources[2] && resources[2] === thngId){
        if (resources[3] && resources[3] === "properties"){
          var property = JSON.parse(message);
          console.log('Property was updated:
            '+property[0].key+'='+property[0].value);
        } else if (resources[3] && resources[3] === "actions"){
          var action = JSON.parse(message);
          handleAction(action);
        }
      }
    }
  });

function handleAction(action) {
  switch(action.type) {
    case '_setStatus':
      console.log('ACTION: _setStatus changed to:
        '+action.customFields.status);
      status=Boolean(action.customFields.status);
      updateProperty ('status',status);
      break;
    case '_setLevel':
      console.log('ACTION: _setLevel changed to:
        '+action.customFields.level);
      break;
    default:
      console.log('ACTION: Unknown action type: '+action.type);
      break;
  }
}
```

Check the type
of this action.

If action type is _setStatus,
display the new value and
do something with it.

You can now run this second code, and you'll still see when properties are updated.
But for now, open a second terminal and send a _setStatus command to the Thng in
your engine, using the following request:

```
curl -X POST "$SERVER/actions/_setStatus?project=$PROJECT_ID" \
  -H "Authorization: $EVRYTHNG_API_KEY" \
  -H "Content-Type: application/json" \
  -d '{ "type": "_setStatus", "thng":"'$THNG_ID'", "customFields":
  {"status":"false"} }'
```

Study carefully the content of the response payload because it contains much more
information that you've sent. Our cloud uses your IP address to determine the location of the action. If you refresh the page, you'll see this action appear on your Thng
page in the dashboard, along with a map of it.

7.4.4 *Create a simple web control application*

So far, you've written a Node application that allows a Pi to connect to a cloud service
and receive push notifications instantly, even if your device is behind firewalls or NAT
boxes. The benefit of using a cloud service is that it allows you to use a uniform interface such as a REST API, properties, or actions to talk to any device connected to the
cloud, regardless of whether the device talks to EVRYTHNG using the REST API, MQTT,

or another protocol. This means you can build a generic client application and it will work with any Thng in the platform. It also makes access to your Things much more scalable because clients don't talk to your Things directly, but rather through a cloud intermediary representing the state of the Thng, like a mirror or a shadow.

A SIMPLE WEB APPLICATION USING THE CLOUD

The next step is to build a simple web application that can interact with the device via its Thng, subscribe to its properties using WebSockets, and display them as soon as the device sends them. This application should also be able to push commands to the device via the REST API of the cloud platform.

We built such an application for you, so go ahead and open the file part3-cloud/client/plug.html in your editor—or, of course, feel free to build your own! Provide the Thng ID and your operator API key here as query parameters in the URL:

```
file:///.../plug.html?key=XXX&thngId=YYY
```

You can now start the plug-with-control.js Node application we used in the previous section and open plug.html in your browser. Within a few seconds, you should see the properties changing and a graph being updated in real time. This application connects to your Thng in EVRYTHNG, subscribes to its properties using WebSockets, and updates the page as soon as property updates are received from the engine. Because the code is long and uses quite a few excellent libraries to do the heavy work, we'll show only the most interesting bits here. First, you create a toggle button that sends a _setStatus action each time it's used, as shown in the following listing.

> **Listing 7.19   client/plug.html: attach a handler to the toggle button**

```
<input type="checkbox" id="toggle-status"/>
<script>
  $(function() {
    $('#toggle-status').bootstrapToggle({
      on: 'On',
      off: 'Off'
    });
  });

  $(function() {
    $('#toggle-status').change(function() {
      sendAction("_setStatus",{"status": $(this).prop('checked')});
    });
  });
</script>
```

You create a button and use the Bootstrap Toggle[23] library to make it look pretty. Each time this button is triggered, the sendAction() function will be called, which looks like the code shown in the next listing.

---

[23] http://www.bootstraptoggle.com/

Listing 7.20   client/plugs.html: the `sendAction()` function

```
function sendAction(type,value){
  $.ajax({
    url: 'https://api.evrythng.com/actions/'+type+'?access_token='+key,
    dataType: 'json',
    type: 'post',
    contentType: 'application/json',
    data: JSON.stringify({"type": type, "thng": thngId,
      "customFields":value}),
    processData: false,
    success: function( data, textStatus, jQxhr ){
        $('#response pre').html( JSON.stringify( data ) );
    },
    error: function( jqXhr, textStatus, errorThrown ){
        console.log( errorThrown );
    }
  });
}
```

The custom actions endpoint in EVRYTHNG.

The payload to POST

POST a JSON document.

If successful, update the response html element.

If an error, display in the console.

Each time this function is called, it will POST an action in the engine that will be received by your device—exactly as you saw in the previous section.

Oh, and don't forget to turn on the plug with the button you just created; otherwise you won't see anything on the graph!

SUBSCRIBING VIA WEBSOCKETS

Second, you need to subscribe your client application to all property updates using WebSockets. In principle, this is similar to what you did with MQTT in the previous section. The idea is that you create a few HTML placeholders to display the current property values. For each property you want to display, you create a list item that looks like this:

```
<li class="list-group-item">
  <span id="value-status" class="badge">false</span>
  status
</li>
```

Note that the id must be set to value-status and the same property name as in the engine. Let's now see how to connect and process WebSockets messages, as the following listing shows.

Listing 7.21   Connecting to WebSockets and handling property updates

```
var url = 'wss://ws.evrythng.com:443/thngs/'+thngId+'
  /properties?access_token='+key;
var socket = new WebSocket(url);

socket.onmessage = function (message) {
  var content = JSON.parse(message.data);
  console.log('Property update : ', content[0]);
  if (content[0].key === "power"){
```

Parse the message content; note that it's an array!

Subscribes to all properties of this Thng via secure WebSockets

Each time you receive a WS message, this will be called.

Call this to update the power graph (function not shown).

```
      updateCharts(content[0].key, content[0].value, content[0].timestamp);
    }
    $('#value-'+content[0].key).html( content[0].value );
};
```

Use the property name to update the badge.

```
socket.onerror = function (error) {
  console.log('An error occurred while trying to connect to a
    WebSocket!');
  console.log(error);
};
```

This is similar to MQTT but entirely web-based and running in your web browser with no dependencies to install. Each time any property is updated you'll receive a corresponding JSON message over the WebSocket channel because you subscribed to the properties topic.

USING QR CODES TO IDENTIFY THINGS

Before we finish this section, let's do a final trick. For this, you'll need to deploy plug.html and the ui/ folder file somewhere in the cloud—for instance, on GitHub pages.[24] If you want to take the short route, we've deployed this file for you as well, and you can access it here (after replacing XXX with your operator API key and YYY with your Thng ID): https://webofthings.github.io/wot-book/plug.html?key=XXX& thngId=YYY. If you ran the script earlier in the previous section, it will have created a redirection for your Thng automatically; scan the QR code or click the short URL and you'll land on that link automatically. Otherwise, you can create it using the Setup Redirector button as shown in figure 7.11.

3. Get a short URL.   **2. Enter the full target URL for the redirection.**

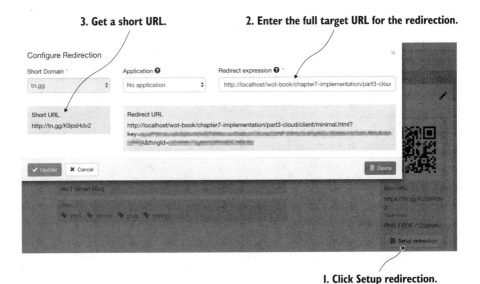

1. Click Setup redirection.

Figure 7.11   How to create a short URL redirecting to the user interface of your device

---

[24] https://pages.github.com/

Put the full path to the file in the redirect expression—the previous URL with your own credentials—and click Create Redirection. You now have a short URL and a corresponding QR code that you can update anytime and that allows you to see and control your device by scanning it with your phone. QR codes or NFC tags are a great way to serialize the URLs of Things and make them physically discoverable by mobile phones.

Note that you should not share this QR code or URL with anyone: it contains your operator API key! This was only to make a point, but you should never expose your API keys in this manner.

7.4.5   *Summary—cloud integration pattern*

Let's take some time to reflect on all you've done in this section. How did it feel to be able to do so much in so little time? Thanks to the open and flexible APIs of a Web of Things cloud platform such as EVRYTHNG, you've written a simple Node application that can talk to its digital identity in the cloud using MQTT. You've also built a basic HTML/JavaScript application that displays data from your device in real time and can send commands to it even if it doesn't have a REST API.

This is where the cloud integration pattern shines. Because most of the complexity of this system lives inside the cloud platform, you have less need to worry about scalability, reliability, or security. A cloud platform allows you, a digital product developer, to drastically reduce the time it takes to build web-connected devices and provides various powerful features, such as visualization, data storage, and access control. Because the front-end application uses only HTML/JS/CSS, you have a uniform interface to control any device regardless of whether it speaks HTTP or not, because the cloud system can seamlessly handle the translation across protocols.

Why would you ever use the direct connectivity pattern? There are several good reasons for still natively providing APIs on Things. Think, for instance, about latency: a local call is almost always faster than a call through the cloud. Or think about monitoring and control when the internet is down. Because of this, the best compromise for real-world WoT products is quite often to offer both local and cloud access.

7.5   **Summary**

- There are three main integration patterns for connecting Things to the web: direct, gateway, and cloud.
- Regardless of the pattern you choose, you'll have to work through the following steps: resource design, representation design, and interface design.
- Direct integration allows local access to the web API of a Thing. You tried this by building an API for your Pi using the Express Node framework.
- The resource design step in Express was implemented using routes, each route representing the path to the resources of your Pi.
- We used the idea of middleware to implement support for different representations— for example, JSON, MessagePack, and HTML—in the representation design step.

- The interface design step was implemented using HTTP verbs on routes as well as by integrating a WebSockets server using the ws Node module.
- Gateway integration allows integrating Things without web APIs (or not supporting web or even internet protocols) to the WoT by providing an API for them. You tried this by integrating a CoAP device via a gateway on your cloud.
- Cloud integration uses servers on the web to act as shadows or proxies for Things. They augment the API of Things with such features as scalability, analytics, and security. You tried this by using the EVRYTHNG cloud.

Now that we've created web APIs for Things, the next few chapters will be about making these APIs even more powerful and interesting. In the next chapter, we'll explore the resource-linking design step as well as the issues of findability and discoverability. In essence, we'll look at how a web Thing can expose its API in a way that makes it easy to be found, understood, and used by other applications, web Things, or even human beings!

Find: Describe and discover web Things

This chapter covers

- Learning the basics of discoverability (methods and protocols)
- Understanding how to do web-level discovery (linking/crawling)
- Proposing a model to describe web Things and their capabilities
- Extending the basic model with additional Semantic Web formats

In the previous two chapters, we explored extensively the various integration patterns for connecting your Things to the web, which is the first layer of the WoT architecture we introduced in chapter 6. We illustrated how using web standards as the connective tissue between heterogeneous devices significantly improves interoperability between components in an internet-scale system and thus is the core foundation of the Web of Things. Nevertheless, without a universal format to describe web Things and their capabilities, integrating web Things and applications still requires a consequent effort for developers. Having a single and common data model that all web Things can share would further increase interoperability and ease of integration by making it possible for applications and services to interact without the need to tailor the application manually for each specific device. This is an essential cornerstone of the WoT because it means that the hotel control center example we introduced in chapter 1 could seamlessly discover, understand, and read data and send commands to any device on the Web of Things, regardless of its capabilities or its manufacturer. The ability to easily discover and understand any entity of the Web of Things—what it is and what it does—is called *findability*.

How to achieve such a level of interoperability—making web Things findable—is the purpose of the second layer, Find, of the WoT architecture and is what this chapter focuses on. The goal of the Find layer is to offer a uniform data model that all web Things can use to expose their metadata using only web standards and best practices. *Metadata* means the description of a web Thing, including the URL, name, current location, and status, and of the services it offers, such as sensors, actuators, commands, and properties. First, this is useful for discovering web Things as they get connected to a local network or to the web. Second, it allows applications, services, and other web Things to search for and find new devices without installing a driver for that Thing. By the end of this chapter, you'll understand how to expose the metadata of any web Thing in a universal and interoperable way using network discovery protocols, such as mDNS; lightweight data models, such as the Web Thing Model; and Semantic Web standards, such as JSON-LD.

8.1 The findability problem

Once a device becomes a web Thing using the methods we presented in the previous two chapters, it can be interacted with using HTTP and WebSocket requests. This sounds great in theory, but for this to also work in practice, we must first solve three fundamental problems, as shown in figure 8.1:

1 How do we know *where* to send the requests, such as root URL/resources of a web Thing?
2 How do we know *what* requests to send and *how*, for example, verbs and the format of payloads?
3 How do we know the *meaning* of requests we send and responses we get, that is, semantics?

To better understand these problems, let's get back to the smart hotel scenario from chapter 1. Imagine Lena, an Estonian guest staying in room 202 of the hotel. Lena would like to pop up her phone so she can turn on the heat. The first question is how can Lena—or her phone, or an app on her phone—find the root URL of the heater? This is often called the *bootstrap problem*. This problem is concerned with how the initial link between two entities on the Web of Things can be established. The simplest solution to this problem would be to write the root URL on the desk or on the wall of the room. Another solution would be to encode the URL into a QR code printed on a

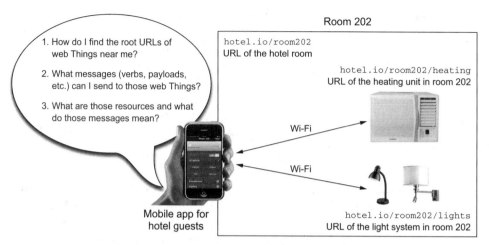

Figure 8.1   The three problems of findability in the Web of Things. How can a client application find nearby web Things, interact with them, and understand what these things are and do?

card or use an NFC tag upon her check-in, so Lena could scan it with her phone. A more complex solution would be to install an application on her phone that searches for devices with heating capabilities nearby. These approaches will be the subject of section 8.2. Finally, a web-friendly solution would be for her to Google for nearby heaters; we'll look into that in section 8.4.

Let's assume for now that Lena enters the root URL of the heater on her phone. Ideally, she would see a pretty user interface in her native Estonian that allows her to figure out right away which button turns on the heat. In this case, a clean and user-centric web interface can solve problem 3 because humans would be able to read and understand how to do this. Problem 2 also would be taken care of by the web page, which would hardcode which request to send to which endpoint.

But what if the heater has no user interface, only a RESTful API?[1] Because Lena is an experienced front-end developer and never watches TV, she decides to build a simple JavaScript app to control the heater. Now she faces the second problem: even though she knows the URL of the heater, how can she find out the structure of the heater API? What resources (endpoints) are available? Which verbs can she send to which resource? How can she specify the temperature she wants to set? How does she know if those parameters need to be in Celsius or Fahrenheit degrees?

Usually, application developers rely on written documentation that describes the various API endpoints and resources available on the Thing (problem 2) and the meaning of those (problem 3). But in some cases, a more automated way to discover the resources of a REST API at runtime might be useful. If there was a way for Lena—or the app she wrote—to interrogate on the fly any web Thing and find out what

---

[1] If the manager ever finds this out, he should probably fire the guy who was responsible for selecting this heater in the first place because it fails to address design rule #2 of chapter 6 by not providing a user interface.

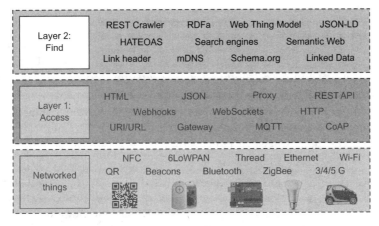

Figure 8.2 The Find layer of the Web of Things. This layer relates to how one can easily understand the nature of things, what they relate to, how to access their documentation, what their API endpoints are, and how to access those (what parameters and their types). It also relates to the meaning of these properties in a standard way.

services/data it offers, without having to read the documentation, her app would work with any heating device, regardless of its manufacturer.

Providing a web-based solution for these three problems is the goal of the Find layer, as shown in figure 8.2. In the rest of this chapter, we'll propose a set of tools and techniques for how web Things can expose their data resource so that users, applications, and Things can easily find and interact with them.

8.2 Discovering Things

We begin our journey in findability by comparing several solutions to the bootstrap problem. In short, how can an app or Thing find the root URL of a web Thing it has never encountered before? This problem deals with two scopes: first, how to find web Things that are physically nearby—for example, within the same local network—and second, how to find web Things that are not in the same local network—for example, find devices over the web. Finding web Things in a local network can be done using network discovery methods described in section 8.2.1. To find web Things beyond the same local network, we'll rely on resource discovery and search, as described in section 8.2.2. Let's now look at these methods in more detail.

8.2.1 Network discovery

In a computer network, the ability to automatically discover new participants is common. In your LAN at home, as soon as a device connects to the network, it automatically gets an IP address using *DHCP*[2] (*Dynamic Host Configuration Protocol*). But only the DHCP

---

[2] DHCP: http://en.wikipedia.org/wiki/Dynamic_Host_Configuration_Protocol.

server knows the device is in your network, so what about the other hosts in your network? Once the device has an IP address, it can then broadcast data packets that can be caught by other machines on the same network. As you saw in chapter 5, a broadcast or multicast of a message means that this message isn't sent to a particular IP address but rather to a group of addresses (multicast) or to everyone (broadcast), which is done over UDP. This announcement process is called a network discovery protocol, and it allows devices and applications to find each other in local networks. This process is commonly used by various discovery protocols such as multicast Domain Name System (mDNS),[3] Digital Living Network Alliance (DLNA),[4] and Universal Plug and Play (UPnP).[5] For example, most internet-connected TVs and media players can use DLNA to discover network-attached storage (NAS) in your network and read media files from it. Likewise, your laptop can find and configure printers on your network with minimal effort thanks to network-level discovery protocols such as Apple Bonjour that are built into iOS and OSX.

MDNS

In mDNS, clients can discover new devices on a network by listening for mDNS messages such as the one in the following listing. The client populates the local DNS tables as messages come in, so, once discovered, the new service—here a web page of a printer—can be used via its local IP address or via a URI usually ending with the .local domain. In this example, it would be http://evt-bw-brother.local.

Listing 8.1   An mDNS message from a printer

```
service up:  {
  interfaceIndex: 4,
  type:
  { name: 'http',              ◀── A service of type TCP and
    protocol: 'tcp',               HTTP was discovered.
    subtypes: [],
    fullyQualified: true },
  replyDomain: 'local.',
  flags: 3,
  name: 'Brother MFC-8520DN',
  networkInterface: 'en0',
  fullname: 'Brother\\032MFC-8520DN._http._tcp.local.',   ─┐ The service is reachable on
  host: 'EVT-BW-BROTHER.local',              ◀───────────┘ http://evt-bw-brother.local.
  port: 80,                     ── The service
  addresses: [ '192.168.0.6' ] }  ◀── local IP address
```

This is also the protocol that your Pi uses to broadcast its raspberrypi.local URL (see chapter 4) to all nearby computers listening with an mDNS client.

The limitation of mDNS, and of most network-level discovery protocols, is that the network-level information can't be directly accessed from the web. You could, of

---

[3]   http://en.wikipedia.org/wiki/Multicast_DNS
[4]   http://en.wikipedia.org/wiki/Digital_Living_Network_Alliance
[5]   http://en.wikipedia.org/wiki/Universal_Plug_and_Play

course, write JavaScript code that relies on predefined .local domains, but this would be merely a hack not supported by all browsers. This is also the reason why many mobile browsers can't resolve these addresses: they don't have an mDNS client populating the local DNS record in the background.

The nerd corner—I want my Pi to say "Bonjour!"

Your Pi already enables mDNS via the Avahi library to broadcast its .local URL, but you could do a lot more with mDNS, such as describing the HTTP services your WoT server provides (just like for the printer in listing 8.1). The experimental `node_mdns` Node library[a] builds on top of Avahi and lets you programmatically implement this and more. To get started with the library, look at the code sample we provided in the mdns folder of this chapter on GitHub.

Note: this module doesn't always run smoothly on the Pi, so you might have to fall back to your PC. If you'd still like to try it on the Pi, make sure you install the additionally required Debian packages via `apt-get install libavahi-compat-libdnssd-dev`.

[a] https://github.com/agnat/node_mdns.

NETWORK DISCOVERY ON THE WEB

If mDNS doesn't work in all browsers, how can a web application running on your mobile phone or tablet find nearby web Things? Or, why can't you find the web Things in your house by following links on a page? An easy solution would be to write a custom plugin for Firefox or Chrome that can talk to those network-level discovery protocols. But this doesn't solve the problem because in place of enabling web-based resource discovery using web standards, devices would still need to implement one or more non-web network discovery protocols. In consequence, web Thing client applications would also need to speak and understand these protocols, which defeats the purpose of the Web of Things.

Because HTTP is an Application layer protocol, it doesn't know a thing about what's underneath—the network protocols used to shuffle HTTP requests around. It also doesn't need to care—that is, unless a web Thing or application needs to know about other resources in the same network. The real question here is why the configuration and status of a router is only available through a web page for humans and not accessible via a REST API. Put simply, why don't all routers also offer a secure API where its configuration can be seen and changed by others' devices and applications in your network?

Providing such an API is easy to do.[6] For example, you can install an open-source operating system for routers such as OpenWrt[7] and modify the software to expose the

---

[6] This was proposed in Vlad's PhD thesis: http://www.slideshare.net/vladounet/vlad-trifa-final-phd-thesis-defense-at-eth-zurich.

[7] https://openwrt.org/

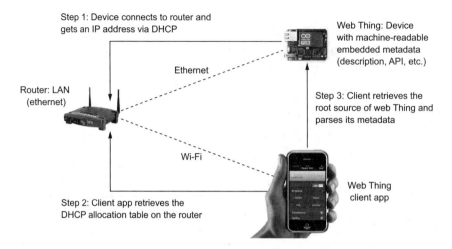

Figure 8.3   LAN-level resource discovery. Assuming that all web Things expose their root resource on port 80, web Thing clients can get their IPs from the router and then query each device to extract their metadata.

IP addresses assigned by the DHCP server of the router as a JSON document. This way, you use the existing HTTP server of your router to create an API that exposes the IP addresses of all the devices in your network. This makes sense because almost all networked devices today, from printers to routers, already come with a web user interface. Other devices and applications can then retrieve the list of IP addresses in the network via a simple HTTP call (step 2 in figure 8.3) and then retrieve the metadata of each device in the network by using their IP address (step 3 of figure 8.3).

Because routers usually have the base network address of the local network, you can easily write a web app that periodically queries the routing table, keeps track of the new devices connected to the network, and registers the devices in the network. The same pattern can be used with any other device on the network, where any web Thing—say, a set-top box or NAS—could continuously search for new devices in the network using various protocols, understand their services, and then act as a bridge to these devices by generating on the fly a new WoT API for those devices.

8.2.2   *Resource discovery on the web*

Although network discovery does the job locally, it doesn't propagate beyond the boundaries of local networks. Thinking in wider terms, several questions remain open: in a Web of Things with billions of Things accessible on the World Wide Web, how do we find new Things when they connect, how do we understand the services they offer, and can we search for the right Things and their data in composite applications?

The web faced a similar challenge when it shifted from a catalog of a few thousand pages with text and images in the early nineties to an exponentially growing collection of web applications, documents, and multimedia content including movies and music, games, and other service types. In those early days, AltaVista and Yahoo were successful in curating this growing collection of documents. But as the web started to grow exponentially, it became obvious that managing the list of resources on the web manually was a dead end. Around this time (~1998), Google appeared out of nowhere and pretty much wiped out any other search engine because it could automatically index millions of pages and allow users to rapidly and accurately find relevant content in this massive catalog.

On the web, new resources (pages) are discovered through hyperlinks. Search engines periodically parse all the pages in their database to find outgoing links to other pages. As soon as a link to a page not yet indexed is found, that new page is parsed and added to directory. This process is known as *web crawling.*

CRAWLING THE API OF WEB THINGS

We can apply the process of web crawling to Things as well: in chapter 2 you used an HTML-based UI for the WoT Pi, and in chapter 5 you saw how to create HTML representations of resources. By adding links to the sub-resources in the HTML code, we make it possible to crawl web Things with the simple pseudo-code shown in the next listing.

Listing 8.2   Pseudocode for crawling the HTML representation of Things

```
crawl(Link currentLink) {
  r = new Resource();
  r.setUri = currentLink.getURI();
  r.setShortDescription = currentLink.text();
  r.setLongDescription =
    currentLink.invokeVerb(GET).extractDescriptionFromResults();
  r.setOperations = currentLink.invokeVerb(OPTIONS).getVerbs();
  foreach (Format currentFormat: formats) {
    r.setAcceptedFormats =
      currentLink.invokeVerb(GET).setAcceptHeader(currentFormat);
  }
  if (currentLink.hasNext()) crawl(currentLink.getNext());
}
foreach(Link currentLink: currentPage.extractLinks())
{ crawl(currentLink); }
```

From the root HTML page of the web Thing, the crawler can find the sub-resources, such as sensors and actuators, by discovering outgoing links and can then create a resource tree of the web Thing and all its resources. The crawler then uses the HTTP OPTIONS method to retrieve all verbs supported for each resource of the web Thing. Finally, the crawler uses content negotiation to understand which format is available for each resource. As an exercise, we suggest you try implementing this crawler for the API of the Pi you created in chapter 7.

HATEOAS AND WEB LINKING

This simple crawling approach is a good start, but it also has several limitations. First, all links are treated equally because there's no notion of the *nature* of a link; the link to the user interface and the link to the actuator resource look the same—they're just

URLs. Then, it requires the web Thing to offer an HTML interface, which might be too heavy for resource-constrained devices. Finally, it also means that a client needs to both understand HTML and JSON to work with our web Things.

A better solution for discovering the resources of any REST API is to use the HATEOAS principle we presented in section 6.1.6 to describe relationships between the various resources of a web Thing. A simple method to implement HATEOAS with REST APIs is to use the mechanism of *web linking* defined in RFC 5988.[8] The idea is that the response to any HTTP request to a resource always contains a set of links to related resources—for example, the *previous, next,* or *last* page that contains the results of a search. These links would be contained in the Link: HTTP header of the response. Although a similar mechanism was already supported with the LINK[9] element in the HTML 4 specification, encoding the links as HTTP headers introduces a more general framework to define relationships between resources outside the representation of the resource—directly at the HTTP level. As a result, links can be always described in the same way regardless of the media type requested by the client, such as JSON or HTML. This type of linking is also the one supported by the Constrained Application Protocol we discussed in the previous chapters.[10]

When doing an HTTP GET on any Web Thing, the response should include a Link header that contains links to related resources. In particular, you should be able to get information about the device, its resources (API endpoints), and the documentation of the API using only Link headers. Following is an example HTTP query sent to a WoT gateway:

```
HTTP 1.1 GET /
Host: gateway.webofthings.io
Accept: application/html

200 OK
Link: </model/>; rel="model", </properties/>; rel="properties", </actions/>;
      rel="actions", </things/>; rel="things", <http://model.webofthings.io/>;
      rel="type", </help>; rel="help", </>; rel="ui"
```

In this example, the response contains a set of links to the resources of the web Thing in the Link header. The URL of each resource is contained between angle brackets (<URL>) and the type of the link is denoted by rel="X", where X is the type of the rela-tion. If the URL is not an absolute URL—that is, it doesn't start with http:// or https:// —it's interpreted in the context of the current request path, to which the relative URL will be appended. In this example, the documentation of the web Thing will therefore become devices.webofthings.io/help. Note that the link element can be any valid URI and therefore could well be hosted on the device itself, on a gateway, or anywhere else on the web. Some reserved and standardized relationship types are defined by

---

[8] https://tools.ietf.org/html/rfc5988
[9] http://www.w3.org/TR/html401/struct/links.html#edef-LINK
[10] https://tools.ietf.org/html/rfc6690

IANA, but those are mainly relevant to the classic web of multimedia documents. Because no set of relationship types has been proposed for physical objects and for the Web of Things, we'll propose one in this chapter. In the previous example, you could see that the root page of the Web of Things gateway contains links to the following four resources.

REL="MODEL"
This is a link to a Web Thing Model resource; see section 8.3.1.

REL="TYPE"
This is a link to a resource that contains additional metadata about this web Thing.

REL="HELP"
This relationship type is a link to the documentation, which means that a GET to `devices.webofthings.io/help` would return the documentation for the API in a human-friendly (HTML) or machine-readable (JSON) format. The documentation doesn't need to be hosted on the device itself but could be hosted anywhere—for example, on the manufacturer's website, in which case the header would look like this:

```
Link: <http://webofthings.io/doc/v/1.1>; rel="help"
```

This allows maintaining and continuously updating the documentation of multiple devices deployed in the wild and running various firmware versions, without the need to host it directly on the device but in the cloud.

REL="UI"
This relationship type is a link to a graphical user interface (GUI) for interacting with the web Thing. The UI must be implemented using HTML so that it can be accessed with any browser, and it should be responsive to allow various device types to interact with the web Thing. Note that the GUI can—but doesn't have to—be hosted on the device itself as long as the GUI application can access the web Thing and its resources. In the following example, the GUI is hosted on GitHub and takes as a parameter the root URL of the web Thing to control:

```
Link: <http://webofthings.github.io/ui?url=devices.webofthings.io>; rel="ui"
```

In some situations you won't be able to modify the HTTP headers of the response returned by a web Thing. If this is the case, you'll need to insert them in the HTML or JSON representation of the resource. We'll show how you do this in sections 8.3.3 for JSON and 8.4.1 for HTML.

8.3 Describing web Things

The ability to discover the root URL and resources of a web Thing solves the first part of the findability problem and is enough to interact with the web Thing if it provides a user interface—the root URL returns an HTML page. But knowing only the root URL is insufficient to interact with the Web Thing API because we still need to solve the second problem mentioned at the beginning of this chapter: how can an application know which payloads to send to which resources of a web Thing? In other words, what

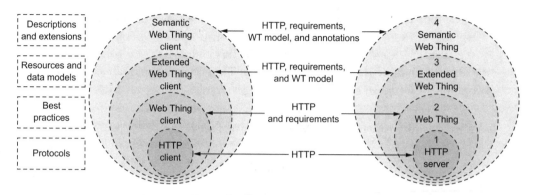

Figure 8.4   The various levels for describing web Things. Any device can have an HTTP API (1). Web Things (2) are HTTP servers that follow the requirements proposed in chapter 6; thus, APIs are more consistent, predictable, and easier to use. Using a shared model will make the web Thing more interoperable (3). Finally, adding semantic annotations will ensure stronger contracts between web Things and also more flexibility to define formally each element of the web Thing API (4).

possible parameters and their type are supported by each end point, what will be the effect of a given request, what possible error/success messages will be returned, and what do those mean?

This question can be summarized as follows: how can we formally describe the API offered by any web Thing? As you can see in figure 8.4, there are various ways to do this, ranging from no shared data model between the API of a web Thing (1), all the way to semantically defining every possible interaction with a web Thing (4). Semantic Web Things maximize interoperability by ensuring that client applications can discover new Things and use them at runtime automatically, without any human in the loop.

The simplest solution is to provide a written documentation for the API of your web Thing so that developers can use it (1 and 2 in figure 8.4). This implies that a developer must read the documentation about your web Thing, understand what requests they can send to it and what each does, and finally implement the various API calls with correct parameters for each call. This approach, however, is insufficient to automatically find new devices, understand what they are, and what services they offer. In addition, manual implementation of the payloads is more error-prone because the developer needs to ensure that all the requests they send are valid. This becomes especially tricky when the API documentation differs from the actual API running on the device, which can happen when the API changes but not the documentation. Or simply when the documentation is…hmm…ungracious in the first place. Sadly, most APIs in the Internet of Things are in this situation because they don't make it easy or even possible to write applications that can dynamically generate a user interface for a device only by knowing its root URL.

As will be shown in the rest of this chapter, all hope is not lost—quite the opposite! By using a unique data model to define formally the API of any web Thing (the Web Thing Model) as described in section 8.3.2, we'll have a powerful basis to describe not only the metadata but also the operations of any web Thing in a standard way (cases 3 and 4 of figure 8.4). This is the cornerstone of the Web of Things: creating a model to describe physical Things with the right balance between expressiveness—how flexible the model is—and usability— how easy it is to describe *any* web Thing with that model. Achieving this balance is necessary in order to achieve global-scale interoperability and adoption, and this is what we'll do in the remainder of this chapter.

8.3.1   *Introducing the Web Thing Model*

Once we find a web Thing and understand its API structure, we still need a method to describe what that device is and does. In other words, we need a conceptual model of a web Thing that can describe the resources of a web Thing using a set of well-known concepts.

In the previous chapters, we showed how to organize the resources of a web Thing using the /sensors and /actuators end points. But this works only for devices that actually have sensors and actuators, not for complex objects and scenarios that are common in the real world that can't be mapped to actuators or sensors. To achieve this, the core model of the Web of Things must be easily applicable for any entity in the real world, ranging from packages in a truck, to collectible card games, to orange juice bottles. This section provides exactly such a model, which is called the *Web Thing Model*.[11]

Because this model is more abstract and covers more use cases than the ones we used in previous chapters, it's also a bit more complex to understand and use, and that's why we only introduce it now. But don't worry—by the end of this chapter, it will all make sense to you and you'll see that you can easily adapt it for any Web of Things scenario you can think of. Not only that, but with the reference implementation of this model you'll find in this chapter, you'll also be able to implement truly interoperable web Things and WoT applications that reach the full potential of the Web of Things. Let's get started!

Note that to make it easier for you to discover the Web Thing Model and try the examples in this section, we deployed a web Thing in the cloud: http://gateway.webofthings.io. In the next section, you'll learn how to implement and run the same web Thing server your Pi or laptop, so feel free to revisit these examples on your own web Things later.

ENTITIES

As we described earlier, the Web of Things is composed of web Things. But what is a web Thing concretely? A web Thing is a digital representation of a physical object—a Thing—accessible on the web. Think of it like this: your Facebook profile is a digital representation of yourself, so a web Thing is the "Facebook profile" of a physical object. Examples of web Things are the virtual representations of garage door, a bottle

---

[11] At the time of writing, the Web Thing Model (http://model.webofthings.io) is also an official W3C member submission. This does not mean it is a standard yet, but it means it will influence the standardization efforts around the Web of Things within the Web of Things Interest Group (http://www.w3.org/WoT/IG/). EVRYTHNG (and hence Vlad and Dom) is part of the Web of Things Interest Group at W3C.

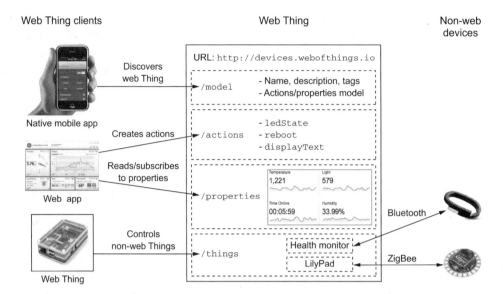

Figure 8.5   The resources of a web Thing. Web Thing clients can interact with the various resources of the web Thing. The model resource provides metadata for discovery, properties are the variables of the Things (data, sensor, state, and so on), and actions are the function calls (commands supported by the web Thing). When the web Thing is also a gateway to other (non-web) Things, the Thing's resource is a proxy to the non-web Things.

of soda, an apartment, a TV, and so on. The web Thing is a web resource that can be hosted directly on the device, if it can connect to the web, or on an intermediate in the network such as a gateway or a cloud service that bridges non-web devices to the web. All web Things should have the following resources as illustrated in figure 8.5:

- *Model*—A web Thing always has a set of metadata that defines various aspects about it such as its name, description, or configurations.

- *Properties*—A property is a variable of a web Thing. Properties represent the internal state of a web Thing. Clients can subscribe to properties to receive a notification message when specific conditions are met; for example, the value of one or more properties changed.

- *Actions*—An action is a function offered by a web Thing. Clients can invoke a function on a web Thing by sending an action to the web Thing. Examples of actions are "open" or "close" for a garage door, "enable" or "disable" for a smoke alarm, and "scan" or "check in" for a bottle of soda or a place. The direction of an action is from the client to the web Thing.

- *Things*—A web Thing can be a gateway to other devices that don't have an internet connection. This resource contains all the web Things that are proxied by this web Thing. This is mainly used by clouds or gateways because they can proxy other devices.

Each web Thing can use this model to expose its capabilities. In the next section we examine these in more detail, especially what they look like. Describing the entire model in this book would take a few more chapters, so we limit ourselves to the strict essentials needed to understand what it is and how you can use it. We invite you to refer to the online description of the Web Thing Model to see the entire description with the various entities and fields you can use. You won't need this information to follow this chapter, but it will help when you will want to adapt the model for your own devices and products. Furthermore, this model is heavily built on the concepts you learned in chapters 6 and 7, so you're definitely not starting from scratch!

8.3.2 Metadata

In the Web Thing Model, all web Things must have some associated metadata to describe what they are. This is a set of basic fields about a web Thing, including its identifiers, name, description, and tags, and also the set of resources it has, such as the actions and properties. A GET on the root URL of any web Thing ({WT} in the following listing) always returns the metadata using this format, which is JSON by default.

> **Listing 8.3 GET {WT}: retrieve the metadata of a web Thing**

```
GET / HTTP/1.1
Host: gateway.webofthings.io
Accept: application/json


HTTP/1.1 200 OK
Content-Type: application/json; charset=utf-8
Link: </model/>; rel="model", </properties/>; rel="properties",
  </actions/>; rel="actions", </things/>; rel="things",
  <http://model.webofthings.io/>; rel="type"

{
  "id": "http://gateway.webofthings.io",
  "name": "My WoT Raspberry PI",
  "description": "A simple WoT-connected Raspberry Pi for the WoT
    book.",
  "tags": ["raspberry","pi","WoT"],
  "customFields": {...}
}
```

As you can see here, the returned payload contains the basic information about the web Thing. The links to the various resources of this web Thing are contained in the `Link:` header of the response; see section 8.2.2. You can then follow each link to get more information about each of those resources. A GET {WT}/model will return the entire model of the web Thing, including the details of the actions or properties available.

8.3.3 Properties

Web Things can also have properties. A *property* is a collection of data values that relate to some aspect of the web Thing. Typically, you'd use properties to model any dynamic time series of data that a web Thing exposes, such as the current and past states of the web Thing or its sensor values—for example, the temperature or humidity sensor readings. Because properties should always capture the most up-to-date state of the web Thing, they're generally updated by the web Things themselves as soon as the value changes and not by web Thing clients or applications. Let's look at the properties of our web Thing by doing a GET on the {WT}/properties resource, as shown in the following listing.

Listing 8.4   GET {WT}/properties: retrieve the properties of a web Thing

```
HTTP/1.1 200 OK
Content-Type: application/json; charset=utf-8
Link: <http://model.webofthings.io/#properties-resource>; rel="type"

[
  {
    "id": "temperature",
    "name": "Temperature Sensor",
    "values": {
      "t": 9,
      "timestamp": "2016-01-31T18:25:04.679Z"
    }
  },
  {
    "id": "humidity",
    "name": "Humidity Sensor",
    "values": {
      "h": 70,
      "timestamp": "2016-01-31T18:25:04.679Z"
    }
  },
  {
    "id": "pir",
    "name": "Passive Infrared",
    "values": {
      "presence": false,
      "timestamp": "2016-01-31T18:25:04.678Z"
    }
  },
  {
    "id": "leds",
    "name": "LEDs",
    "values": {
      "1": false,
      "2": false,
      "timestamp": "2016-01-31T18:25:04.679Z"
    }
  }
]
```

You can see the current values of the various sensors on the Raspberry Pi, such as the temperature and PIR and when they were last changed. Let's now look at one of them in more detail in the next listing.

Listing 8.5　Retrieve the temperature property

```
HTTP/1.1 200 OK
Content-Type: application/json; charset=utf-8
Link: <http://model.webofthings.io/#properties-resource>; rel="type"

[
    {"t":21.1,"timestamp":"2015-06-14T15:00:00.000Z"},
    {"t":21.4,"timestamp":"2015-06-14T14:30:00.000Z"},
    {"t":21.6,"timestamp":"2015-06-14T14:00:00.000Z"},
...
]
```

A GET on a specific property will return an array of value objects like the one shown here. Each value object has one or more fields, such as t for the actual temperature sensor reading, and the timestamp when the value was recorded. Some sensors might have several dimensions; for example, an acceleration sensor will have three dimensions, called values, one for each axis: X, Y, and Z.

8.3.4　*Actions*

Actions are another important type of resources of a web Thing because they represent the various commands that can be sent to that web Thing. Examples of actions are "open/close the garage door," "turn on the living room light, set its brightness to 50%, and set the color to red," and "turn off the TV in 30 minutes." In theory, you could also use properties to change the status of a web Thing, but this can be a problem when both an application and the web Thing itself want to edit the same property. This is where actions can help. Let's draw a parallel to better grasp the concept: actions represent the public interface of a web Thing and properties are the private parts. Much like in any programming languages, you can access the public interface, and whatever is private remains accessible only for privileged parties, like the instance itself or, in this case, the web Thing. But limiting access to actions—that is, the public interface—also allows you to implement various control mechanisms for external requests such as access control, data validation, updating a several properties atomically, and the like.

Actions are also particularly useful when the command you want to send to a web Thing is much more complex than setting a simple value; for example, when you want to send a PDF to a printer or when the action might not be automatically executed. You can find the list of actions a given web Thing supports by sending a GET {WT}/ actions request, as in the next listing.

Listing 8.6　GET {WT}/actions: retrieve the actions supported by a web Thing

```
HTTP/1.1 200 OK
Content-Type: application/json; charset=utf-8
Link: <http://model.webofthings.io/#actions-resource>; rel="type"

[{"id":"ledState","name":"Changes the status of the LEDs"}]
```

The response payload contains an array with the name and ID of each action the web Thing supports. More details about these actions are available in the {WT}/model resource, which describes what each action does and how to invoke it (which parameters to use, what their value should be, and so on). Let's examine the details of the action ledState in the model in the following listing.

Listing 8.7   GET {WT}/model: **the** actions **object of a web Thing model**

```
HTTP/1.1 200 OK
Content-Type: application/json; charset=utf-8
Link: <model.webofthings.io>; rel="type"

...
"actions": {                                        The link to the actions
  "link": "/actions",                               resource; can be
  "title": "Actions of this Web Thing",             changed if needed
  "resources": {
    "ledState": {
      "name":"Changes the status of the LEDs",
      "values": {                                   New actions must contain two values, ledId
        "ledId": {                                  specifying which LED is to be addressed
          "type": "string",                         and state for turning the LED on/off.
          "required": true},
        "state": {
          "type": "boolean",
          "required" : true}
      }
    }
  }
},...
```

The definition of the ledState action

The actions object of the Web Thing Model has an object called resources, which contains all the types of actions (commands) supported by this web Thing. In this example, only one action is supported: the "ledState":{} object, where ledState is the ID of this action. The values object contains the possible parameters that can be sent when creating the action. Here, the action accepts two values: ledId (the ID of the LED to change as a string) and state (the target state as a Boolean), both of which are required. Actions are sent to a web Thing with a POST to the URL of the action {WT}/actions/{id}, where id is the ID of the action (ledState), as shown in the next listing.

Listing 8.8   POST {WT}/actions/ledState: **turn on LED 3**

```
POST {WT}/actions/ledState
Content-Type: application/json

{"ledId":"3","state":true}

HTTP/1.1 204 NO CONTENT
```

You can see that the payload is an object where the different fields correspond to the values object for that action (see listing 8.7). The response of the request will usually be 204 NO CONTENT if it is executed immediately or 202 ACCEPTED if the action will be executed at a later time. If the web Thing keeps track of all actions it receives, you can see the list of all actions with a GET on the {WT}/actions/{actionId} resource. You'll find more details about actions and how to use them in the Web Thing Model reference online.

8.3.5 *Things*

As shown in figure 8.5, a web Thing can act as a gateway between the web and devices that aren't connected to the internet. In this case, the gateway can expose the resources—properties, actions, and metadata—of those non-web Things using the web Thing. The web Thing then acts as an Application-layer gateway for those non-web Things as it converts incoming HTTP requests for the devices into the various protocols or interfaces they support natively. For example, if your WoT Pi has a Bluetooth dongle, it can find and bridge Bluetooth devices nearby and expose them as web Things.

The resource that contains all the web Things proxied by a web Thing gateway is {WT}/things, and performing a GET on that resource will return the list of all web Things currently available, as shown in the following listing.

Listing 8.9 GET {WT}/things: the things object of the Web Thing Model

```
HTTP/1.1 200 OK
Content-Type: application/json; charset=utf-8
Link: <model.webofthings.io/things>; rel="meta"

[
  {
    "id":"http://devices.webofthings.io/pi",
    "name":"Raspberry Pi",
    "description":"A WoT-enabled Raspberry Pi"
  },
  {
    "id":"http://devices.webofthings.io/camera",
    "name":"Fooscam Camera",
    "description":"LAN-connected camera."
  },
  {
    "id":"http://devices.webofthings.io/hue",
    "name":"Philips Hue",
    "description":"A WoT-enabled Philips Hue Lamp."
  }
]
```

You can then access the web Thing for each of those resources by accessing its ID if it's an absolute URL, or by appending it to the Things resource URL ({WT}/things/{id}) and send actions or retrieve its properties like you would with any other web Thing. The Things resource is mainly relevant when a web Thing is a gateway or a cloud service but also if the web Thing has a number of other devices connected to it; for example, via USB, Bluetooth, or any other type of interface.

8.3.6 *Implementing the Web Thing Model on the Pi*

Now that you've seen the basics of the Web Thing Model, it's time to dig into the most important parts of its implementation.

> #### How to get the code
>
> There's a copious amount of code behind the implementation of the Web Thing Model we just presented, so instead of describing each line of code, we'll focus on the most important or tricky parts. You'll find the full code on GitHub; see http:// book.webofthings.io. The examples for this chapter are located in the chapter8-semantics folder. Go to the webofthingsjs-unsecure folder and run `npm install` followed by `node wot.js`.
>
> Because the code is using the webofthings.js project (the reference implementation of the Web Thing Model), you *must* clone the Git repository with the `--recursive` option to make sure all the sub-modules of this chapter are also retrieved.

THE WOT PI MODEL

The first thing we want to do now is to use the Web Thing Model to describe the Pi and its capabilities. This means extending the simpler sensor/actuator model we wrote in chapter 7. The tree structure of the Pi modeled using the Web Thing Model is shown in figure 8.6 and the corresponding JSON model can be found in the / resources/piNoLd.json file.

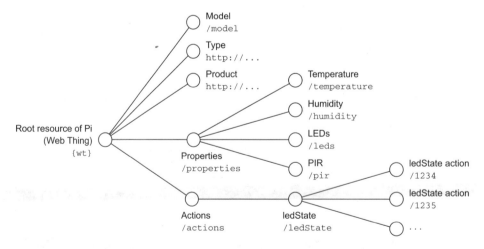

Figure 8.6   Resource tree of the Pi implementing the Web Thing Model. The notion of sensors and actuators is replaced by the idea of properties (variables) and actions (functions). Some of the resources, such as type or product, can be external references.

The listing that follows shows the model of the temperature property shown in listing 8.5.

Listing 8.10 Temperature property for Pi

```
"links": {
  "product": {
    "link": "https://.../products/raspberry-pi-2-model-b/",
    "title": "Product this Web Thing is based on"
  },
  "properties": {
    "link": "/properties",
    "title": "List of Properties",
    "resources": {
      "temperature": {
        "name": "Temperature Sensor",
        "description": "An ambient temperature sensor.",
        "values": {
          "t": {
            "name": "Temperature sensor",
            "description": "The temperature in celsius",
            "unit": "celsius",
            "customFields": {
              "gpio": 12
            }
          }
        }
      },
      "tags": ["sensor","public","indoors"]
    } [...]
```

Properties are also link resources.

The model contains a link object respecting the web linking format.

The temperature property can contain several values, but here it contains just one, t.

Remember that the properties of our model are variables or private interfaces of the web Thing and therefore shouldn't be changed by external clients, only by the device itself. Properties can be modified through actions, which you can see as functions or public interfaces a web client can invoke on a web Thing.

An action is a contract between the clients and the Things. When an action is created, the web Thing must know what to do with it; you'll see an implementation of an action shortly. Likewise, the client must know the format and semantics of the action, such as which parameters can be sent.

In order for clients to easily access the resources of a web Thing, the entire model of the Thing should be easily retrievable by the client. Once the model is ready, we make it accessible through the /model resource, which returns the entire piNoLd.json file.

VALIDATING YOUR MODEL WITH JSON SCHEMA

Creating your model file so that it complies with the Web Thing Model can be a daunting task because this model is significantly more complex than the one we used in chapter 7, for example. This is unfortunately the price we pay for better interoperability and real-world readiness. Luckily, there's a tool that can help us: JSON schemas.[12]

---

[12] http://json-schema.org/

A JSON schema is a way to formalize the model of a JSON payload; it's basically the XML schema (XSD) of JSON. The Web Thing Model provides a Web Thing Model–compliant JSON schema that you can use to validate the JSON model of your Things. To use it, download it[13] and then use a JSON schema validator library such as JSON-Schema for Node.js,[14] or use an online validator such as the good JSON Schema Lint.[15]

EXTENDING THE WOT SERVER FOR DISCOVERY—ARCHITECTURE

There are many ways to implement this model on the Pi, but the simplest way to do it is to extend the architecture on top of what you implemented in chapter 7. The key idea is to put the Web Thing Model in the middle. The properties of the model will be updated by the different plugins connected to the sensors; for example, the temperature or PIR plugins. The plugins managing actuators will listen for incoming actions by observing the model. Finally, clients request resources and the server sends them a subset of the model as a response. Look at figure 8.7 to see the key parts of this implementation.

DYNAMIC ROUTING

In chapter 7, we manually created Express routes. Here, because we implemented a well-known contract (the Web Thing Model), we're able to automatically generate the

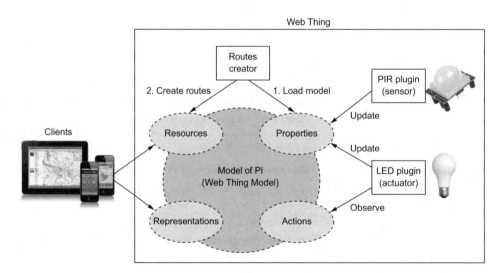

Figure 8.7   Implementation strategy of our Pi web Thing: the model is in the middle. It's used by the routes creator to create the REST resources and their corresponding endpoints. Sensor plugins—for example, PIR—update the model whenever fresh data is read from a sensor. Actuator plugins listen for actions sent by clients, execute the action, and finally update the model when the action has been executed successfully; for example, they update the properties that have changed as a result of the action.

---

[13] http://model.webofthings.io/models/wot-schema.json
[14] https://github.com/tdegrunt/jsonschema
[15] http://jsonschemalint.com/

routes with little effort. To do this we first load the model and create the routes accordingly inside the /routes/routesCreator.js file. The code in the next listing shows the creation of the root resource.

Listing 8.11 /routes/routesCreator.js: root resource route

```
function createRootRoute(model) {
  router.route('/').get(function (req, res, next) {          ◄─┐ Handle the root
    var type = 'http://model.webofthings.io/';                │ resource (/).
    res.links({
      model: '/model/',
      properties: '/properties/',
      actions: '/actions/',
      things: '/things/',                       ┐ Create the Link header
      type: type                                │ containing links to the other
    });                                      ◄──┘ resources (HATEOAS).

    var fields = ['id', 'name', 'description', 'tags', 'customFields'];
    req.result = utils.extractFields(fields, model);          ◄───┐
                                                                  │
    next();                                   Extract the required fields from
  });                                         the model; add the resulting
};                                                     object to the results.
```

Call the next middleware (representation middleware).

The code for the Thing (/), model (/model), properties (/properties/...), and actions (/actions/...) resources is similar. The next listing how to create the routes related to actions.

Listing 8.12 /routes/routesCreator.js: actions resources routes

```
[...]
function createActionsRoutes(model) {
  var actions = model.links.actions;
                                                              ┐ GET /actions
  router.route(actions.link).get(function (req, res, next) {  ◄─┘ route
    req.type ='actions';
    req.entityId = 'actions';
    type = 'http://model.webofthings.io/#actions-resource';
    res.links({
      type: type                              ┐ Transform the model into
    });                                       │ a Web Thing Model
                                              │ actions resource.
    req.result = utils.modelToResources(actions.resources, true);  ◄──┘
    next();
  });

  router.route(actions.link + '/:actionType')               ┐ POST /actions/{:actionType}
  .post(function (req, res, next) {                       ◄──┘ route
    var action = req.body;
    action.id = uuid.v1();                    ┐ Create a unique identifier for the
    action.timestamp = utils.isoTimestamp();  │ new resource and add a timestamp.
    action.status = "pending";
```

Populate the Link header for the actions resource.

Extract the request body (action JSON).

```
        actions.resources[req.params.actionType].data.push(action);

        res.location(req.originalUrl + '/' + action.id);
        next();
    });
    [...]
```

Add the URL of the new resource to the standard Location header.

Add the new action to the model; we add a data field to the model to contain the actual instance of actions.

You can see that the routes are created using two helper functions, defined in utils.js, that map the model to the resource representation as specified in the Web Thing Model:

- `extractFields(fields, model)` creates a new object by copying only the necessary fields from the model.
- `modelToResources(subModel, withValue)` transforms a subset of the model into an array of resources; for example, it extracts all the properties from the model with their latest values to create the `/properties` resource.

PLUGINS

Because the Web Thing Model is based on the concepts of actions, not just properties (like our implementation in chapter 7), we need to adapt the plugins to react to incoming actions. The basic concept is shown in figure 8.7: sensor plugins (for example, the temperature and humidity plugin, the PIR plugin) still update properties just like in the code of chapter 7. But actuator plugins will listen for incoming actions by observing the model and will update properties when changing their state after an action has been executed.

You can find the code for the new plugins in the /plugins/internal directory. You'll notice that unlike in chapter 7, all plugins inherit now from a corePlugin.js module. This helps us group the code common to all plugins into an abstract plugin that other concrete plugins will inherit from and extend. This can be done using a JavaScript feature called *prototypal inheritance*. If you have no clue what we're talking about here, don't worry. All you need to remember is that the all the code shared by all plugins is implemented in corePlugin.js, whereas all the functionality that's specific to a plugin is implemented in the concrete plugin modules themselves; for example, pirPlugin.js.[16] The most important part of the corePlugin.js file is shown in the next listing.

Listing 8.13   /plugins/corePlugin.js: generic plugin for common features

```
[...]
var CorePlugin = exports.CorePlugin = function (params,
                                                propertyId,
                                                doStop,
                                                doSimulate,
                                                actionsIds,
                                                doAction) {
```

---

[16] If you'd like to learn more about prototypical inheritance in JavaScript, the Mozilla JavaScript portal is a good place to start: https://developer.mozilla.org/en-US/docs/Web/JavaScript/Inheritance_and_the_prototype _chain. Or you can use any of the JavaScript or Node.js books we recommended in chapter 3.

```
                  if (params) {
                    this.params = params;
                  } else {
                    this.params = {'simulate': false, 'frequency': 5000};
                  }

                  this.doAction = doAction;
                  this.doStop = doStop;
                  this.doSimulate = doSimulate;
                  this.actions = actionsIds;
                  this.model = utils.findProperty(propertyId);
                };

                CorePlugin.prototype.start = function () {
                  if (this.actions) this.observeActions();
                  if (this.params.simulate) {
                    this.simulate();
                  } else {
                    this.connectHardware();
                  }
                  console.info('[plugin started] %s', this.model.name);
                };
                [...]

                CorePlugin.prototype.observeActions = function () {
                  var self = this;
                  _.forEach(self.actions, function (actionId) {
                    Object.observe(resources.links.actions.resources[actionId].data,
                    function (changes) {
                      var action = changes[0].object[changes[0].object.length -1];
                      console.info('[plugin action detected] %s', actionId);
                      if (self.doAction) self.doAction(action);
                    }, ['add']);
                  });
                };
```

Initialize a new concrete plugin with the given parameters and functions.

doActions is provided by the concrete plugin and contains what to do when an action is received.

A list of the identifiers of actions to observe

This helper function returns the property of this plugin.

Start observing the actions.

For each action ID, find it in the model and register a callback to doAction.

The changes object contains an array of all registered changes; we take the last change.

As a result, concrete plugins are much shorter and simpler because they can use the functionality from the corePlugin.js module. All these plugins have to do now is register which property they will update and which actions they will listen to (observe). Obviously, they also have to implement the hardware connectivity part (GPIOs) as well as what to do with the hardware when an action they listen to is performed through the REST API. All the plugins are in the /plugins directory. To understand how all this works, take a closer look at the LED plugin shown in the next listing.

Listing 8.14   /plugins/ledsPlugin.js: LED plugin working with the Web Thing Model

```
[...]
var actuator, model;
var LedsPlugin = exports.LedsPlugin = function (params) {
  CorePlugin.call(this, params, 'leds',
```

Call the initialization function of the parent plugin (corePlugin.js).

```
                    stop, simulate, ['ledState'], switchOnOff);
                  model = this.model;
                  this.addValue(false);
                };
```

Make the LedsPlugin inherit from all the corePlugin.js functionality.

Pass it the property you'll update (leds) and the actions you want to observe (ledState) as well as the implementation of what to do when a ledState action is created (switchOnOff).

```
              util.inherits(LedsPlugin, CorePlugin);

              function switchOnOff(value) {
                var self = this;
                if (!this.params.simulate) {
                  actuator.write(value.state === true ? 1 : 0, function () {
                    self.addValue(value.state);
                  });
                } else {
                  self.addValue(value.state);
                }
              }
```

Add a new data entry to the property in the model.

Change status to 'completed' as the LED state is changed.

```
                value.status = 'completed';
                console.info('Changed value of %s to %s', self.model.name, value.state);
              };

              function stop() {
                actuator.unexport();
              };

              function simulate() {
                this.addValue(false);
              };

              LedsPlugin.prototype.createValue = function (data){
                return {"1" : data, "2" : false, "timestamp" : utils.isoTimestamp()};
              };

              LedsPlugin.prototype.connectHardware = function () {
```

Change the state of the LED using the onoff library.

```
                var Gpio = require('onoff').Gpio;
                var self = this;
                actuator = new Gpio(self.model.values['1'].customFields.gpio, 'out');
                console.info('Hardware %s actuator started!', self.model.name);
              };
```

Extend the function connect-Hardware of corePlugin.js.

If you have other devices at home, we invite you to extend the Web Thing Model for your devices and adapt this implementation so you can expose those devices as web Things so that they can be part of the Web of Things.

8.3.7 *Summary—the Web Thing Model*

In this section, we introduced the Web Thing Model, a simple JSON-based data model for a web Thing and its resources. We also showed how to implement this model using Node.js and run it on a Raspberry Pi. We showed that this model is quite easy to understand and use, and yet is sufficiently flexible to represent all sorts of devices and products using a set of properties and actions. The goal is to propose a uniform way to describe web Things and their capabilities so that any HTTP client can find web Things and interact with them. This is sufficient for most use cases, and this model has all you need to be able to generate user interfaces for web Things automatically, as we'll show in chapter 10. If the hotel room where our Estonian friend Lena is staying would only offer a Web Thing Model and an API like this for all the devices and services in the room, she would be happy and could build her dream app in no time! Sadly, the Web of Things is nowhere near this vision yet because such a model for the Web of Things has been missing. Until now, that is!

8.4 The Semantic Web of Things

In an ideal world, search engines and any other applications on the web could also understand the Web Thing Model. Given the root URL of a web Thing, any application could retrieve its JSON model and understand what the web Thing is and how to interact with it. But this is not yet the case because the Web Thing Model we proposed isn't a standard. The question now is how to expose the Web Thing Model using an existing web standard so that the resources are described in a way that means something to other clients. The answer lies in the notion of the Semantic Web and, more precisely, the notion of linked data that we introduce in this section.

Semantic Web refers to an extension of the web that promotes common data formats to facilitate meaningful data exchange between machines. Thanks to a set of standards defined by the World Wide Web Consortium (W3C), web pages can offer a standardized way to express relationships among them so that machines can understand the meaning and content of those pages. In other words, the Semantic Web makes it easier to find, share, reuse, and process information from any content on the web thanks to a common and extensible data description and interchange format.

8.4.1 Linked data and RDFa

When search engines find and index content from the web, most of the data on web pages is unstructured. This makes it difficult to understand what a web page is about. Is this page about someone? Or is it about a restaurant, a movie, a birthday party, or a product? HTML pages have only a limited ability to tell web clients or search engines what they talk about. All you can do is to define a summary and a set of keywords. The HTML specification alone doesn't define a shared vocabulary that allows you to describe in a standard and non-ambiguous manner the elements on a page and what they relate to.

LINKED DATA

Enter the vision of linked data,[17] which is a set of best practices for publishing and connecting structured data on the web, so that web resources can be interlinked in a way that allows computers to automatically understand the type and data of each resource. This is particularly appealing because any application that understands the type of a resource can then collect, process, and aggregate data from different sources uniformly, regardless of where it was published.

---

[17] http://linkeddata.org/

This vision has been strongly driven by complex and heavy standards and tools centered on the Resource Description Framework[18] (RDF) and various controlled vocabularies, known as ontologies. Although powerful and expressive, RDF would be overkill for most simple scenarios, and this is why a simpler method to structure content on the web is desirable.

To overcome the limited descriptive power of the web without the heavy machinery of RDF, RDFa[19] offers an interesting tradeoff. This standard emerged as a lighter version of RDF that can be embedded into HTML code. Designed for both humans and machines, RDFa is a simple and lightweight way to annotate structured information such as products, people, places, and events directly within HTML pages. Most search engines can use these annotations to generate better search listings and make it easier to find your websites.

Using RDFa to annotate the elements of the Web Things Model directly in the HTML representation of your device is particularly useful because search engines could then find and understand your web Things, without having to understand the JSON representation of the Web Thing Model. Putting it bluntly, using RDFa to describe the metadata of a web Thing will make that web Thing findable and searchable by Google. Although Google supports several data types, such as products, recipes, and events,[20] there is no specific type for the Web of Things. Let's look at how we can create our own data types and use them within RDFa.

RDFA PRIMER

To annotate any content using RDFa, we must either reuse an existing vocabulary or create a new one. A *vocabulary*,[21] also called a *taxonomy*, is a set of terms (fields) that can be used to annotate a certain type of element, along with a definition of what each field refers to. For example, if we only want to expose basic information about a Raspberry Pi, such as its name, description, or an image, we could use the products vocabulary supported by Google.[22]

Unfortunately, this format doesn't allow exposing the properties or actions of our Web Thing Model because there isn't a vocabulary for the web Things we can reuse. But we can define our own based on the Web Thing Model reference found here: ·http://model.webofthings.io.

In the following listing,[23] we show how the WoT Pi can expose its JSON model using RDFa and our own Web of Things vocabulary. Start the WoT Pi server from our

---

[18] http://www.w3.org/RDF/

[19] http://rdfa.info/

[20] Learn more about Google's support for markups: https://developers.google.com/structured-data/rich-snippets/.

[21] RDFa offers a simple explanation: http://www.w3.org/TR/rdfa-lite/#vocab-typeof-and-property.

[22] Google's Product annotation format: https://developers.google.com/structured-data/rich-snippets/products.

[23] Note that to improve readability, the extract shown in listing 8.15 is a shorter version of the actual HTML code returned by the web Thing implementation you're using in this chapter.

GitHub repository, as shown in section 8.3.6. By accessing the root resource of your WoT Pi with your browser, you'll see the following HTML code.

Listing 8.15   The HTML representation of the root resource with RDFa annotations

```
<div vocab="http://model.webofthings.io/" typeof="WebThing">
  <h1 property="name">Raspberry Pi</h1>
  <div property="description">
    <p>A simple WoT-connected Raspberry PI for the WoT book.</p>
  </div>
  <p>ID:<span property="id">1</span></p>
  <p>Root URL:<a property="url" href="http://devices.webofthings.io">http://
  devices.webofthings.io</a></p>
  Resources:
  <div property="links" typeof="Product">
    <a property="url" href="https://www.raspberrypi.org/products/raspberry-
  pi-2-model-b/">
    Product this Web Thing is based on.</a>
  </div>
  <div property="links" typeof="Properties">
    <a property="url" href="properties/">
    Properties of this Web Thing.</a>
  </div>
  <div property="links" typeof="Actions">
    <a property="url" href="actions/">
    Actions of this Web Thing.</a>
  </div>
  <div property="links" typeof="UI">
    <a property="url" href="ui/">
    User Interface for this Web Thing.</a>
  </div>
</div>
```

You can see that most HTML tags have some unfamiliar attributes[24] defined by RDFa:

- vocab defines the vocabulary used for that element, in this case the Web of Things Model vocabulary defined previously.
- property defines the various fields of the model such as name, ID, or description.
- typeof defines the type of those elements in relation to the vocabulary of the element.

This allows other applications to parse the HTML representation of the device and automatically understand which resources are available and how they work. In particular, because Web of Things search engines will become increasingly popular (or will when Google supports and understands the Web Thing Model), physical devices, their data, and services will be easily indexed and searchable in real time.

---

[24] Lean more about HTML attributes here: http://www.w3schools.com/html/html_attributes.asp.

ADDING RDFA TO YOUR WOT PI

To offer RDFa annotations for your WoT Pi, you'll need to extend the HTML representation of its resources. In chapter 7 you saw a simple way of returning HTML based on converter middleware. The problem with this approach is that you had to create the HTML code inside the converter middleware, which wasn't very clean. A much better method in Express is to use *templating engines*. These modules offer the ability to create HTML templates that are dynamically filled with data when an HTML representation is requested. We installed a templating engine called Handlebars[25] in the project of chapter 8, but feel free to install it yourself as described in the nerd corner that follows.

Once the templating engine is installed, all you need to do is to create HTML templates that contain your RDFa code. As an example, listing 8.16 is a snippet of the HTML template for the root resource of the Pi.

The nerd corner—Install a templating engine

To use a templating engine for your WoT Pi, install the `consolidate` module[a] (`npm install --save consolidate`); this module facilitates the integration of many templating engines to Express. In our case we'll use the Handlebars templating module, which you can install via NPM as well (`npm install --save handlebars`). Once it's installed, you need to tell your Express app to use it by adding the following code to the http.js file:

```
app.engine('html', cons.handlebars);
app.set('view engine', 'html');
app.set('views', __dirname + '/../views');
```

---

[a] https://github.com/tj/consolidate.js

Listing 8.16 Templating HTML view in Express with RDFa tags

```
<p>ID:
  <span property="id">
    {{req.result.id}}
  </span>
</p>
<p>Name: <span property="name">{{req.result.name}}</span></p>
<p>Description: <span property="description">{{req.result.description}}</span></p>
<p>Tags: <span property="tags">{{req.result.tags}}</span></p>
<p>Root URL:<a property="url" href="http://devices.webofthings.io">http://devices.webofthings.io</a></p>
<h3>Custom Fields</h3>
  {{#each req.result.customFields}}
    <p>Key: {{@key}} = {{this}}</p>
  {{/each}}
```

RDFa annotations located in HTML span tags

Handlebars variables that will be filled with the correct information by Express when the view is rendered

---

[25] https://github.com/wycats/handlebars.js/

Then, extend the converter.js middleware to inject the variables needed for your RDFa and to invoke the templating engine, as shown in the next listing.

Listing 8.17   /middleware/converter.js: extending the converter

```
function represent(req, res, next) {
  console.info('Representation converter middleware called!');
  if (req.result) {
    if (req.accepts('html')) {

      var helpers = {
        json: function(object) {
          return JSON.stringify(object);
        },
        getById: function(object,id) {
          return object[id];
        }
      };

      if (req.type) res.render(req.type, { req: req , helpers: helpers });
      else res.render('default', { req: req , helpers: helpers });

      return;
    }
  [...]
}
```

The render() function calls the templating engine configured in Express.

Inject the variables needed in the HTML+RDFa representation.

That's it! The HTML pages of your Pi now offer RDFa annotations, ready for the actors of the Semantic Web (for example, clients and search engines) to consume that data.

8.4.2   Agreed-upon semantics: Schema.org

The tools of the Semantic Web can be used to describe pretty much anything. For instance, we could use RDFa to add more semantic description on top of our Web Thing Model. We could create a vocabulary that describes that a web Thing is a washing machine or smart door lock. The issue with the approach would be that only applications in our ecosystem would understand these specific vocabularies. We could push it one step further and turn these vocabularies into standards. But this is time-consuming and would often lead to competing standards because each manufacturer would want their own vocabulary.

A more recent approach is to rely on more lightweight collaborative repositories. These repositories offer simple schema for specific semantic descriptions. They provide de facto ways of describing simple concepts such as things, people, and locations.

Schema.org[26] has become the most popular of these collaborative repositories. It hosts a set of well-defined schemas for all sorts of structured data on the internet. In their own words,

> *Schema.org is a collaborative, community activity with a mission to create, maintain, and promote schemas for structured data on the Internet, on web pages, in email*

---

[26] http://schema.org/

messages, and beyond. Schema.org vocabulary can be used with many different encodings, including RDFa, Microdata and JSON-LD. These vocabularies cover entities, relationships between entities and actions, and can easily be extended through a well-documented extension model. Over 10 million sites use Schema.org to markup their web pages and email messages. Many applications from Google, Microsoft, Pinterest, Yandex and others already use these vocabularies to power rich, extensible experiences.

Extract from http://schema.org/

In other words, not only can anyone directly reuse the models from schema.org to describe their web resources in a more standard way, but doing so will also make them automatically findable and understandable by many other websites and services. Google, Yahoo!, and Microsoft Bing, for instance, can parse the schema.org vocabulary for people. If you create a product description page using a serialization of this vocabulary—for example, using RDFa—to describe a product, a search engine will know you're talking about a product and will render the results accordingly. Similarly, the Person vocabulary is used to identify pages that describe human beings, and the Place vocabulary is used to attach physical locations to web pages that are taken into account when using location-based search queries, such as via Google Maps. Search engines aren't the only clients that use these vocabularies; mail clients such as Gmail,[27] web browsers, and other web-based discovery tools are also starting to understand them.

In the Web of Things, these agreed-upon vocabularies can readily be used to improve the findability of Things, as we'll illustrate next with a small example using a growing format called JSON-LD.

8.4.3   *JSON-LD*

The schemas available on schema.org aren't bound to a particular format. You can obviously use them in RDFa but you can also use them in Microdata[28] as another way of representing linked data within HTML. On top of that, the schemas are available in a more recent format called JSON-LD (JSON-based serialization for Linked Data).

JSON-LD is an interesting and lightweight semantic annotation format for linked data that, unlike RDFa and Microdata, is based on JSON.[29] It's a simple way to semantically augment JSON documents by adding context information and hyperlinks for describing the semantics of the different elements of a JSON objects.

Getting started with JSON-LD can be a little tricky because at the time of writing JSON-LD is not yet an official standard, but rather an evolving W3C recommendation.[30] A good place to start is the official JSON-LD page,[31] where you'll find a number of

---

[27] https://developers.google.com/gmail/markup/overview
[28] https://html.spec.whatwg.org/multipage/microdata.html
[29] JSON-LD can also be embedded in HTML: http://www.w3.org/TR/json-ld/#embedding-json-ld-in-html-documents.
[30] The latest version of the recommendation is available here: http://www.w3.org/TR/json-ld/.
[31] http://json-ld.org

tutorials, examples, and a playground to test your JSON-LD payloads. In this section, we focus on only the bare minimum you'll need to understand how to use it for the examples we provide.

JSON-LD extends the JSON language with a number of keywords represented by the special names of JSON properties starting with the @ sign. The most important keywords are summarized in table 8.1.

Table 8.1 The three main reserved keywords the JSON-LD language adds to JSON

Key	Description	Example
@context	URL referencing a particular schema	http://schema.org/Person
@id	Unique identifier (usually a URI)	http://dbpedia.org/page/Mahatma_Gandhi
@type	A URL referencing the type of a value	http://www.w3.org/2001/XMLSchema#dateTime

On its own, JSON-LD is just another format for adding semantics to data. But when using it with standard schemas, such as those available on schema.org, it can be powerful because it lets you reference an agreed-upon context to semantically describe your data.

JSON-LD FOR THINGS

Let's look at a simple example. We'll use the Product schema described on schema.org[32] to add some semantic data to our Pi. After all, our Pi is also a product, so it does make sense! The following listing shows a modified version of the `pi.json` model that uses the JSON-LD vocabulary for products.

Listing 8.18 resources/piJsonLd.json: adding JSON-LD to our JSON model

```
{
    "@context": "http://schema.org/Product",        ← A link to the vocabulary for describing
    "@id": "http://localhost:8484",                    a product, available on schema.org
    "name": "My WoT Raspberry PI",
    "description": "A simple WoT-connected Raspberry PI for the WoT book.",
    "productID" : "asin:B00T2U7R7I",
    "manufacturer" : "Raspberry Pi",
    "model" : "100437",
    "image" : "https://www.raspberrypi.org/wp-
content/uploads/2015/01/Pi2ModB1GB_-comp-500x283.jpeg",
    [...]
```

The URL identifier for this web Thing →

References an image for the Pi →

name, description, productID, manufacturer, and model have an agreed-upon meaning in a schema.org product context.

---

[32] http://schema.org/Product

JSON-LD uses a different MIME or media type than JSON. Thanks to HTTP's content-negotiation mechanism you saw earlier, you only have to add a small bit of code to your converter.js middleware, as shown in the next listing, to start serving JSON-LD.

> **Listing 8.19   middleware/converter.js: adding support for JSON-LD representations**

```
[...]
var jsonld = require('./../resources/piJsonLd.json');   ◄─┐ Return just the model as an
                                                          │ example; extend this to return
function represent(req, res, next) {                      │ JSON-LD for all resources.
  [...]

  if (req.accepts('application/ld+json')) {   ◄─┐ application/ld+json is
    console.info('JSON-ld representation selected!');  │ the media type
    res.send(jsonld);                                  │ for JSON-LD.
    return;
  }
  [...]
}
```

Now go ahead and try to request JSON-LD on the root resource of your Pi with the `Accept: application/ld+json` header, and you'll get JSON-LD data returned.

FINDABILITY AND BEYOND

This simple example already illustrates the essence of JSON-LD it gives a context to the content of a JSON document. As a consequence, all clients that understand the http://schema.org/Product context will be able to automatically process this information in a meaningful way. This is the case with search engines, for example. Google and Yahoo! process JSON-LD payloads using the Product schema to render special search results; as soon as it gets indexed, our Pi will be known by Google and Yahoo! as a Raspberry Pi product. This means that the more semantic data we add to our Pi, the more findable it will become. As an example, try adding a location to your Pi using the Place schema,[33] and it will eventually become findable by location.

We could also use this approach to create more specific schemas on top of the Web Thing Model; for instance, an agreed-upon schema for the data and functions a washing machine or smart lock offers. This would facilitate discovery and enable automatic integration with more and more web clients.

8.4.4   *Beyond the book*

As you've realized, a common Application layer protocol is essential but not sufficient to achieve interoperability. A higher-level model to describe the metadata and functionality of the Web of Things along with a standard set of APIs are needed to build interoperable applications and devices. The Web Thing Model we introduced in section 8.3 bridges this gap and is an excellent starting point for building your next Web of Things device, gateway, or cloud.

---

[33] http://schema.org/Place

At the time of writing, this model has been published as a W3C Member Submission. Although it isn't an official standard, it might serve as a basis for working groups, and we invite you to follow the upcoming standardization efforts within the W3C Web of Things consortium.[34]

The battle for semantics and models for the IoT is strategic and will not only involve open standards. In the home automation space, Apple HomeKit and Google Weave will likely play an important role. We're at a critical turning point in the development of the IoT, and relying on standards created by large companies might not be the best option for individual consumers. Therefore, independent institutions such as the W3C will have to play a vital role in the future of the web and WoT.

8.5 Summary

- The ability to find nearby devices and services is essential in the Web of Things and is known as the bootstrap problem. Several protocols can help in discovering the root URL of Things, such as mDNS/Bonjour, QR codes or NFC tags.

- The last step of the web Things design process, resource linking design (also known as HATEOAS in REST terms), can be implemented using the web linking mechanism in HTTP headers.

- Beyond finding the root URL and sub-resources, client applications also need a mechanism to discover and understand what data or services a web Thing offers.

- The services of Things can be modeled as properties (variables), actions (functions), and links. The Web Thing Model offers a simple, flexible, fully web-compatible, and extensible data model to describe the details of any web Thing. This model is simple to adapt for your devices and easy to use for your products and applications.

- The Web Thing Model can be extended with more specific semantic descriptions such as those based on JSON-LD and available from the Schema.org repository.

Although internet access is the bare minimum required to be part of the Web of Things, you've seen that a shared and open data model to describe a web Thing will maximize interoperability without sacrificing flexibility and ease of use.

Now that you've learned how to open, expose, find, and use web Things in the World Wide Web, you're ready for the next challenge—and layer—of the Web of Things: how to share web Things securely over open networks such as the web. In the next chapter, we'll first show you how to secure your web Things using state of the art methods and best practices. Afterward, you'll learn how to use your existing social network account in order to share your devices with your friends. Finally, we'll show how to implement best practices of web security and data sharing on your WoT Pi.

---

[34] http://www.w3.org/WoT

Share: Securing and sharing web Things

This chapter covers

- A short overview of security risks and issues on the Web of Things
- A brief theoretical introduction to HTTPS, certificates, and encryption
- Best practices and techniques for web-based authorization and access control
- Learning to implement these best practices and tools on your Raspberry Pi
- Implementing the Social Web of Things in the WoT gateway

In most cases, Internet of Things deployments involve a group of devices that communicate with each other or with various applications within closed networks—rarely over open networks such as the internet. It would be fair to call such deployments the "intranets of Things" because they're essentially isolated, private networks that only a few entities can access. But the real power of the Web of Things lies in opening up these lonely silos and facilitating interconnection between devices and applications at a large scale.

Why would you even want this? When it comes to a critical IoT system such as a network of industrial machines in a large factory in Shenzhen, the security system of the British Museum, or simply own collection of smart devices at home, you certainly don't want these networks to be open to anyone. But when it comes to public data such as data.gov initiatives, real-time traffic/weather/pollution conditions in a city, or a group of sensors deployed in a jungle or a volcano, it would be great to ensure that the general public or researchers anywhere in the world could access that data. This would enable anyone to create new innovative applications with it and possibly generate substantial economic, environmental, and social value. Another use case is the smart hotel scenario presented in chapter 1, where hotel guests (and only *they*) should have access to some services and devices in their room (and only *there*) during their stay (and only *then*). Because the public infrastructure is becoming not only digital but also pervasive, the earlier we could build, deploy, and scale those systems while maximizing the ability to share data between devices, users, and applications, the better it would be for all of us. How to share this data in secure and flexible way is what Layer 3 provides, as shown in figure 9.1.

The prerequisite for this is to use a common protocol and data format between devices and applications, which we covered extensively in the previous chapters. But once devices are connected to a public network, the most important problem to solve is how to ensure that only a specific set of users can access only a specific set of resources at a specific time and in a specific manner. In the next sections we'll show

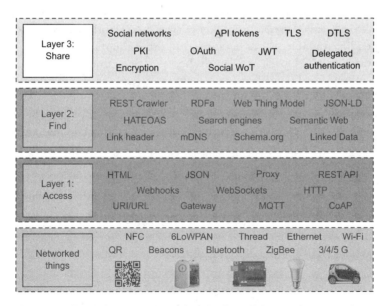

Figure 9.1 The Share layer of the Web of Things. This layer focuses on how devices and their resources must be secured so that they can only be accessed by authorized users and applications.

how to do this by building on the concepts and tools you've already seen. First, we'll show how Layer 3 of the WoT architecture covers the security of Things: how to ensure that only authorized parties can access a given resource. Then we'll show how to use existing trusted systems to allow sharing physical resources via the web.

9.1 *Securing Things*

Right now, the hottest topic (or potato, to be more accurate!) of the IoT world is arguably security.[1] We keep hearing all over the news about the IoT and the endless possibilities of an all-connected world. Sadly, this vision is also continuously tainted by major security breaches: personal information, credit card data, sensitive documents, or passwords from millions of users being stolen by hackers. Such happenings not only can severely hurt the reputation of a company but also can have disastrous effects for the users. Ultimately, every security breach hurts the entire web because it erodes the overall trust of users in technology. No one wants their smart fridges sending spam emails[2] about dubious pills, inheritances, or unclaimed lottery gains.

Security in the Web of Things is even more critical than in the web. Because web Things are physical objects that will be deployed everywhere in the real world, the risks associated with IoT attacks can be catastrophic. Digitally augmented devices allow collecting much more information about people with a fine-grained resolution, such as when you got your last insulin shot, what time you go jogging and where, and the like. But more important, unauthorized access to physical objects can be dangerous—remotely controlling your brand new BMW[3] or house,[4] anyone? Despite those risks, recent reports have shown a sad state of affairs in the world of IoT security.[5] Although many vulnerabilities—called *exploits* in hacker parlance—are widely known and patches for them are readily available, it has been reported that the majority of IoT solutions don't comply with even the most basic security best practices; think clear-text passwords and communications, invalid certificates, old software versions with exploitable bugs, and so on. In other words, you don't even have to be a security expert to use existing weaknesses in many services or devices and gain access to unauthorized content.

This book is not about network security, so don't expect to become an expert in this field by the end of this chapter. But because it's such a crucial issue for any production system or consumer product connected to the internet, we'll cover the basics you need to know when building IoT solutions in the form of a set of best practices for building secure and reliable devices and applications. If you can't wait any longer, an excellent resource is the Open Web Application Security Project (OWASP) Internet of Things project,[6] which contains useful, down-to-earth, and practical information about how to build safer IoT applications and systems.

---

[1] http://venturebeat.com/2016/01/16/ces-2016-the-largest-collection-of-insecure-devices-in-the-world
[2] http://www.theguardian.com/technology/2014/jan/21/fridge-spam-security-phishing-campaign
[3] http://www.wired.com/2015/08/bmw-benz-also-vulnerable-gm-onstar-hack/
[4] http://www.forbes.com/sites/kashmirhill/2013/07/26/smart-homes-hack/
[5] See "Insecurity in the Internet of Things," https://www.symantec.com/iot/.
[6] https://www.owasp.org/index.php/OWASP_Internet_of_Things_Project

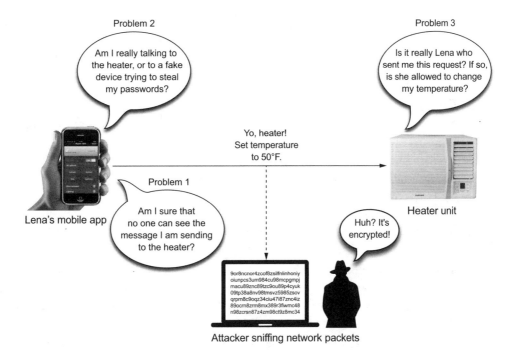

Figure 9.2 **The three principal challenges in securing the IoT. First, communications must be encrypted to prevent unauthorized entities from reading the messages between a client and a server. Second, the client must be sure they are really talking to whom they they are. Third, the server must be sure that a message comes from an authorized client allowed to send that request.**

Roughly speaking, securing the IoT comes down to solving three major problems summarized in figure 9.2:

- First, we must consider how to encrypt the communications between two entities (for example, between an app and a web Thing) so that a malicious interceptor—a "man in the middle"—can't access the data being transmitted in clear text. This is referred to as securing the channel and will be covered in section 9.1.1.

- Second, we must find a way to ensure that when a client talks to a host, it can ensure that the host is really "himself," which is the topic discussed in section 9.1.2. For example, in chapter 4, you downloaded and installed NOOBS from our website. But you did so via HTTP instead of HTTPS, and we didn't provide an SHA checksum available for that image over HTTPS. In essence, you had to trust that whatever you downloaded was really what we gave you and not a corrupted OS image inserted by an attacker.

- Third, we must ensure that the correct access control is in place. We need to set up a method to control which user can access what resource of what server or Thing and when and then to ensure that the user is really who they claim to be. This topic will be covered in section 9.2.

After exploring these three problems and their solutions, in section 9.3 we'll blur another line: the one between the Social Web and the Web of Things. We'll put together everything you've learned so far to build an application that allows you to use third-party social network identities to share Things with your friends.

9.1.1   *Encryption 101*

As you've seen before, there's more to security than encryption. Nevertheless, encryption is an essential ingredient for any secure system. Without encryption, any attempt to secure a Thing will be in vain because attackers can sniff the communication and understand the security mechanisms that were put in place.

Using a web protocol without encryption can be compared to sending a postcard via snail mail: anyone can read the content of the postcard at any stage. Adding encryption to a web protocol is like putting the postcard in a thick and sealed envelope: even if you can see the envelope, you can't read the card!

SYMMETRIC ENCRYPTION

The oldest form of encoding a message is *symmetric encryption*. The idea is that the sender and receiver share a secret key that can be used to both encode and decode a message in a specific way; for example, by substituting or shifting some characters by a number. This type of encryption is the easiest to put in place for resource-limited IoT devices, but the problem is that as soon someone discovers the key, they can decode and encode any message. To use a symmetric key successfully, the key has to be shared with trusted parties securely, such as by giving the key to the recipient in person.

ASYMMETRIC ENCRYPTION

In the internet era, another method called *asymmetric encryption* has become popular because it doesn't require a secret to be shared between parties. This method uses two related keys, one public and the other private (secret), as shown in figure 9.3. A host

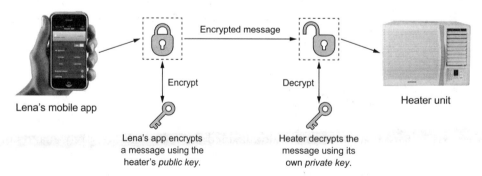

Figure 9.3   Asymmetric encryption in an IoT context. The heater shares its public key with Lena. It's then up to Lena's mobile app to encrypt messages sent to the heater. Thanks to the power of cryptography, the only way to decrypt the message is with the private key of the heater.

can freely share its public key with anyone over the internet. When any client wants to send a message to the host, it can use the public key to encode the message before sending it. Once a message is encoded with the public key, it can be decoded only with the private key that's known only by the host. This way, any message sent by a client (for example, a web app) to a server (for example, a web Thing) can be opened only by the server and not by an eavesdropper.

9.1.2 *Web security with TLS: the S of HTTPS!*

Fortunately , there are standard protocols for securely encrypting data between clients and servers on the web. The best known protocol for this is Secure Sockets Layer (SSL). SSL has long been the technology that sits behind the *S* in HTTPS, which is the method used to encrypt all the communications between your browser and a web server. But a number of important vulnerabilities in the SSL protocol have been discovered over the years, making it possible for attackers to crack the security SSL provides. In 2014, major vulnerabilities in the SSL 3.0 protocols were found; for example, POODLE,[7] Heartbleed,[8] and Shellshock.[9] These events inked the death of this protocol, which was replaced by the much more secure but conceptually similar Transport Layer Security (TLS).[10]

This highlights two important points. First, no method or system is secure forever. Second, open protocols—and especially web protocols—are closely monitored and fixed as soon as flaws are identified. In consequence, all communications over the Web of Things are to be encrypted with TLS. We won't give a full description of TLS here because it would take a chapter on its own—or a whole book, for that matter—but we'll review the basics of TLS and focus on the key concepts while simplifying the complex bits.

TLS 101

Despite its name, TLS is an Application layer protocol (see chapter 5). TLS not only secures HTTP (HTTPS) communication but is also the basis of secure WebSocket (WSS) and secure MQTT (MQTTS). TLS has two main roles. First, it helps the client ensure that the server is who it says it is; this is the SSL/TLS authentication. Second, it guarantees that the data sent over the communication channel can't be read by anyone other than the client and the server involved in the transaction (also known as SSL/TLS encryption).

---

[7] https://blog.mozilla.org/security/2014/10/14/the-poodle-attack-and-the-end-of-ssl-3-0/
[8] https://en.wikipedia.org/wiki/Heartbleed
[9] https://en.wikipedia.org/wiki/Shellshock_(software_bug)
[10] The long legacy of SSL means that today the acronym SSL is used as an umbrella term for both TLS and SSL.

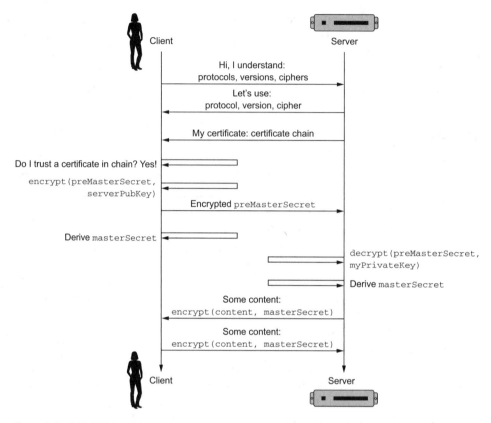

Figure 9.4   SSL/TLS handshake: the client and the server first negotiate the protocols and encryption algorithms, and then the server sends its certificate chain to prove who it is to the client. Finally, the client sends a preMasterSecret from which the client and server derive a masterSecret used to encrypt all the future messages.

A typical TLS exchange between a client and a server is shown in figure 9.4.[11] This is what happens when you use your browser to connect to an HTTPS website, such as https://manning.com. Here's a summary of the most important steps:

1 The client, such as a mobile app, tells the server, such as a web Thing, which protocols and encryption algorithms it supports. This is somewhat similar to the content negotiation process we described in chapter 6.

2 The server sends the public part of its certificate to the client. The goal here is for the client to make sure it knows who the server is. All web clients have a list of certificates they trust.[12] In the case of your Pi, you can find them in /etc/ssl/

---

[11] If you want an even simpler way of explaining TLS to your cat, check "What's Behind the Padlock": https://casecurity.org/wp-content/uploads/2013/01/ssl-1200.jpg.

[12] Firefox and Chrome, for example, trust certificates signed by those CAs; see https://mozillacaprogram .secure.force.com/CA/IncludedCACertificateReport.

certs. SSL certificates form a trust chain, meaning that if a client doesn't trust certificate S1 that the server sends back, but it trusts certificate S2 that was used to sign S1, the web client can accept S1 as well.

3 The rest of the process generates a key from the public certificates. This key is then used to encrypt the data going back and forth between the server and the client in a secure manner. Because this process is dynamic, only the client and the server know how to decrypt the data they exchange during this session. This means the data is now securely encrypted: if an attacker manages to capture data packets, they will remain meaningless.

9.1.3 *Enabling HTTPS and WSS with TLS on your Pi*

Now that you've seen the theory, it's time for a bit of practice! Let's secure the API of your WoT Pi to ensure that traffic between the Pi and its clients is encrypted. Note that the process we define here works as well on all the other Linux devices we talked about—for example, the Intel Edison or the BeagleBone—as well as on any Linux- or Unix-based machines. Go ahead and generate a certificate. First, you need to make sure the OpenSSL library is installed. On your Pi go to the /resources directory and run

```
sudo apt-get install openssl
```

This should tell you something along the lines of `openssl is already the newest version`. Or it will be installed if not present. Now, to generate the certificates, run

```
openssl req -sha256 -newkey rsa:2048 -keyout privateKey.pem -out caCert.pem
    -days 1095 -x509
```

Because this command is self-explanatory we won't detail it. No? Fine, let's dig into it! The command does two things in one. First, it generates a private key (`-newkey rsa:2048 -keyout privateKey.pem`) that will be used to sign the certificate using the sha256 hashing algorithm. While it does this, you'll see a `Generating a 2048 bit RSA private key` message followed by a prompt to provide a passphrase, essentially a password to protect your private key. Make sure you keep this one safe because you'll need it soon!

Second, it will generate a new certificate (`-out caCert.pem`) that will last for 1,095 days using the x509 data format, and it also prompts you with a few questions, as shown in listing 9.1. The common name is the hostname for which this certificate should be valid; for example, `raspberrypi.local` if you're on your Pi or `localhost` if you're running these examples on your machine. The information you provide here will be exposed in the certificate and will be visible to all clients.

> **Listing 9.1 Information requested when generating a self-signed certificate**

```
You are about to be asked to enter information that will be incorporated
into your certificate request.
What you are about to enter is what is called a Distinguished Name or a DN.
There are quite a few fields but you can leave some blank
```

```
For some fields there will be a default value,
If you enter '.', the field will be left blank.
-----
Country Name (2 letter code) [AU]: UK
State or Province Name (full name) [Some-State]: London
Locality Name (eg, city) []:London
Organization Name (eg, company) [Internet Widgits Pty Ltd]: Web of Things
Organizational Unit Name (eg, section) []: Web of Things
Common Name (e.g. server FQDN or YOUR name) []: raspberrypi.local
Email Address []:book@webofthings.io
```

> **This should be the hostname, IP, or domain name corresponding to your Pi or the local machine you test the code from.**

At the end of this process, two files will be generated:

caCert.pem is the public part of the certificate your Pi server will send to the clients when connecting to it via TLS.

privateKey.pem is the private key of your Pi server and hence should be kept, well...private.

You're now ready to turn your Pi unencrypted HTTP and WS APIs into secure HTTPS and WSS APIs. All you need to do is modify the code of the wot-server.js file at the root of your WoT PI project (see chapters 7 and 8). Copy the content of wot-server.js into a new wot-server-secure.js file and modify it as shown in the following listing, which enables HTTPS and WSS.

Listing 9.2   Modifying the WoT Pi server to serve HTTPS and WSS content

```
[...]
var createServer = function (port, secure) {
  if (process.env.PORT) port = process.env.PORT;
  else if (port === undefined) port = resources.customFields.port;
  if (secure === undefined) secure = resources.customFields.secure;

  initPlugins();

  if(secure) {
    var https = require('https');
    var certFile = './resources/change_me_caCert.pem';
    var keyFile = './resources/change_me_privateKey.pem';
    var passphrase = 'webofthings';

    var config = {
      cert: fs.readFileSync(certFile),
      key: fs.readFileSync(keyFile),
      passphrase: passphrase
    };

    return server = https.createServer(config, restApp)
      .listen(port, function () {
        wsServer.listen(server);
        console.log('Secure WoT server started on port %s', port);
      })
  } else {
    var http = require('http');
    return server = http.createServer(restApp)
```

- *Start the internal hardware plugins.* (pointing to `initPlugins();`)
- *If in secure mode, import the HTTPS module.* (pointing to `var https = require('https');`)
- *The actual certificate file of the server* (pointing to `var certFile = './resources/change_me_caCert.pem';`)
- *The private key of the server generated earlier* (pointing to `var keyFile = './resources/change_me_privateKey.pem';`)
- *The password of the private key* (pointing to `var passphrase = 'webofthings';`)
- *Create an HTTPS server using the config object.* (pointing to `return server = https.createServer(config, restApp)`)
- *By passing it the server you create, the WebSocket library will automatically detect and enable TLS support.* (pointing to `wsServer.listen(server);`)

```
            .listen(process.env.PORT | port, function () {
                wsServer.listen(server);
                console.log('Unsecure WoT server started on port %s', port);
            })
        }
    };

function initPlugins() {
    var LedsPlugin = require('./plugins/internal/ledsPlugin').LedsPlugin;
    var PirPlugin = require('./plugins/internal/pirPlugin').PirPlugin;
    var Dht22Plugin = require('./plugins/internal/dht22Plugin').Dht22Plugin;

    pirPlugin = new PirPlugin({'simulate': true, 'frequency': 5000});
    pirPlugin.start();

    ledsPlugin = new LedsPlugin({'simulate': true, 'frequency': 5000});
    ledsPlugin.start();

    dht22Plugin = new Dht22Plugin({'simulate': true, 'frequency': 5000});
    dht22Plugin.start();
}

module.exports = createServer;

process.on('SIGINT', function () {
    ledsPlugin.stop();
    pirPlugin.stop();
    dht22Plugin.stop();
    console.log('Bye, bye!');
    process.exit();
});
```

Finally, modify the wot.js file to require wot-server-secure.js, and start the server by running `nodewot.js`. Now, go to https://localhost:8484/properties/pir in your browser. You should get a warning saying that the connection is not private. What this really means appears in the small print: ERR_CERT_AUTHORITY_INVALID. This means that the certificate was generated by you and not by a certificate authority (CA) trusted by your browser. There are two ways to fix this: you can buy a certificate from a trusted CA, as explained in the next section, or you can tell your computer to trust the certificate you just created. The best way to do this is by adding the certificate to the trust store of your browser. The operation will differ depending on which environment you're using, but here's how to add it to Firefox: click I Understand The Risk (because now you do, don't you?), Add Exception, and finally Confirm Security Exception. Other browsers like Chrome use the trust store of the underlying operating system. Hence, to ensure Chrome accepts your certificate, go to Preferences > Settings > Show Advanced Settings; in HTTPS/SSL click Manage Certificates. This should open the trust store of your operating system, where you can import the certificate. Adding self-signed SSL certificates directly to your operating system[13] will make it much easier for you to develop secure applications for your Pi.

---

[13] http://blog.getpostman.com/2014/01/28/using-self-signed-certificates-with-postman/

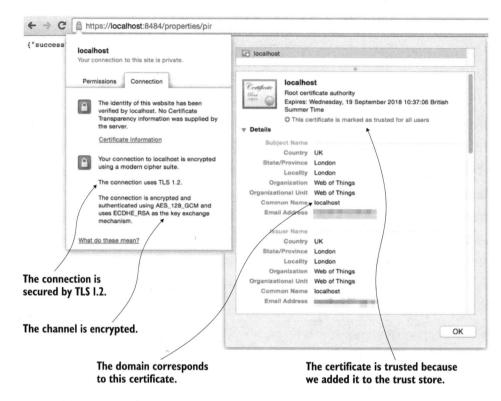

The connection is secured by TLS 1.2.

The channel is encrypted.

The domain corresponds to this certificate.

The certificate is trusted because we added it to the trust store.

Figure 9.5   The server of the WoT Pi can now be accessed via HTTPS. The details of the secure connection and certificates can be reviewed by clicking the small lock icon on the address bar.

Once your browser trusts the certificate of your WoT Pi, you should be able to get the content returned and the browser should display the usual lock icon on the address bar. If you click it, you'll see the details of your TLS certificate, as shown in figure 9.5.

BEYOND SELF-SIGNED CERTIFICATES

Clearly, having to deal with all these security exceptions isn't nice, but these exceptions exist for a reason: to warn clients that part of the security usually covered by SSL/TLS can't be guaranteed with the certificate you generated. Basically, although the encryption of messages will work with a self-signed certificate (the one you created with the previous command), the authenticity of the server (the Pi) can't be guaranteed. In consequence, the chain of trust is broken—problem 2 of figure 9.2. In an IoT context, this means that attackers could pretend to be the Thing you think you're talking to. This isn't a big deal when your Things are accessible only on the local network, but as soon as you make them available on the web, this becomes critical.

The common way to generate certificates that guarantee the authenticity of the server is to get them from a well-known and trusted certificate authority (CA). There are a number of them on the web, such as Thawte, Symantec, and GeoTrust. The good thing about certificates issued by such CAs is that they verify who created the certificates, albeit with various degrees of rigor. This means that a client has a greater certainty of which server it's talking to (authentication). In consequence, these certificates, or certificates generated using these, are trusted by a number of clients such as web browsers. More concretely, this means that web browsers and operating systems have these certificates in their trust store.

The problem is that certificates issued by well-known CAs are certainly not free. The business of selling web security is a lucrative one! A direct and unfortunate consequence of this is that a number of sites use cheaper CAs that do a poorer job of checking to whom they deliver certificates, or they decide to not use secured connections at all. But this is rapidly changing: a number of major actors on the web, such as Mozilla, Akamai, Cisco, and the Internet Security Research Group, got together to create the Let's Encrypt[14] project, an automated CA providing free and secure certificates for the public's benefit. There are even ways to automatically generate certificates using Let's Encrypt from a Raspberry Pi running a Node server with Express.[15] Now that you have the basics of TLS, you should consider this when moving your Pi to the World ~~Wild~~ Wide Web.

The nerd corner—I want my Pi to be on the web!

Once the development and testing phase of your WoT Pi is finished, you'll likely want to make it accessible over the web with its own public domain; for example, mypi.webofthings.io. To do this, you could use Yaler,[a] which is a great service and open source project that offers a relay to securely access your embedded devices through your firewall and supports mobile Things connecting to different networks. Alternatively, if you want to go the DIY route, you can use a dynamic DNS service—unless you already have a fixed IP address—that keeps monitoring the IP address of your home router to determine when it changes. There are a number of those, but Duck DNS is straightforward and free. Moreover, it provides clear explanations of how to install it on a Pi.[b] Once this is set up, you'll also have to set up port forwarding on your home router.[c] Then, you might also need to generate (or buy) a certificate with a common name corresponding to the new Duck DNS subdomain of your Pi; for example, mypi.duckdns.org. Once you've done all of this, your Pi should be truly on the world-wide Web of Things. But your Pi will also be ready for attackers to try to hack it, so make sure you protect it well, at the very least by reading to the end of this chapter and implementing the concepts we describe!

---

[a] https://www.yaler.net/raspberrypi

[b] http://www.duckdns.org/install.jsp#pi

[c] http://portforward.com/

---

[14] https://letsencrypt.org
[15] https://github.com/DylanPiercey/auto-sni

9.2   *Authentication and access control*

Once we encrypt the communication between Things and clients as shown in the previous section, we want to enable only some applications to access it. Let's get back to our hotel scenario to understand this issue. The hotel control center application needs to have full access to all devices in the network and the ability to configure and administer them. But Lena, who stays in room 212, only needs to access the devices and services in that room. Besides, she shouldn't be able to configure them, only to send a limited set of commands. First, this means that the Things—or a gateway to which Things are connected—need to be able to know the sender of each request (*identification*). Second, devices need to trust that the sender really is who they claim to be (*authentication*). Third, the devices also need to know if they should accept or reject each request depending on the identity of this sender and which request has been sent (*authorization*). If encryption is like sending a postcard in a sealed envelope, authentication and authorization are like sending that envelope via registered mail: the postman will deliver the letter only to the correct recipient as long as they can prove their identity with a valid ID.

9.2.1   *Access control with REST and API tokens*

Nowadays, we go through this authentication process all the time on the web, namely every time we enter our username and password on a website. When we use our username/password to log into a website, we initiate a secure session with the server that's stored for a limited time in the server application's memory or in a local browser cookie. During that time, we can send other requests to the server without authenticating again. This method (called *server-based authentication*) is usually stateful because the state of the client is stored on the server. But as you saw in chapter 6, HTTP is a stateless protocol; therefore, using a server-based authentication method goes against this principle and poses certain problems. First, the performance and scalability of the overall systems are limited because each session must be stored in memory and overhead increases when there are many authenticated users. Second, this authentication method poses certain security risks—for example, cross-site request forgery.[16]

To circumvent these issues, an alternative method called *token-based authentication* has become popular and is used by most web APIs. The idea is that a secret token—a long string of characters—that's unique for each client can be used to authenticate each request sent by that client. Because this token is added to the headers or query parameters of each HTTP request sent to the server, all interactions remain stateless. Because no session or state needs to be kept on the server(s), applications can be scaled horizontally without having to worry about where the session of each user is stored.

---

[16] This method exploits the fact that a malicious website can use your browser to send requests on your behalf to another website you're logged into. See https://en.wikipedia.org/wiki/Cross-site_request_forgery.

Obviously, the API token should be generated using a cryptographically secure pseudo-random generator[17] and should be treated like a password: stored in an encrypted manner.

To generate an API token with Node.js, you can use the `crypto.randomBytes()` function.[18] You'll find the function in the /utils/utils.js file shown in the next listing.

Listing 9.3   utils/utils.js: generate a crypto-secure API token

```
exports.generateApiToken = function(length, chars) {
  if (!length) length = 32;
  if (!chars) chars =
  'abcdefghijklmnopqrstuvwxyzABCDEFGHIJKLMNOPQRSTUVWXYZ0123456789';
  var randomBytes = crypto.randomBytes(length);
  var result = new Array(length);

  var cursor = 0;
  for (var i = 0; i < length; i++) {
    cursor += randomBytes[i];
    result[i] = chars[cursor % chars.length];
  }

  return result.join('');
};
```

You can call this function by uncommenting the following line in the http.js file:

```
console.info('Here is a crypto-secure API Key: ' + utils.generateApiToken());
```

When you launch the WoT Pi server, you'll see in the terminal a new API token, which you can copy and paste into the value of the `apiToken` key in the resources/auth.json file. This will be the API token you need to send any request to your Pi.

You'll now modify the WoT Pi application so that for each request that comes in, you check if the request is signed using a valid API token; see the following listing. The best way to do this is to use the middleware pattern shown in the previous section. You'll create an auth.js file in the middleware folder, which has a function that will be called each time a new request comes to your API and which checks if it is signed and valid.

Listing 9.4   auth.js: authentication middleware

```
var keys = require('../resources/auth');

module.exports = function() {
  return function (req, res, next) {
    console.log(req.method + " " + req.path);
    if (req.path.substring(0, 5) === "/css/") {    ◀─┐ Allow unauthorized
      next();                                          access to the css folder.
```

---

[17] https://en.wikipedia.org/wiki/Cryptographically_secure_pseudorandom_number_generator
[18] https://nodejs.org/api/crypto.html#crypto_crypto_randombytes_size_callback

Check header or URL parameters or POST body for token.

If no token provided, return 401 UNAUTHORIZED.

If token is not the valid API token, return 403 FORBIDDEN.

If everything is good, save to request for use in other routes.

```
    } else {
      var token = req.body.token || req.get('authorization') ||
        req.query.token;
      console.log(req.params);
      if (!token) {
        return res.status(401).send({success: false, message: 'API token
          missing.'});
      } else {
        if (token !== keys.apiToken) {
          return res.status(403).send({success: false, message: 'API
            token
            invalid.'});
        } else {
          next();
        }
      }
    }
  }
};
```

Finally, you need to add this middleware function to the middleware chain in servers/ http.js. Start by requiring the middleware with `auth = require('./../middleware/ auth')`, then add it to the chain using `app.use(auth());` right after the CORS middleware. Now, run the WoT server once again and then try accessing https://localhost:8484/properties/pir. You should now get an error message. Try again with https://localhost:8484/properties/pir?token=YOUR_TOKEN (or with Postman by adding the `Authorization` header with your token as value) and it should work: your API now requires a valid token!

In this minimal example, you manually check each request against a hard-coded API token. We wanted to show you the basics of how token-based authentication works, so this is not a robust and scalable solution ready for production applications. You'll need to use a more elaborate solution that suits your use case and devices. Will you have many different users that all need to have their own API token, or is it fine to have only a single token? How granular does your access control need to be? How often will you need to add, remove, or change these permissions? As an exercise, you're welcome to extend this simple token-based implementation to support many users and tokens and also the various end points of your Thing (including WebSockets interactions; see /servers/websocket.js for a solution).

The nerd corner—I want better tokens!

Generating tokens manually and implementing a minimal token-based authentication system from scratch as shown before is a great exercise to help you understand how it works. But for anything more than that, you'll be better off using an actual standard. JSON Web Tokens[a] (JWT) is particularly interesting here because it not only generates

---
[a] https://jwt.io

secure tokens but also offers a standard mechanism to send encrypted payloads over insecure connections. In other words, JWT makes it possible to send secure content over HTTP and WebSocket packets without using TLS. This is particularly appealing for the WoT because it removes the self-generated certificate warnings in the browser you encountered earlier because certificates aren't required for interactions between an app and Thing within a local network. It's certainly not as standard and battle-tested as TLS, but we've had some promising results in our own tests. There are JWT libraries for many languages including Node.js, so go ahead and give it a try!

9.2.2 *OAuth: a web authorization framework*

In the previous section, we gave a brief introduction to API tokens, how they work, and how you can implement them on web Things. API tokens are a good starting point, and along with encryption (TLS), they are arguably the bare minimum a WoT device should offer in terms of security. But as soon as we need to share the resources of a device with several users having different authorization rights, simple API tokens like the ones we've introduced present two challenges.

First, we need a process for web applications to generate and retrieve tokens dynamically, ideally through an API. Obviously, we can't just create an API endpoint that returns tokens. This would be insecure and we'd be back where we started because we'd need to secure that API as well. Besides, creating a bespoke mechanism to get tokens wouldn't foster interoperability; it would make the process complicated and bespoke for each device and/or API.

Second, API tokens shouldn't be valid forever. API tokens, just like passwords, should change regularly. We should also be able to invalidate any token manually when needed. This ensures that when an API token has leaked, we can disable it. But again, creating a custom API to renew tokens wouldn't foster interoperability between web clients and web Things.

What to do? It turns out there's a web standard coming to our rescue: OAuth.[19] OAuth is an open standard for authorization and is essentially a mechanism for a web or mobile app to delegate the authentication of a user to a third-party trusted service; for example, Facebook, LinkedIn, or Google. OAuth makes this delegated authentication process secure and simple by dynamically generating access tokens using only web protocols. OAuth also allows sharing resources and between applications. For instance, you can allow some of your Facebook friends to securely access some of your documents on Google.

In short, OAuth standardizes how to authenticate users, generate tokens with an expiration date, regenerate tokens, and provide access to resources in a secure and standard manner over the web. Sound like exactly what we need, doesn't it? Let's see

---

[19] https://tools.ietf.org/html/rfc6749

how to do this in practice using the most recent version of the OAuth standard: OAuth 2.0.

OAUTH ROLES

A typical OAuth scenario involves four roles:

- *A resource owner*—This is the user who wants to authorize an application to access one of their trusted accounts; for example, your Facebook account.
- *The resource server*—Is the server providing access to the resources the user wants to share? In essence, this is a web API accepting OAuth tokens as credentials.
- *The authorization server*—This is the OAuth server managing authorizations to access the resources. It's a web server offering an OAuth API to authenticate and authorize users. In some cases, the resource server and the authorization server can be the same, such as in the case of Facebook.
- *The application*—This is the web or mobile application that wants to access the resources of the user. To keep the trust chain, the application has to be known by the authorization server in advance and has to authenticate itself using a secret token, which is an API key known only by the authorization server and the application.

The flow of a typical OAuth-delegated authentication mechanism is shown in figure 9.6. At the end of the token exchange process, the application will know who the user is and will be able to access resources on the resource server on behalf of the user. The application can then also renew the token before it expires using an optional refresh token or by running the authorization process again.

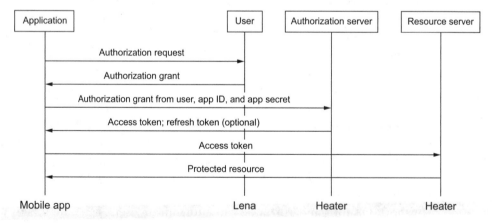

Figure 9.6   OAuth delegated authentication and access flow. The application asks the user if they want to give it access to resources on a third-party trusted service (resource server). If the user accepts, an authorization grant code is generated. This code can be exchanged for an access token with the authorization server. To make sure the authorization server knows the application, the application has to send an app ID and app secret along with the authorization grant code. The access token can then be used to access protected resources within a certain scope from the resource server.

OAuth has become a successful protocol, and as a consequence, a large number of services on the web such as social networks (for example, Facebook, Google+, LinkedIn, and Twitter), developer services (for example, GitHub and BitBucket), and many other websites (such as TripAdvisor and Meetup) support OAuth. But what about the IoT? How does OAuth relate to our web Things?

OAUTH AND THE WEB OF THINGS

For a start, if all Things become OAuth servers in place of generating API tokens, web clients will then have a standard way to obtain tokens to access the resources of devices.

Let's get back to our hotel scenario once again. Lena is the user in figure 9.6 and she has a user account on the heater unit of figure 9.2, which is both the authorization server and the resource server. Lena uses a mobile app to control the heater, as shown in figure 9.6. The application asks Lena to log into the heater with her user account, and then the application exchanges the resulting authorization grant for an access token from the heater unit. The heater unit accepts the access token and provides access to the heater to the application on behalf of Lena.

If Lena was interacting with her heater in her home, this would be a practical scenario. But in the case of the hotel, that means that the heater and all other devices would need to know about Lena and all the other hotel clients. Besides, all devices would also need to know all the applications that would interact with them and would need to have generated a secret token for each of them. It's pretty obvious this approach would be a nightmare to maintain!

Implementing an OAuth server on a Linux-based embedded device such as the Pi or the Intel Edison isn't hard because the protocol isn't really heavy. But maintaining the list of all applications, users, and their access scope on each Thing is clearly not going to work and scale for the IoT. We'll look at a better approach in the next section.

> ### The nerd corner—I want my Pi to be an OAuth server!
>
> If you do want to turn your Pi into an OAuth server, go ahead! It will be a good exercise to help you better understand the protocol and will actually make the implementation in the next section more secure. A good place to start is the `node-oauth2-server` Node.js module for Express, which should run seamlessly on your Pi, Edison, or BeagleBone.

9.3 The Social Web of Things

Using OAuth to manage access control to Things is tempting, but not if each Thing has to maintain its own list of users and application. This is where the gateway integration pattern we discovered in chapter 7 can help. What if you had only a single proxy that would know the Things you have at home (or in the entire hotel) and also know the various users involved, so it could manage access control in place of these Things? "But then I still have to create user accounts on this proxy for each user," we hear you say. Of course, you could do that, but a much better approach would be to use the notion of delegated authentication offered by OAuth, which allows you to use the accounts you already have with OAuth providers you trust, such as Facebook, Twitter, or LinkedIn.

Not only does this approach allow you to reuse the user accounts you already have in other web services, but it also allows you share access to your devices via existing social network relationships. These concepts are often referred to as the Social Web of Things.[20] Let's see what this would look like in more detail. As with all things security, this won't be the easiest ride but will definitely be a rewarding one.

9.3.1 A Social Web of Things authentication proxy

The idea of the Social Web of Things is to create an authentication proxy that controls access to all Things it proxies by identifying users of client applications using trusted third-party services. The detailed steps for this workflow are shown in figure 9.7.

Again, we have four actors: a Thing, a user using a client application, an authentication proxy, and a social network (or any other service with an OAuth server). The client app can use the authentication proxy and the social network to access resources on the Thing. This concept can be implemented in three phases:

1 The first phase is the *Thing proxy trust*. The goal here is to ensure that the proxy can access resources on the Thing securely. If the Thing is protected by an API token (device token), it could be as simple as storing this token on the proxy. If the Thing is also an OAuth server, this step follows an OAuth authentication flow, as shown in figure 9.6. Regardless of the method used to authenticate, after this phase the auth proxy has a secret that lets it access the resources of the Thing.

2 The second phase is the *delegated authentication* step. Here, the user in the client app authenticates via an OAuth authorization server as in figure 9.6. The authentication proxy uses the access token returned by the authorization server to identify the user of the client app and checks to see if the user is authorized to access the Thing. If so, the proxy returns the access token or generates a new one to the client app.

3 The last phase is the *proxied access* step. Once the client app has a token, it can use it to access the resources of the Thing through the authentication proxy. If the token is valid, the authentication proxy will forward the request to the Thing using the secret (device token) it got in phase 1 and send the response back to the client app.

In order not to leak any tokens at any step, all the communication has to be encrypted using TLS. The details for each phase are summarized in figure 9.7.

---

[20] The Social Web of Things was a concept developed in Dom's thesis (http://webofthings.org/2011/12/01/phd-web-of-things-app-archi/) based on the Friends and Things project: http://webofthings.org/2010/02/02/sharing-in-a-web-of-things/.

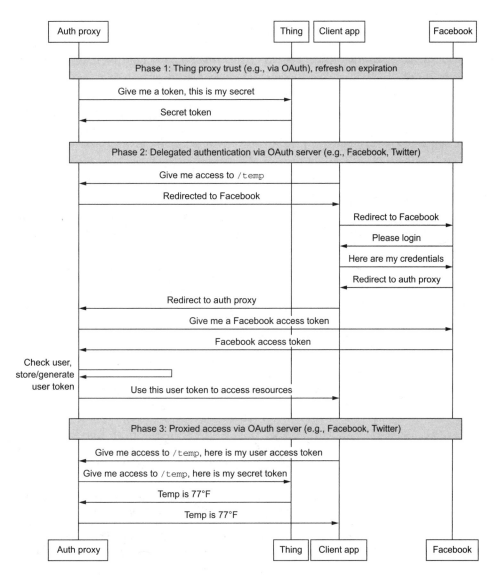

Figure 9.7 Social Web of Things authentication proxy: the auth proxy first establishes a secret with the Thing over a secure channel. Then, a client app requests access to a resource via the auth proxy. It authenticates itself via an OAuth server (here Facebook) and gets back an access token. This token is then used to access resources on the Thing via the auth proxy. For instance, the /temp resource is requested by the client app and given access via the auth proxy forwarding the request to the Thing and relaying the response to the client app.

LEVERAGING SOCIAL NETWORKS

You might have noticed that we overlooked one step in the process: how does the auth proxy know what resources a user can access, or even if they can access any resources at all? Someone needs to configure the proxy with a number of user identifiers corresponding to the users who can access the system along with a list of resources they can access. In the case of our hotel, we could ask the guests to log in with their Facebook accounts or, even better, with the Booking.com profile they used to book the hotel room in the first place! Then we could save their social identifiers in the auth proxy, along with the paths to the devices in their room. In the case of a home automation system, you can even imagine granting access to lists of friends or relatives. Figure 9.8 is an example of a user interface on the auth proxy that can let you share resources with your friends.

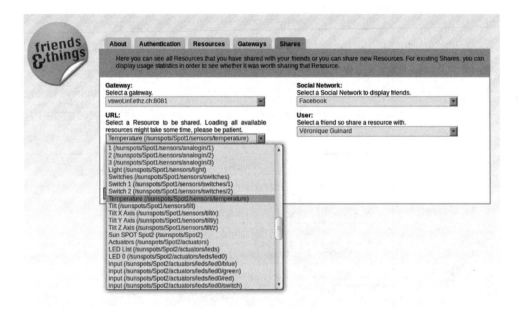

Figure 9.8   User interface of a Social Web of Things authorization proxy: First (upper left), the UI allows the user to select a Thing to be shared and (lower left) the resource of the Thing that should be shared; for example, /temperature. Then (upper right) it lets the owner of the Thing log into their social network, such as Facebook, and (lower right) select a friend to share with or a list of friends. Here we share the temperature sensor of the Spot1 device with Dom's sister via Facebook. [Source: Friends and Things Social Web of Things project[21]]

The good news is that nothing here needs to be hard-coded. Thanks to the fact that our Things speak web (see chapters 5 and 6), we can discover their resources (see chapter 7) and map them to our connections on various OAuth-compliant social networks! This is the very idea of the Social Web of Things: instead of creating abstract access control lists, we can reuse existing social structures as a basis for sharing our

---

[21] hhttp://webofthings.org/2010/02/02/sharing-in-a-web-of-things/

Things. Because social networks increasingly reflect our social relationships, we can reuse that knowledge to share access to our Things with friends via Facebook, or work colleagues via LinkedIn.

9.3.2 Implementing a Social WoT authentication proxy

Now that you've seen the theory, let's put this into practice and implement a simple authentication proxy for the Social Web of Things, as shown in figure 9.9.

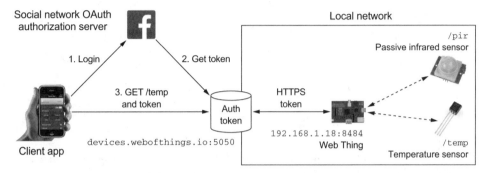

Figure 9.9 A Social Web of Things authentication proxy for your Pi: client apps obtain a token via OAuth on Facebook; this token can then be used to access the Pi resources via the auth proxy. The auth proxy must be accessible on the web, or at least on the same network as the client app, but the Pi can be on a local network as long as the auth proxy can access it.

The complete code for this part is located in the chapter9-sharing/social-auth folder, but we'll only look at the details of some parts here. The proxy could be built directly on top of the WoT Pi code we built in the previous chapters, but as we said before, it makes more sense to implement it as a standalone proxy that can be deployed either on the Pi or somewhere else because it might proxy the access to more than one device.

CREATING A FACEBOOK APPLICATION

Before we can begin coding, we need to make sure that Facebook knows our auth proxy as an authorized Facebook application. To create a Facebook app, you'll need a Facebook account and to apply for a Facebook developer account. If you're not into cat videos or holiday selfies and therefore don't have a Facebook account, feel free to pick another OAuth provider such as Google, Twitter, or GitHub and replace "Facebook" with the OAuth provider you picked in all the following sections. We won't detail how to implement support for other providers, but the principle will be similar, so you shouldn't have too much trouble doing this exercise.

Go to https://developers.facebook.com and apply for a Facebook developer account if you don't already have one. Under My Apps select Register As A Developer. Then you can select My Apps > Add A New App. Select Website, give your app a name,

App ID and secret

Give your app a name

The domains you will use for your app

The main page of your auth proxy

Figure 9.10   Setting up a new Facebook application for our Social WoT auth proxy. The app ID and secret will be used by Facebook to authenticate our app.

and select Skip Quick Start. You should now have a new Facebook app; fill the fields as shown in figure 9.10 by clicking Settings under your app name.

Once you've done this, you can note the two bits of information you need: the app ID and the app secret of your Facebook application. You'll need to send these to Facebook to authenticate your client app. Note that until your app is published publicly, only you and the people you invite as developers/admins will be able to log in via this Facebook app.

PASSPORT.JS: THE AUTHENTICATION MIDDLEWARE FOR EXPRESS

Now that your Facebook app is ready, you need to integrate it into your code. You begin by creating a simple Express application with an HTTPS server. You can find this application in chapter9-sharing/social-auth/authProxy.js, but we won't detail it here because it's similar to the Express apps you created in chapter 8 and the previous sections. Next, you'll create the component that authenticates users via Facebook. You implement it using one of the most popular Node.js modules, Passport.js.[22] Passport is an impressive authentication middleware that provides simple integration of a number of authentication techniques—more than 300!—including OAuth and, hence, all the social networks implementing it.

After installing Passport via `npm install --s passport`, you install the Facebook authentication module of Passport, called a *strategy*, via `npm install --s passport-facebook`. If you want to authenticate via Twitter, LinkedIn, or GitHub, you'll need to

---

[22] http://passportjs.org/

install the corresponding Passport strategy; for example, `passport-twitter` or `passport-linkedin`. As long as you pick a network that supports OAuth, the implementation of the proxy with your chosen authentication strategy will be almost the same as the one used for Facebook.

IMPLEMENTING A FACEBOOK AUTHENTICATION STRATEGY

You're now ready to add Facebook authentication support to your proxy. The providers/facebook.js file shows you how to do that. As shown in the following listing, you have to implement a number of functions to work with a Passport strategy.

Listing 9.5 providers/facebook.js: a Facebook authentication strategy

```
var passport = require('passport'), [...]

var acl = require('../config/acl.json');
var facebookAppId = 'YOUR_APP_ID';
var facebookAppSecret = 'YOUR_APP_SECRET';
var socialNetworkName = 'facebook';
var callbackResource = '/auth/facebook/callback';
var callbackUrl = 'https://localhost:' + acl.config.sourcePort +
  callbackResource;
```
> Configuration variables: FB app ID, app secret, name, and the URL to call back after a user authentication on Facebook

```
module.exports.setupFacebookAuth = setupFacebookAuth;
function setupFacebookAuth(app) {
  app.use(cookieParser());
  app.use(methodOverride());
  app.use(session({secret: 'keyboard cat',
      resave: true, saveUninitialized: true}));
  app.use(passport.initialize());
  app.use(passport.session());
```
> Initialize Passport and support storing the user login in sessions.

```
  passport.serializeUser(function (user, done) {
    done(null, user);
  });
```
> If you had a database of users, you'd use these two methods to load and save users.

```
  passport.deserializeUser(function (obj, done) {
    done(null, obj);
  });

  passport.use(new FacebookStrategy({
      clientID: facebookAppId,
      clientSecret: facebookAppSecret,
      callbackURL: callbackUrl
    },
    function (accessToken, refreshToken, profile, done) {
```
> The credentials used to authenticate your auth proxy as a Facebook app

> This URL will be called by Facebook after a successful login.

```
      auth.checkUser(socialId(profile.id), accessToken,
        function (err, res) {
          if (err) return done(err, null);
          else return done(null, profile);
        });
    }));
```
> The "verify" function, called by the framework after a successful authentication with the provider; here you check if the user is known by the proxy and store their token if so.

Trigger the authentication process, and redirect the user to facebook.com.

```
app.get('/auth/facebook',
  passport.authenticate('facebook'),
  function (req, res) {});
```

Facebook.com will redirect the user to the callbackUrl, so this function will never be called!

```
app.get(callbackResource,
  passport.authenticate('facebook', {session: true,
    failureRedirect: '/login'}),
  function (req, res) {
    res.redirect('/account');
  });
```

This route will be called by Facebook after user authentication. If it fails you, redirect to /login; otherwise to /account.

```
app.get('/account', ensureAuthenticated, function (req, res) {
  auth.getToken(socialId(req.user.id), function (err, user) {
    if (err) res.redirect('/login');
    else {
      req.user.token = user.token;
      res.render('account', {user: req.user});
    }
  });
});
```

If the user is authenticated, you get their token and display their account page; otherwise redirect to /login.

```
function socialId(userId) {
  return socialNetworkName + ':' + userId;
};
[...]
};
```

A unique social identifier is formed by concatenating the social userId and the social network name.

At first sight, this flow might seem a bit complex. It consists of a number of routes that redirect the user to a Facebook login page and back from Facebook to your proxy alongside a code that can be exchanged for a token. Passport takes care of all the nitty-gritty details for you. The good news is that all authentication strategies have to implement the same methods, so what you learned here can be applied to other social networks as well!

This was the core of the Facebook authentication mechanism, and now you also need to make sure users have a user interface (HTML views) for all the routes you created. You can certainly write HTML pages from scratch, but it's easier to reuse Handlebars, the templating engine we used in the previous chapters. The pages we created are located in the /views folder. At a minimum you'll need a login.html page with a link to /auth/facebook to trigger the authentication process. You'll also need an account.html page to which the user will be redirected upon a successful Facebook authentication.

IMPLEMENTING ACCESS CONTROL LISTS

Now that your application allows users to authenticate via Facebook using OAuth, you need to decide which user can access which resource on which Thing. In essence, you need to create an access control list (ACL). There are various ways to implement ACLs, such as by storing them in the local database. To keep things simple, you'll use a JSON configuration file, which can be found in config/acl.json and is shown in the next listing. This file keeps track of which users can access which resources on your Pi.

Listing 9.6 config/acl.json: the access control list JSON file

An array of the resources you want to protect →

User IDs are concatenations of the social network name and the social network ID. ←

The resources you want to allow access without authentication →

The list of resources user facebook:10207489314897153 is allowed to access; replace the number with your Facebook ID.

The list of Things this proxy covers alongside their root URL and secret token; could also be generated dynamically via OAuth if the Thing supports it. ←

```json
{
  "protected": [
    {
      "uid": "facebook:10207489314897153",
      "resources": [
        "/properties", "/properties/temperature",
        "/properties/humidity",
        "/properties/pir", "/leds/1", "/leds/2", "/actions/ledState"
      ]
    }, {...}
  ],
  "open": [
    "/", "/model", "/account", "/login", "/logout", "/auth/facebook",
    "/auth/facebook/callback"
  ],
  "things": [
    {
      "id": "WoTPi",
      "url": "https://127.0.0.1:8484",
      "token": "cKXRTaRylYWQiF3MICaKndG4WJMcVLFz"
    }, {...}
  ],
  "config": {
    "sourcePort" : 5050
  }
}
```

A difficulty might be finding the user IDs of users you want to share with using their social network identifier. A good way is to ask them to log in first because this will display their social network ID on the account page you got back from Facebook. Alternatively, you can use the Facebook Graph API explorer[23] tool. Make sure you add your own ID in the ACL!

Now that your ACL is in place, you need to check what you get back from Facebook against it to ensure the users who are trying to log in are really welcome. Similarly, you need to check that they can access the Things' resources requested. You implement this using a middleware in /middleware/auth.js, as shown in the next listing.

Listing 9.7 Authorizing user requests: /middleware/auth.js

Require your ACL config file. ←

If the request is for an open path, call the next middleware. ←

```javascript
var acl = require('../config/acl.json'), [...]

exports.socialTokenAuth = function (req, res, next) {
  if (isOpen(req.path)) {
    next();
  } else {
    var token = req.body.token || req.param('token') ||
```

---

[23] https://developers.facebook.com/tools/explorer/

```
        req.headers['Authorization'];
      if (!token) {
        return res.status(401).send({success: false, message: 'API token
          missing.'});
      } else {
        checkUserAcl(token, req.path, function (err, user) {
          if (err) {
            return res.status(403).send({success: false, message: err});
          }
          next();
        });
      }
    }
  };
```

Otherwise, get the access token and check the ACL for this token. → (points to `checkUserAcl(token, req.path, function (err, user) {`)

Otherwise, the user is good to go, and you call the next middleware. → (points to `next();`)

If there's an error, return a 403 Forbidden status code. → (points to `return res.status(403).send({success: false, message: err});`)

```
  function checkUserAcl(token, path, callback) {
    var userAcl = findInAcl(function (current) {
      return current.token === token && current.resources.indexOf(path)
        !== -1;
    });
    if (userAcl) {
      callback(null, userAcl);
    } else {
      callback('Not authorized for this resource!', null);
    }
  };
  function findInAcl(filter) {
    return acl.protected.filter(filter)[0];
  };

  function isOpen(path) {
    [...] if (acl.open.indexOf(path) !== -1) return true;
  }

  exports.checkUser = checkUser;
  function checkUser(socialUserId, token, callback) {
    var result = findInAcl(function(current) {
      return current.uid === socialUserId;
    });
    if(result) {
      result.token = token;
      callback(null, result);
    } else {
      callback('User not found!', null);
    }
  };
  [...]
```

Can we find a user with the given token and the given path? → (points to `function checkUserAcl(token, path, callback) {`)

Handle open resources. → (points to `function isOpen(path) {`)

Called by facebook.js when a user is authenticated → (points to `function checkUser(socialUserId, token, callback) {`)

If the user ID you got from Facebook is present in your ACL, you have a winner! → (points to `return current.uid === socialUserId;`)

Store the user token to allow them to make subsequent calls to resources they can access. → (points to `result.token = token;`)

PROXYING RESOURCES OF THINGS

Finally, you need to implement the actual proxying: once a request is deemed valid by the middleware, you need to contact the Thing that serves this resource and proxy the results back to the client. This part is no different from any other HTTP proxy. To implement it, you'll use a blazing-fast Node module for building proxies called node-http-proxy.[24] Install it via `npm install --save http-proxy`. Then use this module to build another middleware in /middleware/proxy.js, as shown in the next listing.

Listing 9.8 Proxying requests to Things: /middleware/proxy.js

```
var https = require('https'),
  fs = require('fs'),
  config = require('../config/acl.json').things[0],      ◄ Load the Thing that
  httpProxy = require('http-proxy');                          can be proxied
                                                              (there's only one here).

var proxyServer = httpProxy.createProxyServer({            ◄
  ssl: {
    key: fs.readFileSync('./config/change_me_privateKey.pem', 'utf8'),
    cert: fs.readFileSync('./config/change_me_caCert.pem', 'utf8'),
    passphrase: 'webofthings'
  },                                                        Initialize the proxy server,
  secure: false    ◄ Do not verify the certificate (true   making it an HTTPS proxy to
});                   would refuse a local certificate).    ensure end-to-end encryption.

module.exports = function() {                              Proxy the request; notice
  return function proxy(req, res, next) {                  that this middleware doesn't
    req.headers['authorization'] = config.token;           call next() because it should
    proxyServer.web(req, res, {target: config.url});   ◄   be the last in the chain.
  }
};
```

Proxy middleware function; add the secret token of the Thing.

That's it! You should now have a full Social Web of Things authentication proxy. To test it, run `node authProxy.js`. Then, start the WoT Pi using `node wot.js` with simple token authentication enabled, as shown in section 9.2.1, or with OAuth if you implemented it.

Try to access a resource of your Pi via the proxy with an invalid token; for example, https://raspberrypi.local:5050/properties/pir?token=1234. As expected, this will return an error: `Not authorized for this resource!`

Now, let's get an access token to issue a valid request: start by browsing to https://IP:5050/login. This should prompt you to log in on Facebook (if your browser doesn't have a Facebook login cookie sitting in the cupboard) and then should ask you if you authorize the proxy Facebook app to access your profile. If you accept, you'll land on your profile page, as shown in figure 9.11, where you can see your access token. Copy it and open https://raspberrypi.local:5050/properties/pir?token=YOUR-TOKEN once again, but this time with your new token. If everything works, you should get the HTML representation of the PIR sensor. Take a deep breath and think about what you just did: you merged the Social Web with the physical world!

---

[24] https://github.com/nodejitsu/node-http-proxy

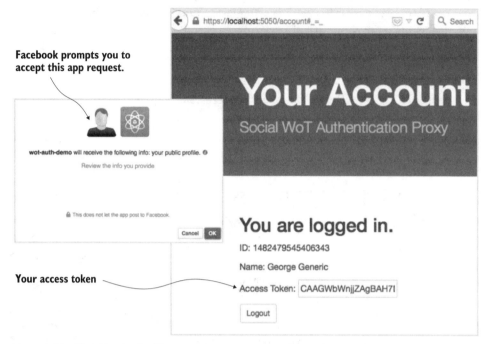

Figure 9.11   First, Facebook will prompt the user to accept the application request. After a successful Facebook authentication, the user is redirected to their Account page on the auth proxy, where they can retrieve their access token to be used in subsequent calls to the Things behind the proxy.

The nerd corner—I want more of this!

As usual, there are many possible ways of extending this example because we kept the implementation simple. Here are a few extension ideas: you could use what you learned in chapter 8 to implement a system for the proxy to automatically discover web Thing model-compliant Things. You could also make the ACL much easier to deal with by implementing wildcards; for example, `/properties/*`. Or you could create a UI for the proxy that lets you share with your friends or that lets you add authorized users dynamically (for our hotel scenario). If you're still hungry for more, you could also implement proxying for WebSockets; `node-http-proxy` supports it as well. Finally, you could implement an OAuth server on the Pi—for example, using `node-oauth2-server`—and change the proxy to dynamically get an OAuth access token from the Pi instead of a simple token; this would make the flow more secure and much more flexible.

9.4   Beyond the book

In this chapter, you learned how to blend the Social Web and the Web of Things to get to the Social Web of Things. Not a small achievement for a single chapter! Although you should certainly enjoy the moment, you should also realize that we barely scratched the surface of security for the IoT and the WoT. We didn't cover a number of aspects, from ensuring privacy to protecting Things against distributed denial of service attacks or securing software and firmware updates.

By definition, perfect security is unattainable. Securing computer networks is a constant battle between security experts and hackers, where security systems always need to be one step ahead because the better our machines and tools get, the easier it is to break secure systems. Network security should be a constant discipline rather than a one-off event, and you need to keep informed and updated as you pursue your IoT adventure.[25]

As the IoT moves out of its teenage years and into adulthood, different focal points will appear. First, security will become ubiquitous and a must-have, rather than a nice-to-have. But just as HTTP might be too heavy for resource-limited devices, security protocols such as TLS and their underlying cypher suites are too heavy for the most resource-constrained devices. This is why lighter-weight versions of TLS are being developed, such as DTLS,[26] which is similar to TLS but runs on top of UDP instead of TCP and also has a smaller memory footprint. Although such protocols represent interesting evolutions, some researchers are looking at revolutions! For example, some researchers started looking at a concept they refer to as *device democracy*.[27] In this model, devices become more autonomous and favor peer-to-peer interactions over centralized cloud services. Security is ensured using a blockchain mechanism: similar to the way bitcoin transactions are validated by a number of independent parties in the bitcoin network, devices could all participate in making the IoT secure. Without a doubt, IoT security will change drastically in the next few years, as the web itself will evolve to match today's needs.

The nerd corner—I want the future of secure application management!

As mentioned before, managing applications or firmware updates on an embedded device can be tricky to get right and secure: if you don't do it right, such as by using an insecure HTTP server, attackers could use your update mechanism to inject whatever they like on your customers' devices! Luckily, as the IoT matures, interesting, secure, and scalable solutions appear to help you deploy code on your Things. As an example, resin.io lets you use Git to push new versions of your code to all your Things or to a selection of them. It also uses Docker containers to package and run

---

[25] Some good bedside readings:
- http://h30499.www3.hp.com/t5/Fortify-Application-Security/HP-Study-Reveals-70-Percent-of-Internet-of-Things-Devices/ba-p/6556284
- https://www.owasp.org/index.php/Main_Page
- http://arstechnica.com/security/2016/01/how-to-search-the-internet-of-things-for-photos-of-sleeping-babies/
- http://techcrunch.com/2015/10/24/why-iot-security-is-so-critical

[26] https://en.wikipedia.org/wiki/Datagram_Transport_Layer_Security

[27] http://www-935.ibm.com/services/us/gbs/thoughtleadership/internetofthings/

(continued)

several applications in isolation on embedded devices, which improves portability, security, and stability. Finally, it works well with Node.js and the Pi and is free if you have a small number of devices, so go ahead and try it.[a]

---
[a] https://resin.io

9.5   Summary

- You must cover four basic principles to secure IoT systems: encrypted communication, server authentication, client authentication, and access control.
- Encrypted communication ensures attackers can't read the content of messages. It uses encryption mechanisms based on symmetric or asymmetric keys.
- You should use TLS to encrypt messages on the web. TLS is based on asymmetric keys: a public key and a private server key.
- Server authentication ensures attackers can't pretend to be the server. On the web, this is achieved by using SSL (TLS) certificates. The delivery of these certificates is controlled through a chain of trust where only trusted parties called certificate authorities can deliver certificates to identify web servers.
- Instead of buying certificates from a trusted third party, you can create self-signed TLS certificates on a Raspberry Pi. The drawback is that web browsers will flag the communication as unsecure because they don't have the CA certificate in their trust store.
- You can achieve client authentication using simple API tokens. Tokens should rotate on a regular basis and should be generated using crypto secure random algorithms so that their sequence can't be guessed.
- The OAuth protocol can be used to generate API tokens in a dynamic, standard, and secure manner and is supported by many embedded Linux devices such as the Raspberry Pi.
- The delegated authentication mechanism of OAuth relies on other OAuth providers to authenticate users and create API tokens. As an example, a user of a Thing can be identified using Facebook via OAuth.
- You can implement access control for Things to reflect your social contacts by creating an authentication proxy using OAuth for clients' authentication and contacts from social networks.

Now that you've seen how to secure your web-connected Things so that their data and services can be securely shared and accessed over the web, it's time to move to the final layer of the WoT architecture: Compose. In the next chapter, you'll see how to take all the components you learned about in this book and combine them to build a whole new generation of web applications: physical mashups. Integrating real-time data from numerous physical sources directly within web applications and services is without doubt the future of the web. We want to make sure you have the tools you need to get there in no time!

10

Compose:
Physical mashups

This chapter covers

- Automatically generating user interfaces for web Things using their model
- Using box and arrow mashup editors to combine web Things and web resources.
- Creating complex workflows for web Things in minutes with wizard mashup editors

We've come quite a long way since the beginning of this book! We've implemented web protocols on Things to make them accessible over the web. We've modeled and semantically described Things with web-friendly formats and languages to facilitate their discovery and interoperability. We've secured Things with state-of-the-art web security protocols and best practices and then shared them over the web to make their resources accessible to our friends on various social networks. Now is probably a good time to step back and understand why we've worked through all these different layers. Things that are accessible through these layers can now be integrated to any web application or service seamlessly and effortlessly because web Things have become first-class citizens of the web!

279

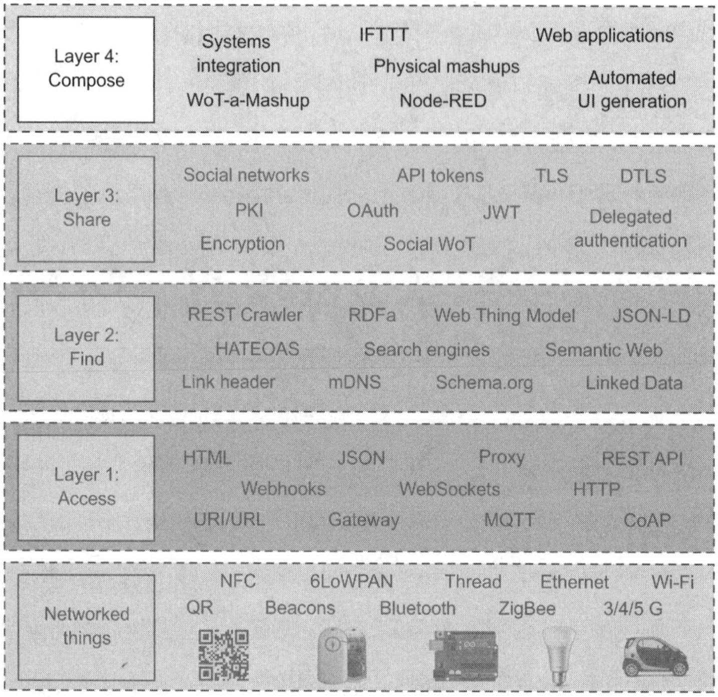

Figure 10.1   The Compose layer of the Web of Things architecture. This layer focuses on building web applications that can control Things or combine data and services from various sources to deliver complex processes. It brings the concept of web mashups to the Internet of Things.

The last layer—Compose, shown in figure 10.1—is all about using what you've learned and built so far to create new applications. You turned Things into web LEGO® bricks; now it's time to unleash your inner artist and create a collection of amazing sculptures! In this chapter, we'll first show you how to use the API of Things to build user interfaces that can accommodate and adapt to the things they discover.

Then we'll look at *physical mashups*: composite web applications that combine Things and web services. You'll learn how to use mashup tools to rapidly build complex workflows by wiring together data and services from various sources. Because all components of your application are web APIs, you don't have to worry about data integration and can focus solely on the wiring and logic of your application.

10.1   *Building a simple app—automated UI generation*

The ultimate goal of the various layers of the Web of Things architecture is to enable as many applications as possible to discover, understand, and interact with other Things with minimal effort. Many IoT scenarios involve users interacting with all sorts of devices using various applications. As you saw earlier, one of the problems of the

IoT is that every device needs a custom application, which is inconvenient for users. If we could have a universal application that's capable of controlling any device, it would be much more interesting. The Web of Things makes this possible by using the Web Thing Model, and this section will show you how to start building this universal remote control.

10.1.1 A universal user interface for web Things

The Web Thing model you implemented in chapter 8 and secured in chapter 9 describes in a standard format the various actions supported by a device, along with its properties and additional metadata. Based on this you can easily write a client application that automatically generates a user interface for any web Thing and then displays the properties in real time and sends commands (actions) to the web Thing. The architecture of this application is shown in figure 10.2 and is the first step toward a universal remote control for web Things: even without having any a priori knowledge about a specific web Thing it just discovered, it can use the Thing's Web Thing Model document to generate a custom user interface and bind it to the Thing to control it and/or visualize its data in real time.

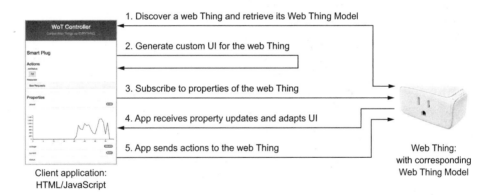

Figure 10.2   The universal remote control for web Things. A web Thing client application (pure JavaScript/HTML) can find nearby devices, retrieve their Web Thing Model description, and use it to generate a custom user interface tailored for that specific device.

You can find a simple application that does that on the GitHub repository of this book in the folder chapter10-mashups/UI, so let's open the file UI.html and analyze its contents.

The first thing this web application does is retrieve the model of a Thing with the getModel() function shown in the following listing. This function is called when the page is loaded with the URL of the model given as parameter.

Listing 10.1   Retrieve the JSON model of a web Thing with jQuery

```
function getModel(sourceUrl){
  $.ajax({
    type: 'GET',
    url: sourceUrl,
    dataType: 'json',
    headers: {Accept : "application/json"},
    success: function( data ){
      baseUrl=data.customFields.hostname+":"+data.customFields.port;
      $('#wt-name').html(data.name);
      $('#wt-description').html(data.description);
      generateActions(data.links.actions.resources);
      generateProperties(data.links.properties.resources);
    },
    error: function( jqXhr, textStatus, errorThrown ){
      console.log( errorThrown );
    }
  });
}
```

Ask explicitly for JSON in the HTTP headers.

Do a GET on the sourceUrl to retrieve the model.

Upon success, store the hostname for future requests, such as sending actions.

Update the page with the device metadata.

Generate the UI for the actions.

Generate the UI for the properties.

Once you've retrieved the JSON model of the web Thing, you use its contents to generate the user interface for it. First, you use the metadata of the web Thing—name, description, hostname, port, and so on—to generate a human-friendly description of the web Thing and its purpose. Then, you use the description of the actions to create UI elements that send commands to the web Thing, as shown in figure 10.3. Finally, you use the description of the properties to generate UI elements that render the data of the web Thing (you can see this in action in figure 10.4).

Before we dive headfirst into the code that generates the HTML form, start the WoT Pi server as you did in the previous chapters with node wot.js and make sure the secure version is started (the first line of the wot.js should require './wot-server-secure'). You can now open the UI.html file in your browser and pass the token of your WoT Pi as a query parameter in the URL (UI.html?token=YOUR_TOKEN).

Now GET the model of your WoT Pi and review the Actions element of the model, as shown in the next listing. You can see that the Pi has only one action, called led-State. This action requires two input parameters, or values: ledId (an enum that can be 1, 2, or ALL) and state (a boolean for the desired state of the LED).

Listing 10.2   The actions object of the Web Thing Model for our Pi

```
"actions": {
  "link": "/actions",
  "title": "Actions of this Web Thing",
  "resources": {
    "ledState": {
      "name": "Change LED state",
      "description": "Change the state of an LED",
      "values": {
        "ledId": {
          "type": "enum",
```

The first parameter, ledId, takes as a value I, 2, or ALL and specifies which LED should change its state.

```
      "enum": {
        "1": "LED 1",
        "2": "LED 2",
        "ALL": "All LEDs"
      },
      "required": true
    },
    "state": {
      "type": "boolean",
      "required": true
    }
  }
  }
  }
}
}
```

The second parameter, state, takes a Boolean value and represents the desired state to which to switch the LED(s).

The corresponding web form to create such an action is shown in figure 10.3.

Figure 10.3 An HTML form to create `ledState` actions based on the web Thing model for a Raspberry Pi

Now, let's see the corresponding HTML code behind this HTML form, shown in the following listing. It's certainly not the simplest piece of code because we use the Boot-strap library to make it look pretty (hence the complex tree of HTML elements), so please bear with us.

Listing 10.3 The HTML code of the form to create an `ledState` action

```html
<div class="panel panel-default">
  <div class="panel-heading">
    <h3 class="panel-title">Change LED state</h3>
  </div>
  <div class="panel-body">Change the state of an LED
    <form class="form-horizontal" id="wt-actions-ledState">
      <div class="form-group" id="wt-actions-ledState-ledId-f">
        <label class="col-sm-2 control-label">ledId</label>
        <div class="col-sm-4" id="wt-actions-ledState-ledId-field">
          <select class="form-control" name="ledId" id="wt-actions
            -ledState-ledId-value">
            <option value="1">LED 1</option>
```

```
        <option value="2">LED 2</option>
        <option value="ALL">All LEDs</option>
      </select>
    </div>
  </div>
  <div class="form-group" id="wt-actions-ledState-state-f">
    <label class="col-sm-2 control-label">state</label>
    <div class="col-sm-4" id="wt-actions-ledState-state-field">
      <select class="form-control" name="state" id="wt-actions
        -ledState-state-value">
      <option value="true">True</option>
      <option value="false">False</option>
      </select>
    </div>
  </div>
  <p>
    <a class="col-sm-offset-2 col-sm-4 btn btn-primary btn-lg"
       id="send-ledState" href="#" role="button">Create Action:
       ledState</a>
  </p>
</form>
  </div>
</div>
```

In summary, here's a simple HTML form with two inputs—the LED ID and the desired state—and a button to send the action. For each action of any web Thing, we need to generate such a form with the appropriate input parameters they support. Let's now dissect the `generateActions()` function shown in the following listing, which does exactly this.

Listing 10.4   The `generateActions()` function

```
function generateActions(actions){
  $.each(actions, function(i,item){                        ◄─┐ Iterate over each action
                                                             │ of this web Thing.
    $("<div>").attr("class","panel panel-default")
    .appendTo("#wt-actions")
    .append($("<div>")
    .attr("class","panel-heading")
    .append($("<h3>")
    .attr("class","panel-title")
    .html(item.name)))
    .append($("<div>")                                     ┌─ For each action create a UI element
    .attr("class","panel-body")                            │  (form) that will hold the parameters
    .html(item.description)                                │  of the action; el is the element ID of
    .append($("<form>")                                    │  the form for this action.
    .attr("class","form-horizontal").attr("id","wt-actions-"+i)));   ◄─┘

    var el = "#wt-actions-"+i;                              ◄──
    $.each(item.values, function(vi,vitem){       ◄─ Iterate over
      $("<div>").attr("class","form-group").attr("id","wt-actions-"+i+"-   each input
                                                      parameter for
                                                      this action.
```

Create the div element that contains the value of this parameter.

Create a div element that will contain the form input element for this parameter; vel is the ID of this div element.

Look at the type of this parameter.

It's a Boolean, so create a true/false dropdown.

It's an enum, so create a dropdown selector with the possible values.

Iterate over the enum object to generate the possible values.

It's something else, so a basic input element will do.

```javascript
          "+vi).appendTo(el);
      var vel=el+"-"+vi;
      $("<label>").attr("class","col-sm-2 control-
          label").html(vi).appendTo(vel);
      $("<div>").attr("class","col-sm-8").attr("id","wt-actions-"+i+"-
          "+vi+"-f").appendTo(vel);

      switch(vitem.type) {
      case 'boolean':
          $("<select>").attr("class","form-
              control").attr("name",vi).attr("id","wt-actions-"+i+"-"+vi+"-
              v").appendTo(vel+"-f");
          $("<option>").val(true).html("True").appendTo(vel+"-v");
          $("<option>").val(false).html("False").appendTo(vel+"-v");
          break;
      case 'enum':
          $("<select>").attr("class","form-
              control").attr("name",vi).attr("id","wt-actions-"+i+"-"+vi+"-
              v").appendTo(vel+"-f");
          $.each(vitem.enum, function(enumi,enumv){
              $("<option>").val(enumi).html(enumv).appendTo(vel+"-v");
          });
          break;
      default:
          $("<input>").attr("class","form-control").attr("type","text")
              .attr("name",vi).attr("placeholder",vitem.type)
              .appendTo(vel+"-f");
      };
  });
```

Create the button for this action.

Attach a handler to this button.

Store all the input fields of this form in the data variable.

Finally, send the action to the web Thing.

```javascript
  $("<p>").html("<a class=\"col-sm-offset-2 col-sm-4 btn btn-primary
      btn-lg\" id=\"send-"+i+"\" href=\"#\" role=\"button\">Create Action:
      "+i+"</a>").appendTo(el);
  $('#send-'+i).click(function() {
      var data = {};
      $(el).serializeArray().map(function(x){
          if (x.value==="true"){
              data[x.name] = true;
          } else if (x.value==="false") {
              data[x.name] = false;
          } else {
              data[x.name] = x.value;
          }
      });
      sendAction(i,data);
  });
  });
}
```

Once this code has generated a form for each action of the web Thing, we can now do the same for its properties. Look at the PIR and LED properties of the model of our Pi in the next listing.

Listing 10.5   The PIR and LED properties of the Pi Web Thing Model

```
...
"pir": {
  "name": "Passive Infrared",
  "description": "A passive infrared sensor.",
  "values": {
    "presence": {
      "name": "Presence",
      "description": "Current sensor value (true=motion detected)",
      "type": "boolean",
      "customFields": {"gpio": 20}
    }
  },
  "tags": ["sensor","public"]
},
"leds": {
  "name": "LEDs",
  "description": "The LEDs of this device.",
  "values": {
    "1": {
      "name": "LED 1",
      "customFields": {"gpio": 17}
    },
    "2": {
      "name": "LED 2",
      "customFields": {"gpio": 19}
    }
  },
  "tags": ["sensor","public"]
}
...
```

We want our generator to create the HTML output shown in figure 10.4 to display those properties.

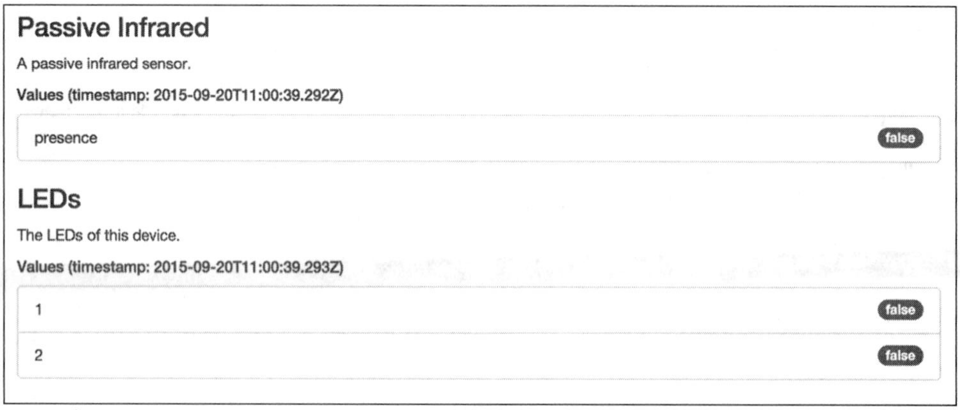

Figure 10.4   An HTML view of the PIR and LED properties of the WoT Pi

Just as we did for actions, we'll generate the HTML elements to display the properties as shown in figure 10.4 and then create a WebSocket subscription to each property so we can display the latest value of each property as it's sent by the web Thing. All of this is done with the generateProperties() function shown in the next listing.

Listing 10.6 The generateProperties() function

```
function generateProperties(properties){
  $.each(properties, function(i,item){
    $("<h3>").html(item.name).appendTo("#wt-properties");
    $("<p>").html(item.description).appendTo("#wt-properties");
    $("<h5>").html("Values (timestamp: <span id=\"property-"+i+"-value
      -timestamp\">unknown</span>)").appendTo("#wt-properties");
    $("<ul>").attr("class","list-group").attr("id","property
      -"+i).appendTo("#wt-properties");

    $.each(item.values, function(vi,vitem){
      $("<li>").attr("class","list-group-item").html("<span
        id=\"property"+i+"-value-"+vi+"\"
        class=\"badge\"></span>"+vi).appendTo("#property-"+i);
    });

    var wsUrl = (secure ? 'wss://' : 'ws://') + hostname
      +'/properties/'+i;
    var socket = new WebSocket(wsUrl);

    socket.onopen = function (message) {
      console.log("Subscribed to Property : "+wsUrl);
    };

    socket.onmessage = function (message) {
      var content = JSON.parse(message.data);
      console.log("Property "+i+" updated : ", content);
      $.each(content, function(vi,vitem){
        $("#property-"+i+"-value-"+vi).text(vitem);
      });
    };

    socket.onerror = function (error) {
      console.log('Error while connecting to a WebSocket!');
      console.log(error);
    };
  });
}
```

For each property, create a set of HTML elements. →

For each value of this property, create a list item. →

Subscribe to the property via WebSockets.

Called when the WebSocket connection is successfully opened. ←

Each time a WS message has been received, unpack it. →

For each value received, update its content. ←

Start a secure WoT Pi server and open https://raspberrypi.local:8484/?token=X. Make sure you replace X with the actual API token of your WoT Pi, as you did in section 9.2.1. Once you accept the certificate by adding a security exception (see section 9.1.3), you should see the root page of your Pi. After that, you can open the UI.html file and append ?token=X (again, with X being your Pi token) to the URL, and you should see the WoT UI page that was automatically generated, along with the actions and properties.

SO WHAT?

In this section, we explored a simple web application that can generate on the fly a custom user interface to interact with any web Thing without knowing anything other than the web Thing's URL. We hope this was a convincing illustration of the important role played by the Find layer we presented in chapter 8. By now, it should be clear why having a uniform format—the web Thing model—to describe physical objects and their capabilities is a key enabler of the Web of Things at scale.

With fewer than 200 lines of code, the example we provided is only a starting point and certainly not a real, production-quality application. There are many more things we could improve, but we'll leave this part as an exercise to stimulate your imagination. For example, you could extend the `generateActions()` function to display a slider for numeric input values, or you could validate that all required parameters are provided before sending an action. Also, you can explore more interesting ways to display the properties in real time. Let us know what you come up with, and don't hesitate to send us pull requests with your improvements and ideas—we're looking forward to hearing from you!

10.2   *Physical mashups*

Implementing layers 1–3 of the WoT architecture allows you not only to automatically create UIs and applications to interact with web Things but also to seamlessly blend web Things with any other services and data sources on the web.

Layer 4 focuses on this problem: how to easily combine data from various sources to create more-complex applications. A web mashup is an application that takes several web resources and uses them to create a new, hybrid application. Unlike traditional forms of integration, mashups focus mainly on opportunistic integration occurring on the web for an end user's personal use. The concept of mashups can also be applied to the Web of Things, in the form of *physical mashups*.[1] These are web applications that combine services from physical Things with services from virtual web resources.

If you read chapter 2, you should already be familiar with the notion of physical mashups. In section 2.6 (exercise 5), you combined a temperature sensor on the Pi with weather data from the web, an LCD screen, and a webcam—all of this with JavaScript and web APIs.

Now that your Pi has a web API, you can create mashups with any programming language that supports HTTP, WebSockets, JSON and TLS (hint: pretty much all of them). In this chapter you'll see that you can also create physical mashups without writing a single line of code! Thanks to great web tools such as boxes and wires or wizard-based editors, you'll be able to create complex and powerful composite applications within minutes!

---

[1] We first described the concept of physical mashups in a research paper called "Towards the Web of Things: Web Mashups for Embedded Devices," and this became one of the core topics of Dom's PhD thesis. Both are available from http://webofthings.org/publications/.

10.2.1 *Boxes and wires mashups for the Physical Web: Node-RED*

Creating physical mashups using JavaScript gives you the most flexibility. The fact that all the Things you include in your mashups are using web protocols makes it straightforward. But it still requires a significant amount of work and programming skills when compared to the mashup technique we'll look at next: *boxes and wires* editors. The idea of these tools is to make the mashup-creation process a lot easier by transforming programming into a visual experience consisting of connecting boxes to form a workflow.

Basically, the *boxes* are ready-made modules that abstract operations, such as GETting data from a REST API, and the *wires* between the modules represent the flow of data or control. You can see an example in figure 10.5. There are a number of boxes and wires mashup tools on the web, but one of them is especially geared for creating IoT mashups: Node-RED.[2] Node-RED is a visual tool for wiring the Internet of Things. It's an open source project supporting a number of protocols but with a strong focus on web protocols and benefiting from a large community of developers creating new modules on an almost daily basis.

The nerd corner—Let's do it in the browser!

Node-RED is built on top of Node.js and hence is a server-side JavaScript mashup tool. This has the big advantage of being able to run mashup workflows even when your browser is closed, but it requires installing and running more tools. Running mashups entirely in the browser, without the need for server code, is also possible. Back when Node-RED didn't exist, we created our own client-side physical mashup editor called *wot-a-mashup*. This tool was built on top of ClickScript,[a] a nice visual programming language environment running in the browser. You're more than welcome to give it a try by cloning it on GitHub.[b]

---

[a] http://clickscript.ch
[b] https://github.com/webofthings/wot-a-mashup

GETTING STARTED WITH NODE-RED

The good news is that Node-RED is a Node.js application, so you should be familiar with the tools around it. Node-RED can be installed only on your computer or in the cloud via NPM,[3] but it's also available out of the box on your Pi. If you want the mashups you create to run continuously, it makes sense to deploy Node-RED on your Pi. This way, your Pi will become an always-on gateway that can orchestrate all the mashups in your home/hotel/business while consuming much less power than a PC. A number of additional Node-RED community modules are available specifically for the Pi; for instance, to interface with Pi hardware modules.

---

[2] http://nodered.org/
[3] http://nodered.org/docs/getting-started/installation.html

Let's see how you can use Node-RED to create physical mashups on top of your WoT Pi or any other web Thing. To start it on your Pi, use the following command:

```
$ node-red-start
> Once Node-RED has started, point a browser ...
```

That's it! Note that Node-RED is started as a service, which means that closing the SSH window from which you started it won't stop Node-RED. To stop it, use `node-red-stop`. If everything works, you should now be able to use the web UI of Node-RED by accessing http://raspberrypi.local:1880 with any recent version of Firefox or Chrome.

The nerd corner—I want to secure Node-RED!

If you made your Pi directly accessible on the web, you definitely should ensure Node-RED requires authentication to access it; otherwise, anyone will be able to reprogram your Pi as they wish! This process is straightforward. It requires you to generate a password and change a configuration file. This process is well documented online.[a]

---
[a] http://nodered.org/docs/security.html

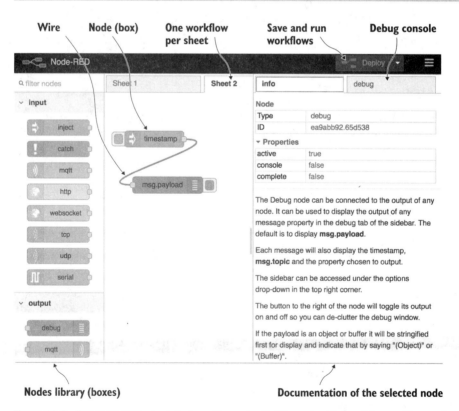

Figure 10.5   The Node-RED user interface: the nodes (left) are dragged and dropped to create workflows by connecting them with wires, sending the data from one node to another.

The Node-RED interface is composed of three main parts, as shown in figure 10.5. First, you have a library of *nodes* on the left. This is where you can find all the boxes representing the functional bits of your mashups. Second, in the flow designer (center), you create your workflows (or just flows) by connecting different nodes together. You can configure nodes by double-clicking them in the flow designer. Third, the rightmost part is where you can see the documentation of nodes by clicking them and is also where you see the debug console.

HELLO WORLD NODE-RED

To test all of this, let's start by creating a simple flow that displays the traditional "Hello World" message. The flow is shown in figure 10.5; to build it, first drag the `inject` input node and the `debug` output node onto the flow designer. Then, connect the extremities of both nodes together. Double-click the `inject` node to change the content injected by this node. Change the `Payload` property to a string and to contain "Hello World!" as shown in figure 10.6.

That's it. Your first flow is ready! Now deploy it by clicking the Deploy button on the top right. This translates your flow into Node.js code and runs it inside the Node-RED process. Now, to test your flow, make sure you have the Node-RED debug console (on the right of the Node-RED window) visible and click the blue dot to the left of the `inject` module.

When you do this, the "Hello World" string is added to a special object called `msg`. This object holds the data to be passed from one node to another and can be either

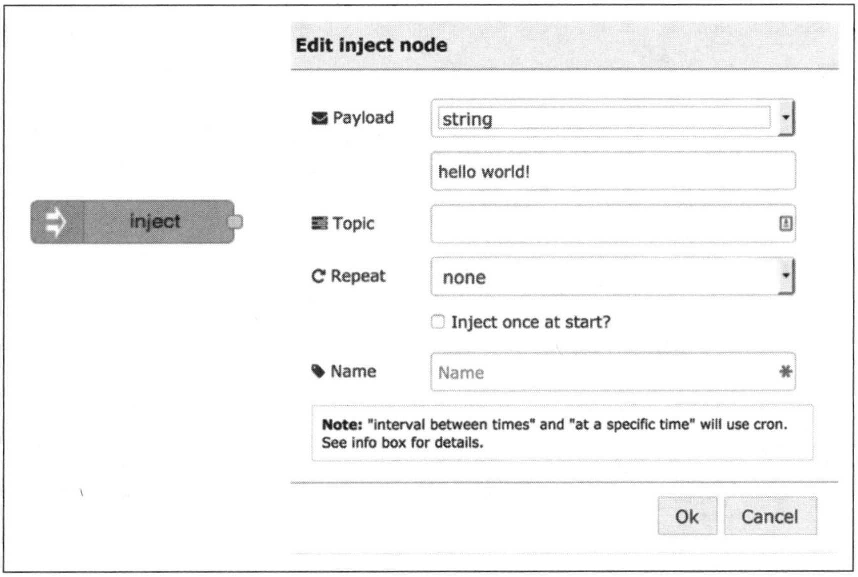

Figure 10.6   Editing nodes: when double-clicking a node, the edit dialog pops up where the node can be configured. This edit dialog shows the configuration of an `inject` output node.

an object or an array of `msg` objects, one for the result of each node in the flow. In this particular case, `msg` is a single object containing the "Hello World" string in a `msg.payload` property. After clicking the blue Inject button, the workflow engine passes the `msg` object to the next node: the `debug` node, which displays data it receives in `msg.payload` in the debug console. This system basically allows you to pass data between the nodes to build workflows. Imagine using this to visually pass the temperature data from a node representing your Pi to a node representing a database.

SAVING WORKFLOWS

Node-RED flows can be represented and saved as JSON documents to reuse later or to share on the Web. To save a flow, select the flow by dragging a selection enclosing all nodes you want to include in the export, and click the menu next to Deploy on the far right of the screen. Select Export and then Clipboard. You'll get the JSON document corresponding to your flow, and you can save it wherever you want. Then, you can use this JSON representation to share your mashup on the web[4] or to reimport a mashup into Node-RED by using the Import menu.

A PHYSICAL MASHUP WITH NODE-RED

Now that you've successfully created a simple virtual mashup with Node-RED, let's see how to include the physical world using the web API of your Pi.

The flow you'll build is shown in figure 10.7 and is available in the book source code in chapter10-mashups/node-red/pir-websockets-twitter.json. The idea is to create a smart alarm mashup that receives notifications when the state of the PIR changes, updates the state of an LED accordingly, and sends an intrusion alert via Twitter. If you decided to buy one of the suggested webcams from the shopping list of

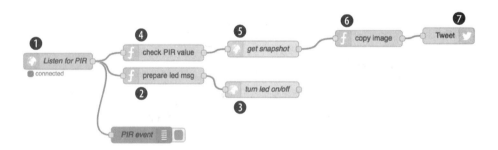

Figure 10.7   The flow of a physical mashup built with Node-RED. This physical mashup is a smart intruder alarm that listens for state changes of the PIR sensor via the WebSocket API ❶. When an event arrives, Node-RED POSTs a `ledState` action to change the state of the LED ❷–❸, and if the event contains a PIR sensor value of `true` ❹, it GETs a snapshot from the webcam ❺ and POSTs it on Twitter ❻–❼.

---

[4]   For instance, on the Node-RED community website: http://flows.nodered.org/.

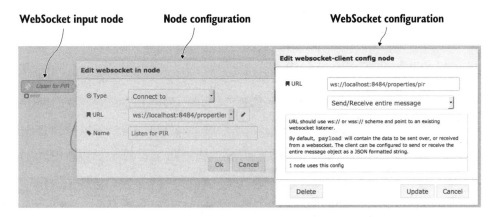

Figure 10.8 Configuration of the WebSocket input node and configuration of a new WebSocket client

chapter 2, it should also take a snapshot of the intruder via the webcam and attach it to the tweet. All of this by connecting boxes and wires!

Let's get started with building your workflow by referencing the steps of figure 10.7. First, drag and drop a `websocket` input node (step 1) and configure it by double-clicking it. The configuration of this node is shown in figure 10.8; basically, you make it listen to the PIR WebSocket resource of your Pi. To do this, select Add a new websocket-client and configure it to ws://raspberrypi.local:8484/properties/pir[5] (the WS address of the PIR sensor), and make sure you select the Send/Receive Entire Message option.

Next, you'll create a function node (step 2). These nodes contain bits of JavaScript code that can be used to transform the messages passed from one node to another based on certain conditions. In step 2, you use the function node to prepare a corresponding POST request to turn the LED on or off depending on the value of the PIR that was sent over WebSockets. The code of this function node is shown in the following listing.

Listing 10.7 Prepare LED message function node

```
msg.headers = {
  'Accept' : 'application/json',
  'Content-Type' : 'application/json',
  'Authorization' : 'cKXRTaRylYWQiF3MICaKndG4WJMcVLFz'
}
if(msg.presence) {
  msg.payload = {"ledId" : 1, "state" : true};
  return msg;
} else {
```

◄── **Prepare the headers for the next node (an HTTP request node).**

◄── **If the WebSocket message contains a value of true for presence, prepare a turn LED on request; otherwise a turn LED off request.**

---

[5] Secure WebSockets with self-signed certificates don't work well on Node-RED, which is why we use the non-secure version of the WoT Pi for this example. If you have a non-self-signed certificate for your Pi, you can use the secure URL instead: wss://PI_URL/properties/pir.

```
    msg.payload = {"ledId" : 1, "state" : false};
    return msg;
}
```

In step 3, you create an `http request` function node that creates an action on the Pi via a POST request to http://raspberrypi.local:8484/actions/ledState. The payload of this action is available to the node in `msg.payload` as prepared by the previous node; see listing 10.7.

You should be able to test this first part of the workflow. Click Deploy and observe what happens when changing the state of the PIR. You just wired a sensor (PIR) with an actuator (LED) on the Pi using an external mashup tool!

Let's not stop here but build the second part of the workflow. The function node of step 4 is a conditional node: if the `presence` value of the PIR sensor is `true`, it passes a message to the next node; otherwise, it interrupts this branch of the flow. The corresponding code is simple, the trick being that when a function node returns `null` the rest of the flow stops, as follows:

```
return msg.presence ? msg: null;
```

If the `presence` value is `true`, you move on to step 5, where you take a snapshot using a WoT-enabled webcam. As mentioned before, if you don't have a webcam offering an HTTP API, you can simply remove the nodes of steps 5 and 6. If you do have a webcam, create an `http request` function node. Using the GET method, call the snapshot URL of the webcam (for example, http://[IP]/snapshot.cgi?user=USER&pwd=PWD in the case of a Foscam) and select binary buffer as a return type. In step 6, create a function node that prepares the tweet:

```
msg.media = msg.payload;
msg.payload = 'Intruder Detected!';
return msg;
```

You must copy the image in `msg.media` because this is where the `twitter` node expects an image to be. Step 7 is where you put the cherry on top: you send an intruder alert via Twitter. To do this, use a `twitter` output node and double-click it to configure your Twitter account by selecting Add new Twitter credentials, which uses OAuth (see chapter 9) to obtain a Twitter API token for your account.

That's it! You can now test your intruder alert workflow. Note that closing your browser won't interrupt the workflow. As long as the Node-RED server runs, your workflow will be running, watching for the next intruder.

The nerd corner—I want more nodes!

Node-RED goes well beyond what we've implemented here. Try creating other mashups with your Pi and all the available nodes; for example, the `MQTT` node connecting to MQTT clients or the `sentiment` node analyzing if an input string is positive or negative.

> **(continued)**
>
> There are also hundreds of nodes from the community, ranging from database integrations like `node-red-node-redis` to IoT device integrations like `node-red-node-arduino` or IoT cloud integrations like `node-red-contrib-evrythng` (maintained by yours truly). All these nodes are available online.[a] You install them just as you'd install any Node.js module via npm. You might also want to create your own nodes; Node-RED also lets you do this without too much effort.[b]
>
> ---
>
> [a]   http://flows.nodered.org/
> [b]   http://nodered.org/docs/creating-nodes/

10.3   *Using wizards for physical mashups: IFTTT*

Visual mashup editors such as Node-RED drastically reduce the time it takes to build IoT prototypes. They also significantly simplify the programming process, but you still have to *program* your mashups. The next mashup technique we look at further pushes the abstractions to simplify even more the creation of mashups. Wizard-based mashup tools consist of a user interface that guides you through a number of steps to create a customized workflow. If you've ever used the filter editor of your mail client, you must know what a wizard interface looks like: a number of steps to create a rule.

A number of wizard mashup tools are available, with Zapier[6] and IFTTT[7] being the most popular. Both tools integrate with a large number of web services ranging from Google Drive to Instagram or Facebook. IFTTT stands for stands for "If This Then That" and is especially relevant here because it's on a mission to incorporate many IoT devices and platforms, so let's take a closer look at this tool.

Basically, the tool lets you create an `if (conditions) then (actions)` statement without having to write a single line of code. The `conditions` and `actions` must be selected from a growing list of prepackaged web integrations ranging from Twitter to Google Drive, as well IoT integrations such as the Nest Thermostat, the Philips Hue lighting system, the SmartThings home automation devices, and the Misfit wearable devices. To create these `if-then` statements, IFTTT takes you through a seven-step wizard process. Once the process is finished, the newly created workflow will run for as long as you want it on the IFTTT servers in the cloud.

IFTTT is a simple yet powerful system, but it doesn't allow the general public to make any integration in any way you want beyond the channels offered. It does, however, offer the Maker channel,[8] which allows you to integrate with arbitrary REST APIs.

---

[6]   https://zapier.com
[7]   https://ifttt.com
[8]   https://ifttt.com/maker

10.3.1   *Pushing intruder alert tweets to a Google spreadsheet*

Let's experiment with IFTTT and create a simple integration of our smart intrusion-detection system. Here's the first workflow we want to create:

- If a new Intruder Detected tweet is posted…
- then log an entry in a Google spreadsheet document.

First, you should create a free IFTTT account[9] and log into your account. In the IFTTT world, workflows are called *recipes*. Start by creating a new recipe, as shown in figure 10.9.

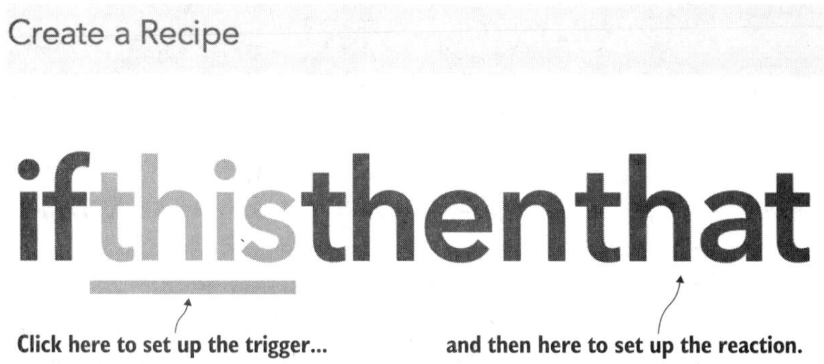

Create a Recipe

ifthisthenthat

Click here to set up the trigger...   and then here to set up the reaction.

Figure 10.9   IFTTT workflows are called recipes. They are composed of two parts: a condition (this) and a reaction (that) triggered when the condition is met.

By clicking the "this" link you set up the condition. In IFTTT, both conditions and reactions are called *channels*. The channels are essentially the prepackaged integrations we were talking about before. Select the Twitter channel and then the New Tweet By A Specific User trigger, and when prompted for a Twitter user, provide the handle of the Twitter account you want to use—@wotbook in this example. That's it for your condition. Basically, what you've created so far is an `if (new Tweet by @TwitterAccount)`.

Next, you need to create the reaction. Click the "that" link. Same story: select a channel for the reaction. We selected the Google Drive Channel and the Add Row To Spreadsheet option. This prompts you to connect your Google account and then to set up the spreadsheet and the content you want to be written to the spreadsheet. This step is shown in figure 10.10.

Finally, in step #7 of the wizard you're ready to create your workflow by selecting Create Recipe, as shown in figure 10.11. This saves the workflow to your account and runs it continuously for you in the cloud.

---

[9] https://ifttt.com/join

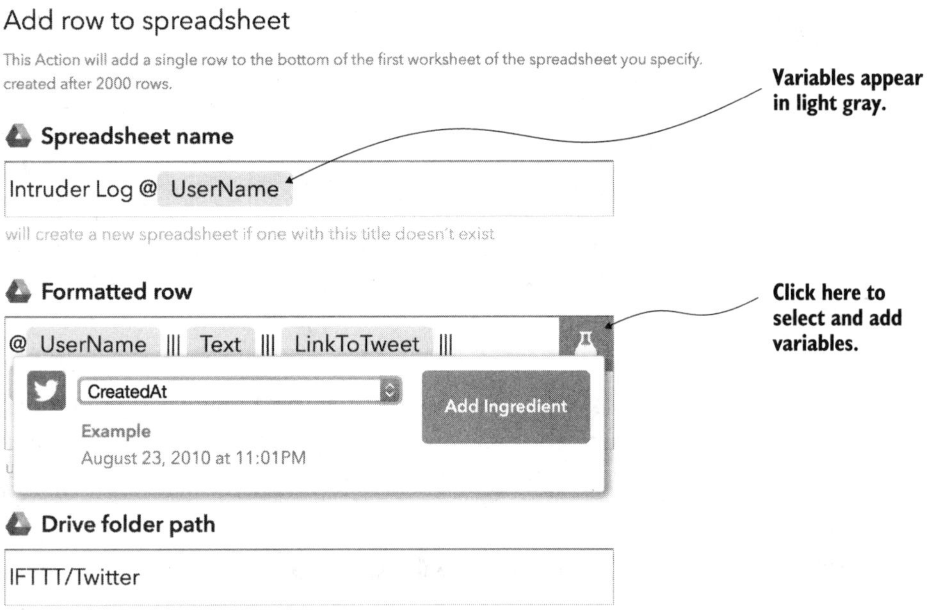

Add row to spreadsheet

This Action will add a single row to the bottom of the first worksheet of the spreadsheet you specify, created after 2000 rows.

Variables appear in light gray.

☁ Spreadsheet name

Intruder Log @ UserName

will create a new spreadsheet if one with this title doesn't exist

Click here to select and add variables.

☁ Formatted row

@ UserName ||| Text ||| LinkToTweet ||| 🧪

CreatedAt   **Add Ingredient**
Example
August 23, 2010 at 11:01PM

☁ Drive folder path

IFTTT/Twitter

Figure 10.10   Setting up the spreadsheet. IFTTT lets you add variables by clicking the Erlenmeyer flask icon. Here we use variables such as the Twitter user name (UserName), the content of the tweet (Text), and the timestamp of the Tweet (CreatedAt). All these fields will appear in the new row created in the Google spreadsheet located in an IFTTT/Twitter folder.

Create and connect   step 7 of 7   back ▲

if 🐦 **then** ▲

New tweet by specific user
@wotbook

Add row to spreadsheet in
Google Drive

Recipe Title

If new tweet by specific user @wotbook, then add
row to spreadsheet in

use '#' to add tags

Create Recipe

Figure 10.11   Step 7 is the final step of the workflow creation process. It summarizes the workflow you just created: if a tweet is pushed, then add a row to the Google Drive spreadsheet.

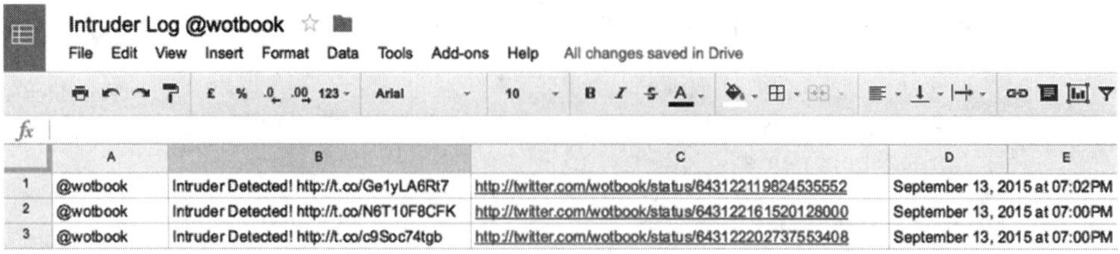

Intruder Log @wotbook

File Edit View Insert Format Data Tools Add-ons Help All changes saved in Drive

	A	B	C	D	E
1	@wotbook	Intruder Detected! http://t.co/Ge1yLA6Rt7	http://twitter.com/wotbook/status/643122119824535552	September 13, 2015 at 07:02PM	
2	@wotbook	Intruder Detected! http://t.co/N6T10F8CFK	http://twitter.com/wotbook/status/643122161520128000	September 13, 2015 at 07:00PM	
3	@wotbook	Intruder Detected! http://t.co/c9Soc74tgb	http://twitter.com/wotbook/status/643122202737553408	September 13, 2015 at 07:00PM	

Figure 10.12 When an intruder is detected by the PIR sensor on your Pi, it tweets it via Node-RED. IFTTT detects this and adds a corresponding entry in your Google spreadsheet. Here you can see three intruder detection events.

To test it, run the Node-RED code of section 10.2 and trigger the PIR sensor, or simulate this by tweeting from the account you selected. If everything works according to plan, you should see a new entry in your Google spreadsheet document in the IFTTT/Twitter folder, as shown in figure 10.12.

10.3.2 Sending requests to a Thing with the Maker Channel

The mashup we just created is pretty impressive but it impacts only the virtual world, a spreadsheet. What if it could also impact the physical world, such as by changing the state of actuators on your WoT Pi? Wouldn't this be pretty powerful? It turns out you can do this via the IFTTT Maker channel. This WoT-friendly channel allows you to send REST requests via HTTP in the "then" part of a workflow, like this:

- *If*—A new Intruder Detected tweet is posted
- *Then*—Turn on the LED of your Pi.

Start by creating a new recipe. The "if" part of the workflow is exactly the same as before: select the Twitter channel and then New Tweet By A Specific User. For the "then" part use the Maker channel and configure it as shown in figure 10.13.

Note that in order to create this recipe, your Pi needs to be securely accessible on the web because IFTTT runs on the web and luckily (or hopefully!) doesn't have access to your local network. Refer to chapter 9 for more information on how to do that. If you didn't put your Pi on the web or don't want to, you can instead use the connected Pi you used in chapter 2 and display an alert on its screen whenever an intruder is detected. You can do this by POSTing to the following URL http://devices.webofthings.io/pi/actuators/display/content a JSON object with the message to display; for example, `{"value":"Intruder Detected!"}`. Finally, create your workflow by selecting Create Recipe. Now, whenever a tweet is sent, you'll see the LED of your Pi turning on—or a message will be displayed on your Pi.

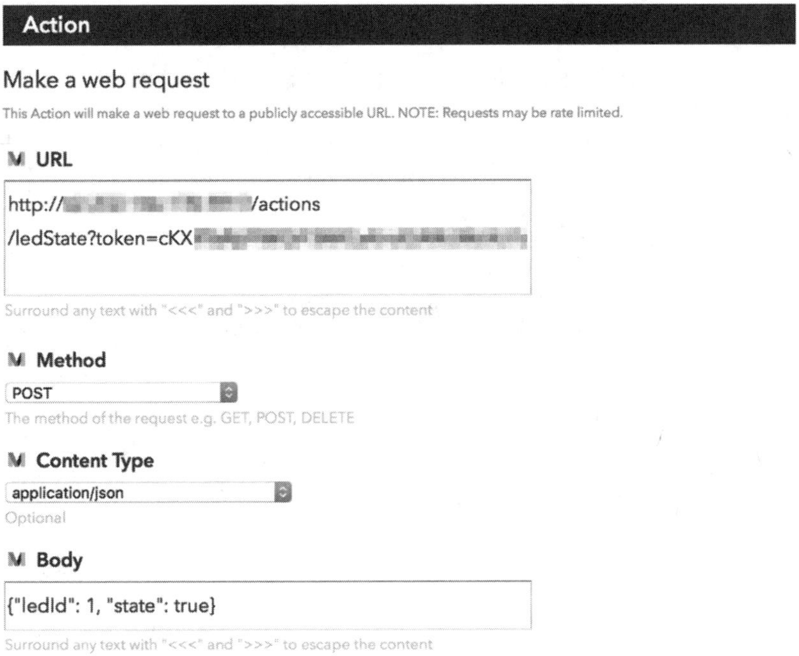

Action

Make a web request

This Action will make a web request to a publicly accessible URL. NOTE: Requests may be rate limited.

ℳ **URL**

http://▒▒▒▒▒▒▒▒▒▒▒/actions
/ledState?token=cKX▒▒▒▒▒▒▒▒▒▒▒▒▒▒▒▒▒▒▒

Surround any text with "<<<" and ">>>" to escape the content

ℳ **Method**

POST

The method of the request e.g. GET, POST, DELETE

ℳ **Content Type**

application/json

Optional

ℳ **Body**

{"ledId": 1, "state": true}

Surround any text with "<<<" and ">>>" to escape the content

Figure 10.13 Make a REST request via HTTP to your WoT Pi. This creates a new `ledState` action on your Pi by POSTing the corresponding JSON payload.

10.3.3 *Pushing intruder alert tweets to a Google spreadsheet*

Let's step back for a second and reflect on what you just built. When your Raspberry Pi detects an intruder via the PIR sensor, Node-RED tweets a picture taken from your webcam. IFTTT listens for such tweets and adds a corresponding entry in a Google spreadsheet. The second rule goes even further and uses REST to turn on the LED of your Pi over the web. We were able to build such complex workflows in minutes thanks to the power and ubiquity of web APIs: all the actors in our workflow can speak to each other via web protocols. Node-RED uses the WoT WebSocket API of the Pi and the HTTP API of Twitter. IFTTT also uses the HTTP API of Twitter and the HTTP API of Google Drive. Finally, IFTTT uses the RESTful HTTP API of your Pi to actuate it via actions. This is the true beauty and power of the Web of Things!

> **The nerd corner—More mashups!**
>
> There are many ways to tweak the workflow you just created. As an example, you could use the Twitter condition "New tweet by you with hashtag" so you trigger the alert only for tweets with a particular # hashtag. Why stop here? IFTTT opens many more doors to create interesting workflows! As an example, we created another recipe that sends us an SMS whenever an intrusion is detected. If you want to create more mashups,

(continued)

browse https://ifttt.com/channels and look for inspiring channels. Need ideas? Try using the other sensors of your Pi such as the temperature or humidity sensor, logging values inside documents, creating visualizations, or sending weather alerts. Be creative; the cloud is the only limit! Note that you don't have to use Twitter to integrate data from your Pi to IFTTT. You can also use the IFTTT Maker channel in the reverse direction to communicate with IFTTT via REST and trigger workflows. Finally, there's a world beyond the mashup tools we looked at here and some are really worth a try. For example, Freeboard[a] allows you create visual dashboards mashing up the data from various devices and integrates nicely with the Web of Things. Some IoT platforms also conveniently have mashup tools built in. EVRYTHNG, for example, provides a tool called the Reactor, which lets you write Node.js scripts that are run in the cloud and can be triggered each time the state of your connected Things change.[b]

---

[a] https://freeboard.io/
[b] https://developers.evrythng.com/docs/reactor

SO WHAT?

The key takeaway of this section is that by moving Things and their services closer to the web, we can seamlessly integrate them with the very large ecosystem of web tools. Had we not built the API of our Pi based on web standards but rather on closed protocols, creating this integration would have taken significantly more time. The two tools we used offer different levels of integration. Node-RED is open and supports many standard web protocols out of the box, but it's primarily a prototyping tool meant for developers and makers. On the other hand, IFTTT takes a much more controlled approach targeting less technically skilled users but doesn't offer the same level of flexibility and configurability. In consequence, devices and services need to go through a selective selection process with the IFTTT team in order to get their own channels.

Nevertheless, the common denominator of both platforms is the web. Using a Web of Things approach radically reduces the prototyping time and open the doors for new ideas and integration opportunities for the Internet of Things. Devices aren't locked in their own closed worlds anymore but become open for integration.

10.4 *Beyond the book*

Mashups are important for the Web of Things because they illustrate the simplicity offered by the WoT approach. Let's talk about what the future of WoT composite applications looks like.

10.4.1 *From simple mashups to big data mashups*

The future will be about big data mashups. Very big data! Things connected to the web will generate an unprecedented amount of data. Think about it: 1 million connected devices sending a sensor reading every second to an IoT cloud means 86.4 billion messages per day (yes, billion!) That's roughly 170 times more than all tweets posted globally that same day[10]!

Put this in perspective with the 20 to 50 billion connected devices predicted for 2020 (see chapter 1) and we have a significant data challenge ahead of us. Yet data is the new gold, so we'd be fools not to exploit it! Although currently much of the focus on the IoT is on raw connectivity, exploiting this data is the next big wave we expect. IoT data has the potential to make our world smarter and more aware, but the amount of data it will generate will crush any of the traditional data tools we were using in the past.

Many of the new big data techniques and technologies will help. As an example, considering events as they come and running queries on a stream of events instead of against databases should help us crunch more IoT data. Large-scale and real-time stream and data processing systems like Spark[11], Storm[12], Flink,[13] or Samza[14] are mushrooming these days and help us deal with these challenges. Real-time analytics techniques will help us create applications that can trigger alerts right when abnormal events happen.

Machine learning methods and tools (a modern term for artificial intelligence) will help us create more intelligent applications that can analyze and learn from huge amounts of unstructured data and allow applications—from logistics, to public transportation, to city management—to adapt their behavior and make optimal decisions in real time. Some devices are already using these techniques. Nest[15] thermostats, for instance, use data patterns to predict the temperature you're likely to prefer in a specific room at a specific time.

Most of this data integration and processing is likely to happen in the cloud, so it makes sense to connect Things to the web to be able to efficiently pipe this data. Having said that, a certain level of filtering and intelligence will also be required on devices. We still have a lot of tools and techniques to build and improve in order to use in the most efficient manner the massive amount of data the IoT will generate!

10.4.2 *A better user experience*

Data will not only make Things smarter but will also improve the way we interact with the physical world. Currently, many consumer products, especially electronic appliances, are still quite cumbersome to use. If everyday products are to become smarter, the way we interact with the digital world will have to change. The way we interact with smart products will especially have to become more intuitive and less obtrusive.

---

[10] See "What Happens in an Internet Minute": http://www.intel.co.uk/content/www/uk/en/communications/internet-minute-infographic.html.

[11] https://spark.apache.org/

[12] https://storm.apache.org/

[13] https://flink.apache.org/

[14] http://samza.apache.org/

[15] https://nest.com/

Because sensing technologies will keep evolving, new ways of interacting with the digital world will become possible—far beyond a keyboard, touchscreen, or mouse.

User experience and interaction design for the IoT are yet in their infancy, but the potential to revolutionize the way we interact with machines—and soon the physical world, for that matter—is absolutely massive.

Rituals that would have sounded weird or futuristic a mere 20 years ago have become an everyday routine for some of us. From swiping your wallet to pay for the bus ride home, to unlocking your door with your phone (or even an RFID body implant!), or the heating turning on automatically when you're 20 minutes away from your home—this is only the beginning of a world that's becoming smarter. Remember, however, that a better user experience ultimately also means a safer one, and the WoT pioneer you became through this book shouldn't forget to put security higher on the list than pure usability. Don't mess with the real world!

10.5 *Summary*

- Thanks to the semantic layer of the Web Thing Model combined with web APIs, a universal remote control web app for Things can be created using straightforward JavaScript code that fetches the model and crawls resources.
- Physical mashups are composite web applications combining virtual services with services provided by Things.
- There are two big types of mashup tools: boxes and wires, and wizards.
- Boxes and wires editors allow you to visually connect different actors of the virtual world and the physical world. A good example of a physical mashup editor is Node-RED.
- Wizard editors guide you through a number of steps to create composite applications. IFTTT is a physical mashup editor based on the wizard principle; it allows you to connect all kinds of physical Things to all kind of virtual services to create simple triggers and reactions.

You've just made it through all the layers of the WoT architecture. Congrats! Consider yourself now ready to build the web of your Things! To keep you inspired for the years to come, we'll leave you with a quote from the famed Mark Weiser, one of the grandfathers of the Internet of Things:

The most profound technologies are those that disappear. They weave themselves into the fabric of everyday life until they are indistinguishable from it.

Mark Weiser, in "The Computer for the 21st Century" (September 1991)

appendix A
Arduino, BeagleBone, Intel Edison, and the WoT

As mentioned before, although we use the Raspberry Pi as a reference device throughout this book, all the concepts, architecture, and patterns you learned in this book are definitely not bound to the Pi: they apply to any embedded device or any other Thing out there. Should you decide to opt for a different device than the Pi, this appendix will help you set it up and build the necessary code to integrate your chosen device with the Web of Things. We won't give you all the nitty-gritty details of each platform but will give you all the necessary pointers for three popular embedded systems: the BeagleBone,[1] the Intel Edison,[2] and the Arduino.[3] For each of them, we'll look at these points:

- Installing the software
- Installing Node.js
- GPIO layout and libraries

A.1 Integrating a BeagleBone to the WoT

Let's start with the closest relative of the Pi: the BeagleBone. This device is made by BeagleBoard.org, a U.S.-based nonprofit corporation that provides education in and promotes the design and use of open-source software and hardware in embedded computing. The foundation works with partners such as Texas Instruments to release the easy-to-use embedded devices called BeagleBones. Although in this appendix we focus on their best seller, the BeagleBone Black (BBB), most of this section applies to all BeagleBone models.

---

[1] http://beagleboard.org/
[2] http://www.intel.com/content/www/us/en/do-it-yourself/edison.html
[3] https://www.arduino.cc/

A.1.1 *Meet the BeagleBone Black*

The BeagleBone Black is a member of the Linux-powered family of embedded devices, and its features and size are similar to those of the Raspberry Pi B+:

- ARM Cortex-A8
- 512 MB of RAM
- 4 GB on-board flash storage
- Onboard Ethernet adapter
- A 3D graphics accelerator

The BeagleBone is well-known for its robustness and stability, which makes it an excellent choice even in production applications. Moreover, the BeagleBone offers both SD card and flash-based storage, making it straightforward to move from a prototype to a real-world trial (it's best not to rely on SD cards because they have a limited life span, they move, and they tend to be slow, among other issues). A BBB will set you back around $50 USD, which is only slightly more than the Pi. Should you want to buy one, you'll find a list of recommended sellers on this book's website.[4]

A.1.2 *Preparing the BeagleBone Black for the book*

As we said earlier, the hardware and software of the BBB are similar to that of the Pi, so most of the setup procedures shown here will be straightforward.

LINUX

The BeagleBone Black comes preinstalled with Debian Linux, so there's little you need to do to have it up and running. Should you feel adventurous, the BB can also support other Linux distributions such as Ubuntu.[5]

SSH

To connect to your BBB via SSH, first follow the online getting started guide,[6] which will teach you how to power your BBB and how to access the default onboard web server. Yes, the BeagleBone is a very WoT-friendly device! Then, connect the BBB to your router with an Ethernet cable and follow the steps in the wiki to set up and use the IP of your BBB and access it via SSH.[7]

NODE.JS

Here again, the BBB plays well with the WoT because Node is the default programming language for the device.[8] Should you want to upgrade the version of Node, you can follow the steps listed in section 4.2.5, but make sure you select a version of Node that's suitable for the processor of your BBB (ARMv7 architecture). The BeagleBones

---

[4] http://book.webofthings.io
[5] http://elinux.org/BeagleBoardUbuntu
[6] http://beagleboard.org/getting-started
[7] http://elinux.org/Beagleboard:Terminal_Shells
[8] http://beagleboard.org/support/bonescript

also come with the Cloud9 IDE that lets you conveniently edit Node.js programs directly on the board.[9]

WOT SERVER CODE

All the code samples in this book, including the one for the full WoT server, will work on the BBB without any changes. Just like for the Pi, the BBB supports Git, so you can fork the book source code from GitHub (see chapter 7).

GPIOS

The `onoff` library we used to interface with the GPIO of the Pi is also compatible with the BBB so you won't have to change much in the code. The only thing that will differ is the layout of the GPIOs; therefore, you'll need to change the GPIO numbers in the code. For instance, for the blink.js examples in chapter 4 (listing 4.6), you'll need to change `led = new Gpio(4, 'out')` to use a valid GPIO pin such as pin 11: `led = new Gpio(11, 'out')`. This also means that you'll have to connect your circuits to different GPIO, GND, or PWR pins on the BBB, so be sure you carefully study the layout of your device.[10]

A.2 Integrating an Intel Edison to the WoT

Unlike the Pi and BeagleBone—and the majority of embedded platforms out there—the Intel Edison isn't powered by an ARM processor but by an Intel one (surprise, surprise!). It's primarily a Linux Yocto device, but it also has a second microcontroller running an RTOS called Viper OS. The Edison is not much bigger than a postage stamp and roughly half the size of a Pi Zero, making it the smallest device covered in this book. Nonetheless, it's packed with an impressive set of features:

- Intel Atom dual-core x86 CPU @ 500 MHz for Linux
- Intel Quark 100 MHz for RTOS
- 1 GB of RAM
- 4 GB onboard flash storage
- Wi-Fi a/b/g/n onboard module
- Bluetooth 4.0 onboard module

All these features come with a price; an Edison and its mini breakout board will cost around $70 USD. Check the list of recommended sellers on the book's website if you want to get one.

A.2.1 Preparing the Edison for the Book

Because the Edison is also a Linux device, getting it ready for the Web of Things isn't fundamentally different than for the Pi or BBB.

LINUX

The Edison comes with a preinstalled version of Yocto Linux, so it's ready to use.

---

[9] http://beagleboard.org/Support/bone101/

[10] See here for more details about the BBB pin layout: http://beagleboard.org/support/bone101/.

SSH

To access your Edison via SSH, you'll first need to establish a serial connection through USB to configure the onboard Wi-Fi. Once the Wi-Fi connection is established, you'll be able to SSH your Edison directly. This process is detailed in the online getting started guide.[11]

NODE.JS

The Edison loves Node.js because it comes preinstalled. Like the BeagleBone, the Edison also has its own IDE that lets you write Node.js code that runs on the board. It's called the Intel XDK IoT Edition and can be installed on Mac OS, Linux, and Windows.[12]

WOT SERVER CODE

The full WoT server you wrote in this book will work on the Edison, except for the part that interacts with the GPIOs; see the next item. Just like for the Pi, the Edison supports Git so you can fork the book code from GitHub; see chapter 7.

GPIOS

Unfortunately, the code in this book that uses the onoff library for GPIO access won't work directly on the Edison. But don't worry; the Edison board also has its own Node GPIO access abstraction library called MRAA GPIO.[13] You should be able swap onoff for MRAA and have the different sensors and actuators up and running. Nevertheless, just like for the BBB, the GPIO layout is different on the Edison than it is on the Pi, so you'll have to make sure you connect the right pins.[14]

A.3   *Integrating an Arduino to the WoT*

The Arduino is an open-source electronics platform based on easy-to-use hardware and software. It's intended for anyone making interactive projects and is probably the most popular—and one of the oldest!—platforms for hardware prototyping. There isn't just one Arduino but rather a dozen Arduino devices, or boards as they're called in the Arduino world. Boards range from the all-time best-seller Arduino Uno[15] to the beautiful and minimal LilyPad,[16] with prices ranging from $80 USD to just a few dollars.

Unlike the Pi, BeagleBoard, and Edison platforms, Arduino boards belong to the family of RTOS devices, not Linux. Arduino boards are also much more resource-constrained than the other platforms we've looked at up to now. The consequence is that you won't be able to run Node.js on Arduino boards (except for some special boards; see the next section). This also means the code samples in this book won't run on the Arduino, and you'll have to rewrite them using the Arduino programming language, which is based on the C/C++ languages.

---

[11] https://software.intel.com/en-us/iot/library/edison-getting-started
[12] https://software.intel.com/en-us/getting-started-with-the-intel-xdk-iot-edition
[13] https://github.com/intel-iot-devkit/mraa
[14] Pin layout of the Intel Edison breakout board: http://bit.ly/1Kjc7mj
[15] https://www.arduino.cc/en/Main/ArduinoBoardUno
[16] https://www.arduino.cc/en/Main/ArduinoBoardLilyPadUSB

The good news is that all the concepts described in this book can be easily ported to the Arduino platform because the APIs for your device will be quite similar if not the same. If this book is your first swim in the IoT world and learning about these concepts and implementing them directly on the Arduino will be tough, we recommend that you get a Pi first. But once you get the gist of it, you'll be able to further explore the world of embedded systems. For this, the Arduino platform is a great place to start, especially if you're looking around for low-power devices.

A.3.1 Linux, SSH, Node.js

As mentioned before, the Arduino boards are running an RTOS environment where the C programming language rules. There's no way to install Linux, SSH, or Node on an Arduino board. There's one exception, though: the Arduino Yún supports both Linux and the Arduino RTOS environment, and although it requires a number of steps far beyond the scope of this book, it is possible to install Node on a Yún.[17]

How do you program the other Arduino boards if you can't SSH them? You use a development environment called Arduino Integrated Development Environment (Arduino IDE). This IDE runs on your computer and lets you develop your programs on your machine before uploading them to the Arduino board. How to do that is also beyond the scope of this book, but you'll find a lot of online resources that can help you. Or better yet, you might want to get a copy of *Arduino in Action* by Martin Evans, et al (Manning Publications, 2013)[18]

WOT SERVER CODE

Although you won't be able to reuse the code samples provided in this book, a number of great Arduino libraries can help you implement a WoT-compliant Arduino.

In particular, the `Webduino`[19] library lets you implement a REST API on your Arduino board. The `ArdunioWebsocketServer`[20] library can be used to implement the WebSocket part of your device's WoT API. This should let you work through all the concepts presented in chapters 4 to 8. Chapter 9 is a bit trickier, because the Arduino platform doesn't support TLS very well. This is because the underlying encryption algorithms are resource-demanding, leading to significant times needed to encrypt/decrypt messages.[21]

GATEWAY PATTERN

There's another way to integrate Arduino boards to the Web of Things: using the gateway pattern we explored in chapter 7. You can, for instance, use MQTT or CoAP on your Arduino board and then use a more powerful embedded device, such as a Pi, to

---

[17] https://blog.arduino.cc/2014/05/06/time-to-expand-your-yun-disk-space-and-install-node-js/

[18] *Arduino in Action*, Manning Publications: https://www.manning.com/books/arduino-in-action?a_aid=wot

[19] https://github.com/sirleech/Webduino

[20] https://github.com/ejeklint/ArduinoWebsocketServer

[21] A great read on the practical considerations of security on very resource constrained devices is available here: https://tools.ietf.org/html/draft-aks-lwig-crypto-sensors-00.

serve as a gateway. Should you want to do this, there's a great MQTT[22] Arduino library that can help you and one for CoAP[23] too.

GPIOS

The Arduino boards are meant to be used to experiment with lots of sensors and actuators and hence they have a number of GPIOs at hand. The good news is that the GPIOs are marked directly on the boards, so there's no need for a picture explaining the layout. All the sensors and actuators we installed on the Pi in chapter 4 can also be used with an Arduino board but, again, the code will be quite different. Although describing the Arduino code is beyond the scope of this book, we provide you with good links for each sensor and actuator used in this book:

- LEDs[24]
- Passive infrared sensor (PIR)[25]
- Temperature and humidity sensor (DHT22)[26]

A.4   *Integrating other embedded systems to the WoT*

Literally any embedded device can be integrated to the web by following the WoT architecture. It will just require a bit of searching or a good book on the device you pick! Should you want to try other platforms as well, a good place to start is the Embedded Linux Wiki[27] for Linux-based devices or the Element14 community[28] for RTOS devices. If you port these concepts on other platforms, please do reach out via our GitHub because we'd love to hear about it and link to your project from our book's website.

---

[22] https://github.com/knolleary/pubsubclient
[23] https://github.com/1248/microcoap
[24] http://playground.arduino.cc/Code/LED
[25] http://playground.arduino.cc/Code/PIRsense
[26] http://playground.arduino.cc/Main/DHTLib
[27] http://elinux.org/Main_Page
[28] https://www.element14.com/community

index

Numerics

6LoWPAN (IPv6 over Low power Wireless Personal Area Networks) 120
101 Switching Protocols code 169
200 Ok code 157
201 Created code 155, 157
202 Accepted code 155, 157, 231
204 No Content code 157, 231
304 Not Modified code 164
401 Unauthorized code 157
404 Not Found code 157
500 Internal Server Error code 157
501 Service Unavailable code 157

A

abstract plugin 236
acceleration sensor 149
Accept header 37–38, 151–152, 186, 188
Accept: application/ld+json header 246
Accept: text/html header 152
access control, with REST and API tokens 260–262
Access layer 136–137
access token 267
Access-Control-Allow-Origin header 158

accessing, Web of Things devices 50–54
ACLs (access control lists) 272–274
action resource, web Thing 226
action type 207
actions 207
Actions element 282
actions object
  of Pi Web Thing Model 282–283
  overview 230
actuation 128
actuator plugins 234, 236
actuators
  connecting to Raspberry Pi 100–108
    accessing GPIOs from Node.js 102–107
    breadboards and electronic components 100–102
    general-purpose input/output ports 100
  overview 5, 31, 36, 180
/actuators end point 225
actuators.js file 181, 188
Add Exception option 257
addressable resources 146–150
Advanced Message Queuing Protocol. *See* AMQP
aggregate resources 150
Akamai 146, 259
AMQP (Advanced Message Queuing Protocol) 131
analog components 100
angle brackets 222

anonymous callbacks 74–77
API (application programming interface) 11
  access control with API tokens 260–262
  overview 32
  using Web as for devices 36–41
    getting details of single sensor 41
    getting list of devices from gateway 37–39
    getting list of sensors on device 40
    getting single device 39–40
API endpoints 222
API key 201
APIs for Things 163–174
  Comet-hacking HTTP 167–168
  from HTTP/1.1 to HTTP/2 172–174
  polling and 164
  publishINSERT FWD SLASH HEREsubscribe model 165–166
  webhooks-HTTP callbacks 166–167
  WebSockets 168–171
APIs for Things, RESTful REST constraints 144–146
  cacheable 145
  client-server 145
  layered system 146
  stateless 145
  uniform interfaces 145

APIs for Things, RESTful
  (continued)
  uniform interface, principles of
    addressable resources
      147–150
    HATEOAS 160–163
    manipulation of resources
      through
      representations 151–153
    self-descriptive
      messages 154–160
  uniform interface, reasons
    for 146–147
apiToken key 261
App API key 203
app.use() function 187
Apple HomeKit 132
application gateways 194
Application layer 114–115, 121,
  123, 130–133, 136, 139
application programming interface. See API
application protocols 130–136
  Apple HomeKit and Google
    Weave 132
  Constrained Application
    Protocol 135
  Message Queuing Telemetry
    Transport 132–134
    for Sensor Networks 134
    for Sensor Networks
      (MQTT-SN) 134
    persistent connections 134
    quality of service 133
    security and
      encryption 134
  selecting 135–136
  ZigBee and Bluetooth applica-
    tion stacks 130
application role, OAuth 264
Application-level protocols 113
application/json 37–38, 49, 56,
  188
application/x-msgpack 188
application/x-www-form-
  urlencoded format 49–50
architecture of Web of
  Things 136–140
  Access layer 136–137
  Compose layer 138
  Find layer 137–138
  importance of 138–139
  Share layer 138
Arduino 17, 87, 306–308

Arduino Uno 195
ARM processors 97
ASCII protocol 172
Ashton, Kevin 13
asymmetric encryption 252
Async library 79, 81
async.parallel libary 81
asynchronous I/O
  operations 72
asynchronous programming,
  Node.js and 73–82
  anonymous callbacks 74–77
  control flow libraries 78
  named callbacks 77–78
/auth/facebook 272
authentication, social Web of
  Things authentication
    proxy 266–276
  creating Facebook
    application 269–270
  implementing access control
    lists 272–274
  implementing Facebook
    authentication
    strategy 271–272
  Passport.js 270–271
  proxying resources of
    Things 274–276
authorization 260
Authorization header 262
authorization proxy 267–269
authorization server role,
  OAuth 264
automated generation of user
  interface 280–288
  actions object of Web Thing
    Model for Pi 282–283
  generateActions()
    function 284–285
  generateProperties()
    function 287
  HTML code of form to create
    ledState action 283–284
  PIR and LED properties of Pi
    Web Thing Model 286–287
  retrieving JSON model of web
    Thing with jQuery 282
  universal user interface for
    web Things 281–288
Automatic Identification
  methods 6
Avahi library 219
Avahi mDNS server 95

B
BBB (BeagleBone Black)
  303–305
  GPIOs 305
  Linux 304
  Node.js 304–305
  overview 304
  SSH 304
  WoT server code 305
BCM 2835 C Library 106
BeagleBoard 88
BLE (Bluetooth Low
  Energy) 122
blink.js 103–104
blue line, breadboards 101
Bluetooth protocol 121–122,
  130
body-parser module 189
Bootstrap library 209, 215, 217,
  283
boxes and wires editors 289
breadboards 100–102
brightness property 46
Brillo 86
broadcast 218
Brock, David 13
broker 133
browsability support 162
buildings, smart 17

C
CA (certificate authority)
  257–258
caCert.pem file 256
callback function 105
callback hell 77
callbacks 72
  anonymous 74–77
  named 77–78
camelCase 153
camera element 39
Cantelo, Mike 63
Carriots 200
CDNs (content delivery
  networks) 146
central node 111
certificate authority. See CA
channels 296
Cisco 259
cities, smart 18
clean dependencies, with pack-
  age.json and npm 68–69

cloud integration pattern 176, 199, 212–213
  creating MQTT client application 204–206
  creating simple WebSockets control application 208–212
    cloud integration pattern 212
    subscribing via WebSockets 210–211
    using cloud 209–210
    using QR codes to identify things 211–212
  setting up EVRYTHNG account 201–204
    changing properties 204
    creating device API key 204
    creating first products and thngs 203–204
    creating project and application 202–203
  using actions to control power plug 206–208
cmd.exe 95
CO2 sensor 197
CoAP (Constrained Application Protocol)
  overview 120, 131, 135
  proxying via gateway 196–198
  running CoAP server 195–196
Comet-hacking HTTP 167–168
command prompt 95
communication 5
complex commands 207
Compose layer 138, 280
compressed headers 172
compression format 172
computation 5
concrete plugins 236–237
concurrent requests 71
config-sample.json file 205
config/acl.json file 272
Confirm Security Exception option 257
connected objects use cases 14–22
  connected hotel 6–8
  Marketing 2.0 21–22
  smart cities and energy grids 18
  smart homes and buildings 17
  smart logistics and supply chains 19–20

  smart manufacturing and Industry 4.0 19
  wearables and quantified self 16–17
  wireless sensor networks and distributed sensing 14–15
connectHardware() function 184
connection-oriented protocol 119
connectionless protocol 118
console.log() 43, 72–73, 207
consolidate module 242
Constrained Application Protocol. *See* CoAP
consumer packaged goods. *See* CPGs
content delivery networks. *See* CDNs
content negotiation 37, 151, 153
content property 46–48
Content-Type header 65, 151, 159
Content-Type: application/json header 169
contentType method 50
Contiki 15, 86
control flow libraries 78
control flow mechanism, TCP 119
controlled vocabularies 240
converter middleware 188
Copper plugin 196
corePlugin.js module 236–237
CORS (cross-origin resource sharing) 158
coupling between elements
  with Internet of Things 25
  with Web of Things 25
CPGs (consumer packaged goods) 19
crawling API of web Things 221
Create Redirection option 212
CRUD (create, read, update, and delete) 154
crypto.randomBytes() function 261
cURL 36
Cylon.js library 62

D

Dahl, Ryan 62
Dashboard tab 206

data-intensive real-time application. *See* DIRT
database.query() function 72, 74
Debian Linux system 91
debug output node 291
default representation 153
delegated authentication step 266
dependencies, clean 68–69
describing web Things 223–239
  actions 229–231
  metadata 227
  properties 227–229
  Things 231–232
  Web Thing Model, implementing on Pi 232–238
    dynamic routing 234–236
    extending WOT server for discovery-architecture 234
    plugins 236–238
    validating your model with JSON schema 233–234
    WO T Pi Model 232–233
  Web Thing Model, overview of 225–227
descriptive names 150
Details page 36
devDependencies 69
device discovery 51
devices.webofthings.io server 170
DHCP (Dynamic Host Configuration Protocol) 217
DHT22 (AM2302) sensor 105–107
digital actuator 100
Digital Living Network Alliance. *See* DLNA
digital sensor 100
direct integration pattern 176–194
  creating WoT server 178–179
  interface design 189–191
    adding body parser 189
    binding actuators to server 190–191
    supporting other HTTP verbs 189–190
  pub/sub interface via WebSockets 191–194
  representation design 186–189

direct integration pattern
    (continued)
    resource design 180–186
        binding sensors to
            servers 183–185
        creating Express
            application 182–183
        creating Express
            routes 181–182
        creating resource
            model 180–181
        testing with real hardware
            on PI 185–186
DIRT (data-intensive real-time)
    application 73
discovering Things 217–223
    network discovery 217–220
    mDNS 218–219
    on web 219–220
    resource discovery on
        web 220–223
        crawling API of web
            Things 221
        HATEOAS and web
            linking 221
        REL= 223
distributed sensing 14–15
DIY (do it yourself) 7
DLNA (Digital Living Network
    Alliance) 218
Dom Pérignon button 21
domotics 17
doPoll() function 42
DPWS (Devices Profile for Web
    Services) 23
Duck DNS 259
duration property 46
Dynamic Host Configuration
    Protocol. See DHCP
dynamic routing 234, 236

E

Edison 305–306
embedded devices 84–88
    beyond Pi 87–88
    for hobbyists vs. industrial
        devices 84–85
    industrial prototypes 87–88
    real-time operating systems vs.
        Linux 85–86
encryption 252
energy grids, smart 18

Engels, Daniel 13
EnOcean protocol 123
entities 225–227
environment variables 202
EPCglobal network 20
err parameter 74
ERR_CERT_AUTHORITY_INV
    ALID 257
error parameter 74
event loop, Node.js 71–73
    multi-threaded web servers 71
    single-threaded, non-block-
        ing web servers 71–73
event-driven programming 105
Evian Drop 21
EVRYTHNG_API_KEY
    variable 202
EVRYTHNG, setting up
    account 201–204
    changing properties 204
    creating device API key 204
    creating first products and
        Thngs 203–204
    creating project and
        application 202–203
ex-2.3-websockets-temp-
    graph.html file 45
ex-3.2-actuator-ajax-json.html
    file 49
ex-4-parse-device.html file 51
ex-5-mashup.html file 55
exFAT 92
exploits object 250
exports object 70
Express framework 178
external requests 229
extractFields(fields, model) 236

F

F function 74
Facebook application
    authentication strategy
        implementation 271–272
    creating 269–270
Facebook Graph API explorer
    tool 273
fast-moving consumer goods. See
    FMCGs
Find layer 137–138, 217
findability problem 215–217
Fleisch, Elgar 13
Flink 301

FMCGs (fast-moving consumer
    goods) 19
forking 99
forms, using to update text
    46–48
fragments 148
FreeRTOS 86
fs.appendFile() function 76
fs.readFile(filename, callback)
    73
fs.readFileSync(filename) 73

G

gateway pattern 176, 194–199
    Arduino and 307–308
    proxying CoAP via
        gateway 196–198
    running CoAP server 195–196
gateway, getting list of devices
    from 37–39
Geiger counter 127
general-purpose input/output
    ports. See GPIO
generateActions()
    function 284–285, 288
generateProperties()
    function 287
Generating a 2048 bit RSA pri-
    vate key message 255
GeoTrust 258
GET {WT}/actions request 229
GET {WT}/actions/{actionId}
    resource 231
GET {WT}/model 227
GET {WT}/properties
    resource 228
GET method 294
GET request 169
GET tag 227
getLight() function 78
getModel() function 281
getTemperature() function 78
GETting data 289
Git and GitHub, using on Rasp-
    berry Pi 99
git clone command 32
git commit command 32
git push command 32
GitHub page 67
GitHub repository 281
GND (ground) pin 105
Google 263
Google Charts 43

Google spreadsheet, pushing intruder alert tweets to 296–298
Google Weave 132
GParted 92
GPIO (general-purpose input/output) ports 89, 100, 305
    accessing from Node.js 102–107
    Arduino and 308
    Edison and 306
Graph API explorer tool, Facebook 273
graphing, sensor values 43
GUI (graphical user interface) 223

H

Handlebars engine 242
hardware bridges 9
Harter, Marc 63
HATEOAS (Hypermedia as Engine of Application State) 147, 160–163, 221
HDP (Health Device Profile) 130
HEAD verb 154
headless option 94
Heartbleed 253
heating, ventilation, and air-conditioning systems. See HVAC
Hello World HTTP server 64
hello-modules folder 70
hello-node folder 65
hello-npm folder 68
hobbyists, embedded devices for 84–85
homes, smart 17
Host Name field 97
HTML interface/representation 153
HTTP (Hypertext Transfer Protocol)
    Comet-hacking HTTP 167–168
    webhooks-HTTP callbacks 166–167
HTTP GET 40
http module 64
HTTP polling 168
HTTP POST 49
http request function node 294
http.js file 189, 242

HTTPS, enabling with TLS 255–259
humidity sensor 180
HVAC (heating, ventilation, and air-conditioning systems) 17
hyperlinks 221
Hypermedia as Engine of Application State. See HATEOAS

I

I Understand The Risk option 257
I/O (input/output) pins 31
I2C (Inter-Integrated Circuit) 107
IANA (Internet Assigned Numbers Authority) 151, 171
id field 203
@id keyword 245
IDE (integrated development environment) 99
idempotent 154
identification 260
IEEE 802.15.4 standard 120
if-then statements 295
IFTTT (If This Then That)
    wizard 295–300
    pushing intruder alert tweets to Google spreadsheet 296–300
    sending requests to Thing with Maker channel 298
implementing status codes 159
implementing web Things 175–213
    cloud integration pattern 199–213
        creating MQTT client application 204–206
        creating simple WebSockets control application 208–212
        setting up EVRYTHNG account 201–204
        use actions to control power plug 208
        using actions to control power plug 206
    connecting devices to web 176
    direct integration pattern 177–194
        creating WoT server 178–179

direct integration
    pattern 194
    interface design 189–191
    pub/sub interface via WebSockets 191–194
    representation design 186–189
    resource design 180–186
gateway integration
    pattern 194–199
    proxying CoAP via gateway 196–198
    running CoAP server 195–196
industrial prototypes 87–88
Industry 4.0 19
input mode 100
input parameters 207
input text bar 49
input/output pins. See I/O
installing Node.js 63, 97–99
integrated development environment. See IDE
integration strategy 163, 176
Inter-Integrated Circuit. See I2C
interface design 163, 176, 189–191
intermediate hops 112
intermediate nodes 112
Internet Assigned Numbers Authority. See IANA
Internet layer 114
Internet of Things project 250
internet protocols 116–120
    Transmission Control Protocol 119
    transport protocols of Internet 117–118
    User Datagram Protocol 118–120
    versions 4 and 6 116–117
Internet Security Research Group 259
intruder alert tweets, pushing to Google spreadsheet 296–298
IoT (Internet of Things)
    compared with Web of Things 8–12
    defining 4–6
    disadvantages of closed and proprietary protocols 24

IoT (Internet of Things)
(continued)
  insufficient level of
    security 25–26
  maintenance difficulties 24
  programming
    difficulties 23
  tight coupling between
    elements 25
  history of 12–14
IoT attacks 250
IP (Internet Protocol) 114
IPv4 (Internet Protocol version
  4) 116–117
IPv6 (Internet Protocol version
  6) 116–117
IPv6 over Low power Wireless
  Personal Area Networks. *See*
  6LoWPAN

J

JavaScript 60–62, 194
jQuery 42, 282
.js extension 65
JSON (JavaScript Object
  Notation) 153
  returning sensor data as 65–66
  validating Web Thing Model
    with 233–234
JSON Schema Lint 234
JSON-LD format 244–246
  findability and beyond 246
  JSON-LD for Things 245–246
JSON-LD payloads 246
json2html library 186

K

Kiessling, Manuel 63

L

LAN (local area network) 115
layers 113
LCD screen 31, 36, 47–48, 55, 57
LED message function
  node 293
LED property, of Pi Web Thing
  Model 286–287
ledId parameter 282
ledId value 230
ledState action 230, 282–283,
  292, 299

Lets Encrypt project 259
/lib folder 69
light sensor value 65
LINK element 222
Link header 222, 227
Link layer 114
linked data 239–240
LinkedIn 263
links element 53–54
Linux
  BeagleBone Black and 304
  Edison and 305
  vs. real-time operating
    systems 85–86
List of Sensors link 34
listen() function 183, 193
listen(PORT) function 65
loading time 145
local area network. *See* LAN
Location header 155
/log resource 74
login cookie, Facebook 275
login.html page 272
logistics, smart 19–20
logValuesReply() function 78
long polling 168
loose coupling 145
LoRa 125
low-power protocols 194
LTS (long-term support) 99

M

M2M (machine-to-machine)
  communication 133
Made for iPhone program. *See*
  MFi
MagPi magazine 89
maintenance 24
MAJOR version 69
MAJOR.MINOR.PATCH
  pattern 69
Maker channel 295, 298–300
malicious interceptor 251
manipulation of resources,
  through representations
  151–153
manufacturing, smart 19
MAP (Message Access
  Profile) 130
Marketing 2.0 21–22
mashup() function 56, 74
mashups, creating 54–57
masterSecret 254

Mattern, Friedemann 13
mbed OS 86
mDNS (multicast Domain Name
  System) 218
mDNS server 95
mesh networks 112–113
Message Access Profile. *See* MAP
MessagePack 153
metadata 227
MFi (Made for iPhone)
  program 132
Micro USB connector 91
/middleware/auth.js file 273
middleware/converter.js
  file 186
MIME (Multipurpose Internet
  Mail Extensions) 151
MINOR version 69
/model resource 233
model resource, web Thing 226
modelToResources(subModel,
  withValue) 236
modularity, in Node.js 66–71
  clean dependencies with pack-
    age.json and npm 68–69
  first Node module 69–71
  npm- Node package
    manager 67–68
module-client.js file 70
Mozilla 259
MQTT (Message Queuing
  Telemetry Transport) 120,
  131–132, 171
  creating MQTT client
    application 204–206
  persistent connections 134
  quality of service 133
  security and encryption 134
MQTT-SN (MQTT for Sensor
  Networks) 134
MS-DOS (FAT) format 92–93
msgpack5 library 186
mul function 70
multi-threaded web servers 71
multicast 218
multicast Domain Name System.
  See mDNS
multicast messages 118
Multipurpose Internet Mail
  Extensions. *See* MIME
My Apps section, Facebook 269

N

named callbacks 77–78
NAS (network-attached storage) 218
NAT (Network Address Translation) 116
Nest 301
nesting callbacks 77
Network Address Translation. *See* NAT
network discovery of Things 217–220
mDNS 218–219
on web 219–220
Network layer 114
network socket 117
network-attached storage. *See* NAS
Network/Transport-level protocols 113
networking protocols 115–130
internet protocols 116–120
Transmission Control Protocol 119–120
transport protocols of Internet 117–118
User Datagram Protocol 118–120
versions 4 and 6 116–117
personal area networks 120–124
personal area networks (PANs)
Bluetooth 121–122
EnOcean 123
IEEE 802.15.4 and 6LoWPAN 120
Thread 121
Wi-Fi and low-power Wi-Fi 122
ZigBee 120–121
selecting, factors to consider when 127–130
bandwidth, latency, actuation, and sensing 128
cost 127–128
internet integration and openness 128–130
power source 127
range and network topology 128
spatial considerations 115
wide area networks 124–126

wide area networks (WANs)
low-power WANs 125–126
mobile phone networks 124–125
networks of Things 109–140
application protocols 130–136
Apple HomeKit and Google Weave 132
Constrained Application Protocol 135
Message Queuing Telemetry Transport 132–134
selecting 135–136
ZigBee and Bluetooth application stacks 130
network classification models 113–115
network topologies 111
mesh networks 112–113
point-to-point 111
star networks 111–112
Web of Things
architecture 136–140
Access layer 136–137
Compose layer 138
Find layer 137–138
importance of 138–139
Share layer 138
New Out Of the Box Software. *See* NOOBS
new plugins 236
Next Generation Mobile Networks Alliance. *See* NGMN
next() function 186, 188
NFC tags 115, 212, 216
NGMN (Next Generation Mobile Networks) Alliance 125
Nike+ 14, 16
Nipper, Arlen 132
node authProxy.js 275
node blink.js 104
node coap.js 196
Node libraries 178
Node module 67
node module-client.js 70
node simple-plug.js 206
$ node –version 63
node wot.js 232, 257, 275, 282
node_mdns library 219
node_modules/ directory 68
node-dht-sensor library 106–107, 184
node-http-proxy 275–276

node-oauth2-server 265, 276
Node-RED boxes and wires editor 289–294
getting started with 289–291
Hello World message, flow for creating 291–292
physical mashup with 292–294
saving workflows 292
node-red-contrib-evrythng 295
node-red-node-arduino 295
node-red-node-redis 295
node-red-stop 290
Node.js web framework 59–82, 178–179
accessing GPIO ports 102–107
asynchronous programming and 73–82
anonymous callbacks 74–77
control flow libraries 78
named callbacks 77–78
BeagleBone Black and 304–305
Edison and 306
event loop 71–73
multi-threaded web servers 71
single-threaded, non-blocking web servers 71–73
first web server in 63–65
installing 63
installing on Raspberry Pi 97–99
modularity in 66–71
clean dependencies with package.json and npm 68–69
first Node module 69–71
npm- Node package manager 67–68
overview 62–66
returning sensor data as JSON 65–66
nodes 111
non-IoT platforms 185
NOOBS (New Out Of the Box Software) 91–93
Not authorized for this resource! error 275
npm command-line utility 67
npm init command 69
npm install 185, 206, 232
npm install coap 195
npm install consolidate 242
npm install handlebars 242

npm install http-proxy 275
npm install node-dht-sensor 106
npm install node-json2html library 186
npm install passport 270
npm install passport-facebook 270
npm install ws 192
npm- Node package manager 67–68
npm, clean dependencies with 68–69

O

Object.observe() function 190
on/off library 190
"one device, one protocol, one app" pattern 8
online validator 234
onoff library 103, 105, 107
onoff readSync() function 105
@context keyword 245
ontologies 240
OpenSSL library 255
operations module 70
operations.js file 69
operator API key 201
ops variable 70
optional query parameters 148
optionalDependencies object 185
OPTIONS (HTTP verb) 158, 162, 221
Origin header 158
OS (operating system) 85
OSI (Open Systems Interconnection) 9, 113–115
-out caCert.pem 255
OUT pin 104
output mode 100
OWASP (Open Web Application Security Project) 250

P

pages 221
PANs (personal area networks) 120–124
    Bluetooth 121–122
    EnOcean 123
    IEEE 802.15.4 and 6LoWPAN 120
    Thread 121

Wi-Fi and low-power Wi-Fi 122
    ZigBee 120–121
part3-cloud/client/plug.html file 209
passive infrared sensor. *See* PIR
passive RFID tags 20
passport-twitter or passport-linkedin 271
Passport.js 270–271
PATCH version 69
Payload property 291
Physical layer 114, 121–122, 127
physical mashups 288–294
    better user experience 301–302
    creating 54–57
    from simple mashups to big data mashups 300–301
    IFTTT wizard for programming of 295–300
        pushing intruder alert tweets to Google spreadsheet 296–300
        sending requests to Thing with Maker channel 298
Physical Web 90
physically incompatible protocols 129
Pi
    enabling HTTPS and WSS with TLS on 255–259
    implementing Web Thing Model on 232–238
        dynamic routing 234–236
        extending WoT server for discovery-architecture 234
        plugins 236–238
        validating your model with JSON schema 233–234
    WoT Pi Model 232–233
Pi Web Thing Model
    actions object of 282–283
    LED property of 286–287
    PIR property of 286–287
Pi Zero 88
pi-gpio library 103
pi.json model 245
ping command 95
PINGREQ requests 134
piNoLd.json file 233
PIR (passive infrared) sensor 104–105

PIR plugin 164, 180, 183, 234, 236
PIR property, of Pi Web Thing Model 286–287
pirPlugin.js 236
placeholder 202
PLC (Power Line Communication) 127
plug-with-control.js file 207
plugins 183–236, 238
/plugins directory 237
/plugins/internal directory 236
PoE (Power over Ethernet) 127
point-to-point network model 111
polling data from sensors 42–46
    current sensor value 42–43
    real-time data updates 44–45
    values 43
POODLE 253
POST request 204
Postman 36
preMasterSecret 254
prepackaged integrations 296
prepareMessage() function 56
presence value 294
Press for DP button 21
private interfaces 233
private key 253
privateKey.pem file 256
process-forking approach 71
processForm() function 50
Product schema 246
programming 23
project 202
?project=$PROJECT_ID parameter 203
properties 204, 227, 229
property attribute 241
property resource, web Thing 226
protocol stacks 114–115, 127–128, 130–131, 133, 139
protocols 24
prototypal inheritance 236
prototypes, industrial 87–88
proxied access step 266
proxies 9
proxying resources of Things 274–276
proxying, CoAP via gateway 196–198
public interface 229
public key 253

/public/websocketsClient.html
file 193
publishers 165
publish/subscribe 165–166,
191–194
publish-subscribe 133
publishMessage() function 56
PUT request 189

Q

QoS 0: fire and forget level 133
QoS 1: deliver at least once
level 133
QoS 2: deliver exactly once
level 133
QR codes 211–212, 215
quantified self 16–17

R

Raspberry Pi 31–32, 88–97
choosing version of 89–90
connecting sensors and actuators to 100–108
accessing GPIOs from
Node.js 102–107
breadboards and electronic
components 100–102
general-purpose input/out-
put ports 100
connecting to device 96–97
installing Node.js on 97–99
items needed with 90–91
overview 88–89
setting up 91–96
connecting to network
93–94
creating network for
95–96
installing Raspbian with
NOOBS 92–93
remotely accessing 94–95
using Git and GitHub on 99
raspberrypi.local domain 95
Raspbian 91–92
RDFa
adding to WoT Pi 242–243
overview 240–241
real-time operating systems. See
RTOS
recipes 296
-recursive option 232

red line, breadboards 101
Register As A Developer option,
Facebook 269
REL= 223
relays 112
representation design 163, 176,
186–189
req parameter 64
request module 67, 75
request-response
communication 163
request-response pattern 145,
164–165
requests, sending to Thing with
Maker channel 298–300
res parameter 64
res.writeHeader() function 65
resource design 163, 176,
180–186
resource discovery on web 220,
223
crawling API of web
Things 221
HATEOAS and web
linking 221
resource linking design 163, 176
resource owner role, OAuth 264
resource server role, OAuth 264
resource-constrained
devices 195
resource-oriented architecture.
See ROA
/resources/auth.json file 261
resources element 54
resources object 40
/resources/piNoLd.json
file 232
resources, of web Thing 226
resp parameter 74
response parameter 74
REST (Representational State
Transfer) 144
access control with 260–262
constraints 144–146
cacheable 145
client-server 145
layered system 146
stateless 145
uniform interfaces 145
on devices 177–194
creating WoT server
178–179
interface design 189–191

pub/sub interface via
WebSockets 191–194
representation design
186–189
resource design 180–186
RESTful resource 161
RFID (radio frequency identification) tags 13, 160
RGB value 155
ROA (resource-oriented
architecture) 147
roles, OAuth 264–265
root page 34, 37
/routes/routesCreator.js
file 235
RTOS (real-time operating
systems) 85–86

S

same-origin policy 157
Sarma, Sanjay 13
schema validator library 234
schema.org vocabulary 244
scope 202
SD Card Formatter tool 92
SD cards 87
search engines 221
Sec-WebSocket-Protocol request
header 171
Secure Sockets Layer. See SSL
security 25, 250–259
access control with REST and
API tokens 260–262
encryption 252
OAuth web authorization
framework 263–265
TLS (Transport Layer Security)
enabling HTTPS and WSS
with, on Pi 255–259
overview 253–255
with Internet of Things 25–26
with Web of Things 26
self-descriptive messages 147,
154–160
CORS-enabling client-side
JavaScript to access
resources 157–158
DELETE 156
error codes 156–157
GET 154
POST 155
PUT 155–156

semantic Web of Things 239–247
   JSON-LD format 244–246
      findability and beyond 246
      JSON-LD for Things
         245–246
   linked data 239–240
   RDFa
      adding to WoT Pi 242–243
      overview 240–241
   Schema.org and 243–244
sendAction() function 209
sensing, distributed 14–15
sensor plugins 183, 234, 236
sensor.read() function 184
sensors 5
   connecting to Raspberry
      Pi 100–108
      accessing GPIOs from
         Node.js 102–107
      breadboards and electronic
         components 100–102
      general-purpose input/out-
         put ports 100
   getting details of 41
   getting list of on device 40
   graphing values 43
   polling data from 42–46
      current sensor value 42–43
      real-time data updates
         44–45
      values 43
   returning sensor data as
      JSON 65–66
/sensors end point 225
Sensors page 35
sensors.js file 181, 188
sentiment node 294
sequence numbers 119
Serial Peripheral Interface. See
   SPI
SERVER variable 202
/servers/websocket.js file 262
server-based authentication 260
server, creating 178–179
/servers/http.js file 182, 262
set-top box 220
_setStatus command 207–209
Setup Redirector button 211
setup.sh bash script 205
sha256 hashing algorithm 255
Share layer 138, 249
Shellshock 253
SIGFOX 125
SIGINT 103

simple interfaces 145
simple-plug.js file 205
single-threaded, non-blocking
   web servers 71–73
Skip Quick Start option,
   Facebook 270
smart cities 18
smart homes and buildings 17
smart logistics 19–20
smart manufacturing 19
smart thing 5
SoC (system on chip) 127
social Web of Things authentication proxy 266–276
   creating Facebook
      application 269–270
   implementing access control
      lists 272–274
   implementing Facebook
      authentication
      strategy 271–272
   Passport.js 270–271
   proxying resources of
      Things 274–276
socket 117
Socket.io 191
software bridges 9
Spark 301
SPI (Serial Peripheral
   Interface) 107
SSH client
   connecting to BBB via 304
   connecting to PI on Linux or
      Mac OS 96
   connecting to PI on on
      Windows 97
   Edison and 306
SSL (Secure Sockets Layer) 253
SSL certificates 255
SSL Heartbleed 26
SSL/TLS authentication 253
SSL/TLS encryption 253
SSL/TLS handshake 254
standard interfaces 145
standards 24
Stanford-Clark, Andy 132
star networks 111–112
star of stars 111
state parameter 282
state value 230
stateful applications 161
status property 207
Storm 301
strategy 270

sub function 70
subresources 160
subscribers 165
sudo command 107
supply chains, smart 19–20
supporting verbs 159
Symantec 258
symmetric encryption 252
system on chip. See SoC

T

tagged objects 83
takePicture() function 57
taxonomy 240
TCP (Transmission Control
   Protocol) 118–119, 169–170
TCP packets 119
TCP/IP (Transmission Control
   Protocol/Internet
   Protocol) 113–115, 172
/temp resource 267
temperature and humidity
   plugin 236
temperature sensor 180
templating engines 242
text-plain 65
text, using forms to update
   46–48
Thawte 258
thethings.io 200
Thinfilm 20
Thing proxy trust step 266
thing resource, web Thing 226
ThingSpeak 200
ThingWorx 200
third-party trusted service 263
Thngs, creating 203–204
Thread protocol 121
threading approach 71
Thunderbolt adapter 96
timestamp 229
TinyOS 15, 86
TLS (Transport Layer
   Security) 134, 253
   enabling HTTPS and WSS
      with, on Pi 255–259
   overview 253–255
token-based authentication 260,
   262
Transmission Control Protocol.
   See TCP
Transmission Control Protocol/
   Internet Protocol. See
   TCP/IP

Transport layer 9, 114, 117, 121, 127, 129, 133, 135
transport protocols of Internet 117–118
true value 292
trust chain 255
twitter output node 294
@type keyword 245
typeof attribute 241

U

UDP (User Datagram Protocol) 118–120
UI (user interface), automated generation of 280–288
actions object of Web Thing Model for Pi 282–283
generateActions() function 284–285
generateProperties() function 287
HTML code of form to create ledState action 283–284
PIR and LED properties of Pi Web Thing Model 286–287
retrieving JSON model of web Thing with jQuery 282
universal user interface for web Things 281–288
UI.html file 282
ui/ folder file 211
unambiguous interfaces 145
unicast model 118
uniform interface of web
principles of
addressable resources 147–150
HATEOAS 160–163
manipulation of resources through representations 151–153
self-descriptive messages 154–160
reasons for 146–147
universal remote control 281
universal user interface for web Things 281–288
UPD (User Datagram Protocol) 118
updateProperties()function 206
UPnP (Universal Plug and Play) 218
URI (Uniform Resource Identifier) 147

URL (Uniform Resource Locator) 147
url parameter 50
USB dongles 122
USB Ethernet 96
user interface. See UI
user privacy 25
UTF8 encoding 153
/utils/utils.js file 236, 261

V

values object 230
variables properties 233
verb usage, in URLs 150
versioning patterns 69
vocab attribute 241
vocabulary 240
vulnerabilities 250
VxWorks 86

W

W3C (World Wide Web Consortium) 239
WAN (wide area network) 115
watch() function 105
wearables 16–17
Web
using as API for devices 36–41
getting details of single sensor 41
getting list of devices from gateway 37–39
getting list of sensors on device 40
getting single device 39–40
overview 36
using as user interface to devices 32–36
Web Server Software. See WSS
Web Thing Model
implementing on Pi 232–238
dynamic routing 234–236
extending WoT server for discovery-architecture 234
plugins 236–238
validating your model with JSON schema 233–234
WoT Pi Model 232–233
overview of 225–227
webhooks-HTTP callbacks 166–167

webofthings.js project 232
WebSocket input node 293
websocket input node 293
WebSockets 45, 168–171
creating simple WebSockets control application 208–212
cloud integration pattern 212
subscribing via WebSockets 210–211
using cloud 209–210
using QR codes to identify things 211–212
Weiser, Mark 12
Wi-Fi and low-power Wi-Fi 122
wide area network. See WAN
Wireless Protected Access. See WPA
wireless sensor networks. See WSNs
World Wide Web Consortium. See W3C
WoT (Web of Things) 6–14
advantages of
ease of maintenance 24
ease of program 23
loose coupling between elements 25
open and extensible standards 24
widely used security and privacy mechanisms 26
architecture of 136–140
Access layer 136–137
Compose layer 138
Find layer 137–138
importance of 138–139
Share layer 138
compared with Internet of Things 8–12
connected hotel scenario 6–8
disadvantages of 26–28
WoT (Web of Things) devices
accessing 50–54
overview 30–32
using Web as API for 36–41
getting details of single sensor 41
getting list of devices from gateway 37–39
getting list of sensors on device 40
getting single device 39–40

WoT (Web of Things) devices
    (continued)
    using Web as user interface
        to 32–36
WoT gateways 194
WoT Pi Model 232–233
WoT server code
    Arduino and 307
    BeagleBone Black and 305
    Edison and 306
wot-a-mashup 289
WoT-enabled webcam 294
wot-server-secure.js file 256
wot-server.js file 182, 191, 193,
    256

WPA (Wireless Protected
    Access) 94
WSNs (wireless sensor
    networks) 14–15
WSS (Web Server
    Software) 255–259
{WT}/model resource 230
{WT}/things/{id} resource 231
{WT}/things resource 231

X

X-axis 149
x509 data format 255
Xively 200

XML schema 234
XMPP (Extensible Messaging
    and Presence Protocol) 131

Y

Yahoo Weather Service API
    55–56
Yaler 259
Yocto 86
Young, Alex 63

Z

ZigBee 23, 120–121, 130, 194